D0513924

COMPANION TO
2016

Published by Times Books

An imprint of HarperCollins Publishers
Westerhill Road
Bishopbriggs
Glasgow G64 2QT
www.harpercollins.co.uk
timesbooks@harpercollins.co.uk

First edition 2016

© Times Newspapers Ltd 2016
www.thetimes.co.uk

The Times® is a registered trademark of Times Newspapers Ltd

A catalogue record for this book is available from the British Library.

ISBN 978-0-00-821489-0

10 9 8 7 6 5 4 3 2 1

Printed and bound in Great Britain by Clays Ltd., St Ives plc.

MIX
Paper from
responsible sources
FSC™ C007454

FSC™ is a non-profit international organisation established to promote the responsible management of the world's forests. Products carrying the FSC label are independently certified to assure consumers that they come from forests that are managed to meet the social, economic and ecological needs of present and future generations, and other controlled sources.

Find out more about HarperCollins and the environment at
www.harpercollins.co.uk/green

THE TIMES

COMPANION TO

2016

CONTENTS

Winter

Spring

INTRODUCTION

Ian Brunskill

This volume brings together some outstanding writing, photography and graphics from a year in the life of the world's most famous newspaper. It would be wrong to call it "The Best of *The Times*". The best of *The Times* is published every day, as it has been since 1785 when the paper was founded as the *Daily Universal Register*. The daily print editions and their digital counterparts still strive above all to tell readers what is happening in the world and help them to make sense of it. They do it in reports that must be accurate, readable, reliable and clear even when compiled under great pressure of time or in conditions that are far from ideal. It's a daily achievement for which reporters, editors and their newsroom colleagues tend to receive less credit than they deserve. It's not an achievement to which it's easy to do justice in a book.

"What the British public wants first, last and all the time is News," the press baron Lord Copper tells his hapless correspondent William Boot in Evelyn Waugh's comic novel *Scoop*. Well, up to a point. There was no shortage of news in the period covered by this volume, from September 2015 to August 2016, and *The Times*, with its unrivalled team of correspondents around the world, reported it with the immediacy and authority its readers expect. The migrant crisis in Europe; armed conflict in Syria and Iraq; terror attacks in Belgium, France, the US; tensions between Russia, China and the West; the global rise of political populists and extremists amid growing distrust of "elites"; controversy over the investigation of historical sexual abuse; the deaths of much-loved entertainers; the shock of Britain's Brexit vote; sporting triumph at the Olympics in Rio. All these were comprehensively covered, and all are well represented in this book. For the most part, however, they're reflected in these pages more obliquely, not so much in direct reportage (though the volume includes some vivid examples of that) as in expert analysis and commentary, colourful background features and in-depth interviews, witty opinion columns and incisive leading articles.

In other words, *pace* Lord Copper, there's news and news, and there are ways and ways of delivering it. While even the best live news reporting may make for frustrating reading once the news it reports is no longer quite so live, this book is intended as a reminder of just how much there is in *The Times* each day that can claim more lasting appeal. Whatever form the pieces included here may take, they do what the best journalism – what *Times* journalism – has always done: they inform, they explain, they entertain.

ACKNOWLEDGEMENTS

Special thanks to Matthew Lyons, Lauren York, Annabelle Stapleton-Crittenden, Andrew Keys, Annika Rasanen, Tim Shearring, Lisa Pritchard and Isabella Bengoechea, who worked on the book at *The Times*, and to Sarah Woods, Jethro Lennox and Kevin Robbins at HarperCollins.

Thanks also to the contributors and to the following *Times* colleagues: Nicolas Andrews, Grace Bradberry, Peter Brookes, Becky Callanan, Jessica Carsen, Magnus Cohen, Hannah Fletcher, Richard Fletcher, Helen Glancy, Fiona Gorman, Jeremy Griffin, Tim Hallissey, Robert Hands, Suzy Jagger, Nicola Jeal, Alan Kay, Alex Kay-Jelski, Will McQuhae, Robbie Millen, Alex O'Connell, Tim Rice, Monique Rivalland, Fay Schlesinger, Mike Smith, Sam Stewart, Matt Swift, Craig Tregurtha, Emma Tucker, Richard Whitehead, Giles Whittell, John Witherow.

AUTUMN

WHAT IT TAKES TO GET INTO THE SAS

Hugo Rifkind

SEPTEMBER 5 2015

I THINK THEY'RE impressed. Not in the general scheme of things. I'm dreadful at this but they thought I'd be worse. Probably the happiest period during my day of discovering whether I have what it takes to be selected for the SAS is the half hour I spend on the floor of a Land Rover, with a bag on my head and my wrists bound with cable ties, under a bag of rocks.

It's not that I'm comfortable. Really, I'm not. For one thing, I can't breathe very well and am genuinely worried I'm about to have an asthma attack. For another, the car is being driven at high speed the whole time, across bumpy, gravelly tracks, and there are two massive trained killers in the front of it, and they scream, "Get the f*** down, you f***ing f***," whenever I stick my head up. Occasionally we'll stop, start, stop, start, or go backwards suddenly. Vomit looms high on the agenda. Plus, I've a strong hunch that, when they finally take me out, they're probably going to torture me a bit. Still, at least I'm lying down. At least I'm not climbing a hill. Which, after the day I'd had, counts for a lot.

What follows may not be terribly accurate. A vital skill in the SAS, apparently, is the ability to form detailed memories at times of high stress. This, it turns out, is one of many vital abilities I don't have. Still, I've done my best, with scraps of sweat-stained notes and flashes of memory. This ain't gospel. Think of it more like a rant. A shocked, exhausted rant, with streaks of pride and streaks of shame, and an overall sense of relief that I will never, ever have to do anything like this again.

This autumn, Channel 4 is to bring us *SAS: Who Dares Wins*, in which lots of normal-ish men are subjected to an approximation of the selection process used by British special forces. Part of it is physical, part mental. In reality, hundreds enter every selection process, and only a handful are still there by the end. My mission is to see what they go through. On telly, it lasts eight days. For the real deal, it lasts a year. Think of that, as you read what follows. Think of it lasting for a year.

So, it's evening, in the bar of a Premier Inn in East Grinstead. They wanted me there the night before, so we could start early. Start what, though, I am not at all sure. "They did want to abduct you," says Katherine, the PR for the programme.

"Abduct me?" I say.

"Mmmm," says Katherine.

"From a Premier Inn?" I say.

"Mmmm," says Katherine. "Only I don't think they will."

Are the SAS allowed to abduct you from a Premier Inn? This is one of the many things I don't know. Selection is as much psychological as physical. This is what people keep telling me. Last week, I had to speak to a psychologist, to check if I would go mad. He decided I probably wouldn't. Why might I, though? What are they going to do? Is it going to start with an abduction from a Premier Inn in East Grinstead even if the PR said it wouldn't? I don't sleep much, in wary preparation, but no. It doesn't. Instead I'm met outside, at 6am, by a man I will later learn is called Ian Reilly, and 55, and a medic, and formerly of the Royal Engineers, and has trained with the Special Air Service reserves. Right now, though, he's just a man in black, with a car, who won't answer any questions, except with a terrifying stare. So I don't ask many questions.

We end up at Pippingford Park, an army training ground. Here I meet the team. Later, again, I'll find out that they are Colin "Col" Maclachlan (41, former SAS), Matthew "Ollie" Ollerton (44, former Special Boat Service) and Jason "Foxy" Fox (38, former SBS). World-class at training, the British special forces, but, let's be honest, lousy at nicknames. Later, they will all tell me what they were expecting of me. Not much, is the broad answer. Roughly speaking, they all expected what I did, which is that I'd be beyond lousy at the physical stuff, but do better with the mental.

All this, though, is a while away. I'm shown into a hut. Col barks at me. I'm given my clothes and an armband with my number on it. Should I wish to drop out at any point, I'm told, all I need to do is rip the band from my arm. Then I'm given a rucksack. Proper SAS recruits train with a 45lb rucksack and a rifle. For the show, like me, contestants have a mere 35lb. My six-year-old daughter weighs less, and I moan about carrying her all the time. All of this, anyway, doesn't include water, which is more on top.

"We were worried," Ollie will tell me later. "We didn't think you'd manage it. We were going to cut it down if you'd struggled." I wish they'd told me. I'd have struggled. Or, at least, struggled more.

After that, pretty swiftly, we're off. Ollie, Foxy and I, packs on, jogging down the hill. "Bloody hell," I wheeze at Ollie, after about two minutes.

"Never smoking again." He snorts. And after that, we don't stop for 1 hour and 40 minutes, by which point I'll have covered slightly under six miles. Only when it is uphill do you get to walk. When it's flat or downhill, you have to jog. Counter-intuitively, then, it's the easy bits that fill you with dread. Ollie shouts at me to speed up, tells me to suck in air, periodically asks me if I want to quit.

"No," I say.

"Really?" he says.

"No," I say, wishing he wouldn't give me the choice. After a while, I start to make a funny noise. It's a cross between a grunt and a roar, not unlike the sound that hefty female tennis players make. I'm making it with every breath. Foxy jogs off ahead, comes back, strolls around me in circles. Horrifying. "Your body is lying to you," says Ollie, early on. "It says you've reached your limit, and you haven't. Not even nearly." And he's right, too. You start, and you swiftly feel dreadful. But you don't feel any worse. So, after a while, you start to ignore it. I'm not terribly fit. I run a bit, but slowly. I go to the gym, but wholly out of vanity.

So, as the march comes to an end, and we jog back up to the hut, I'm feeling pretty good about myself. Buggered, sure, but invincible, too. "I have stamina," I'm thinking to myself, delightedly. "Who knew?"

"Not sure why you're stopping," says Ollie. "We're doing that again." We don't. We just do quite a lot of it again. And by the end … Jeez. I have not been more tired. When you read about SAS trainees collapsing, being hospitalised and worse? This is what they are doing. Hikes like these. Longer, sure. Far longer. But the same basic idea.

Reilly, now outed as the medic, sits me down and gives me Lucozade. Out of the corner of my eye, I see Foxy and Ollie standing around, chatting. Somebody has been to Costa Coffee. They're drinking lattes.

The next phase is called "Truth & Lies". In the real SAS, says Col, this would be where the selectors go through your army record and quiz you about it. In the show, instead, they've trawled people's web history and Facebook pages, confronting them with criminal convictions and odd details from their CVs. ("Show initiative, be a leader," says Col, scanning the details of one hapless bloke who fancies himself as a human drum machine. "So how far down the list do you think f***ing beatboxing is?")

For my day, they've read up, and plan to ask me invasive questions. Not bothered. I'm on social media. SAS or not, there's simply no way they're going to be nastier than my Twitter feed after I've said something fairly innocuous about Israel. The week I dissed *The Great British Bake Off* in my TV review? That was brutal. This? Nah. They try, though. Col is from Edinburgh, like me, and understands my background pretty well. "Some folk have preconceptions about folk who went to schools like yours," he says.

"They're probably right," I say. He asks about a fairly savage mugging I suffered as a teenager, and I'm happy enough to tell him it was horrible. He asks, sniggeringly, about a feature I wrote for which I got my back waxed, and I snigger happily back.

"Couldn't do that," shudders Foxy.

"Not everybody has the drive and commitment to be a frivolous lifestyle journalist," I tell him. "So I'd understand if you found it a little intimidating."

Then Col asks if I'd die for my country, and I say probably not, but I'd like to think I'd die for the friends and family my country contains. Then he asks about my dad, a former MP who recently stepped down. "I think," he says later, "that you got a bit annoyed then."

"Yes," I say. "That's because I was annoyed. I was making annoyed noises with my voice. To indicate annoyance." Col thinks this is a crack in my otherwise stable demeanour, and he could have chiselled it open a bit more. I'm not so sure. Like I said, I do Twitter. I'm a pro. Although I sound a bit annoyed right now, don't I?

Alas, all this doesn't last nearly long enough. Before long, I'm in a PE kit and out again with Foxy and Ollie, for what is known as a "sickener". Essentially this involves sprints, squats, press-ups and a strange sort of squat press-to-star-jump affair. I run from Ollie to Foxy and back again, over and over. It goes on and on. Normally, this would merely be knackering. After the hike? It's hell.

I couldn't say how long it lasts. Maybe 20 minutes. Maybe an hour. When we pause, Ollie quizzes me on the numberplate of a car we passed on the road. I couldn't even tell him the damn thing's colour. So the pause stops. Then we're back at the hut. I sweat and I drink. Somebody gives me a big, mighty bacon roll, wrapped in kitchen foil and Cellophane. Lunch. Am I halfway? This is good. I'm still alive. And I'm coping, I think. I pick up the roll. I pull back the Cellophane. "Drop it!" shouts Ollie. "We're off."

Maybe it wasn't even a roll. Maybe it was a s*** in a bun. I don't bloody know. Later, the team will all tell me that this deprivation, this powerlessness, is core to special forces training. Sometimes you'll finish a hike and have a whole meal laid out in front of you. Then, before your first bite, you're dragged away and sent out again. You don't know when you eat; you don't know when you sleep. It sounds trivial. It isn't.

This time, anyway, the sickener is worse. Much worse. More running, more squatting, more burpees. After a while, we come to a strange waterfall structure. It has steps up the middle, and pools of hellish black water on every level. I'm to stand with my back to each pool, jump in and submerge. Climb down, do the next. Some of them are 8ft deep, some only 3ft. You don't know until you're in. It's not nice.

From here on, either way, things are hazy. I'm making my noise again. For a while, I'm crawling. Then I'm standing on a … what? A bridge? A high path? Ollie makes me run to Foxy. Foxy makes me run to Ollie. Afterwards, Foxy, who has a streak of rugged kindness, will tell me that the dynamic bothered him. He's used to being one of several trainers, with a large number of recruits. He's not used to being one of three, all focused on one. It felt a bit like bullying, he'll say, apologetically. Same here. "Carry me to Foxy," says Ollie, and I do, over the shoulders, as I've been shown. "I'm glad," I wheeze, "I'm not carrying him to you. Because he's f***ing massive."

"Carry me to Ollie," says Foxy, after that. Ollie asks me the numberplate again when we get back. I get it right, this time. Can I have a brag? Allow me one, not least because much of what comes later doesn't reflect upon me nearly so well. The thing is, I think they're impressed. Not in the general scheme of things, obviously. Really, I'm dreadful at this. But they thought, nonetheless, I'd be worse. Even big, hard, scary men, apparently, are often quite reluctant to leap backwards into murky pools of water, and I have done so without complaint. In short, they expected me to pull off my number, long before now, and quit.

"I think," Col will say, "you would have just kept on until your body gave up." I'm still not wholly sure why. Speaking as a surprised observer of myself, it interests me. Afterwards, they will tell me about the things that kept them going through their own selections; the various seeds of their resolve. For Ollie, who came to the SBS via the Royal Marines, it was the doubts of others; people who had always told him he simply wasn't that sort of person. I can understand that. For Foxy, also a Marine beforehand, it was more internal; for a year of training, he simply allowed no alternative possibility to enter his mind.

For Col, it was something else. Having joined the Army at 15, he'd found himself in what felt like a dead end in the Royal Scots, and couldn't get excited about a future of, as he puts it, "standing around outside Balmoral". It was the thought of a special forces career, and missing out on one if he stopped, that kept him struggling on.

All of these guys are clever, and eloquent, and in fearsome shape. In our later chats, they will all talk about their military experiences up to a certain point, when they suddenly won't. None is in the services any more. Ollie served in Northern Ireland, Iraq and elsewhere, and now works in corporate training, as well as helping veterans with post-traumatic stress disorder. For a while he was in Asia, working for an organisation that smashed child-prostitution rings. Col served in the Balkans, Iraq, Northern Ireland, Sierra Leone and Afghanistan. Once, at a siege at Stansted, he was a sniper. He's now a security consultant, and occasionally does motion work for computer games, to the extent that he's in the credits for *Grand Theft Auto*.

Foxy left most recently, in 2012. He did multiple tours in various places, including Afghanistan, and worked in hostage rescue. I, meanwhile, am a former gossip diarist who now writes a humorous opinion column. The sickener ends eventually, and we break for lunch. Real lunch, this time, although I eat it warily, like a Dickensian orphan, fearful it will be snatched away. I ache.

Next morning, I will catalogue my various injuries. All of my toes are mince. One has a blood blister on it the size of a baby tomato. I have been chafed bloody on my inner thighs, hips, shoulders and, worst of all, my nipples. Seriously. Scabs on the nipples. Like a new mother. It's nothing. Only a few days into his own, real selection, Ollie will afterwards tell me, he fully inverted his ankle, to the extent that medics wanted him to drop out. He didn't. "I was crying the next day through the marches," he says.

After lunch, I'm told, I'm going on a mission. Before this mission, I'm briefed about what to do if I get captured. "So I'm probably going to get captured," I think, cunningly. Col, I discover much later, actually was captured in Iraq, in 2006. Stopped at a police checkpoint, and given little clue as to who was friend or foe, he ended up stripped naked in a cell, handcuffed and blindfolded. His rescue came about more or less by chance, when an army patrol passed nearby. He knew full well, at the time, what his fate was likely to be. Once, back in the days when war was simple, the instructions for what to do if you were captured were simple, too.

You gave your name, rank, number and date of birth. And, while your captors may have been cross, the Geneva conventions prohibited them from doing much about it.

Today, though, the world brims with potential war zones where silence means death. So, the military has developed a strategy called "controlled release". You give information, but slowly, and only when you're confident it will do no harm. All of this I absorb through an exhausted haze. Then I'm back into my bloody, gravel-filled, nipple-chafing rucksack, and I'm off.

My mission, essentially, is to accompany a "local agent" to a checkpoint, without being seen. If that checkpoint becomes endangered, we are to go to another checkpoint further away, instead. All of this is against the clock. The first checkpoint is declared endangered immediately. The local agent turns out to be Reilly. Unlike before, he's smiling and chatty. I've done well, he tells me, which is thrilling. On a map, he shows me where we're going, and how we're going to get there. Needless to say, it involves climbing a big hill. For the SAS, I am learning, pretty much everything does.

"We'll go the long way round," he says. "They won't be expecting that." At this point, I feel conflicted. On the one hand, I do quite like the idea of tagging along with Reilly while he outwits the team. On the other, I'm not actually sure if I can trust him. On the third hand, which I haven't even got, I'm pretty sure the plan for the day involves me eventually getting captured anyway. So I'm not entirely sold on the logic of voluntarily taking another bloody great hike first.

We climb, we duck, we crawl. We freeze, suddenly, when he spots things I can't see on the skyline. Reilly is full of little nuggets of bushcraft, such as the wisdom of filling your water canteen before drinking when you come to a river, so that if you get shot at and have to run away, you won't be empty-handed. Before long, I'm very nearly enjoying myself. Even with the nipples. With minutes to spare, we're down the hill again, and crashing through an enormous jungle of ferns.

I'm enthused now; it's a game and it seems to be going well. I'm exhausted, obviously, and I'm still carrying the bloody pack, but I know, one way or another, it'll all be over soon. Up we run, on to a bridge. "Hang on," says Reilly. And all hell breaks loose. Like I said, my recollection is not to be trusted. Still, I remember bangs and flashes, and strange objects whizzing past my feet. I remember Reilly lying flat, and myself crouching, and then a lot of shouting.

"Get the f*** down!" somebody is screaming. Suddenly, there are people in masks. My pack is ripped off my back, which gives a moment's blessed release. "Shut your f***ing eyes!" I'm told, and I do. I simply have no fight left in me. Then a bag goes over my head and my wrists are tightened together. I'm dragged, somewhere, by the thumbs. And then I'm in the back of the car. At one point we stop, clearly at some sort of checkpoint, which I suppose could be my chance to escape. There are three of them, though, and they're the best-trained soldiers in the world. And there's one of me, and I'm a slightly fat journalist, who has already run a marathon and has hurty nipples and his wrists tied together. So I don't really get the point.

By the end of our drive, I'm feeling sick as a dog. Then I'm being dragged out again by the thumbs and sat down, roughly, and I wait, and I wait, and I wait. Then the bag comes off, and I'm looking at Col. Only, he's not quite being Col. This is an interrogation. First, I'm told to change my clothes. Off comes the army gear, and on go a pair of giant overalls and some huge, slip-on trainers. Nobody could run in this.

In my briefing, I was told that the worst thing you can do when captured is sign anything. Col wants me to sign a list of my clothes. I refuse. He asks if I'll just write, "This is accurate," or something like that instead. I shrug, and do, even though, as he'll explain later, this is just as stupid. Then he shouts, "Guard!" and somebody in a mask bursts in, puts the bag back over my head, and drags me away by my thumbs.

I end up in another shed next door. I'm forced to my knees, with my hands behind my head. Goggles go over the bag so I can see nothing at all, and a pair of headphones go over my ears. Then I start to hear the sound of a woman screaming. Occasionally I'm moved, roughly, into different squats, or to lean against walls. These are stress positions and they're not pleasant, but they're a damn sight more pleasant than climbing a hill. None of this is nice, but I know it can't go on for long. On the show, they do this stuff for 36 hours, interspersed with interrogations. In true selection, they do it for days, with no sleep at all. For me, I know there's an end in sight. I'm due on a train at six. It's a non-refundable ticket.

After half an hour, I'm dragged back to Col. Thumbs again. Man, I'm sick of that. This time he has lots of questions, and I give him lots of answers. So many, in fact, that he'll later be quite disappointed with me. "I thought you'd be better than that," he'll say. "You wouldn't shut up."

I thought I'd be better, too. I think I'm trying to outwit him, although the facts I'm alternately revealing and withholding are pretty random.

I've a vague idea that I ought not to let him know how my mission began, so that the theoretical comrade who drove me there (Ollie, who I also know is the bad guy who put the bag on my head) has a chance to escape. Other details, though, I'm blurting out quite voluntarily. Essentially, I just don't want to go back in the other shed.

I'm near the end, I know, and the only thing that seems to matter is not quitting before I get there. I'm not breathing right, particularly in the bag. I haven't had an asthma attack since I was 12, but I haven't felt like this, either. Plus, I really, badly need the toilet (with all the hiking, I have drunk pints and pints) and I feel that wetting myself would be a bit humiliating, not least because there's a photographer.

The longer I'm next door, the more likely I am to throw in the towel. I do go back, all the same. This time the sound in the headphones is a crying baby. I almost start laughing. A baby? Really? I have two kids. You think I can't stand this for half an hour? I've stood it for the past six f***ing years. Plus, you recognise your own kids' crying, and this isn't them. You know what this sounds like to me? Somebody else's problem. Bring it on.

The next time, though, in the interrogation shed, Col is in a mask, and screaming. "We're going to kill one of you," he says. "You or him?"

"That depends what you want to get out of it," I stammer.

"You or him?" he screams, right up in my face, and I just collapse.

"Him," I say. "Kill him."

I like to think it would be different if I thought it were real. Frankly, who knows? I've had enough. And then the guard comes back, and on goes the bag, and he drags me off to the other shed, and … off comes the bag again. "It's over," says Ollie, grinning now. "You're done."

AN INJUSTICE THAT FOLLOWED
A DYING MAN TO HIS GRAVE

David Aaronovitch

OCTOBER 7 2015

ON JANUARY 21 this year Leon Brittan, the former home secretary, died after suffering for a long time with cancer. His family mourned and on Twitter his former cabinet colleague John Gummer expressed sadness at the news. Noting Gummer's comments, Tom Watson, the MP and now Labour deputy leader, wrote the single word: "Hmm".

Those who had not been following Mr Watson's two-year campaign concerning a possible Westminster paedophile network might have been bemused. If so, a column by Mr Watson in the *Daily Mirror* three days later explained all. He knew, he said, that what he was about to write would distress the Brittan family greatly, but he felt obliged to speak out where others had remained silent. Mr Watson then itemised the charges that, during Lord Brittan of Spennithorne's life, he had not made publicly for fear, he said, of prejudicing any trial.

"I've spoken to a woman who said he raped her in 1967. And I've spoken to a man who was a child when he says Brittan raped him. And I know of two others who have made similar claims of abuse." Mr Watson quoted their belief that the recently deceased peer was "as close to evil as a human being could get, in my view", and then added, slightly unconvincingly: "It is not for me to judge whether the claims made against Brittan are true".

All Mr Watson wanted, he said, was for a proper investigation to happen and justice to be done. And he concluded boldly: "Former home secretary Leon Brittan stands accused of multiple child rape. Many others knew of these allegations and chose to remain silent. I will not." Last night, however, Mr Watson was indeed silent. For the past three years, since he stood up in the House of Commons and suggested the existence of a "powerful paedophile network linked to parliament and No 10", journalists have been trying to investigate the truth of the allegations — some of them very general — made against Britain's political establishment.

For more than a year the BBC's *Panorama* programme has been looking at the sources for the claims made about Brittan and others and effectively repeated by Mr Watson. What the programme discovered added important information to reports that have already appeared in this newspaper, which is that the claims are so badly flawed that it calls into question whether they can be relied upon.

Yet despite these flaws, pressure from Mr Watson and other up-and-coming politicians, such as Zac Goldsmith, the new Tory candidate for London mayor, has helped to persuade the police to put scarce resources into investigations that have led nowhere and that are in danger of undermining campaigns against genuine child abuse.

Unfortunately Mr Watson declined to be interviewed by *Panorama* on the basis, I gather, that he was "too busy". The origin of the great Westminster "paedo scandal" — described by the Australian television current affairs programme *60 Minutes* in July as "without question the biggest political scandal that Britain has ever faced"— lies in information passed to Mr Watson in 2012 by Peter McKelvie, a social worker.

The case was that of a convicted paedophile called Peter Righton and Mr McKelvie told Mr Watson that documents implicating powerful people had been discovered and not acted upon. One was a letter sent by Charles Napier, another convicted paedophile, and half-brother to John Whittingdale, who was political secretary to Mrs Thatcher during her last years in Downing Street and who had been chairman of the Commons media committee during the phone-hacking affair — the committee where Mr Watson had made such an impact.

My understanding is that although a police scoping exercise led to new charges against Napier being proved, nothing remotely actionable implicating anyone in Downing Street has ever emerged. However, following Mr Watson's Commons performance a series of new and unrelated accusations began to be made concerning Westminster politicians (most of them dead). Long dormant and unreliable writers suddenly discovered memories of lost politicians' diaries and some tabloids gave their front pages over to preposterous claims involving illegal gay orgies in the Grand Hotel on the eve of the Brighton bombing. The late Conservative MP and anti-Satanist Geoffrey Dickens, whose famous file of who-knows-what had disappeared in the bowels of the Home Office (as had so much else) was transformed from eccentric to Carl Bernstein almost overnight.

Once the exotica had been dealt with, however, three main strands of claim remained, two at least of them featuring in Mr Watson's repetition of claims about Brittan. The first was the story, repeated now in many newspapers, in documentaries, in books, interviews and speeches, that a private guesthouse in southwest London — the Elm Guest House — had, during the 1980s, been a place where boys from a nearby children's home had been trafficked and sexually abused by a whole series of celebrities and politicians, one of whom was supposedly Brittan. This story had been on the edges of the internet for years (I came across it on a site run by a follower of the bizarre David Icke cult), but was now given credibility by a police operation set up to examine allegations.

Almost everything to do with Elm Guest House originates with a man called Chris Fay. Once a social worker in the area and then a Labour councillor, it is Fay who claims to have been given the list of "attendees" by the now deceased owner; Fay who claims to have spoken to many boys who were trafficked and Fay who "saw" photographs of Brittan at the guesthouse abusing under-age boys — photos now missing. On last night's *Panorama*, reporters spoke to one boy who Fay claimed was at the guesthouse and who said clearly that he was not there. *Panorama* also found a man who acted as a gay masseur in the house, who said that though sexual activity certainly went on, he never saw anyone famous or any children. Fay, it should be noted, is a convicted fraudster who went to prison in 2011.

The second strand of the accusations against Brittan concerned the supposed happenings at Dolphin Square in London in the early Eighties. Again this place had been the subject of internet rumours for years, but in the end the hard evidence boiled down to the testimony — most of it obtained by the Exaro news agency and then elsewhere — of three "survivors": "Nick", "Darren" and "Andrew". Nick's account even made it as the top item of the BBC's *Six O'Clock News* last year. *Panorama* chased down one of the key claims from Nick, that he witnessed the hit-and-run murder of a schoolboy in Kingston, committed as a warning to him from his abusers. They established that no such accident happened and that no child was killed in this way in that location and time frame. If that murder didn't happen, then a huge doubt must exist about his other stories, the most lurid of which (involving Edward Heath and a knife) were itemised by Harvey Proctor in a press conference last month where he protested his innocence and accused police of a witch-hunt.

Furthermore, the supposed corroboration from Darren was also highly dubious, since he is a convicted bomb-hoaxer and has been classified as delusional. The third witness, Andrew, told *Panorama* that he felt pressured into saying he was at Dolphin Square by Fay and the Exaro team.

Then there is the accusation of (unusually for a supposed homosexual paedophile) heterosexual rape. "Jane" contacted Mr Watson through a fellow Labour MP and claimed to have been raped by Brittan in 1967. When the police investigated her claim a number of problems quickly arose. She said he had taken her to his basement flat, but at the time he had lived on the third floor. And friends of hers who she said could corroborate parts of her story flatly contradicted it. Finally, what she was alleging didn't match the criteria for rape. The police concluded that they had no grounds for interviewing or arresting Brittan, who was obviously terminally ill.

And then Mr Watson wrote a remarkable letter to the DPP, in effect demanding that Brittan be interviewed and citing in addition to the case of Jane some of the other spurious allegations against him. The DPP leant on the police. The subsequent interview of the dying man resulted in Brittan's name becoming public. In my opinion this was partly a deliberate ploy to try to "flush out" other complainants. Now Lady Brittan is attempting to find out from the Metropolitan police what has happened to the investigation, reopened at the insistence of Mr Watson. Last night, hours before the programme was broadcast, she received a letter from the Met finally confirming that inquiries had ceased for want of evidence. I fear it is more of a reply than she'll get from the Labour deputy leader.

LABOUR'S GUILTY MEN SHOULD ALL HANG TOGETHER

Philip Collins

OCTOBER 9 2015

CAMERON'S CONQUEST OF the political centre ground has been made possible by the vanity and incompetence of his foes.

Long before he was Labour's most ill-suited leader to date, Michael Foot made his name with a book of withering scorn. In 1940, under the pseudonym of Cato, the Liberal Frank Owen, the Tory Peter Howard and Mr Foot jointly wrote *Guilty Men*, an assault on 15 appeasers of Hitler's Germany. The book was a sensation and a significant reason for the declining careers and reputation of Baldwin and Chamberlain.

Would that Mr Foot were alive now, not necessarily as leader (although we could promote him to merely Labour's second most unsuitable leader), but to update the book.

On Wednesday in Manchester, David Cameron, like George Osborne before him on Monday, sought to seize the ground that the Labour party, under Gordon Brown, Ed Miliband and Jeremy Corbyn, has vacated. Mr Cameron's speech was a bit of a Humpty Dumpty affair, in which words stood for deeds. His fine lines on poverty will not survive Mr Osborne's last budget, the effect of which will be to redefine 200,000 working households as poor. The speech contained a lot of high hopes and even more low cunning.

However, as the Labour party has decided that politics is best conducted by being on a perpetual protest march, Mr Cameron commanded the scene like an invading general. He gave a speech that Tony Blair might easily have given, although he always leaves the impression that his cover is not quite the equal of the original. Mr Blair singing You Can't Hurry Love sounded like a Supreme; Mr Cameron's version is a bit more Phil Collins. Which is to say, still pretty good and a lot more melodious than the bizarre tuning-up that the Labour party was doing in Brighton the week before.

The consensus on Mr Cameron contains a clue about the behind-the-hands conversation that was being had all over Brighton. Mr Cameron wants to pitch his party to the political centre because the winning formula in British politics is still to be tough on both the causes of crime and on crime itself. If the Labour party had not abandoned its own recent history it would be able to claim that the Tory conversion to the living wage, gay marriage, free schools, NHS reform, active government in infrastructure projects and social mobility was the lesson it taught them. Labour could say that the Tories' hold on popularity exists only insofar as it has turned itself into a cover version of the Labour party. In government, Labour shifted political logic to the left and Cameron and Osborne are Blair's unwitting creations.

Hating Blair even more than Cameron and Osborne, Labour is unable to say any of this. How did it come to this, that Labour should be so inveterately, stubbornly stuck to losers and so aggressively angry about a winner? If Cato were able to trace the decline and name the guilty men where would the accusations start and end? The analysis from the left of the Labour party is the remarkable suggestion that, as he "lost" a few million votes from the height of 1997, the rot set in under Tony Blair. The guilt was formed by a tolerance of inequality, accelerated by the disaster of Iraq and confirmed by the former prime minister's cupidity after leaving office.

It is true to say that the Blairites did not stand and fight, but to blame the winner for a series of defeats after he was forced out is what a party of losers is inclined to do. It's not a serious attempt to locate the blame, which is a game that is being played in Labour circles right now. The candidates are plenty.

The decline really begins with Gordon Brown whose premiership tested to the destruction the idea that political tactics and news management are adequate substitutes for ideas. Mr Brown offered the Labour party the comforting illusion that he could take the edge off Mr Blair's reforms and pro-market zeal and win a more vintage Labour victory. The consequence was that intellectual inquiry ceased. Since the introduction of tax credits Mr Brown had been barren of policy invention. When people accuse the Blairite Labour party of having run dry of ideas they really mean that, after 2007, Labour had nothing more to say. The Blairites had been largely expunged even by then. It was under Mr Brown that the decline began because he arrived at the top already finished.

The same suspicion, that in reaching a senior position in the party he has achieved all he ever wanted, has to attach to Labour's deputy leader, Tom Watson. The Labour intake of MPs in 2015 was, with a few clear exceptions such as Wes Streeting and Peter Kyle, the worst in living memory. The selection of candidates has been too tightly controlled by Unite and the man who held the auditions was Mr Watson, I presume. It is one of life's ironies that Mr Watson now has to wield the knife to rid the party of the monster he has had a large hand in creating. To add to the roster of charges, Mr Watson also had a hand in the plot to install Mr Brown and was implicated in the farrago in Falkirk which prompted Ed Miliband to panic and change the party leadership rules, thereby clearing a path for Mr Corbyn.

Here, of course, lies the rub. It is an insult to the intelligence of the party beyond anything he perpetrated as leader that Ed Miliband has shown no contrition about what he did. At the centre of the text of the revised *Guilty Men* stands the self-righteous, self-justifying figure of Mr Miliband. He kidded himself and his party, with no evidence to speak of, that Britain had shifted to the left. He threw out everything Labour had done well and clung to spending, on which it had made errors. He yielded control to the unions over selections, the price of his narrow leadership victory over his brother. He rushed through a calamitous change to the character of the party. He led his party to a terrible 30 per cent share of the vote in a wholly winnable election. Then, when the whole sorry hollow nonsense of it was exposed by the electorate, Mr Miliband's precipitous resignation plunged Labour into a leadership contest peopled by candidates who were unready and an analysis of defeat that was risible.

Senior figures in the party, such as Neil Kinnock, connived in the illusion that Labour could be more nearly itself and win. It is a fallacy. George Osborne showed he knows it this week and so did David Cameron. Mr Corbyn calls to mind La Rochefoucauld's maxim about the popular song that we only sing for a short time. Whatever comes next, whenever it comes, Labour needs to arraign the guilty men and remember what they did. The gap in quality between Tory and Labour has never been so wide, never been so embarrassing.

'IF I WAS FRUMPY THERE WOULDN'T BE THIS BACKLASH'

Michelle Mone interviewed by Stefanie Marsh

OCTOBER 10 2015

A BLONDE, DIVORCED Scottish woman with a world-famous cleavage is about to join the House of Lords and every last person in Britain seems to have it in for her. But Michelle Mone or Baroness Mone of Mayfair, as she will be known, is surely everything that a functioning democracy ought to be proud of. *My Fight to the Top*, the blood, sweat and tear-saturated autobiography she published this March, details her rise from the lowest ranks of squalid poverty in Glasgow's East End to here, a London pad with a large balcony overlooking the Thames. She has already designed her coat of arms: a Scottish deer and a labrador, in memory of Ozzie, the family's much loved dog, who died last year.

This morning Michelle Mone, 44, is done up to the nines but rather stiff when I first meet her. I can understand why. The tabloids oohed and aahed all over her in the years she built Ultimo, her bra company, into a global brand from scratch. But now that David Cameron has unexpectedly fast-tracked her to the very apex of the British establishment, a shiver of what one might interpret as stricken horror seems to be passing down the spines of members of that elite club: posh Dave has gone all weak-kneed, is the assumption, under the steady gaze of this newly minted bra boss.

There's the view, also, that she's going to make a mockery, just by being there, of the Upper House. And it's for these reasons that, since Cameron's announcement in August, the muckrakers have been working overtime. She's a fibber, they allege, prone to exaggerate the degree of both her own achievements and the size of her company's profits; she's a PR machine on steroids; she made sure that Ultimo benefited from a "morally questionable" tax avoidance arrangement; the life peerage is a pay-off for having been one of the tiny handful of famous Scots to come out so vocally against Scottish independence in the run-up to the referendum earlier this year. Plus, Rod Stewart called her "a manipulative cow".

That last bit is true. Proof that her critics were right, they said, came last month in the form of a tweet. She'd been travelling in a tax-funded government Jaguar (which is out of character, as Mone is actually Bentley's global ambassador), when she decided not only to drape her top on the car's heater but to take a picture of it, along with the words, "The things you do in Government car drying my travel top love it so much. See you soon #Stockport #betheboss." She's since deleted the tweet.

She was in the car in the first place because of another Tory brainwave: shortly before she was announced as a life peer, Iain Duncan Smith announced that Mone was going to be the country's new start-up tsar, with ten months to deliver her recommendations. Even the people who admire her fret that she's joined a doomed political conga line. Cameron seems to have made a habit of choosing glamorous women for high-profile shopkeeping roles that go nowhere, making Carol Vorderman a maths tsar, Tamara Mellon, the Jimmy Choo founder, a global trade ambassador and Karren Brady, vice-chairman of West Ham, an ambassador for small businesses. Nothing much seems to have come of these vague roles. Mary Portas's high-profile appointment as high street rejuvenator ended in a damp squib: one gets the impression that her recommendations were sidelined. Now it's Mone's turn to be put on a pedestal, and before long ... discarded?

Douglas Anderson, who runs the GAP Group, a plant hire company, went public to say Cameron had "lost his marbles", elevating Mone to the House of Lords. He described her as a "small-time businesswoman" who'd done practically nothing to boost British employment. "Because she is flogging bras and knickers she gets PR way ahead of anything she should get," he grumbled. "I mean," says Mone in her steady voice, when I read this quote out to her, "I don't know who he is to begin with. I can't stand people who say things when they have never met you and don't know you and don't know what investments you have, and everything else."

The House of Lords gig is a job, not a photo opportunity, she says. "I want to do really well in the House of Lords. I want to contribute. I'm going to go in there and learn the ropes and progress." Anderson's is not the first slight that's been thrown Mone's way. "I would just say that with me, I don't know why, there has been a lot of jealousy and a lot of negative comments." She's not bothered. "That's just life. I'm not one to sit with a box of tissues and cry myself to sleep."

It does seem to get under her skin, though. "The criticism, it's as if I have robbed a bank." For the record all she's ever done is roll up her sleeves, and "work really, really hard". "I've never asked anyone for any favours. Never asked anyone for anything. And I can assure you it will be a brilliant review." She delivers everything she says evenly, calmly, unblinkingly: she really can hold that gaze for a long time. "Just stare them in the eye. And stare at them. And stare at them," was Grandpa Mone's advice if ever little Michelle worried about having her pocket money stolen in one of the tenements where she grew up. "When they look away, you've won."

Is it possible, in these explicit days, that the great and the good still find underwear unsettling? "Yes. I mean, if I was designing the pen that you're holding now, I don't think I would be getting as much flak as I am getting. But I'm not going to sit here and say poor me. I've courted the media for many years." She is four shots (coffee) into her morning, which, like every morning, began at 5.30, was built on a maximum of five hours of sleep and kicked off with a gym session with her trainer: her goal is to achieve the personal fitness of a professional footballer (male).

Her OBE hangs framed in her hall. The open-plan lounge, where we're sitting on an L-shaped sofa, has views of the river. This is a clutter-free zone, thanks to Mone's obsessive compulsive disorder. How is her OCD these days? She laughs but — "I'm going to tell you the truth: that cushion over there is annoying me a wee bit." Which one? "The one lying on its back on the terrace," she says. When Mone's three children were growing up, "I would take out the pencil cases and put their pencils all the right way up. I'd get rid of the dirty rubbers and replace them with a batch of new ones."

So many questions. Mone's polite but coolly distant manner this morning makes me worry that she'll shut me down when I ask them. Take the financial nosedive Ultimo experienced while she was still fully on board. She has since sold 80 per cent of the company and stepped down as chairman, but wasn't the company in financial trouble since 2011? "What is true," she says, her laser-beam eyes are still on, "is that in the six to nine months before the divorce, my husband [with whom she set up and ran the business] was saying, 'You need to be sectioned. You need to be locked up.' And that had an effect on the business. Of course it did. Before that, the company was flying and then the divorce put it in a very difficult situation. It almost went under. It almost went bust, excuse the pun. It wasn't being managed properly. The thing was a nightmare. And I fought my way to save the jobs and save the brand, and I did. And I did it with not that much time to go. Now it has 63,000 people. It's part of MAS Holdings. Turnover is £1.4 billion; they are committed to turning it into a global brand."

She describes herself as "very private", a self-description that contrasts oddly with all the things we now know about her divorce, thanks to her autobiography. Unusually for a life peer, she's written about how, in a fit of humiliation, she trashed her husband's Porsche and put laxatives in his coffee the morning he was due to go to a public event. Mone's behaviour flared up after it emerged that Michael was having an affair with a member of his wife's bra designing team, a woman Mone had hired.

When Mone confronted her husband, he told her she was imagining things, hence the reference to being sectioned. Shortly before her book was published, Michael muttered something to the effect that nothing in it was true. Mone says, "Well, he would say that, wouldn't he?"

Michael is getting married in two weeks, to the woman he still says he wasn't having the affair with. Mone says she has proof that he was, having obtained it from a detective she'd hired. She "wishes him well" now. They have three children. Michael Mone's wedding will coincide with his ex-wife taking her seat in the House of Lords, almost to the day. "I take no prisoners" — this is Mone describing to me her business MO. "I don't let people mess me about. I don't go looking for trouble, but if someone attacks me I make sure I win before I leave. Sorry for saying that. But that's the truth. I never, ever lose."

By the way, she's got a new boyfriend (lives abroad, identity is still under wraps): "I've never felt this way before."

She's made a lot of her rags to riches story. Mone was born in Glasgow's East End, the daughter of a printer and a home help. Her brother died of spina bifida; her father was confined to a wheelchair. The family were close, but so poor that when little Michelle needed a wash, her mother had to take her to the public baths. But, to paraphrase her autobiography, there was always something special about Mone, even as a girl, her grandmother often said so: perhaps it was the poster of Richard Branson that the teenage Michelle pinned over her bed; perhaps it was the way, aged ten, she had two dozen children working for her once she'd monopolised the paper round.

She met Michael when she was 17. He was middle class. The two of them spent their nights fantasising about how to get rich. When Mone was 18, they had a child, then another one, then she got a job at Labatt brewers. "I am very, very, very competitive," she says, meaning she wiped the floor with all of her colleagues. Unfortunately, Labatt found out that she'd fibbed about her qualifications. She was the best thing that had ever happened to the company's Scottish marketing department (see autobiography). But they sacked her anyway.

Twenty-four and jobless, it occurred to Mone that she could never find a comfortable push-up bra. Then — she happened to be in Florida — she came across a squidgy silicone substance, "chicken fillets," as they became known in the biz. It was her lightbulb moment. There she was, a completely unknown bra inventor, persuading Selfridges to give Ultimo — it sounded classy and Italian — a whirl. Sales went through the roof on Day 1. This was because Mone had hired a group of actors to picket the department store: they'd dressed up as plastic surgeons who'd lost their livelihood because of the Ultimo bras. The stunt was all over the news.

And then America went nuts for the bras as well. There'd been an article in the *New York Post*, she says, stating that Julia Roberts owed her juicy cleavage in *Erin Brockovich* to an Ultimo bra. "Like Erin, I had to fight and learn not to take no for an answer," Mone told journalists when they called her for a quote. The bras were a worldwide phenomenon (this is still Mone talking). Flat-chested women came up to her in the street to give thanks.

Her other love when growing up, besides Richard Branson, was *Dynasty*. She longed for that life, and when she and Michael hit the jackpot, she got it: spiral staircases, expensive cars, a house with a turret. Money went to her head. She became a diva, an alcoholic, fat, suicidal. Ultimo had taken over her life. She'd be lying in bed next to Michael at night, on her BlackBerry. Her marriage was falling apart; her OCD was rampant: she had four dishwashers installed in her home. A mark of her newfound happiness is that she gets by on just the one dishwasher these days.

Mone is recognised on the street because of another one of her publicity stunts. Four years ago, she found the perfect model for her new bra campaign: herself. "I was on a beach with [the model and Rod Stewart's ex-wife] Rachel Hunter. She said, 'Michelle, when you lose the weight, do a shoot to show women what can be done and encourage them.'"

She was at the time unhappy, a fact that she says was reflected by her weight. At Hunter's words, her goal-orientated spirit went into overdrive. She lost eight stone. She bought new teeth. The result was a metaphorphosis: sweet-faced pudgy entrepreneur turns into a blonde Elizabeth Hurley. Photographs taken of the Mones from this period show a tanned, beach blonde goddess, usually on a red carpet, wearing a camera-ready smile, an enormous cleavage and a lot of jewellery. Next to her is a man who looks like he's been accidentally cut and pasted into the scene direct from a cosy evening of telly-watching in his front room. The man is Michael. They looked more natural together before Mone had her upgrade.

One can imagine that there are among Mone's male critics a sizeable proportion who find themselves caught between drooling over her flashy looks and wanting to oust her from their universe: perhaps the two things are connected. Today she's wearing Christian Louboutin wedge heels and a jumpsuit by Diane von Furstenberg, cut into a V as deep as it is wide: the Ultimo bra she's wearing underneath ensures that you'd have to be blind to miss her cleavage. Yes, she'd wear this to work, she says. Sad tidings, however, for the codgers hoping to get an eyeful on October 12. "When it comes to the House of Lords, yeah, my wardrobe needs to change slightly."

We've been speaking for an hour, and Mone has relaxed. She is showing flashes of humour, mainly when imitating the debates she often has about her career with her mother. The worm turned when she came out against Scottish independence. Anti-unionists hated her; she says it was the first time in Scotland she felt "unsafe". "My mother asked me, with the referendum, to stop talking about it publicly: 'Stop! You're getting death threats. For the sake of your family, stop please.' And I said, 'Mum! I love what this country is all about. I love being Scottish. I love being British. Why should we after all these years split up? It's bad for business.' And I said, 'Mum, no! I believe in it. And I'm not going to stop.'"

There were other reasons she moved to London: her son, Declan, has started university in the capital (he lives at his mum's) and her business interests are better taken care of here: fake tan, fake jewellery, motivational speaking. There are, she says, a heap of board positions up for grabs. And, of course, the advisory role. Did Cameron single her out for the job because she was a woman? "I'm sure he's picked men as well. I don't think it comes down to gender. It comes down to your skills set. And I'm not saying I'm wonderful, I'm Miss the-bee's-knees, but I do have a skills set. I am talented. I do know what I'm talking about in the areas that I specialise in. So if people think I'm only getting it because I've got blonde hair and am wearing nice shoes and a nice outfit, I would just say to them, 'Get in the real world.'"

Had she been the old Mone, "If I had turned up frumpy, there would be no trace of this. I'm no supermodel or glamour queen but I'm not the way I used to be, which is a size 22. I was quite frumpy then. If I was that person now, going into the House of Lords and everything else, would I be getting this much backlash? I don't think I would. But, you know, I keep fit. I'm now a size 12. I look after myself. I do love glamorous things. I think the blonde hair has got a lot to do with it as well."

Criticism never has the desired effect on her: it only makes her more determined to succeed, "because, I suppose, my whole life I've had to work hard and prove myself". She's also been successful despite not having a single qualification. "I've always had the opinion it doesn't matter where you're from or whether you have a good education or a bad one. If you've got that determination, if you stick in there, you'll do it. Have I had to stick in there more than someone that's gone to Eton or whatever? Possibly."

A few months ago, the costume designer on *Erin Brockovich* popped up — or, more likely, was hauled out by Mone-haters — and told the world that Julia Roberts wasn't wearing an Ultimo bra in that film after all. Did Mone lie? "It's a very, very, very long time ago," she says. "All I know about is the amount of samples that we sent to the wardrobe person, who we were told adjusted them to fit. Was I there when he did that? No. But it was all over the American press, that's the reason I found out about it."

Later, I look up the original American "news story": Ultimo can give you breasts like Julia Roberts, it claims, but there's no mention of Roberts wearing an Ultimo bra. It reads like a story written off the back of a press release. The kind of press release the PR department of a lingerie company might send out. She's raised three children. "I would say I'm a planner and everything was planned out to the minute. Their uniforms would get left out; the shoes would be polished at night; their school bags would be tidied out. Every day at school was like their first. It was like an army. Right?" The children even had "their KPIs growing up". What are KPIs? "Key performance indicators," she says. The concept amuses her but I'm 90 per cent certain she's not joking.

It is a bore that she won't say anything about any thoughts she might have had — and she says she's already had loads — for her small business review. Nevertheless, an idea she's had for improving diversity in the City hints at things to come. Employers obsess to their detriment about CVs, she says. "For example, HSBC: wouldn't it be incredible if they were to have like an *X Factor* for people who wanted to come and work there?" The idea delights her. It's clear that it's been rattling around in her head for some time. "Simon Cowell started it for singing. Maybe I can start it for business."

Mone's mantra is "Get out of your comfort zone." It's why she did that lingerie shoot. It's a mantra that, if inflicted on them by Mone, would likely terrify the brittle bankers and businessmen of the world, not to say this country's politicians. "You know, if they got my CV — straight in the bin. I'll tell you something, if I went to that open day I'd get straight through. That's what I'd love to see, because I'm nothing on paper. In terms of qualifications. Absolutely nothing."

You would have thought her parents would have been thrilled about their daughter's House of Lords appointment, but the first thing her mother said, this is during one of the regular calls Mone has with her parents, was, "Can't you change your mind?" "We're not used to this, right?" says Mone. "We're from the East End of Glasgow. My mum and dad are scared. But why can't someone come from where I've come from and be part of the House of Lords, be part of this country and what it stands for? Why?"

And it was her mother who told her to take down the tweet. She remembers their exchange: "'You cannot dry your top in a government car! Get that down.' 'Mum!' 'Get it down.' Then she hangs up. And, again, hindsight is a wonderful thing. I shouldn't have removed it, because I said what I said and I'd say it again. My top was wet; we were laughing about it. I said, 'How am I going to dry this?'" And so she put the air con on hot and dried it. "And I shouldn't have done it. But for God's sake, do we all have to be so doom and gloom? I was drying a top! OK, it was a government car, I'm sorry. Right? But I didn't rob a bank."

She's not getting paid for the 50 days she's taking out to draft her government review, she reminds me. She travels economy, even though you can only charge your laptop in first class, because everyone in government travels economy too, she says. You have to hold yourself back a bit, as a businesswoman, she says. "Don't get me wrong, but some of the amazing business guys out there — Lord Alan Sugar, Sir Philip Green — if I were to say some of the things they say or do, I would be an absolute bitch. And they seem to get applauded for it."

Rod Stewart, I say. Didn't he describe you as a … I read out the words hesitantly … "'Manipulative cow'?" The friction arose between the rocker and the bra designer when Mone hired Stewart's ex-wife, Rachel Hunter, to replace his girlfriend, Penny Lancaster, as the new face, and breasts, of Ultimo. She must have known what would happen?

"Yeah. I'm not going to sit here and lie to you. I'm going to tell you as it is. And, yes, it was planned. Why was it planned? Because I was, phhhhwww" — she makes the sound of a jet taking off — "straight out there with the business. I would have done anything, nothing illegal or anything, for that business. And at some point I almost died for the business, because it sucked me in so much that I took pills and almost ended it all because I couldn't cope any more. I did it for the business. I did it for the team. I did it for the brand and I knew it was going to create lots of publicity."

The campaign was "huge", she is saying now. "It was all over the world. Do I feel bad about upsetting Rod? Yeah. I replaced his girlfriend with his ex-wife. I didn't create a crime." This is exactly the kind of ruthless business tactic, she says, that men carry off and women aren't supposed to. "It was a business decision. Would I do it again? Yeah."

She had to buy her husband out of the business. "You couldn't make it up: in a board meeting, food flying across the table." Being cheated on is terrible, she says. "I was her boss! Every minute of the day. It was bad." I can't imagine, I say, but Mone hasn't finished. "And she lives in your guesthouse! And when you get in having been on the red eye, and coming in and seeing her sitting in your kitchen. With a bottle of red wine. Yes. It was tough."

She throws off the memory with a laugh. "I'm so over it now." Tax avoidance? "I have not done anything wrong. I use a big accountancy firm in Scotland. They've looked after me for 12 years. I have checked with them since the divorce: 'Have I done anything that I shouldn't have done?' 'Michelle, no.' And everyone knows my ex dealt with all the finance and dealt with all the lawyers. I was never, ever allowed to get involved in his side and he never got involved in my side." They wouldn't let her in to the House of Lords, she says, if they hadn't checked her out.

"A Tory poster girl," she's been called. This surprises her. "I believe in what they're doing. But when I don't think they're doing a good job, am I still going to agree with them? No. They don't own me."

It's her maiden speech that's worrying her. "It's a huge thing. And it's all, 'My Lord, my … ' you can't say 'You'. My 'Fellow Lord'. I don't want to screw up. I've been reading the manuals and I'm almost done." There aren't many famous people who would own up to manual-reading so as to understand the archaic rules of etiquette in the Lords. I think most would pretend that they know these things. "I never, ever, will lose," she says, "and if I have to work ten times harder and put in more work than that person I will get past the finish line before them. And that's the way I've always been. And I'm never going to change. I don't work for the government. I'm doing this for free off my own back and it's all new to me and I'm out of my comfort zone."

It's time for me to go. The glamourpuss has relaxed. She's much easier going than she was two hours ago. It must have been all that fighting talk: you can see how fired up she gets about success. It's a drive that seems to have a weirdly relaxing effect on her. "I would love one day," she says, "for the kids in Peckham and the East End of Glasgow to say, 'Wow. If we can make it in business we can get in to the House of Lords, we can get an OBE.' Because I was a complete write-off before I even started. Just because of where I was from and no education and no money."

On October 12 she'll doubtless reinvent herself again. Where will it end? "When I'm mentoring people," she said earlier, "they start off with, 'Oh, it's my mum's fault I'm overweight, or my dad's fault I can't get a job.' I say, 'Stop blaming everyone. You're in charge. If you don't want to be overweight there's just one way of doing it: cut out the crap and go to the gym.'"

It's not impossible that David Cameron still has plans for Michelle Mone: does a job as Tory health or employment minister beckon?

A PREP SCHOOL TRAGEDY

Andrew Norfolk

OCTOBER 10 2015

THE BOY WHO will one day kill himself is devouring a new *Harry Potter* novel. Too bulky for small hands, it sits on a reading stand at the family's holiday home in Brittany. Eight-year-old eyes scan each line at lightning speed, sparkling with curiosity and just a hint of mischief. It is a fleeting glimpse of childhood, captured in a home movie that charts the joy-filled early years of one upon whom nature's gifts seemed liberally showered. He was unusually intelligent, multitalented, born into a secure, loving family and soon to join a prestigious London preparatory school. Even his name carried an echo of the boy wizard. Harry Parsons was a child with the world at his feet.

Two years ago, aged 21, Harry placed a plastic bag over his head and killed himself. He left no note. It was the final act of a young man so stripped of self-worth, in the opinion of the psychiatrist who treated him for severe depression from the age of 19, that he could see no purpose in living. He felt that at his core lay something rotten and he was increasingly drawn "to a place of intense self-loathing that sometimes overwhelmed him".

The little boy in the film is so full of life, laughter and adventure. He scrambles over rocks, slides down banisters, climbs trees, messes about in boats. What catastrophe happened here? How could darkness have descended with such savage consequences? Mental illness rarely lends itself to simple explanations, but Harry's tormented parents feel they know when and where the seeds of his self-hatred were first planted. Aged 12, in the scholarship class at Colet Court, the junior division of St Paul's School, a cheerful boy with an insatiable passion for learning was transformed into one who sobbed himself to sleep and jabbed holes in his arm with a pen. He found it difficult to speak about what was wrong, but told his parents that his teacher "really hates me".

Increasingly worried about their son's welfare during that academic year, 2004-2005, they tried — in writing and at meetings with senior staff and the headmaster — to warn the school of their concern. No investigation took place and the classics teacher of whom he was so scared, Anthony Fuggle, was not questioned about his conduct.

The boy's misery seemed to vanish after he won a scholarship to the 500-year-old senior school, which stands side by side with Colet Court on the banks of the Thames in Barnes, southwest London. Harry enjoyed his time at St Paul's and won a place at Oxford. What happened during his final year at the prep school would in time, perhaps, have begun to fade from his parents' memory. Not even those who were closest to him know what triggered his terrifyingly rapid descent into a state of suicidal depression after one term of his first year at university. What subsequently made the crushing illness so difficult and eventually impossible to treat was that, defences down, this was a young man so convinced of his own worthlessness that even to talk about it caused him physical pain.

As psychiatrists sought the underlying cause of his self-revulsion, attention once more focused on Colet Court. The search for answers would expose a dark chapter in the history of one of England's most famous schools. It was a story of sexual obsession, emotional abuse and of a man entirely unfit to teach boys who, for 21 years, had daily access to some of the country's brightest young minds.

For a parent, a child's death in any circumstances is devastating. Harry's parents watched the mental disintegration of their beloved boy, "this magical creature with his exceptional mind", to the point where suicide became his only refuge. More than two years on, so raw is their grief that to be in a room with them is to feel its weight pressing down, squeezing out air. Harry's father, Roger, is a television director and producer. His mother, Henrietta, was a garden designer but has barely worked since their son's death.

She apologises for the "filthy and chaotic" state of their terraced home, in an affluent west London street, but what really hits you is its stillness. It feels like a house where laughter is a distant memory. "Every day, every hour, we beat ourselves up that we didn't recognise what was happening to him ten years ago. We feel we failed him catastrophically. We knew he was crying and didn't want to go to school any more, but we didn't realise that how he felt about himself had changed for ever. He used to love being Harry. After that year he felt deep down that something was wrong with him. I don't think that feeling ever went away."

French windows in a large kitchen gaze towards a garden of dappled sunlight. Inside, the surface of a large wooden table is barely visible as we sort through hundreds of photographs: Harry on his own; with his younger sister, Emma; with his parents; with friends. His mother speaks without self-pity, but it is a voice of exhausted despair. "I was told by a psychologist that a mother is only ever as happy as her least happy child," she says. "If that child has killed himself because he's so unhappy, because he didn't know how to be alive any more, how do you cope with that? You've given life to a child and the child has rejected it. Suicide victims don't put an end to their pain; they just pass it on to those who loved them most."

That the Parsonses now know far more about what happened at Colet Court in 2004-2005 than they did at the time is largely due to a decision, taken last year by the current leadership of St Paul's, to order an independent review of Harry's case to examine how it was handled by their predecessors. The school said it wanted to leave "no stones unturned".

Led by one of the country's top barristers, Jonathan Laidlaw QC, it was commissioned after fresh concerns about the classics teacher came to light in September 2013, five months after Harry's death. A member of Colet Court's IT department was carrying out routine maintenance of the school's computers. The photographs and stories that he found on Anthony Fuggle's hard drive triggered a criminal inquiry that led to the 58-year-old's conviction this year for possessing almost 3,000 indecent images of young boys. None was of pupils at the school.

A 93-page copy of Laidlaw's findings was delivered to Roger and Henrietta Parsons in August. Fuggle, who in June received a suspended prison sentence, refused to participate in the review, but the QC, who was given access to the school's confidential records, conducted a series of interviews with staff, past and present, former pupils, parents and medical professionals. His report, unflinching in its criticism of the former headmasters of St Paul's and its prep school, gives details of incidents involving the teacher and other pupils that should have led to his dismissal several years before Harry fell under his sway.

Laidlaw says Fuggle became infatuated with some young boys while subjecting others to the misery of emotional bullying and humiliation.

He was "an entirely unsuitable man ever to have taught". Two members of staff claimed that his inappropriate closeness to certain boys "was known at the highest levels of Colet Court". Harry, the review concludes, was "initially something of a favourite in Mr Fuggle's eyes", but was later singled out for cruel and deliberate mistreatment.

Why that happened remains a mystery, but the QC "certainly would not exclude the possibility that his suffering extended beyond emotional abuse". The boy and his parents were, he said, failed by both schools, whose inadequate response to their complaints additionally meant that "nothing was done in the years that followed to protect any other child" who may have been at risk from the teacher. In a letter to Harry's parents, the school's chairman of governors, John Robertson, accepted the review's findings in full and offered them his unreserved apology.

At the kitchen table where their young child once used pen and paper with boundless creativity, Henrietta Parsons picks up a photograph of her son, taken in September 2000. Aged eight, he is in uniform on the morning of his first day at the prep school. "When he was born, I felt daunted by the responsibility we had to protect him," she says.

"I had no idea that the place where we wouldn't be able to keep him safe was an incredibly expensive private school. Parents and teachers need to be taught how fragile a child's psyche can be. It doesn't take much to derail them, and schools carry a huge responsibility to protect them from harm. If Harry's story makes even one teacher or one parent more alert to the dangers of emotional abuse, then perhaps it'll help us to feel that his short life was not for nothing."

Harry was offered places at two top London prep schools. The Parsonses chose Colet Court largely because of its extensive grounds. Their son felt he needed "space to run". Asked to write a self-portrait, he introduced himself as a "happy boy who feels lucky about his life and interested in the way the world works". He loved his first three years at the new school.

Fuggle, a single man who lived alone with his elderly mother, first taught Harry when he was ten and initially took a liking to the child, nicknaming him "HP Sauce" because he was so cheeky. One of the teacher's colleagues recalls him admiringly describing Harry, during that year, as "very bright and brilliant at Latin".

For their final two years at Colet Court, the brightest boys were selected to join the scholarship class in preparation for the St Paul's entrance examination. None of Harry's friends made it into the form and the Parsonses sensed that their free-spirited son, disorganised and no conformist at the best of times, was not enjoying the pressure of an increasingly competitive culture.

In Harry's penultimate year they raised the possibility of withdrawing him from the scholarship form. Their sole concern was his happiness, but the consensus among staff was that this was "an extremely bright pupil with a lot of potential". They felt he would be bored in a lower stream and that his occasionally "silly behaviour" might escalate.

Towards the end of that year came the first warning that Harry was becoming wary of the master who, in addition to teaching him Latin and Greek, would also be his form teacher for his final year. Harry told his parents he didn't want to be in that class because "Mr Fuggle really hates me". The child seemed fearful and anxious, which was very unlike him. His Latin grades plummeted.

If they could turn back time, this was the moment when his parents wish they had removed Harry from Colet Court. That they did not, and instead tried to work with the school to resolve what initially seemed no more than a severe clash of personalities, is near the top of a long list of "things we might have done differently" that has become, since Harry's death, part of their daily torture.

Born in 1956 and educated at Harrow and Oxford, Fuggle joined Colet Court as head of classics in 1992, when the future Oscar-winning actor, Eddie Redmayne, was among its young pupils. Long before Harry's arrival, Fuggle additionally took on the role of form teacher for 5F, the final-year scholarship class. He was, by all accounts, a highly gifted teacher of Latin and Greek, popular with most boys and their parents, but there were hints of The Prime of Miss Jean Brodie in the way he treated the pupils of 5F, encouraging them to feel that they were an elite within the school. His classroom was set apart from the others and he guarded his territory jealously. The school and his boys were his life.

The judge who spared Fuggle a prison sentence this year at Kingston-upon-Thames Crown Court heard glowing but anonymous character references, one of them from a Colet Court teacher, in which he was described as a "kind, caring and considerate" man who was "dedicated to the welfare of the pupils in his charge" and "always maintained the correct boundaries between public and private".

Each accolade passed unchallenged. The court was left with the impression that a man who in private possessed thousands of indecent images of young boys, who collected stories of erotic encounters between adults and children and whose internet searches included terms such as "12-year-old stroked his c***", had not once allowed his sexual inclinations to intrude upon his role as a teacher of 12-year-olds.

Fuggle told the police that the images of naked schoolboys, collected over many years, gave him "sexual gratification". Laidlaw was "not able to say" that the senior management of Colet Court knew of his sexual interest in boys, but this "might well have emerged" had the school properly investigated the Parsons' complaints ten years ago, when "very serious concerns about Mr Fuggle's suitability to continue to teach would certainly have been revealed".

Three members of staff told the Laidlaw review about "Boy A", a few years older than Harry, with whom Fuggle allegedly fell in love during the child's time in his scholarship form. He was said to have become so infatuated with the boy that he wrote love letters to him, followed him around the school and bought him presents. Fuggle "openly cried at the prospect that A was to leave the school for St Paul's, saying he didn't know how he could live without [the boy]". The teacher even "dyed his hair at one point so that it was the same colour as pupil A". No disciplinary action resulted.

Shortly before Harry joined Fuggle's form came the case of "Boy B", who described Fuggle giving him money and encouraging him to stay behind in the classroom. On one occasion, "Mr Fuggle stood over him and stroked his hair." In Fuggle's employment file was a note made by Colet Court's headmaster, Geoff Thompson, of a complaint that "apparently Anthony [Fuggle] has sent [Boy B] an email saying that he had a present for him, but it would be better if he didn't tell his mother about it". The head questioned Fuggle, who admitted to buying the boy a gift and having previously given him £20. Thompson told Fuggle he had been "incredibly foolish" and must have no more contact with the child. He took no further action.

Laidlaw additionally established that Fuggle tended to have not only favourites but also "one or two members of the same class who became scapegoats". One teacher said that "when Anthony Fuggle decided he didn't like a boy, he really took against him" and "would have a physical reaction when their name was mentioned in the common room".

It was into the latter category that the 12-year-old Harry now fell. A senior member of staff recalled that the classics master was "very hard" on him. He remembered Harry arriving late for a lesson and explaining apologetically, "Mr Fuggle's been shouting at me again."

Back at home it was rapidly becoming apparent to his parents that something was seriously wrong. They found him sobbing in bed at midnight. He began self-harming. A boy who, until recently, had loved going to school now dreaded it.

After Henrietta Parsons spoke to the school's deputy headmaster, Harry was seen by the St Paul's psychologist, who felt his mental health was fine. He was merely "a child who wanted life to be enjoyable and for whom school was no longer a place of any enjoyment". Survive the rest of the year and he would encounter a much less pressurised atmosphere at the senior school. They did not discuss teachers and Harry did not mention Fuggle.

The advice seemed reassuring, but in February 2005 Harry, now 13, came home and collapsed in tears. He'd hit his head on a cupboard while alone in the classroom with Fuggle. The teacher, he said, told him he hoped he'd get a brain tumour. The incident convinced the Parsonses that it was time to act. In a letter to the headmaster, Harry's mother listed a series of "nasty and vindictive" incidents and described her son as "close to breaking point".

"Harry frequently comes home from school and buries his head in his hands on the table, saying, 'Why does Mr Fuggle hate me so much?' Initially, we thought that Harry was bringing this dislike upon himself by his silly behaviour. Increasingly, however, we see Mr Fuggle's behaviour as nothing short of petty bullying. He enjoys his power over the boys and toys with it. [Harry] loved his first three years at the school. Look at him now. He used to be bursting with interest in everything around him. Now he says, 'I feel like a used-up Biro with no ink left.' He is 13 years old."

Laidlaw says that when the headmaster read the "articulate and extremely carefully written" letter, "it should have been clear that this was a complaint of substance requiring urgent and serious attention", not least because Thompson received it within months of learning of the "Boy B" incident. Harry's parents were invited to meet the head, but their recollection is that he asked them no questions about the issues they had raised and showed no interest in their son's welfare. He also told them that no one had previously raised any concerns with him about Fuggle.

Ten years on, Thompson's explanation for his failure to investigate the complaint was to blame Henrietta Parsons for having asked him not to show her letter to Fuggle "until Harry has left his class". The former head, who did not think the "Boy B" incident had "any bearing whatsoever" on Harry's case, said he was "dismayed that Mr and Mr Parsons didn't think that I did everything I could at the time". He had wanted to carry out a thorough investigation, but his hands were tied by their desire for confidentiality.

The Parsonses feared that, if Fuggle learnt of their letter, he would make life even more hellish for their son. In the pressure-cooker atmosphere of 5F, where academic success was paramount, they sensed that poor pastoral care was viewed by some parents as a price worth paying. Henrietta Parsons remembers being told by one mother that you put up with Colet Court in order to secure a place at St Paul's. Harry limped to the end of the year, then remarkably won a top scholarship to the senior school.

Fuggle's parting shot was a confidential report for St Paul's in which he described Harry as "self-centred and obsessive", traits he blamed on the boy having been brought up "in a very liberal, laissez-faire way". Laidlaw observes that such a damning opinion was "entirely out of step with everyone else's view of him".

The Parsonses were so dismayed by Thompson's handling of the matter that a year later, with Harry safely established at St Paul's and his spirits seemingly lifted, they wrote a second letter, this time to the governors of the senior school. They explained their desire to ensure that should further concerns about Fuggle come to light in the future it would not be possible for anyone to claim that he had never before "made life hellish for individual boys in his class". Enclosed with the correspondence was a copy of their earlier letter to Thompson.

The new letter led to a meeting with Dr Martin Stephen, the high master (headmaster) of St Paul's. They recall him explaining that he could take no action unless they were prepared to make a formal complaint. This would trigger an inquiry that Harry would have to "spearhead". They told him they were "not prepared to put Harry through such an ordeal" and were left with the clear impression that Stephen "did not want to investigate the matter at all".

Harry's mother remembers having asked more than once why St Paul's could not initiate its own investigation, for which they and Harry would give evidence. She and her husband felt "astonished at the school's failure to recognise that this was now their problem, not ours, because they had a duty of care to other pupils".

Stephen told the Laidlaw review that an investigation in the absence of a formal complaint would have been "contrary to natural justice". He said he had wanted to take matters further, was keen to minimise Harry's role in any formal investigation and would never have used the word "spearhead". The boy's parents must have "misremembered the meeting".

There the matter rested until Harry fell ill in 2011. Neither Thompson in 2005 nor Stephen in 2006 investigated Fuggle's conduct. Each blamed their inaction on the Parsonses reluctance to make a formal complaint. The review gives this explanation short shrift. So troubling were the concerns the Parsonses raised that at each meeting it should have been the objective of both heads "to make it clear that the complaint raised issues of such seriousness that it could not be ignored and would have to be investigated".

A thorough investigation would have brought to light not only Fuggle's emotional abuse of Harry, but "further evidence of inappropriate behaviour" towards other pupils. Thompson retired in 2007 and Stephen left St Paul's in 2010. Each rejected the report's findings and "disagreed very strongly" with its criticism of their actions. Thompson, 68, who described Fuggle as an "excellent teacher", said he had "analysed and re-analysed" his handling of the Parsonses concerns "and I don't think that I could have reacted any differently". Stephen, 66, said the report was "not a fair or accurate representation" of his role.

In 40 years of teaching he had "never to my knowledge been accused of not placing the welfare of the children in my care as my top priority". Speaking through his solicitors, Fuggle categorically rejected all accusations of bullying. He said no allegation of sexual abuse has ever been put to him. Any such claims would be equally "incorrect and unfounded".

Laidlaw's review found that Fuggle emotionally abused Harry and described his treatment as "deliberate cruelty". He did not think that Fuggle "intended that Harry would suffer any long-term harm". But, "Whether or not [he] even considered how much damage he may have been causing, the bullying should never have occurred."

Much happened in Harry's life after he left Colet Court. The child became an adolescent and then a young adult. Along the way, he made many friends, nearly died from peritonitis and won glittering academic prizes. There were parties, girlfriends and a place at Wadham College, Oxford, to read chemistry. Harry was so gifted that his teachers said he could have gone on to study "almost any subject". The school's reference for his university application described him as "wonderfully passionate, intellectually curious, perpetually smiling and bursting with ideas". He was, it concluded, "someone who is likely to do something very special with his life".

Home at Christmas after his first term at Oxford, Harry's mental health collapsed. He began talking about suicide. Within days he was referred to a psychiatrist and in February 2011, two months after his 19th birthday, was briefly admitted to a mental health ward at Charing Cross hospital before he was moved to the Priory hospital in Roehampton. There, Harry received every form of treatment for severe depression — medication, biological and psychological therapy, even electroconvulsive therapy — but Dr Mark Collins, the psychiatrist who treated him for more than two years, said his illness was relentless.

That summer Harry made his first suicide attempt. He was found in a coma after taking a huge overdose of antidepressants. After a further year of struggle, he applied again to university, this time accepting a place at Glasgow. He completed two terms. In April 2013, alone in his bedroom in a shared flat, he killed himself.

In his 25 years as a psychiatrist, Collins says he has encountered suicide "too many times", but has "never felt so emotionally affected as I was by Harry's death". In the course of their many sessions, it became evident that "deep inside, despite being this extremely bright young man, was a huge self-loathing and a core belief that, 'I'm bad. I'm a bad person.'"

There was "a sense of intense physical and psychological pain, which manifested itself when Harry talked about his self-esteem. When someone presents with an illness like this you go through all the usual causes: drugs, alcohol, leaving home, issues to do with identity, forming intimate relationships, worries that he might be gay. Becoming a grown-up can be difficult, but none of those seemed to apply."

Another potential factor was "trauma from the past that had surfaced later". Collins says that Harry "found it almost impossible to talk about his experience with Mr Fuggle". Laidlaw's review states that Harry did not say anything to suggest there had been any type of sexual abuse, but "that does not, of course, mean it did not happen".

Harry did reveal to Collins that he was so scared of the teacher he would hide from him at school and always tried to ensure that someone else was with him when he was in Fuggle's presence. Collins believes that verbal bullying and humiliation "would certainly have had an impact on Harry in terms of his self-esteem". It was "undermining and bewildering if a master suddenly turns on you", especially one who previously made you feel special.

"That core self-loathing is absolutely the sort of stuff you get when children are abused, in whatever way," he says. "There was no sense whatsoever of anything of that nature coming from within the family. The Fuggle stuff is the only preceding event of any note that would go any way towards explaining it. It may well have damaged his psyche in a way that left a scar."

Neither Collins nor Laidlaw felt it was possible to be certain that what happened at his prep school was the direct cause of the self-hatred that emerged when Harry's depression struck six years later, but the QC's report states that, "One certainly cannot rule that possibility out. Harry's parents will, naturally, continue to believe that Mr Fuggle's behaviour played its part in Harry's death. They may well be right."

In March 2011, with Harry desperately ill, his mother wrote to the current headmaster of Colet Court, Tim Meunier, to let him know of the "terrible event that has descended on our family" and of their growing conviction that its roots lay "in our son's experience at Colet Court".

Meunier's reply briefly offered sympathy for the family's distress, but insisted that both the prep school and St Paul's had dealt with the concerns raised by the Parsonses "entirely appropriately". He went on to suggest that the family must be "very proud" of Harry's subsequent academic achievements and told them he had "no concerns whatsoever regarding Mr Fuggle's suitability to teach young boys".

Laidlaw does not criticise Meunier for the letter. The head was "doing no more than following legal advice". There was no evidence of a cover-up at any stage, but the QC's opinion is that the school's defensive response in 2011 and in correspondence after Harry's suicide in 2013 merely intensified his family's agony "at the very time they were witnessing the terrible struggles of their son and then reeling from his death".

The past two years have not been the easiest in the proud history of an institution, founded in 1509, whose former pupils include John Milton, Samuel Pepys, Viscount Montgomery of Alamein and the chancellor of the exchequer, George Osborne. Multiple allegations surfaced in 2014 that implicated more than a dozen former teachers at St Paul's and Colet Court in the sexual abuse of boys from the Sixties to the Eighties. The resulting criminal inquiry has led to five ex-members of staff being charged with sexual offences against children. They are the alleged crimes of an earlier generation.

Fuggle's cruelty towards Harry, however, and his earlier infatuation with at least two Colet Court boys, were not sins of the distant past. It was as recently as 2006 that the former high master of St Paul's seemed, according to Laidlaw, not to understand "how to run a proper investigation with the welfare of the child being as important at least … as the rights of the individual who stood accused".

Annual day fees are £18,100 at Colet Court and £22,600 at St Paul's. For their money, parents are entitled to expect for their sons an education of the highest quality in an environment whose values and systems are structured to keep them safe from harm. Stephen's successor, Professor Mark Bailey, acknowledged that the school's correspondence with the Parsonses in 2011 and 2013 lacked compassion. Letters were sent under professional advice, but he regretted "not allowing my humanity to intervene".

He ultimately decided to confront the Fuggle affair head-on. "We wanted, belatedly, to give [the Parsonses] the investigation they should have had all along and to identify ways we can learn and make the school safer and better." In an otherwise damning report, Laidlaw asserts that, "Had these events occurred when Professor Bailey was in charge I am quite certain the outcome would have been very different."

Separate reviews have found that the school's child protection procedures in 2015 are unrecognisable from those of ten years ago. Colet Court's scholarship class has also ceased to exist. It was felt to create "too much pressure". At his former school, the story of a boy who once felt lucky about his life will not be forgotten. St Paul's plan is that in future all second-year pupils will attend an annual talk about mental health and young people. With his parents' blessing, it will be called the Harry Parsons memorial lecture.

Harry cycled through a park every day on his way to and from school. Today, a wooden bench carries a simple plaque: "Harry Waldo Parsons, 1991-2013. Loved beyond words."

POACHERS LEAVE THE FOREST BARE
FOR HUNGRY PYGMIES

Jerome Starkey

OCTOBER 10 2015

HOW MANY PYGMIES can you fit in a Lexus? The answer would determine the size of our hunting party and whether or not we caught our lunch in the forests of the Central African Republic.

The Bayaka pygmies and their Aka cousins, genetically distinct from much of humanity, have lived off the forests of central Africa for tens of thousands of years. But their way of life is under threat as those forests are denuded by poachers, loggers and commercial bushmeat hunters.

The Lexus wasn't part of the plan, but it was the only car available, and if we were going hunting for a day, rather than a month or more as is the Bayaka way, then it was the only option.

By the time we arrived at Yandoubé, the pygmy village, the car was already full with a retinue of helpers. There was Papi, the driver, whose absurdly sumptuous 4x4, complete with cream leather seats and electric windows, had broken down three times the previous day. There was Yafu, who came with a chainsaw in case any trees had fallen across the forest tracks. There was Mosset, the tracker and translator. Finally, there was Leance, a guide and interpreter from the national parks authority. Leance announced our arrival in Yandoubé by leaning out of the window and yelling "Bokia! Bokia!" or "Hunt! Hunt!" as we passed a cluster of thatched huts.

By the time we stopped moving, the car was surrounded and it took me a moment to notice the wiry white man, with a pencil moustache, who had come out of his house to see all the fuss. Louis Sarno, from New Jersey, has spent 30 years living with the pygmies and recording their music. His house, which had a verandah and was slightly larger than the rest, was looted when Muslim Seleka rebels from the north toppled the government in 2013.

Mr Sarno, 61, fled into the forest for three months with his girlfriend of six years, Agati, and their neighbours, but he lost four years' worth of manuscripts and a hard-drive full of photographs. "When I first came here, no one had seen motor vehicles. No one had seen paper money," he said. "But that's all changing. Logging companies came in. Poaching came in. People started working. They are no longer self-sufficient and self-reliant in the same way."

We left Yandoubé with 12 extra passengers, six men and six women, each with a hand-woven net made from forest twine. There were 15 people inside the car and two clinging on the back. The most traditional form of hunting is with nets. Sometimes the Bayaka use dogs to hunt porcupines, or spears for hogs. Increasingly they use guns to kill monkeys, which they scare down from the tree tops with a whistle that imitates an eagle's call. "Monkeys have been decimated by shotguns," Mr Sarno said. "I have spent weeks in the forest and haven't even heard a monkey."

The Bayaka have long used bushmeat to barter with neighbouring Bantu tribes for cigarettes and flour, but the advent of logging and better roads has encouraged locals to trade bushmeat with much larger markets. "They are killing far too much for local consumption," Mr Sarno said.

"People are just trying to make a bit of money but it has devastated the wildlife in the forest." There was no attempt at stealth when we moved into the trees. The hunters were constantly calling to each other as they linked their nets into a large circle, before hurling logs into the centre and waving handfuls of leafy branches to try to flush out their quarry. But there were no signs of any animal.

"It is bad luck if one of the hunters had had sex with their husband or their wife the night before the hunt," explained Mungambe Anise, one of the hunters. "It is bad luck if someone is pregnant. The animals can sense it and run away." There appeared to be an argument over who might have had sex. The men looked at the ladies' tummies for any signs of pregnancy. "Maybe they don't know," Mr Anise said.

DIPLOMATIC MISCHIEF: PUTIN MUST WORK HARDER TO WIN BACK BRITISH TRUST

Leading Article

OCTOBER 26 2015

IN AN INTERVIEW with *The Times*, Alexander Yakovenko, Moscow's ambassador to London, calls for Britain to be more co-operative. It is of course his duty to urge a resumption of regular talks between all levels of government, including the intelligence agencies. Since relations dropped just below freezing point, Mr Yakovenko has been underemployed; like others in that position, he has taken to writing an often impenetrable blog.

It would be easier to feel sorry for this unfulfilled envoy if his diplomacy added up to more than inverting the facts. He claims that the Anglo-Russian froideur began with the Syrian conflict and intensified during the Ukraine crisis. In truth, relations are bad because Russia is in multiple breach of international law and because of the reckless brinkmanship of Vladimir Putin. Intelligence co-operation with Russia became impossible after the dissident ex-KGB officer Alexander Litvinenko was poisoned in London. The refusal of the Russian authorities to help fully in the investigation of his death has made pointless a meaningful exchange of intelligence.

Some exchange of information was conducted in the lead-up to the Winter Olympics in Sochi last year, aimed at reducing any terrorist threat to the Games. When, soon after the closing ceremonies, Mr Putin moved against Ukraine, it was plain that there was little scope for a trusting relationship. The annexation of Ukraine was a violation of the postwar world order.

The active subversion of eastern Ukraine signalled that Mr Putin's strategic aim was to destabilise Europe. His use of hybrid warfare — a limited conflict in which Russian troops were deployed in disguise — was a way of dodging the rules of war and neutralising Nato. Mr Putin's bombers have come close to British airspace and have violated that of other Nato allies. In no respect has Russia behaved like a country willing to work in the spirit of partnership.

Now Mr Yakovenko calls on Britain to share targeting intelligence on Islamic State positions in Syria. This would be absurd. Russia shares military intelligence with Iran (and therefore the Hezbollah militias), with the Syrian government and with Iraq. While they are all engaged in some aspect of the war against Isis, their shared purpose is to keep the Syrian dictator, Bashar al-Assad, in power — and to thwart, indeed kill, those western-backed groups who are fighting his regime.

Russia has not been openly engaged in the Syrian conflict for long and yet has managed to shatter the basic laws of war. Airstrikes in northern Homs this month killed 59 civilians including 33 children, according to Human Rights Watch. One airstrike at Ter Maaleh struck close to a bakery, hitting a queue, supposedly with the intention of killing a western-backed Free Syrian Army commander. Neither Russia nor the Syrian government ever identifies intended targets, nor gives warning to civilian populations in affected areas.

Mr Yakovenko bemoans the lack of a personal relationship between the British and Russian leaders. Yet the history of this friendship is that it favours Kremlin manipulation; that one of the leaders seizes on conciliatory gestures as a token of weakness and gullibility.

Perhaps the ambassador can persuade Jeremy Corbyn that there is no room for suspicion in Anglo-Russian relations. For the rest of us, he will have to try a little harder.

There is no diplomacy, Mr Yakovenko, like candour.

BRITAIN NEEDS TO SMASH
THE CUT-GLASS CEILING

Clare Foges

OCTOBER 27 2015

IS THERE A PHRASE more dull or disconnected from its meaning than "social mobility"? It should evoke the triumphs of hard-working people over the obstacles that stand between them and success, but sounds more like something beige, rubbery and clinical you'd find advertised in the back of *Saga Magazine*.

Still, what's in a name? Quite a lot, according to the prime minister. In his speech to the Conservative Party conference this month, he highlighted the scandal of those with white-sounding names being nearly twice as likely to get called for job interviews as those with ethnic-sounding names who had exactly the same qualifications.

Yesterday he announced the remedy: applications for graduate-level jobs across government are to be name-blind. The civil service will be sifting through Jane and John Does, as will big recruiters like Deloitte, HSBC and the BBC. Universities are following suit. It's a good move but if the government wants to tear down the barriers holding people back and actually shift social mobility, they need to do more on class discrimination.

In Britain the salary you earn is more closely linked to your father's wage than in any other major country. Our class system is like some vast mountain of sedimentary rock formed over centuries: layer upon layer of wealth, education and marriage making it super-strong and impervious to government intervention. Lord knows they have tried, chipping away with grammars, assisted places, Sure Start and social mobility task forces.

The government's academy and free schools programmes might prove to be the game-changer. We will only know for sure if 30 years from now the prime minister, London mayor and would-be mayor come not from Eton College but Eton Academy.

But there's more that could be done now. At university application, it's time to ditch the Ucas personal statement; a great chance for middle-class kids to mention their violin Grade 6 and conversational Mandarin but not so good for those denied such opportunities. Graduate job recruitment should become university-blind as well as name-blind. Teach First, which recruits 1,600 graduate teachers every year, does blind applications in every sense: name, school, university. The results are remarkable: 42 per cent of recruits were the first in their family to go to university and 27 per cent were on free school meals. If you can fix graduate recruitment like this, you can help to boost social mobility.

But one thing above all others stands in the way of true social mobility. We need to talk about talking: about voices, accents, pronunciation — and the way speech can hold some people back. In his preface to Pygmalion, George Bernard Shaw believed it "impossible for an Englishman to open his mouth without making some other Englishman despise him". The great variety of British accents and pronunciation styles means we've got the measure of each other at "hello" and have decided within the space of a glottal stop on someone's status, education and even ability.

Earlier this year the Social Mobility Commission found that law and accountancy firms were applying a "poshness test" to job applicants, which favoured middle-class mannerisms and accents. Alan Milburn, its chairman, said that "young people with working-class backgrounds are being systematically locked out of top jobs".

Chumbawamba might have sung a song called RIP RP that danced on the grave of Received Pronunciation ("Let our words go free/ Coo and howl/ Lay flat your vowels/ Ah ay ee/ Goodbye RP") but in many professions a cut-glass ceiling remains.

When recruiters talk about the need for "polished" candidates they mean not just the dry-cleaned M&S suit but the way they speak. Just as important as financial capital and social capital is linguistic capital. That doesn't mean speaking with the purple plumminess of the late, great Brian Sewell. On the BBC Huw Edwards, Adrian Chiles and Steph McGovern use Standard English: grammar correct, each consonant and diphthong clearly enunciated. But some accents do come with quirks that, like it or not, won't please employers: h-dropping: 'ow now brown cow; the use of "what" as a relative pronoun ("the story what was in the paper was offensive".)

The fastest-growing dialect is known as "multicultural London English", a fusion of Cockney, Caribbean and African American, spoken by young people of all races. MCLE regularises the past tense of the verb "to be": "You was there, I weren't." We can pretend that the Ali G school of speaking is different but equal. But that won't help the bright young man who is turned down for numerous jobs because he doesn't have "it", little knowing he was doomed from the moment he opened his mouth.

Those who speak sloppily will always be locked out of an invisible club and we do them no favours by denying its existence. Because there is a proper way of speaking, whatever your accent. There is Standard English, there is virtue in clarity and crispness, and these things can make a huge difference to our chances in life.

So if the government is serious about social mobility, it is time to revive the tweedy old concept of elocution. Schools should teach children how to speak as well as how to think. Lessons on pronunciation and projection should come as standard. One school in Basildon has led the way. At Cherry Tree Primary the children learn to pronounce "thought" instead of "fought", "both" instead of "bofe". Ambitious parents have long sent their children to elocution lessons to help them to get on. Why shouldn't we extend those same opportunities to all children?

Having polled a smattering of the chattering classes there is clearly profound squeamishness about elocution lessons. One likened them to "verbal social cleansing". Others saw it as a capitulation to prejudice: the world needs to change its view, not the children their voices. All very right on but it won't break this invisible sound barrier.

Children should leave school not just with a clutch of GCSEs but with the gift of clear and proper speech. As Henry Higgins tells Eliza Doolittle: "Remember that you are a human being with a soul and the divine gift of articulate speech: that your native language is the language of Shakespeare and Milton and the Bible; and don't sit there crooning like a bilious pigeon."

GCHQ LIFTS THE LID ON ITS MISSION TO PROTECT BRITAIN

Ben Macintyre

OCTOBER 28 2015

IN A CONCRETE AND steel-lined room deep in the bowels of GCHQ stands a grey metal machine, roughly the size of a large fridge, emitting a low hum. The room, known as the Cage, is where the hi-tech cryptographic "keys" are made that protect all secret government communications.

The Cage is the most secure place in GCHQ, the vast circular building in the suburbs of Cheltenham universally known as the Doughnut. These cryptographic keys are the most valuable tools in the intelligence trade, enabling the passing of coded information without fear of interception. The room is sealed off from the rest of the building. The grey machine is a random-number generator, producing the raw material from which all cryptographic keys are made.

It is the most secret machine in the most secret department of the most secret branch of British intelligence. And no journalist has ever seen it before. The mere fact that I am standing here is a measure of the cultural change that is taking place at GCHQ, the home of British signals intelligence (Sigint), as distinct from MI5 and MI6, which deal largely in human intelligence. In the tradition of Bletchley Park, this was for decades the most closed and mysterious branch of the secret intelligence services. Most British citizens had little idea that it existed, which was exactly how the spooks and geeks of GCHQ wanted it.

The explosion of the internet, the astonishingly rapid evolution of communications technology and the revelations of the NSA whistleblower Edward Snowden have changed that for ever: GCHQ is opening its doors, at least a crack, to reveal what it does, if not exactly how it is done. This is the first time that GCHQ has allowed its most senior officials to be interviewed, on the record, and even, in the case of those with a public profile, by name. "GCHQ has to be out there," one of the senior officials says. "We can't operate behind veils of secrecy any more."

Ensuring secure communications for the government and armed forces is only one small aspect of the work of GCHQ. Its most prominent (and controversial) role is the tracking of terrorist threats to the UK by means of intercepting and analysing "bulk data", the great mass of electronic communications, a process that its opponents call snooping, and which GCHQ insists is the proportionate invasion of privacy necessary to keep Britain safe.

GCHQ performs myriad other functions less apparent to the public: using electronic interception to combat serious and organised crime, liaising with MI5 and MI6 to provide internal security and external intelligence, tackling online child abuse, working with the military on operations worldwide, developing new technological tools, liaising with outside business, and training up a new generation of digital spooks.

In addition, GCHQ is increasingly preoccupied with cyber threats: the danger posed to Britain by electronic espionage and hackers seeking to steal information, disrupt or destroy British interests using the weapons of the internet age. In the words of Robert Hannigan, GCHQ's director: "The organisation detects a wide range of cyberattacks every day. The threat is growing in number, sophistication and impact."

If the conflict of the future is cyberwar, then this otherwise sleepy corner of Cheltenham is on the front line. The Doughnut stands out like a vast and incongruous spaceship, surrounded by car parks, on the edge of Cheltenham. Visitors approach via a series of security gates, and then up a broad avenue of beeches and lavender beds. A man mows the grass, possibly the most secret gardener in Britain. We might be on the campus of a Midwestern university save for the high fences, razor wire and satellite dish on the lawn the size of a swimming pool.

At a curved reception desk, I am required to hand in all electronic devices. GCHQ is the hub of Britain's government communications but it is impossible to call out of it on your personal mobile, or receive calls while in it. I am about to enter the first of several swipe-card barriers and entry pods when I remember the flash-drive attached to my key ring. I return and hand it in. "What would have happened if I had walked in with that in my pocket?" I ask. My guide simply gives me a weighty look.

GCHQ employs 6,000 people, as well as heavily vetted outside contractors. The corridors are thronged with staff. Some are in business suits and ties, but most are casually dressed. Many are in jeans, shorts, even flip flops. One young man with an earring sports a T-shirt reading: "Occupy Mars." James Bonds they are not.

The impression is of a highly successful internet technology company that, like Google, has dispensed with normal corporate behaviour in favour of informality, innovation and working on the move. Signs have been posted on the glass doors: "Beware, we have a red badge visitor here today: keep all conversations to official." "Official" is the classification of material below "top secret" and "secret"; in other words, un-secret. The red badge visitor is me.

The Doughnut consists of three circular floors running around the entire building. In case of emergency, a terrorist attack for example, the building can be divided into separate sections, meaning that operations could continue in one area even if disabled or destroyed in another.

The ground floor is known as the Street and in many ways it superficially resembles a shopping mall: there is a Starbucks and a Costa, an internet café and a gym, a recreation room with television and a library of books. Posters on the wall advertise social gatherings and talks, as if this were an ordinary company. In reality, it could hardly be less normal: beneath our feet is the most powerful computing facility in the country, bank after bank of processors covering an area the size of two football pitches, crunching data of staggering scale and complexity.

The man serving coffee in Costa is no ordinary barista: every two years he has to pass a legal security exam. I am told I may not enter the dining hall in case I pick up some non-official tidbit, "because people converse differently when they are eating — they tend to be more relaxed". It is a surreal experience to wander around a packed building in the knowledge that everyone knows you are there but no one acknowledges that they know you are there. A line of people are sitting at computer terminals. As I pass, I glance over their shoulders. The screens are blank; one man is sitting staring fixedly at the image of a tiger cub. They have seen me coming. I am not going to overhear, or see, anything I am not supposed to.

GCHQ's essential role is twofold, and in a way combines the two functions of MI6 and MI5: intelligence and security, discovering secret information that will serve and protect British interests, and defending the nation against external (and often internal) threats. The technique by which this is done is, broadly speaking, the same, whether the target is a terrorist, drug smuggler, Taliban fighter or child abuser. GCHQ's priorities are set by the government, in the Joint Intelligence Committee and the weekly meetings of the National Security Council, chaired by the prime minister.

Bulk data is gathered and maximised to collect foreign communications, suspicious patterns of behaviour are sought and identified, often working on a tip-off or other sources of intelligence. All acquisition of bulk data is collected under ministerial warrant, and authorised in the UK: this, of course, is how classic espionage works.

GCHQ is not in the business of routinely reading your emails. The myths that Britain is subject to mass surveillance by GCHQ, or that certain trigger words set off alarm bells in the Doughnut, are just that. The data harvested is foreign in focus; given the global nature of internet traffic, this may well include communications to and from people in Britain. To investigate an individual in Britain any further, an additional warrant would be required. Having identified a target, additional steps must be taken before any content can be examined — to go after a specific internet user, mobile phone or Facebook account.

At each stage, the hunters must clearly explain and justify why the action being taken is both "necessary" and "proportionate", that it will achieve the desired result, that the outcome is demonstrably important, and that the process intrudes upon privacy no more than is required. As one GCHQ official put it: "The challenge is how do we fillet out information without looking like the Stasi? The mission is about saving lives but also obeying the letter of the law."

Such a bald simplification of the role of GCHQ hardly reflects the bewildering range of applications, and the range of skills needed to collect, analyse, interpret and pass on intelligence and security information to GCHQ's "customers": MI5 (internal security), MI6 (external intelligence), the armed forces, the Foreign Office, No 10 and the National Crime Agency. The popular image of the GCHQ spook is of a technological boffin, and to be sure a level of technical expertise is essential. As the director-general of technology put it: "If you are afraid of cookies, this is not the place for you."

But the process of turning raw intercepted data into usable intelligence also requires a host of linguists, lawyers, psychologists, anthropologists, international affairs specialists, trained analysts and experts in the entire range of human life. My guide, who has worked in various departments of GCHQ for more than ten years, is a music graduate. "You would be surprised where excellence comes from," the head of strategy said. "We are not all academics." Some people in the building speak eight languages; some virtually speak in computer code.

The emergency rapid-response hub of GCHQ is the GCHQ Sigint Operations Centre, or Gsoc (this is an organisation that cherishes its acronyms). This event response centre operates around the clock in reaction to crises. If a hacker launches a cyberattack on a key element of the country's economic infrastructure, if a bomb goes off, if a known terrorist suddenly pops up, this is the first line of electronic action. It is, in effect, a mini-GCHQ, able to deploy the full technological power of the organisation at speed. "There is what we call the golden hour — after, say, a kidnapping — when the signals intelligence may be buzzing around and still accessible before the baddies shut it down," explains the head of the Gsoc team, consisting of 11 analysts and a technology expert.

TV screens hang down from the ceiling; analysts sit at desks around a central hub; there is the low murmur of extreme concentration. To my eyes, it resembles nothing so much as a miniature newspaper office. In a boardroom a few doors away, the head of tradecraft, a bouncy young man with the fizzing energy of a zealot, outlines the sheer magnitude of the task facing GCHQ. "Going back to Bletchley Park and the Cold War, GCHQ has always found ways to exploit vulnerabilities in the communications system and turn that into intelligence. But the exponential growth of digital communications is unprecedented in history. It's one hell of a problem."

Before the First World War, some three quarters of the world's telegraphic cables, the "Victorian internet", passed through the UK or key colonies. The official censor could simply read them. Even the codebreakers of Bletchley Park, though dealing with a vastly increased volume of communications traffic, could intercept and gather the large though limited number of wireless messages sent by the Axis powers.

The collection of bulk data is not new; but the definition of what "bulk" actually means has changed utterly and the scale of communications data today is on an unimaginably vast scale. Half the world, more than three billion people, are active internet users.

"Everybody is on the internet," my guide says. "It's like the air." These users communicate in a vast and growing variety of ways; every day apps appear offering new ways to pass information. Between 2006 and 2013 the whole of online data increased tenfold. "The amount we can process is tiny, because big data is really big. It's about trying to keep up."

The contrast between what the private sector is investing in the internet, and what government can afford to spend, poses another dilemma. The head of technology says: "The growth of the internet is relentless; $3.7 trillion a year is being invested every year on developing the internet. The only way we can keep up is to be clever."

Internet communications are now routinely encrypted, vastly complicating the job of GCHQ. Moreover, even when data is decoded, it is increasingly difficult to pinpoint who really sent it, and who actually received it, because it is extraordinarily easy to hide on the internet, and getting easier. Any single user can conceal themselves behind hundreds of false identities. "It's not like looking for a needle in a haystack. It's like looking for a piece of hay in a haystack. The good guys look very like the bad guys."

The talk of bad guys is ubiquitous. Almost every person I speak to refers, at some point, to "the mission", and there is a distinctive missionary ethos to the place, the sense of fighting a battle for good against evil.

"Our mission is saving lives but also obeying the letter of the law. Our job is about finding the new threats and tying them to real people and real targets that others can do something about," the head of tradecraft says. How does GCHQ physically access the foreign cables carrying the data it wants to look at? Now there is a pause. "That's the crown jewels. That's the magic. We can't tell people how we do that."

Access to bulk data clearly depends, in large part, on internet companies either agreeing, or being forced, to open up their databanks. In the post-Snowden world, such companies are unwilling to be seen colluding with intelligence services. Yet those such as Google routinely, with the permission of users (though they may not realise they have given it), gather personal data to use for commercial purposes.

Here, for the first time, a note of real passion enters the voice of the head of tradecraft: "If the internet is being used to sell you things, why is it wrong for little GCHQ to use a tiny bit of the data to stop you being blown up on holiday?" That, in essence, is the conundrum of GCHQ: where the right to privacy ends and the right to pry begins.

'DON'T CALL ME BLONDE'

Charlotte Proudman interviewed by Will Pavia

NOVEMBER 7 2015

WE'RE IN A photographer's studio in Boston. Charlotte Proudman, the young barrister who took a stand against sexism, is standing on a box. She's wearing what I think would be deemed a black trouser suit, although I'm nervous to ask. It is almost exactly six weeks since Proudman's very public reprimand of a heavyweight City solicitor named Alexander Carter-Silk.

She had contacted Carter-Silk on the business networking site LinkedIn; he had replied saying he was "delighted" to make her acquaintance, before complimenting her on the head shot on her profile page. "This is probably horrendously politically incorrect but that is a stunning picture!!!" he wrote. "You definitely win the prize for best LinkedIn picture I have ever seen." This was not a prize that Proudman was hoping to win.

She wrote back, informing Carter-Silk that she was "on LinkedIn for business purposes and not to be approached about my physical appearance or objectified by sexist men. The eroticisation of women's physical appearance is a way of exercising power over women. It silences women's professional attributes as their physical appearance becomes the subject." Then she published a screenshot of the exchange on Twitter, asking how many other women on LinkedIn spent their time batting away comments about their looks, instead of inquiries about their professional skills.

Thus began the great sexism debate of 2015. Within a few days, Proudman was at the centre of one of those sudden media storms that seem to rise up suddenly and blot out the sun. On the one hand, she was a newly minted feminist icon, prepared to risk her own career for the sake of gender equality at work. On the other, she was a "feminazi" who was seeking to purge all life and colour from human interactions by publicly shaming a man who dared to compliment her. Journalists sought out her relatives, trolls besieged her Twitter account and she got death threats.

Now here we are, in the calm after the media storm. More specifically, we are in the studio of Josh Andrus. Proudman has agreed to tell her story, and naturally, we want to take her picture. "Great cheekbones," shouts Andrus, as he shoots her. I imagine some men may be a little careful about complimenting Proudman on her looks in the light of recent events, but Andrus is not one of them. He is young, with tousled hair. He's dressed in a zip-up jumper and jeans, like a surfer on a day ashore, and he has a breezy, teasing way with his subjects. "Girl, you are glowing!" he shouts.

I try to warn him that he may be eroticising Proudman's physical appearance in order to exercise power over her, but he says it is fine because he does the same with men. He is an equal-opportunities eroticiser. He says men, in his experience, are more likely to be upset by physical compliments.

Proudman, in this case, does not seem to mind. She chuckles at his jokes — "Yeah, girl! Put that on your LinkedIn page!" — until Andrus declares that the shoot is complete. "Now we've just got to add the Hitler moustache," he says. Fortunately, Proudman laughs. Then the two of us get a taxi to a café at the edge of the campus of Harvard University, where she is currently a visiting researcher. I had vaguely assumed that Proudman came to Harvard Law School as a sort of refugee, fleeing the press, like Salman Rushdie fleeing a fatwa. In fact, Harvard had accepted her in June. She had booked a flight on September 11.

On September 7 she was at her desk, at King's College, Cambridge, working on her PhD thesis on female genital mutilation and gender-based violence, when she noticed the LinkedIn message from Carter-Silk. "I have had other inappropriate messages, but this was the first from a senior solicitor in a position of power over me," she says. He was more than twice her age — she is 27, he is 57. He was a partner at a major London firm. "And the solicitor-barrister dynamic is always imbued with power relations because it's the solicitor who gives the barrister work, so you are not on an equal footing. This is somebody who can make or break your career."

If that is true, I say, there must have been a temptation to let this slide. To take the compliment. "No, absolutely not!" she replies. "It's unacceptable, this behaviour, and it needs to be challenged wherever it happens because if you do not challenge it, then this form of insidious and endemic sexism becomes normal and acceptable and incredibly difficult for any woman to challenge, because when you do, the woman becomes the issue as opposed to sexism being the issue." In her view, what happened afterwards — the personal attacks, the waves of vitriol — proved her point.

We're sitting on a sofa now in her local café. Proudman is sipping a hot chocolate. How should I describe her? Should I compare her to a summer's day? Proudman obviously has a view on this. She says that if you believe in equality, you should either offer equally detailed descriptions of men and women in an article such as this one, or you should "minimally describe their appearance".

"I would prefer the latter," says Proudman, who has small blue eyes, pale skin, a patina of freckles about the nose and high, elegant cheekbones. She thinks one should give merely "a minimal description [of the subject] and concentrate on the substance of the article, which I assume is about this person's contribution to society, and hopefully that's not solely reliant on physical attributes".

She has the short, sleek bob of the consummate professional: like Anna Wintour or Mary Portas, two women not known for their relaxed and accommodating manner around the office. Occasionally, as we speak, Proudman runs a hand through it, or clutches at her temples, until her ruler-straight fringe has vanished and her pale blonde hair sprays up above her brow.

And what about Carter-Silk? He's not with us, of course, but there's a lovely picture on LinkedIn. He has deep-set blue eyes, a rich-looking tan, a large nose and a strong jawline. His hair is brown, side-parted, and greying at the temples. He looks extremely pleased with himself — although in one outdoorsy shot, he sits in profile on a misty hillside wearing a black anorak, and seems quite rugged: like a very well-fed Harrison Ford.

Some of the joy the media took in this contretemps between the two of them must relate to how perfectly they seemed to fit their allotted roles in this social drama. On the one side, you had Carter-Silk, whose very name recalls something the late John Mortimer would have invented for a character in a *Rumpole* story. He soon began to sound like a *Rumpole* character, too: anonymous "friends" told reporters he was a lovely man with no verbal filter. It soon emerged that he had form when it came to making politically incorrect comments. A year earlier, on Twitter, he had posted a photo of his daughter in skimpy sportswear: "Whilst I should not encourage lascivious comments about my daughter," he began, "… Yeee gods, she is hot."

Charlotte Proudman played the plucky young woman from the provinces who takes on the establishment. She hails from Leek, in Staffordshire, and grew up in a middle-class home, although she will not say much more about it because she does not want to talk about her family. So I ask, a little desperately, what do they — Mum and Dad — make of this controversy? She sighs and rolls her eyes. "I'm sure they are very proud," she says.

I ask if she is a coddled millennial. This was a charge laid at her door by several commentators, who suggested that she was one of a generation raised by overly protective parents, who emerge blinking into the real world and are instantly offended by the smallest of unintended slights. "I worked while I was at college and at university," Proudman replies. "From the age of 16 to 21, I worked as a cashier at my local supermarket, so I am grounded in the real world. I'm not someone who has grown up with an Oxbridge-type background." So, you went to a comprehensive? "Yes!" she laughs. "Wouldn't you have just died if I had said, 'Oh no, I went to Cheltenham Ladies' College'?"

On the other hand, she does not take offence at the idea that she takes offence too easily. "What's the criticism?" she asks. That you are more touchy, as a generation, you millennials. "Yeah, damn right!" she exclaims. "Damn right! Sexism is not to be tolerated. It's a form of violence against women and girls." During the holidays before her final year at school, Proudman volunteered as a teacher in Tamil Nadu, India. "That was the first time I realised I wanted to become a lawyer," she says. She met women who had suffered abuse. "Often their only remedy was through the legal system, although that in itself was haphazard."

Some of her fellow volunteers were law students: back in Staffordshire, she applied and was accepted to study law at Keele University. Her role model was the barrister Michael Mansfield, who helped exonerate the Guildford Four and the Birmingham Six, and who served as a powerful advocate for the family of the murdered teenager Stephen Lawrence. "He was a real hero, particularly when he was involved in the Dodi Fayed and Princess Diana inquest," she says.

I find this particular choice of reference point surprising. I covered the inquest, and remember Mansfield giving some grandstanding performances in the service of Mohamed Al Fayed, who believed that the Duke of Edinburgh, Tony Blair, MI6 and assorted police commissioners and ambulance drivers were all involved in a conspiracy to murder Diana. "This is a radical lawyer who really challenges vested interests, takes on the establishment and is fearless in doing so," says Proudman. Mansfield also happens to be an alumnus of Keele (along with a fellow named Alexander Carter-Silk).

At Keele, Proudman successfully took on the university over its parking system — she says it was issuing more parking permits than there were spaces, and students were running up fines. She also began seeking work experience in lawyer's offices and chambers. She says the partner of one firm of solicitors told her to send in a picture of herself in a bikini. "As opposed to my CV. I asked if that was a joke. I was taken aback; I was so young at the time." She said the partner replied saying, "Who knows?" She remembers puzzling over whether this was an isolated incident, a rogue individual, or actually an indicator "of how you have to behave as a criminal-law solicitor".

In any case, she was leaning towards a career as a barrister. She gained a "mini-pupillage" with a criminal-law chambers. In a taxi one day, on the way to court, she says a barrister placed a hand on her thigh. "He was rubbing up and down, and while he was doing that, he was recounting that some law graduates will have sex with senior members of a firm in exchange for pupillages." Pupillages are effectively places in chambers as trainee barristers, and they are notoriously difficult to secure. Competition, among bright young things who are naturally very good at arguing their case, is fierce. "It was one of the most challenging experiences of my life and I was damned determined to get a pupillage," she says.

Do you think that barrister was telling the truth? Do some young law graduates really have to have sex in order to become a barrister? "He was completely upfront about it," she says. "Friends have told me that they know people who have engaged in transactional sex for pupillages, with men."

In a strictly legal sense, that sounds like hearsay. Proudman offers another example. She says a young law graduate "contacted me this week and told me that she tried to seek out a mentor who was a member of the judiciary. She met this person for lunch. And the person wanted her to be his mistress." A judge? "The judge wanted her to be his mistress," she says. "She wanted a mentor to guide her through being a law graduate and becoming a lawyer, and that was what she faced instead. There are women who are vulnerable to this kind of pressure. It is a coercive pressure that is put upon them by men in positions of power." She said no? "As far as I'm aware she said no, and came to me for advice."

She thinks that sexism is "systemic within the legal profession", which she says is dominated by men with public school and Oxbridge backgrounds. At Bar school, "I felt unwelcome from the get-go because of my accent," she says. "I sound northern, maybe not as much now as I did then, but that was constantly pointed out in conversation, particularly when I was first introduced to someone. Anywhere past Watford Junction is apparently northern ... Then people automatically think you are from a working-class background and that you are never going to make it at the Bar. And, on top of that, you are a woman! It didn't bode well."

Before starting Bar school, Proudman made the equivalent of a statement of intent about the sort of lawyer she hoped to be. She had grown up with her father's surname; now she became Proudman, adopting her mother's family name. "I wanted to have the same surname as my great-grandmother on my mother's side," she says. "She was a supporter of the suffragette movement." She'd been meaning to do this for years. "I was about to start my legal career, so this was the time to change it. I wanted to, I suppose, honour her memory."

Proudman thinks that women who do make it at the Bar tend to get "shoved into so-called 'women's work': family law, child law, soft crime, sex cases. Those types of areas that some women don't want to pursue — they want to be criminal barristers." She wanted to be a criminal barrister, too. "Ultimately, I got a family-law pupillage and I was very fortunate because I enjoyed it." She did well: she won awards and scholarships, she worked on cases of forced marriage, she did pro bono work in Pakistan and Congo, and she gained a place at the chambers of her hero, Michael Mansfield. Then she went to Cambridge to study for a PhD. And there she was, on the afternoon of September 7, checking her LinkedIn messages.

So, this older bloke sent you a message saying, "What a nice picture," and you were shocked? "I guess, surprised, perhaps, but very disappointed." Yours is quite a nice picture, I say. You look like you're about to present the news. "Yeah," says Proudman. She shrugs.

Very professional. "Yeah." And it's striking, I say, like a man tiptoeing to the edge of a cliff, seeing how close he can get. "Yeah." And glamorous.

"That's subjective," says Proudman. "I don't think you would see that photograph in *Glamour* or *Cosmopolitan*, let's put it that way." She says it was taken for the website of her legal chambers. "It's a fairly professional photograph. I'm not prepared to justify what I choose to do and whether I choose to wear make-up or how I choose to have a photo taken of my face. It doesn't warrant or merit objectification or sexism."

After praising her photograph, Carter-Silk said: "Always interest to understant people's skills and how we might work together (sic)," the typos suggesting the missive was dashed off. How long did Proudman take to compose a reply? "A few minutes." And did you think about it for a long time first, or just spit it out at once? "I would say it was more of a considered response." How long did you spend thinking about it? "Maybe about 15 to 20 minutes or so. I thought about the kind of impact it had, and how these types of so-called innocuous sexist comments really cement women's subordinate position in the workplace."

And did you have that moment, just after hitting the button, where, even if you were right, you thought, "Ohhhh …"? "No, no!" she exclaims. "This was, I thought, a to-the-point response." Proudman thinks this line of questioning is itself sexist. "How long did you take to respond, how long did you take to decide this — all it's doing is trying to paint a picture that I'm an irrational woman. I'm not. I'm a rational barrister. I was legally charged and fully understood the dynamics of sexism in society. I will challenge it wherever I see it."

I'm not trying to suggest you're irrational. I'm trying to tell the story. I'm interested in what happened where, when, why. "Perhaps, but maybe subconsciously," she says. "Someone else asked me something very similar. A man who was very senior and supportive, I must say; a feminist. And I thought [there was something] underlying that, subconsciously. And it's not his fault, because we are all peeling back the layers of gender socialisation."

Of course, it was not the response, but the fact that she posted their exchange on Twitter — which she did before the end of the day — that really stirred things up. "I was thinking about how many other women receive these types of messages. I'd received them in the past. I was genuinely interested to know." There had been a discussion, among some of the people she corresponded with on Twitter, about sexism in the workplace, and the use of LinkedIn as a dating site. "I expected maybe a couple of people to retweet or favourite [the tweet] or respond with the messages they had received." Nothing happened for a day. Then, it started.

"There was a lot going on, on my phone," she says. There were calls and emails, and reporters circulating through her faculty, seeking her, or anyone who might know her. But, "It was after the 'feminazi' article, by Sarah Vine, on the front page of the *Daily Mail* — that was when it kicked off," she says. "It became war." Proudman's LinkedIn head shot was on the front page. "The glam lawyer and the Feminazis who hate men who praise their looks," said the strapline. It was an interesting article, I say. "Interesting article!" Well, what did you make of it? "I honestly haven't read it. I have read the headlines, but I haven't read the vitriolic and nasty newspaper articles."

But how do you know what you're responding to? "I have been informed by other people and I think I understand the gist of it," she says. "To be quite frank, I'm not really interested in what other people have to say in response to just one tweet. It's disproportionate. But if Sarah Vine wants people to ... " She pauses. "What did she say?"

She said you should have been pleased to be complimented on your photograph. She said what is the world coming to, if a woman gets offended by a harmless compliment. She said she once got a very thoughtful letter from a male reader, who asked, at the end of it, if she could send him a picture of herself in her nightie. Vine said no, and that she was actually a pyjama girl. But she was delighted to be asked. The nightie anecdote may not actually have been crucial to her piece, but put on the spot, it's almost all I can remember.

"I wouldn't want to deny any woman's feelings towards sending photographs or receiving compliments about their photographs," says Proudman. "If that's something that they enjoy, then that's really a matter for them. But there are many women who don't appreciate unsolicited sexist comments, particularly in the workplace." So what can a man say to a woman at work about her appearance? Where is the line? Proudman rolls her eyes. "I just think it's disappointing that people can't distinguish between an innocuous comment and a sexist message," she says.

Well, I thought she might help us out with this. How about, "Nice shoes"? "No." Gosh, I had a whole list of these from "Nice shoes" to "You remind me of my mother." But we're already in the red. How about, "Have you had your hair cut?" "No. For me, no. I mean, you have to remember that I'm a barrister," she says. "I wouldn't want to receive comments on my appearance from my opponent, because that would be demeaning and patronising. And would I want to receive this comment in chambers? Well, I hope they would rather ask, 'How was your day in court?'" Let's say you are back in chambers and someone says, "Have you been working out?" "Well, no one's ever said that to me." She laughs. "Maybe that's a personal thing."

How about, "Have you lost weight?" "I just don't think we should be focusing on physical attributes, full stop, in a professional context. I mean, would you say the same to a man with the same frequency? 'Nice shoes'? 'Have you lost weight?'" My wife said it yesterday to our neighbour. I worried he might think we thought him fat before, but it turned out he had lost weight. Although he was also wearing a tight jumper.

"I just don't think it's said with the same frequency to men," she says. "Because the ideal of a woman's physical appearance is slim. Skinny. That's a male-determined precept of how a woman's body should be." She talks about how beauty fades, and women judged on their looks will fade out of sight in the office. She says compliments can cement a woman's inferior position, until "they are just Attractive Mary, or Hot Amanda".

The thing about Proudman is that she's right; it's just that she's so absolute in the way she applies the logic. *The Times* columnist Janice Turner summed up the feelings of an older generation of feminists, who agreed with her stand against Carter-Silk, but felt slightly uneasy at quite how hard she walloped him. They felt you were too hard, too rude.

"Oh, boo hoo!" says Proudman. "What else did Janice say?" She said women of her generation perhaps felt that you opened yourself up to criticism. By being quite so, um, forthright. "Well, this is classic," says Proudman. "A woman can't be forthright? A woman can't be assertive or she's considered too bolshie?" Wait, hang on. She was on your side. I feel like the boy in the playground telling tales.

Sarah Vine implied you'd never get a boyfriend — men would be too frightened to approach you. "Well, I have a boyfriend," she replies. "Ha ha! He's my partner and my best friend and a feminist ally. How could you possibly have a meaningful relationship with someone who believes that sexist behaviour is acceptable?" This may be true for Proudman, although I must say my mum manages it.

While the women of Fleet Street, and quite a few men, were writing columns that Proudman did not read, less cerebral responses were flooding in on Twitter. "It's ironic, because I objected to being objectified," she says. "And yet afterwards my appearance was under scrutiny more than ever." One of the death threats she received, informed her that, "They were going to cut off my head," she says. "They knew where I lived." It seemed fortunate that she was about to leave the country. Did it feel like the great escape? "It did, actually. I have never felt such relief arriving in America." Her boyfriend came, too: they had roughly coordinated their work placements.

Proudman is very impressive, really. Almost exhaustingly so. Are you always on it? "My God, I'm on it!" she laughs. "Nonstop, 24-7." There's a pause. Then she says, "I am actually on it most of the time." Occasionally, people at Harvard will ask her if she is the woman who wrote that message to the solicitor. Many have accused her of deliberately inciting the furore, to raise her profile; she says the whole thing has been a huge distraction — from her PhD, and for her colleagues at Mansfield's chambers, who were besieged by reporters asking them about LinkedIn. She reels off a list of grand crises: Syria, migrants dying in sealed trucks. "This is what we should be focusing on," she says. "I'm still pretty astounded by what's happened."

She would much rather it hadn't. "It's been a complete nightmare. No one wants this kind of scrutiny. No one. I would rather be Charlotte Proudman, prior to September 7, than Charlotte Proudman after that date," she says. "You can change your world completely in a matter of minutes."

LETTERS FROM IRIS MURDOCH 1934-1995

Review by Roger Lewis

NOVEMBER 14 2015

THE CHIEF PROBLEM with this bulky book — a diabolical 666 pages — is that Iris Murdoch would not have wanted it to exist. Unlike the brilliant comical prose performances of Larkin and Amis, or the genius poured into his correspondence by Evelyn Waugh, Murdoch's letters are scrappy boring notes ("I wonder if I could see you next Monday or Tuesday afternoon"), which were never intended for preservation, let alone for publication.

"Destroy this and all letters," she commands one of her friends. "You should not keep carbon copies of personal letters," she instructs another chum. When she and her husband, John Bayley, moved from their tumbledown country house in Steeple Aston to central Oxford, in 1986, Albert and Naomi Lebowitz are told that the "destruction of old manuscripts and letters is a major part of this task". What, therefore, is the rationale behind this lavishly produced volume, culled from the 3,200 letters gathered in the archives at Kingston University, and painstakingly edited by Avril Horner and Anne Rowe?

On the face of it what we have is simply so much wastepaper — literally laundry lists: "Shall I buy a white duffel coat?" "Must go now and pack my bathing costume." Nevertheless, Murdoch was "an important figure in British culture", we are reminded, and her 26 novels, which explored "powerful passions and paralysing obsessions", clearly grew out of her riotous and supremely self-indulgent private life, with its sadomasochism and homosexuality, as denoted in these scribbled messages.

In her later years, when I knew her, Murdoch liked to give the impression she was "a somewhat saintly, puritanical figure", but in her prime she was a nymphomaniac, and had she been from the working class, instead of a fellow of an Oxford college with heaps of honorary degrees, she'd have been a candidate for compulsory sterilisation.

From the moment she left school and arrived at university in 1938, she seemed to have felt obliged to sleep with everyone she met, particularly dreary ugly foreign intellectuals such as Elias Canetti: "He subjugates me completely," she panted. On the evidence of her letters, she went to bed with each member of Congregation, as the register of dons is called: Wallace Robson ("Why do you never wash your hair?"), Franz Steiner, Donald MacKinnon, Michael Oakeshott — by whom she was "intoxicated and ravished". Dozens more. She flirted with Denis Healey ("he looked bronze and sleek and rough"), and Murdoch must have been the sole person to find toad-shaped Arnold Goodman "super and so attractive".

Her pupils weren't off-limits ("It had become impossible not to touch you"; "Your fellatio idea is very powerful"), nor were other people's husbands. In one extraordinary though not untypical tangle, which probably took place over an average weekend, Murdoch says: "Pip hated me for making Michael suffer. I hated Michael because he spoilt my celestial relations with Thomas. Later I hated Thomas because he was the devil." You can see why she wrote the sorts of novels she did.

The unalluring erotic kaleidoscope was further agitated by her lesbian alliances. Pip was Philippa Foot, with whom she often had sex. Another lover was Brigid Brophy: "I cannot think that I shall ever stop wanting to see you," Murdoch gushed. It is believed that Murdoch resigned her fellowship at St Anne's, in 1962, not because she wanted to concentrate full-time on her novels but because her relationship with a colleague, Margaret Hubbard, was becoming an open scandal. Murdoch (bafflingly) thought of herself as "a male homosexual in female guise". When she laments "I am really in a hell of an emotional mess at present", clearly she relished the dramas she precipitated.

Her muddy metaphysics — on display in tracts such as *Existentialists and Mystics* — were attempts to rationalise, if not ameliorate, her solipsism and callousness. If she burbled on in interviews about the importance of being "morally good", it is because she knew she herself had failed to attain such a state. "I want to go on being myself," was her chief motivation, preying on people and performing emotional experiments.

"I certainly don't feel any inhibition about asking for your heart," she says to Brophy — yet she never once gave of herself. "It's frightening," she concluded, "how people can deceive themselves and how quickly their moods can change." Her own moods changed capriciously and she was oblivious to the suffering she created; as is the case for many an only child, other people didn't have quite the same degree of reality as she did herself. They were playthings.

One of her lovers, Frank Thompson, went on a suicide mission with the SOE in Bulgaria. Another became a nun in the closed order at Stanbrook Abbey. There were divorces and broken engagements galore. Murdoch's own intensities were transient because she had "an increased horror of all ties, especially marital". Furthermore, "I have also a very strong irrational fear of pregnancy."

She never did become a mother but she did become a wife, in 1956, when she married sexless homunculus John Bayley, an English don who stank of talcum powder and sardine tins. Reading this book I finally understood why Bayley was strangely happy when he could care for Murdoch during her pitiful declining years with the Alzheimer's from which she died in 1999 — an episode sentimentalised in Iris, the film starring Judi Dench and Jim Broadbent. At long last Bayley could have her to himself. Hitherto he had been the biggest cuckold of the 20th century.

Bayley, who died this year aged 89, hardly appears in these letters, save as an accident-prone ninny. "John is still on crutches and cursing away," we are told — after he'd run himself over in the garage, when the starting handle slipped from his grasp. "John managed to fall into a wishing well," another correspondent is informed. It's a nervous moment when it is revealed that Bayley possesses a .22 rifle, "which he keeps licensed, although I never allow him to fire it".

I wonder if this is why Canetti moved from Hampstead to Zurich? What comes across in this book is the charmed, lazy life of overpaid Oxford academics — the short hours, endless long vacations and sabbaticals, the high-table boozing, international conferences, holidays to sponge off the Cecils, the Spenders or the Griggs, the general unaccountability. It was an ideal environment in which Murdoch could exploit her need for total freedom, and where she could observe the chaos that resulted.

"Oh it was all very golden and beautiful," prattles Murdoch, with "a sense of joyous carnival". At least the Quality Assurance Agency for Higher Education will have put a stop to such institutional laxity.

Living on Paper: Letters from Iris Murdoch 1934-1995, Ed Avril Horner and Anne Rowe, published by Chatto & Windus.

IT WAS WAR SURGERY: EASY BULLETS OUT FIRST, LEAVE THE REST FOR LATER

Adam Sage in Paris

NOVEMBER 18 2015

THE FIRST TWO PATIENTS arrived in a taxi at Lariboisière Hospital in east Paris at about 9.30pm after the massacre at the restaurant. The woman had been hit by a bullet in the chest, her husband in the leg.

Patrick Plaisance, the head of the accident and emergency department, was at home watching the France v Germany football match when he got a call from the doctor on duty: "There's been a shooting." Half an hour later, Professor Plaisance arrived at the department for a night that tested France's renowned public hospital system to the very limit.

He had dealt with terrorist attack victims before — after the shooting at *Charlie Hebdo* in January which left 11 dead and 11 injured, and after the explosion outside a shop in Paris in 1986, when seven died and 55 were injured. This was on a different scale. A total of 129 people were killed and 415 wounded on Friday. The injured were taken to 38 hospitals around the capital. Lariboisière, which is near the scene of the shootings, was one of five called upon to handle the worst cases.

Within an hour, 15 or so victims had arrived — one transported in a car with a bullet in his head (he is still in intensive care). They kept on coming, many after police ended the siege at the Bataclan concert. In all, the hospital treated more than 50 victims. Professor Plaisance said that the injuries were reminiscent of a war zone, with "bullets in the chest, arms, thighs, pelvis, stomach and heads".

The Kalashnikovs used by the terrorists ripped holes in the skin so wide that some of the wounds could not immediately be sewn up, and shattered the bones into tiny fragments, he said. Four operating theatres were used throughout the night and into the next day. Teams of surgeons, anaesthetists and nurses — some of them on duty anyway, some requisitioned, some who turned up when they heard what had happened — worked in stints of eight hours. In all, more than 30 patients were operated on over the weekend, some of them twice. None died.

Professor Plaisance said that bullets were extracted if they were close to the surface and could be removed easily. Others were left for another day, another operation. Professor Rémy Nizard, an orthopaedic surgeon, was on duty. "It was war surgery," he said. "Some patients were in a very serious condition. They had a bullet in the head or the neck, or damage to their ocular orbits which meant they could lose an eye. One man had been hit by a bullet which went through his knee before fracturing his tibia. These are wounds due to high-energy projectiles."

Parisian hospitals had carried out a drill in preparation for a terrorist attack that morning, so staff knew what they had to do, says Professor Plaisance. They separated the absolute emergencies — those needing an immediate operation — from those who could wait a few hours while their blood pressure and pulse rates were monitored for signs of internal haemorrhaging. A psychological unit was established to help patients, but also for panicked relatives joining them at the hospital.

Road crash victims arriving in accident and emergency departments tend to cry, moan and demand immediate treatment, a doctor said. Friday's victims responded very differently. "What struck me is how silent they were, how they closed in on themselves," Professor Plaisance said. "Even those with relatively light injuries didn't talk, or very little. It was exactly the same thing after the attack on *Charlie Hebdo*. I remember big imposing police officers being brought in on stretchers and not saying a thing."

Professor Plaisance worked throughout the night. "The first time I looked at my watch, it was 6am," he said. "In the heat of the action, the adrenaline keeps you going, and on the whole all the staff present coped pretty well." When the rush was over, some of the younger nurses and doctors felt the shock. "One doctor who was there on Friday was meant to be on duty again on Sunday. But he couldn't do it," Professor Plaisance said.

Seventy-seven victims of the attacks were still in hospitals in Paris yesterday, including 29 in intensive care.

BLONDE BOMBER APPEARED AT A WINDOW AND BLEW HERSELF UP

David Brown, Adam Sage, John Simpson

NOVEMBER 19 2015

THE BLAST TWO floors up the communal stairwell roused Catalin Stetiu from his sleep at 4.20am, moments before the gun battle that raged above his head. As he cowered with his family, the terrorists above fought with police until the blonde-haired woman at the centre of the gunfight detonated her suicide belt.

The decaying block in the heart of the north Paris suburb of St Denis was the final stand for the gang believed to have terrorised the city in the series of attacks that left 129 people dead on Friday. Jean-Michel Fauvergue, head of the police operation, said that the assault began at 4.16am. The failure by police to blow out the reinforced door of one flat, which had previously been used as a crack den, led to a gunfight during which antiterrorism officers fired 5,000 rounds.

Abdelhamid Abaaoud, 27, the gang's mastermind was believed to be hiding in two adjoining apartments along with his female cousin and suspected wife, Hasna Aitboulahcen, 26, and at least three fanatical followers. The tiny flats were on the third floor of a four-storey block on Rue du Corbillon off the main shopping street leading to the cathedral that was once the final resting place of French monarchs.

On Friday residents heard the blasts a mile away when three suicide attackers blew themselves up outside the Stade de France during the international football match against Germany. Police were told on Monday that Abaaoud was in France. They tracked the group and monitored their telephone calls before 110 armed officers surrounded their hideout. Yesterday's raid was one of 118 operations carried out overnight under emergency powers.

Mr Stetiu, 26, had been asleep with his wife, Roxanna, 21, their son David, 18 months, his mother, Micheka, 47, and father, Yoan, 50, when he was roused by the first explosion. "Then I heard shooting, everyone was shooting," he said. "Of course I was scared, it was just in front of our door. There were hundreds and hundreds of shots, thousands. There was one big explosion and then lots of small ones. The building was trembling. No one was screaming, Even if they were we would not have been able to hear because the gunfire was so loud.

"The police were shouting 'get down on the floor, get down on the floor'. Through the window I could see the flames from the flat on the third floor." Recordings picked up police shouting "Where's your boyfriend?" and a woman replying: "He's not my boyfriend."

Directly below the gang's flat, Sabine was asleep with her husband and their two-year-old son. "I was woken by gunfire," she said. "My ceiling began to collapse, there was dust everywhere. You could feel the whole building shake." She could hear the people in the flat above talking, running around and reloading their guns. "We could see bullets flying and laser beams out of the window," she said. "My baby was gripping on to me when he heard the guns go off. It was never-ending. I stayed on the floor for about two-and-a-half hours."

A police sniper on a rooftop opposite is believed to have shot at least one of the gang. Kamel Khemissi, 60, who works at the nearby town hall, said: "They were aiming at someone. The sound of the shots was like trembling. It was so intense." After an intense 35-minute gunfight, during which the police threw 20 grenades, there was silence. At 4.45am armed officers led three semi-naked men from the block, one with a gunshot wound. It is believed that police managed to seize the men from the adjoining flat.

Christian, 20, who lives opposite the gang's flat said the gunfire resumed after a 15-minute pause. "That's when a woman shouted out of the third floor window: 'Help, help, help me'," he said. "I heard police officers ask her to identify herself and show herself. She put her hands out [of the window] but she did not show her face. She withdrew her hands and showed them again several times. The police shouted at her to put her hands in the air and show them. They said they were going to fire. The shots started up again. Police officers were firing from the roof of the building opposite."

At 5.15am a woman appeared at the window and fired a long burst from a Kalashnikov before detonating her suicide belt. After a further grenade assault by police a man's body fell from the third floor to the second. At 7.35am two men discovered hiding in rubble in the building were arrested and led out in to the street. An injured man was also surrounded by police in a nearby shopping centre.

"There was a lot of shooting in the flat and then there was an enormous explosion," Christian said. "It was probably the woman who was blowing herself up. The windows shattered, a lot of objects from the flat were blown into street, bits of human flesh as well. They are in the street. You can see a bit of head, skin, ribs." The gunfire killed a seven-year-old sniffer dog called Diesel, who had been sent in to look for booby traps.

Jeward Bendaoud, who owns one of the flats used by the gang, said he had been asked by a Belgian friend to let two people stay there for a few days. "I said there was no mattress. They told me, 'It's OK they just want water and to pray'," he said.

Police continued hunting for other terrorists amid fears that some had escaped and there was a second cell based near by. Only at 11.27am, seven hours after Mr Stetiu was woken, did the operation officially end.

Last night there were further explosions as police dismantled booby traps in the apartments. There were reports of a third body in the rubble. Police were waiting for tests on the dead before confirming if Abaaoud and Aitboulahcen were among them.

WHY MUSLIMS ARE TURNING AWAY FROM ISLAM

Matt Ridley

NOVEMBER 23 2015

FIFTY YEARS AGO, after the cracking of the genetic code, Francis Crick was so confident religion would fade that he offered a prize for the best future use for Cambridge's college chapels. Swimming pools, said the winning entry. Today, when terrorists cry "God is great" in both Paris and Bamako as they murder, the joke seems sour.

But here's a thought: that jihadism may be a last spasm — albeit a painful one — of a snake that is being scotched. The humanists are winning, even against Islam. Quietly, non-belief is on the march.

Those who use an extreme form of religion to poison the minds of disaffected young men are furious about the spread of materialist and secularist ideas, which they feel powerless to prevent. In 50 years' time, we may look back on this period and wonder how we failed to notice that Islam was about to lose market share, not to other religions, but to humanism.

The fastest-growing belief system in the world is non-belief. No religion grew nearly as fast over the past century. Whereas virtually nobody identified as a non-believer in 1900, today roughly 15 per cent do, and that number does not include soft Anglicans in Britain, mild Taoists in China, lukewarm Hindus in India or token Buddhists in Japan. Even so, the non-religious category has overtaken paganism, will soon pass Hinduism, may one day equal Islam and is gaining on Christianity. (Of every ten people in the world, roughly three are Christian, two Muslim, two Hindu, 1.5 non-religious and 1.5 something else.)

This is all the more remarkable when you think that, with a few notable exceptions, atheists or humanists don't preach, let alone pour money into evangelism. Their growth has come almost entirely from voluntary conversion, whereas Islam's slower growth in market share has largely come from demography: the high birth rates in Muslim countries compared with Christian ones. And this is about to change.

The birth rate in Muslim countries is plummeting at unprecedented speed. A study by the demographer Nicholas Eberstadt three years ago found that: "Six of the ten largest absolute declines in fertility for a two-decade period recorded in the postwar era have occurred in Muslim-majority countries." Iran, Oman, the United Arab Emirates, Algeria, Bangladesh, Tunisia, Libya, Albania, Qatar and Kuwait have all seen birth-rate declines of more than 60 per cent in 30 years.

Meanwhile, secularism is on the rise within Muslim majority countries. It is not easy being a humanist in an Islamic society, even outside the Isis hell-holes, so it is hard to know how many there are. But a poll in 2012 found that 5 per cent of Saudis describe themselves as fully atheist and 19 per cent as non-believers — more than in Italy. In Lebanon the proportion is 37 per cent. Remember in many countries they are breaking the law by even thinking like this. That Arab governments criminalise non-belief shows evidence not of confidence, but of alarm.

Last week a court in Saudi Arabia sentenced a Palestinian poet, Ashraf Fayadh, to death for apostasy. In 2014 the Saudi government brought in a law defining atheism as a terrorist offence. Abdel Fattah al-Sisi's government in Egypt, though tough on Islamists, has also ordered two ministries to produce a national plan to "confront and eliminate" atheism. They have shut down a café frequented by atheists and dismissed a college librarian who talked about humanism in a TV programme. Earlier this month there was yet another murder by Islamists — the fifth such incident — of a Bangladeshi publisher of secularist writing.

I recently met one of the astonishingly brave humanist bloggers of Bangladesh, Arif Rahman, who has seen four colleagues hacked to death with machetes in daylight. He told me about Bangladesh's 2013 blasphemy law, and the increasing indifference or even hostility of the Bangladeshi government towards the plight of non-religious bloggers. For many Muslim-dominated governments, the enemy is not "crusader" Christianity, it is home-grown non-belief. The jihadists of Isis are probably motivated less by a desire to convert Europe's disaffected youth to fundamentalist Islam than by a wish to prevent the Muslim diaspora sliding into western secularism.

In the Arab world, according to Brian Whitaker, author of *Arabs Without God*, what tempts people to leave the faith is not disgust at the antics of Islamist terrorists, but the same things that have drained church attendance here: materialism, rationalism and scepticism. As the academics Gregory Paul and Phil Zuckerman wrote in an essay eight years ago: "Not a single advanced democracy that enjoys benign, progressive socio-economic conditions retains a high level of popular religiosity. They all go material."

America is no longer much of an exception. Non-believers there outnumber Mormons, Muslims and Jews combined, and are growing faster than southern Baptists. Whitaker found that Arab atheists mostly lost their faith gradually, as the unfairness of divine justice, the irrationality of the teaching, or the prejudice against women, gay people or those of other faiths began to bother them. Whatever your origin and however well you have been brainwashed, there is just something about living in a society with restaurants and mobile phones, universities and social media, that makes it hard to go on thinking that morality derives exclusively from superstition.

Not that western humanists are immune from superstitions, of course: from Gaia to Gwyneth Paltrow diets to astrology, there's plenty of room for cults in the western world, though they are mostly harmless. As is Christianity, these days, on the whole. I do not mean to sound complacent about the Enlightenment.

The adoption of Sharia or its nearest equivalent in no-go areas of European cities will need to be resisted, and vigorously. The jihadists will kill many more people before they are done, and will provoke reactions by governments that will erode civil liberties along the way.

I am dismayed by the sheer lack of interest in defending free speech that many young westerners display these days, as more and more political groups play the blasphemy card in imitation of Islam, demanding "safety" from "triggering" instances of offence. Nonetheless, don't lose sight of the big picture. If we hold our resolve, stop the killers, root out the hate preachers, encourage the reformers and stem the tide of militant Islamism, then secularism and milder forms of religion will win in the long run.

MAKE SURE YOU CALL HIM MR A. THE TRUTH ABOUT ROMAN'S EMPIRE

Oliver Kay

NOVEMBER 27 2015

IN THE COURT OF Roman Abramovich, they have learnt to look out for the telltale signs. He rarely voices his displeasure, but when that often inscrutable face morphs into what they call his "death mask", that is when the chill descends as the wind of change blows through Stamford Bridge.

Among those who mix loosely in Abramovich's circles, there is surprise that José Mourinho has, for now, been spared a second sighting of the death mask, but among the inner circle — which tends to mean those who are privileged to address him as Roman rather than as "Mr A"— it is a different story.

There they reject the portrayal of the Chelsea owner as a man prone to knee-jerk reactions or impulsiveness. "Rash?" one associate asks. "Rash is the last word I would use to describe Roman." So how would you describe him? "Quiet," the associate says. "Private — obviously, you know that — and very loyal, unless of course you let him down, but the main things are calm, measured and businesslike."

Abramovich is not afraid of a bit of spontaneity. Another associate relates tales of evenings when they would be in one of his fleet of cars, with one of his chauffeurs at the wheel, and he would settle on a destination for a night out — London, Paris, Moscow, St Tropez — and simply fire off the instruction to his staff to ready the private jet. Now 49, though, and on his third marriage, he has become a little more sensible. If he is to invest in another yacht or a piece of art — like when he paid £43 million in 2008 for Francis Bacon's Triptych, 1976 — he thinks about it more carefully these days.

He has certainly thought carefully about how to solve a problem such as Mourinho. On October 3, barely eight weeks after the Portuguese signed a new four-year contract, the Chelsea board met to discuss whether they might need to change manager for a tenth time in 11 years. The support of Marina Granovskaia, Abramovich's former PA who is now a highly influential director of the club, helped the billionaire owner to go with his initial instinct, which was to give Mourinho time to sort things out.

Another three Barclays Premier League defeats later, the club's position is unchanged, but the matter will continue to be reviewed and Abramovich will continue to deliberate, asking questions, soaking up opinions, both on Mourinho and alternatives, such as Carlo Ancelotti, until the early-season crisis has either passed or escalated too far.

"Roman makes the decisions at Chelsea, there is no doubt about that," another associate says. "But it isn't a dictatorship. It's a very small, tight board structure; effectively everyone reports in to Marina, who reports to Roman." As an influential but low-profile woman in football, Granovskaia attracts intrigue. It is striking just how many people around Abramovich use the same word to describe her — "brilliant".

An executive at a rival club agrees. "She's charming, but she's formidable, a real asset to Chelsea," he says. "Marina knows Roman's pressure points," another source says. "She knows how to hit them and how to avoid them. You need to know how to communicate with Roman. He asks direct questions and he expects direct, succinct answers. He will soak up those answers, form a view and one day, whether that's in four days, four weeks or four years, he will decide it's time for a change.

"If José wants to delay the inevitable, he has to win matches, be careful what he says in public and be even more careful about what he says in private. If he upsets people behind the scenes, he won't survive."

"Roman doesn't like sacking people, surprising as that might sound," another says. "He's fiercely loyal to those who have worked with him for a long time, like Marina, Eugene Tenenbaum, Eugene Shvidler. They are like family to him. Then there is his actual family. He has been divorced twice, but his family means everything to him. If you consider his background, that is probably not surprising."

Roman Arkadyevich Abramovich was born into what one friend suggests was a "typical Brezhnev-era Soviet Jewish family — not a great deal of money" in October 1966. Before his first birthday, he had lost his mother, Irina, who died during a medical procedure. In May 1969 his father, Arkady, was killed in an accident on the construction site where he worked. At the age of two, an only child, Abramovich was an orphan.

Initially Abramovich was brought up by Arkady's brother, Leib, and his wife in their small apartment in the frostbitten industrial town of Ukhta, 700 miles northeast of Moscow. At the age of seven, he was sent off to Moscow — at first with his grandmother, then with another uncle, Abram — on the basis that the capital would offer him the best chance of making something of himself.

The most familiar and impressive claim about Abramovich's academic achievements — that he attended the Gubkin Institute of Oil and Gas — is questioned by some and rejected by others. At some point he returned to Ukhta to attend the industrial institute there. At 18, he was called up for national service, late enough to avoid being sent to Afghanistan, and it was in the army that he discovered the skills that would make his fortune.

In an interview with *Zhizn*, the Russian newspaper, in 2007, Nikolai Panteleimonov, a former army friend, claimed that Abramovich came up with a scheme whereby delivery drivers would allow fuel to be siphoned out of their vehicles, which would then be sold to other delivery drivers — all of them aware of the scheme — at a reduced price. "Every party involved was happy," Panteleimonov said. "He was head and shoulders above the rest when it came to entrepreneurship. He could make money out of thin air."

Abramovich took his wheeler-dealer skills back to Moscow, selling imported rubber ducks, dolls, retreaded tyres and much more. His reputation and influence in Moscow business circles grew. He befriended the late Boris Berezovsky, who was making fortunes by capitalising on the privatisation of state property in the aftermath of *perestroika*. Between 1995 and 1997, through President Boris Yeltsin's controversial loans-for-shares privatisation auctions, Berezovsky assisted Abramovich with the acquisition of Sibneft, the oil company — "the largest single heist in corporate history", as Paul Gregory, the economist, wrote in 2011.

"If you were a psychologist, you would probably relate a lot of Roman's story to his upbringing — orphaned, as an only child, raised by his uncle and then sent off to Moscow, in theory to make his fortune," one former Abramovich aide says. "But he was also one of those guys who was in the right place at the right time to make a huge amount of money after the break-up of the Soviet Union. He got lucky in one respect, but I don't think anyone would look at his life and say he has been blessed."

Roman Abramovich has five children from his second marriage — one son, Arkady, and four daughters, Ilya, Anna, Sofia and Arina — and two, Aaron and Leah, from his third marriage, to Dasha Zhukova, the 34-year-old daughter of another Russian oligarch. Arkady is already embarking on his own business career, as founder and owner of ARA Capital, a private investment vehicle, and Sofia, a budding showjumper, likes to post photographs on Instagram of family life, whether at the Belgravia residence, the vast Sussex mansion or the villa near St Tropez.

All seven children have been, or are, being educated in the UK, but if that, along with the choice of names for the younger offspring, suggests that Abramovich is slowly being anglicised, the notion is rejected by those close to him. "Their life revolves around Moscow, not London," one says. "Dasha's big project is the Iris Foundation, which invests in contemporary art, notably at the Garage Museum. She is passionate about art and Roman has become so, too." This year's *Sunday Times Rich List* estimated Abramovich's personal wealth at £7.29 billion. That put him at No 10 in the list of Britain's richest people.

Those close to him take issue not with the figure, but with the concept. "You people always claim he lives in London," one says. "He has property there and he visits, but the same goes for France and the United States. If you asked me, I would say he lives in Moscow. If you asked him, he would say he lives on his plane or his yacht."

The yacht, registered in Bermuda but frequently moored off St Tropez, is *Eclipse*, reported to be the world's second-largest (162 metres long) and is valued at hundreds of millions of pounds. Described as a "floating palace", it has two swimming pools, two helicopter pads, a mini-submarine and a missile defence system. The plane is his customised Boeing 767 jet. When asked if the interior is chestnut and gold, an occasional passenger says — presumably in jest — "I could tell you, but I would have to kill you."

Security is a big deal for Abramovich. The cost of his personal security operation in the UK alone, with a staff of 20, mostly former soldiers, is reported to be more than £1.2 million. Then again, when he was described as being surrounded by a grizzled, scruffy-looking bunch of "bodyguards" as they took *Eclipse* on a trip around the Scottish islands last summer, stopping for a spot of cycling and dog-walking, those "bodyguards" turned out on closer inspection to be Shvidler, Alexey Polezhaev, David Davidovich and Oleksandr Yaroslavsky, reportedly worth a combined £4 billion.

Few oligarchs have what Abramovich has: a profile that can lead people to regard him as something other than the beneficiary of Yeltsin's post-Soviet carve-up. He also has strong, if informal, links to President Putin, whom he supported strongly in his candidacy to become prime minister for the first time in 1999, and the Russian government. At the Kremlin, as among many at Stamford Bridge, Abramovich is known as "Mr A".

"Does Roman have any political ambitions? No," one associate says. "He tried that [as governor of Chukotka between 2000 and 2008] and it didn't interest him. He is apolitical. He has a line to Putin, but so do a lot of other important businessmen in Russia. I guess the thing that sets Roman apart is that he has this different image, which is 'cleaner' than it might be otherwise. He is known and recognised, in Russia and worldwide, as the guy who owns Chelsea, rather than the guy who picked up Sibneft in the way he did and then sold it for billions."

So what is Abramovich's grand plan as he moves towards 50? "He's an investor," the associate says. "He isn't involved in the day-to-day running of any of his companies — at Chelsea or anywhere else — but he takes an active interest in all of it. There are investments in steel, gold, nickel, forest products, real estate in Moscow, start-ups in Russia and Israel, green energy."

Where do Chelsea fit into that? "It has never been a business investment in the same way the others are, but nor is it just some rich man's toy. He gets a great deal of excitement from it — and no doubt frustration too, at times — but, more and more these days, it's a mature business.

"The day he bought Chelsea, people were asking, 'What happens when he gets bored of it?' Then when they won the Champions League in 2012, people thought it was mission accomplished and he would sell up and look for something new. But he doesn't get bored of it. He enjoys it and he enjoys the reflected glory that comes with it. Will he ever sell? Who can say, but I really can't see it happening any time soon."

PRICKLY SUBJECT: MORE HEDGEHOGS MEANS FEWER BADGERS

Leading Article

NOVEMBER 28 2015

CHRISTMAS CHARITY APPEALS should ideally be free from controversy. Most good causes, by definition, fit those criteria. The depredations of poverty, conflict or natural catastrophe stir the generosity of our readers irrespective of political or intellectual disagreement. Human empathy, mercifully, and rather wonderfully, is a motivational force more powerful than most others.

That said, one of our chosen causes this year, the plight of Britain's humble hedgehog, embroils us in a contentious debate as to how this crisis of numbers can best be tackled. The causes of the decline from about 30 million to just a million are unclear. Intensive farming and lack of habitat may play a part, as does the one predator that has a taste for hedgehog flesh, the badger.

Hedgehogs and badgers have much in common. Both are indigenous to the UK. Both, as a cursory study of Beatrix Potter reveals, occupy a special place in British affections. Both animals are shy, nocturnal and difficult to count. Even so, it is beyond dispute that in recent decades hedgehog numbers have declined alarmingly (hence our appeal) while badgers have proliferated.

Badgers and hedgehogs largely share the same food: worms, slugs and beetles. If that food becomes scarce, however, due to pesticide use, traffic, the fencing of suburban gardens and so forth, badgers prey on hedgehogs. In one of nature's brutal rock-paper-scissors equations, a badger's claws beat a hog's spines. Evidence suggests that where badger culls are conducted, the hedgehog population recovers.

There are many ways in which concerned citizens can help safeguard the future of our spiky friends. An acceptance of the need to limit the proliferation of the badger, which is in any case spreading bovine tuberculosis among cattle, should form part of this preservation strategy.

BACK TO THE BATTLEFIELDS OF BOSNIA, SCENE OF MY FIRST WAR

Anthony Loyd

NOVEMBER 28 2015

TWO GHOSTS STOOD waiting outside a busy café. They had blue eyes and wore leopard-print jackets. Although I had expected to meet them there, when we caught each other's stares a door opened through which poured a torrent of memory, and I felt rather afraid.

Many times over the past two decades I had thought of those two women, their blood and bullet wounds, and wondered as to their fate.

My working life is filled with shards of stories, of people like them, met then left behind. Some I have known for a few hours, perhaps days; sometimes weeks, rarely more. Then I leave, never to speak with or see them ever again. They populate my experience of war in a mass of fragmented, unfinished sympathies; grabs of conversation and unanswered questions.

In this kaleidoscope of brief encounters, a few stand salient; these women were among them. I wanted to know of them once more. I wanted to tell them something, too.

Walking towards them, the recollection of our first distant meeting came back in a sudden flash. The autumn day faded, replaced by the hot, heaving heat of summer. It was 1994, and I was a correspondent, young enough to be excited by the small battle unfolding around me as troops from the Bosnian army's 5th Corps attacked separatist units belonging to a renegade businessman, Fikret Abdic, in the town of Velika Kladusa.

Already one man had been killed on the road in front of me, and I was looking at his body when fresh firing and cries to my right caught my attention.

Running towards the sound I found two women and three children, all of them wounded. They had been strafed by machinegun fire attempting to flee the fighting in a car. Dajana was among them. She was just four years old at the time. One bullet had scoured away a segment of her skull, exposing her brain. Another round had gone through her stomach. Untreated, she would soon die. Holding the little girl, pleading with her to live, was her mother, Irma, herself shot through the hand and grazed by another bullet to her head.

Two other children, a young girl and boy, were also wounded, one seriously, and lay in the lee of a house with their own distraught mother.

Amid the thump of mortars and peals of machinegun fire, two journalist friends and I picked up the children and ran with the women to a nearby house, rented by the UN, where we borrowed a pick-up. We slung the casualties in the back, then sped off through the middle of the battle towards a French UN base in a limb-tangled sprawl of smeared blood and bandaged bodies. It was a sketchy, instinctive plan, and I thought at the time we could likely get riddled, too.

Seconds later we drove into an advancing gauntlet of Bosnian troops, wild-eyed and pumped with action, who levelled guns at our temples and screamed and bawled while I pleaded with them for safe passage.

We made it through.

In the abandoned factory that served as the French base and medical centre, I interpreted between a French military doctor and Irma over the prognosis for Dajana.

"She could die at any minute. She is very badly wounded," the doctor told me.

"It's very serious, but they are doing what they can," I filtered back to Irma, who, splattered with her own blood and that of her child, stared at me dead-eyed with shock.

Eventually, as the fighting around the town subsided, a French armoured personnel carrier evacuated the three children to a hospital in Bihac, an hour away. UN rules apparently forbade Irma from travelling in the vehicle, too. I held her for a while as she cried. Then a French officer asked me to leave the base, so I trudged back with my two companions through the aftermath of the battle. I left Irma by the gate.

"I am sorry," I said.

So, that was how we met. I knew that they had survived, because I had tracked them down through the Red Cross in the war's final weeks. But that was 20 years ago, in the age before mobile phones, emails and Facebook. After that, I lost them.

Now they stood before me again, alive, dressed up for the occasion. The terribly wounded child I had once carried was a young woman, and her blood-stained mother glamorous.

Feeling the intensity of what we had fleetingly shared, I wanted to embrace them. But I did not want to be ambushed by emotion, and feared that if I did I might weep. So I stretched out my hand to shake theirs, and felt my face twitch and jump with hidden currents.

Bosnia. Before that war, I was clay. Undefined, unthinking, unknowing: just another Etonian who thought opinion was a game. An ill-setting son, something of an outsider in my own caste and hungry for some edge, by my mid-twenties I was an easy candidate for adventures in someone else's war.

So I hitchhiked to Bosnia in early '93, where I found rock'n'roll dreams were real and wreathed in gun smoke.

Staying on throughout the conflict, I became a journalist for *The Times* along the way, returning home after the war ended. Two years later, in a three-month burst of clarity on the run from heroin addiction, I wrote a personal account of the conflict, *My War Gone By, I Miss It So.*

The ineloquent coherence of the book gladdened and surprised me. More than that, though, the work entrenched me in war reporting, the playing field upon which outsiders excel. Thus I felt defined by that war.

For a while, I missed it. But as the years and other wars passed by, Bosnia drifted from my day-to-day thoughts, until the 20th anniversary of the Dayton Agreement loomed, and I found myself curious to return. Whatever happened to those people in the place that I wrote about so long ago?

So the ghosts formed up in cohorts along the roads and villages when I returned last month, exactly 20 years after the ceasefire that halted the fighting in a precursor to the eventual signing of the Dayton Accords in Paris on December 14, 1995.

The ghosts of memories, the ghosts of friends; the ghosts of people I had once known, the ghost of my youth; dead and alive: they were all waiting for me.

At first, when I found Hamdu, it seemed time had little changed him. He was still laughing about Rejo when I met him in a Bihac restaurant. His laughter was contagious and, as I sat with him, drinking coffee and brandy, I found myself laughing at Rejo, too, just as we had done one night on the front line in October '95, waiting for word to move forward on one of the final offensives of the war.

The former brigade commander of a famed Bosnian army unit, Hamdu took his nickname from his one-time command of the 502 Tiger Brigade, and was still called "Tigar" by some locals.

By contrast, Rejo was a chubby gastarbeiter, who had returned from abroad to Bosnia wearing a pair of cowboy boots for the final stage of the war, turning up near the front one evening with a BMW filled with deutschmarks and uniforms – donations to the 502 Brigade from expatriate Bosnians sitting out the action in Germany.

The Bosnian soldiers took a little convincing.

"See any of us looking fat, do you, Rejo? Where have you been all this time?" they chided.

Next day, disaster had befallen us all, and the intended Bosnian offensive had turned into a rout before it began after a Serb force hit the lines to our rear. We had fled across an open field, under fire, joining a small band of survivors for a four-hour exfiltration through no man's land back to Bosnian lines.

Rejo survived but lost his BMW and money, and his blistered feet shook for days afterwards. Now, our memories of the horrors diminished by time, Hamdu and I laughed once more, recalling Rejo's fear and his trembling cowboy boots.

Then the laughter ended.

"There is not a single night that I don't go to sleep thinking about the war," Hamdu murmured. "It seems as if it only stopped yesterday."

I had enjoyed his company in the war. He had the typical humble beginnings of so many men who had risen to command. Tough, courageous, street-smart, he was a former lorry driver elevated through the chaos of conflict to become a local hero. As we sat together again, a middle-aged woman from a nearby table came to shake the hand of "Tigar".

But nothing had quite worked out for him as planned since Dayton. His business ventures had lagged or failed. His marriage had ended. By his own admission he drank and smoked too much, and struggled with his temper. He had done a stretch in jail, too, charged with GBH after a local businessman was set upon by Hamdu's entourage in an extortion attempt.

"We got drunk, there was a dispute, then some of my guys beat him up," he explained matter-of-factly, bloodshot eyes squinting through cigarette smoke.

A sense of continual pursuit haunted him across the years.

"The Serbs are desperate to prove some sort of moral equivalence between our actions and theirs," he continued, "so they send in investigators to offer my old soldiers money for witness statements, trying to prove some sort of command responsibility linking me to a war crime."

"I expect one day they will come for me and I'll be arrested," he added, "although I know that nothing I did was wrong."

It was a familiar refrain. No one in Bosnia is ever guilty of a war crime. They just fall victim to politics. But it was not only war crimes investigators who were interested in him. He had been investigated in the suspected murder of a Bosnian-Croat general, Vlado Santic, who had disappeared one night in Bihac in March 1995.

During the war, Santic was suspected by Bosnian officers of conspiring with renegade autonomists in western Bosnia. He was last seen drinking with a 5th Corps commander in a hotel outside Bihac. There had been a row. He had disappeared. The investigation into the case reopened in 2013 and, not long afterwards, a protected witness guided investigators to a site where a barrel was exhumed. Its contents were too eroded to be identifiable as human, but Hamdu and six others had been questioned after Santic disappeared.

"I'm under huge pressure the whole time," he acknowledged. "The federal police nose around, make up different stories, dig here, dig there."

Gone were his glory days.

"The war was sort of defined," he admitted. "We knew our enemy, our strengths, and our weaknesses. There was loyalty. There was respect."

As we sat speaking, one of his wartime bodyguards, Nedza, with whom I had run across the fields in retreat so long ago, came to join us. Nedza had been in and out of prison in the intervening years on a string of different charges, and when I asked him how he found peace, he shrugged.

"I am trying," he said, shooting Hamdu a quick smile.

Leaving Bihac and its erstwhile heroes, I headed eastwards through a thousand smashing shades of orange into Bosnia's autumn hills. The rain came down and I was glad to be alone.

In a mist-heavy valley, I found another man I was looking for.

Senad was the subject of a famous war image. In the closing days of the conflict he had been in an advance Bosnian unit fighting to drive Serb forces back from around his village, Prhovo, which he had fled in 1992 during a massacre in which many of his family had died.

Battling back into the village as a soldier three years later, he found every house burnt down, and a mound of earth upon the mass grave of his murdered family and friends. Leaning against a tree beside his gutted home, gun in hand, he wept amid the desolation as another soldier, a curiously detached figure, stood behind him smoking.

Magnum's legendary Gilles Peress had photographed him as he wept, and the moment became one of the iconic images of the Bosnian war. I had chosen Gilles' photograph as the cover for *My War Gone By*, because Senad's grief epitomised the ambiguity of the book's title.

Senad was still crying when I found him now. Crying, drunk, apologetic, utterly traumatised: a war wreck. Nevertheless, he clawed himself together. On the second day of our meeting he stood before me sober, in clean clothes, freshly shaved, and humbled me by saying, "I'm really sorry I lost it earlier. The memories are still hard."

In that land of autumn leaves and broken men, in its every detail his story of what happened after the war – the two failed marriages, lost jobs, the booze and breakdowns – was a typical account of grief, misplaced guilt and unprocessed trauma.

We drove back to Prhovo together, partially rebuilt since the war's end, and wandered in the rain through the village, standing briefly by the home before which he had been photographed so long before.

"Whatever happened to the guy who was standing behind you in the photograph?" I asked him, keen to know something of the detached soldier: so cold and remote a witness in that moment of passion. "He was killed a couple of days later in another clash," Senad replied. "I forget his name now."

Against the wretchedness of his present situation, it was the survivor's instinct of his niece Velida, his current mentor although a decade younger, that seemed totemic. Now the mother of a teenage son, as a 15-year-old girl Velida had also been in Prhovo on the day of the massacre, in which her father and sister were among 56 killed. She had stood beside them when they were lined up against a wall, as around them houses burnt and dozens of Serb troops crowded in for the killing.

"I came from a village, so I had never seen so many people gathered together in my life before that day," she recalled. "The rage, the fires, the shooting: if it had gone on any longer, I would have had a heart attack."

In the confused moments of the killing, amid the swirling smoke and dust, she had also managed to escape and fled to the forest. She eventually made it to Switzerland, and did not return to Bosnia until 1999.

Despite her trauma – she told me that she still thinks about the massacre every day, and that even the sound of a raised voice brings back the memory of the shouts and screams – Velida seemed to have escaped the worst depredations of psychological injury in a way that Senad had not. "The love I miss from my father and sister I transferred to my husband and my son," she explained. "I was a victim, but I became a survivor. My ambitions changed. I wanted to be a good daughter, a good mother, a good wife. I achieved all that. Sure, I was lucky and met a good husband. But I worked for it, and it is what I live for: my family."

She pointed to the spot where she had been lined up along with other massacre victims.

"I can still feel anger for those who did this to us," she added. "But it would be too selfish to let my traumas influence my son's life. I want him to know what happened to my sister and father, because by forgetting evil we would do even greater evil. But I don't want that knowledge to prejudice him against someone just because they have a Serb name, say, 'Zoran'.

"I do not wish to hate them as they hated us," she added. "I do not wish them that victory."

I drove onwards into the mist, a slideshow of memory my only companion. A day or so later I stopped at a verge outside Travnik, where once I had been in a firefight and seen two young HVO (Croatian Defence Council) prisoners captured by Bosnian troops. I felt full of sympathy for these young men as they begged and pleaded for their lives. One, hoping it would reinforce his chances of survival, gave me a note to take to his mother. But after they were marched to the rear, a Bosnian soldier found a girl's ear in one of the captured men's ammunition pouches. I remember the ear sitting in his hand, pink and fresh. Amid the fighting, we were eating veal from a slaughtered calf at that moment. I tore up the note. Next day, I wrote an account of the incident. It was the first story I ever filed.

Standing by that verge again, beside busy traffic and rebuilt homes, it seemed that I stood astride parallel worlds of recall and reality.

There were those I met again in Bosnia who did tell me that they had broken the yoke of war and its memory, but they were the minority. In the zombiefied post-Dayton world, most wanted to embrace a future, but seemed unsure how much the key to tomorrow lay in holding on to the memory of the past.

In Vitez, a small town that was once the epicentre of Croat-Muslim fighting in central Bosnia and made famous by the presence of a beleaguered British UN force, I hooked up with a Bosnian friend I had known since '93. He tried explaining the dichotomy.

As an 18-year-old he had been purged from the town, but his family had reclaimed their home after the war. Sitting there now in the warmth of his house, as we drank wine and laughed about mutual friends and life after the war, it seemed for a moment that the past had indeed receded into distant legend. Then I noticed the three bullet holes in the front door.

"Hey, man, why didn't you fix the bullet holes?" I asked.

"Because I wanted to remember the morning in '93 that four masked men in HVO uniform came to that door, fired through it and shouted, 'Muslim motherf***ers out!'" he said. "I am all for being cool, living together, and getting on with life. But if we are going to do that, we shouldn't forget the day it happened."

Justice was supposedly a prerequisite of reconciliation in Bosnia, allowing communities to heal by acknowledging what had been done in their name, while giving victims a sense of redress. In practice, its pursuit seemed only to have reinforced Bosnia's divisions. The Serbs claimed their soldiers in the dock for war crimes were victims of an international conspiracy, while Bosnians and Croats suggested their own guilty men had fallen foul of politics designed to spread the balance of blame.

Hamdu alleged the system was rigged. Irma was to tell me she thought it was better never to know who shot her daughter. Velida said that no prison sentence could ever be long enough to quench her anger.

Yet if the Bosnians I had known wanted to preserve the memory of what had happened in the war, but at the same time ensure that the hatreds did not boomerang back to visit their children, then what part did justice – or its absence – really play in reconciliation and forgiveness?

Looking for answers, I returned to the scenes of familiar war crimes. One day in November '93, a disgusted British officer approached me to say that his troops had just recovered the dismembered remains of three Bosnian prisoners of war from the lines outside Novi Travnik. The men had been rigged with explosives by their HVO captors, forced back into no man's land and blown up at the edge of the Bosnian forward positions.

Among the many war crimes I looked into and wrote about during the war, this one was glaringly appalling, not just for the psychopathic intent of the act, but for its intimacy, too.

Novi Travnik was a typical small-town battlefield: everyone knew one another, friend and foe alike. So it was easy to investigate after the tip from the Brits. The identities of the three dead men – Mevludin "Dino" Muslimovic, Nedzad Mujak and Enes Hajric – were well known. I interviewed their families at the time. The deputy commander of a local HVO brigade in Novi Travnik even admitted to me that his soldiers had committed the crime.

So I was surprised, returning to Novi Travnik again, to find that despite the accumulation of evidence, justice had never been done. No one had ever been charged for the killings, and the families of the victims remained in limbo.

I talked with the dead men's brothers, soldiers in their twenties during the war, now working men in their forties struggling to get by. I spoke with one of the victims' children, and with a wife so traumatised she was on a 22-year course of tranquillisers. And with the mother of another who had never been told the exact manner of her son's death, only that it was "a war crime"; I had to waltz the conversation around without ever mentioning the detail.

Each remained deeply scarred by the atrocity, but each was struggling to come to terms with it against the pressures of Bosnia's crumbling economy.

"My mission is to raise my children and to make them decent human beings," explained Fuad, a 47-year-old former soldier who had to identify the body parts of his brother Nedzad after they were eventually collected from no man's land.

"I will never erase the moment I saw what was left of my brother from my mind," he said, staring out of the window of the café where we met again. "It is a picture laid upon my brain. But I am a plasterer, a tradesman trying to find work in a town with 70 per cent unemployment, who had to put my kids through school and raise my family.

"Time does its thing, and I found a greater struggle after the war was the fight for life and a job. So now, working men of my class, we don't have much time for politics and ethnicity in our struggle. When I have got some work, I don't question whether or not I am working beside a Serb, a Muslim or a Croat."

In their own way, "Dino" Muslimovic's family had also got on with their lives in the absence of justice being done. Articulate and measured, they explained to me that in the hours before "the crime", two HVO soldiers, Dino's former schoolfriends, had tried to protect their captive from an angry mob as Dino was marched to an improvised jail.

"Although I can't ever forget the criminals who killed Dino as a prisoner of war, nor can I forget those two Croats who tried to save him," Dino's brother Sabahuddin, now a 45-year-old postman, told me. "In this way, I have found it is possible to live side by side without 'forgiveness' for an evil minority."

In a tiny flat in Sarajevo I found the wife and children of the third murdered prisoner. Enes Hajric was identified by the names of his children, tattooed on an arm blown across the trench lines. His wife, Kemala, lost her elder son, Hasan, a young soldier, a few days after her husband's murder. The legacy of the war for the family was best described by Kemala's daughter Esmerelda, now 30. Despite being illiterate, having lost the prime of her education to the war and its aftermath, she explained her family's position with persuasion.

"I still need to know what happened to my father and who killed him," she said, "because it would give me some sort of sense that the state for which we gave so much actually cared about us. But it doesn't. Bosnia as a state doesn't seem to exist. Give me an answer, a job, childcare, somewhere to live, and forgiveness might come a bit easier."

Kneeling down beside Kurt's grave in the Lion Cemetery in Sarajevo, I wanted to tell him an update on a story. Kurt Schork was a great man. It has become customary to call almost any man killed in war "a legend", but he was the real deal: the high priest of war correspondents, utterly unique for his courage, moral strength, intelligence and humour. (He was funny as f***.) When he was killed in West Africa in an ambush in 2000, he left his friends the awareness of having known someone truly good, and in death he still inspires us. I thought of him as my mentor, as well as a friend. His death confused me for a long time.

In recognition of his devotion to the Bosnian story, some of Kurt's ashes were buried in Lion Cemetery, beside the tomb of Bosko Brkic and Admira Ismic, two lovers, Serb and Muslim respectively, who were killed by a sniper as they tried to escape the city across the Vrbanja bridge and whose fate Kurt brought to the world's attention.

One day in the autumn of '93, I had entered the village of Stupni Do with Kurt and four friends to discover a terrible massacre. A Croatian HVO unit had stormed the Muslim village and killed everyone they could find there. As dusk fell on the smouldering ruins, Kurt staggered back in shock through the door of a house. I walked in and saw three murdered women. They had been found hiding in a small grain pit beneath a trap door and were killed on the spot by the HVO. We never knew the dead women's identities.

"I have just been back to Stupni Do," I wanted to tell Kurt now. "There was a survivor from the pit. A 14-year-old girl with a bullet in her back was hiding beneath the legs of the dead women. Her name is Mufida Likic and I just found her. One of the dead women was her sister Medina, who had been hiding her when they were found. Mufida escaped. Years later she became a witness at the Hague and testified against the men who led the massacre. They were sent to jail. The thing is, although she had the chance to testify and saw the guilty men imprisoned, she cannot find forgiveness."

So it was. I had been back to Stupni Do two days before reaching Kurt's graveside.

Leaving the Lion Cemetery I walked through the streets of Sarajevo, where my young man's adventure began in January 1993. I passed over Vrbanja Bridge, where Bosko and Admira died. I followed the scuttle run I used with a war friend there, Momcilo, to avoid the snipers as we ran home. And just for a minute as I did so, I became a ghost, too, lost in a new shopping mall, standing still among streams of shoppers, staring at a McDonald's sign, looking for the ruins and remembering the run.

Inevitably, I got blasted drinking whisky in a bar with my old friend from Vitez. Everyone there was in their twenties and I thought I recognised them all, until I realised 20 years had passed and they were just children in the war.

A few years ago, I met my long-lost elder sister for the first time. The rendezvous was in a Caffè Nero. I was grateful for the crowded space and the uninterested hubbub around us. It was overwhelming enough without the added intensity of meeting in an empty and silent room.

Stepping into a similarly crowded café with Dajana and Irma in Velika Kladusa, I felt the same sense of relief now. It was full. Nelly Furtado and John Newman sung out from speakers above our table. As we sat together, my fears of awkwardness or uncontrolled emotion dissipated: we seemed like old blood, as easy in each other's company as cousins.

"I remember that day in its every detail," Irma began. "How could I forget? I remember the fear that my daughter might haemorrhage and die at any minute without proper treatment. I remember the shooting, the French. I remember you pleading with the soldiers to let us through. We shared that intensity."

That Dajana had lived was in itself miraculous. Her head wound was severe, and the bullet in her stomach had hit her liver. She had done more than survive, though. Her cognitive ability undamaged, despite her injuries she had been a perfect student at school, and had just returned home from visiting her boyfriend in Austria.

But this is a war story, not a fairytale. Her head wound had left her with a limp and lasting nerve damage that still causes her pain. At her school leavers' party, she sat by the wall while others danced. Her mother cried very quietly, just once, as she talked about it.

"There are times that I still feel angry with the war, angry with an event I cannot remember that stole part of my childhood," Dajana said. "But I don't want people's sympathy. I don't feel like a victim. I have never given up. I want to achieve things for myself."

After I had left Irma by the gate of the French base that day in '94, she had managed to reach Bihac and found Dajana in hospital. For a while, the little girl was blind with the trauma. Then one day, when Irma left her side to get some food for her daughter, a Serb artillery barrage hit the hospital.

"The shock of the explosions brought back her vision," Irma told me. "I rushed back into the ward and my daughter looked at me and said, 'You've had your hair cut.' That's when I knew she could see again."

I asked if the war had bequeathed them a prejudice against the Serbs or any other group. Despite Bosnia's sectarian divisions, the question seemed oddly irrelevant to these two women, so that I found myself abandoning its logic even as I asked it.

"I spent weeks in that hospital with Dajana," Irma explained. "Weeks in a ward with young people with no legs, with terrible wounds: Serbs,

Muslims and Croats. The experience left me unable to differentiate between them. I considered myself the mother of a wounded child in war, and saw others in that light."

She was a single mother, who had struggled without support across the years to raise her wounded daughter alone. In another life in another country, it may perhaps have been possible for Dajana to be given further treatment for the nerve damage caused by her wounds. In Bosnia, however, that has not been the case. The doctors in Sarajevo have said that nothing more can be done.

"We are close. We have each other, we have life, and God," Irma said.

The café had emptied and we were alone. We walked out into Velika Kladusa. The banks of rain clouds were absent, and the sun threw an autumn glow on the streets.

They tried to thank me.

"Words cannot explain …" Dajana began.

Although it was lovely to hear (who would not want to hear those words from those women?), I wanted to stop them. I wanted to say that I was exhausted by being a witness, watching people around me suffering needlessly at the hands of the great thief that is war; that I had watched so many people die whom I was unable to save; that I was tired of writing portraits of others' pain; that in them, just for once, I had had the chance to do something that actually mattered; that they were an outpost of something worthy in a deluge of darkness.

Luckily, I did not say all of that. But I did manage to say, "You don't have to thank me. It is you I am grateful to."

I drove them to their home and we said goodbye again. This time I managed to hold them.

Back in my hotel room in Bihac, although it was only late afternoon, I felt overcome by an overwhelming urge to sleep, and dropped on my bed fully clothed.

It was 2am when I awoke, confused as to the time and place. Outside my window, the River Una uncoiled thick in spate, black and silver beneath a sky of stars and scudding clouds. I watched it for a long time, that dark and swollen river. Twenty years ran down it as I watched and I grew old. It wasn't such a bad thing.

WINTER

RELAX, STAR WARS REALLY IS OUT OF THIS WORLD

Review by Kate Muir

DECEMBER 18 2015

THE FORCE AWAKENS opens with the chilling sight of a steel-grey Star Destroyer spaceship gliding up the screen, on and on, blocking out all light, a behemoth unlike anything previously seen on any planet. The same might be said for the *Star Wars* franchise, and the weight of expectation on the shoulders of the space opera's new director, JJ Abrams. And lo, he has delivered on his promise, paying witty, nostalgic homage to the 1977 original, while taking the action to pangalactic heights. *Star Wars*, after a barren patch with the prequel episodes I, II and III, has returned to cracking form, with Abrams as its saviour.

Is a modern, Western child more likely to recognise the source of this sentence: "A long time ago in a galaxy far, far away ... "? Or this one: "And it came to pass in those days that there went out a decree from Caesar Augustus that all the world should be taxed ... "? Yes, the latest *Star Wars* is an event of Biblical proportions. While most children celebrate Christmas, their understanding of the *Star Wars* universe is probably greater and more accurate. (That the two events will intersect in the form of *Star Wars* merchandising is a Yuletide miracle!) On the other hand, the eternal appeal of *Star Wars* is partly its simple moral universe: dark versus light, Sith versus Jedi. Kylo Ren, the new Darth Vader-like villain played by Adam Driver (*Girls*), struggles to repress his own attraction to the light and wields a red lightsaber in the shape of a glowing cross.

Episode VII is set 30 years after Episode VI, *Return of the Jedi*, and riffs on George Lucas's original. Luke Skywalker (Mark Hamill) has disappeared off the face of the Universe, and General Leia (Carrie Fisher, eschewing her princess title) sends a search party to find the lost Jedi. A hot-shot pilot, Poe Dameron (Oscar Isaac), teams up with renegade Stormtrooper Finn (John Boyega) and über-cute rollerball droid BB-8 — whose hard drive contains a valuable secret — as the search begins.

But Finn and Poe are not alone in their quest for Skywalker — the dark side is equally keen to find him — and the two men are brought crashing to the ground on the planet Jakku. The inhospitable desert there is home to Rey (Daisy Ridley), an orphan and a scavenger. Rey is young, athletic, and wears a taupe Issey Miyake Pleats Please-style costume that you could easily recreate with bandages for next Hallowe'en. Rey is also a mechanic, a pilot and a swordswoman, and a fine example to us all. Indeed, there is something exceptional about her abilities: the way she instinctively flies the Millennium Falcon spaceship with no training and fights like a tigress with a wooden staff. As those steeped in the series know, occasionally orphans on desert planets have special powers ... and thus begins another mythic *Star Wars* journey, a chosen one who must find her calling.

Ridley, whose previous work is mostly small parts in television, fills the screen with fresh-faced honesty and confidence — a brilliant find by Abrams. Rey pairs up on a journey with Finn, previously Stormtrooper FN-2817, who gains a name, and grows in strength, conscience and character as the movie progresses. Boyega — who came to our attention in *Attack the Block* — has boyish charm and great comic timing once he dumps the white Stormtrooper helmet.

The two innocents become unexpected fighters for the Resistance, battling the dark side, which has a new empire known as the First Order (which seems a bit Third Reich — as do Abrams' magnificent parades of Stroomtroopers below red banners, with a touch of Leni Riefenstahl's cinematography). The First Order is ruled by Supreme Leader Snoke, digitally brought to life by Andy Serkis, who looks like a giant Gollum. His image is projected above his minions on a throne, like a vast statue of Abraham Lincoln. Except Snoke is one gnarly, bad-tempered planet-zapper and if you thought the Death Star was big ...

Snoke's henchmen are Ren and General Hux: Domhnall Gleeson working fascist greatcoats and a stiff mien. Driver is perfect as Ren — beneath the helmet he has the face of a medieval knight, and his face-off with Harrison Ford's Han Solo is one of the movie's great set pieces. Ford's role is major, and he is grizzled but unchanged, bringing a rangy, devil-may-care energy to proceedings. The old generation came back to wild applause at my screening, particularly the droids C-3PO and R2-D2; and when Solo and Chewbacca the Wookie rediscover the Millennium Falcon, the words "Chewie, we're home!" induced whoops.

Chewie, incidentally, has gained a bit of paunch to reflect 30 years of wear and tear. Fisher has a small but serious role, and clearly the days of Leia in a gold bikini are long gone. A new generation of women seems to be running this galactic show, with Rey in woman-warrior form, a tougher creature than even Jennifer Lawrence in *The Hunger Games*. Plus *Star Wars* gains its first villainess in the form of Gwendoline Christie as Captain Phasma, a woman of steely resolve and armour, who in real life is 6ft 3in and on screen seems much bigger.

Avoiding spoiler territory means that the plot must go almost untouched in this review, but suffice to say its tentacles stretch back to the original film, and forward into the sequel. As Maz Kanata (Lupita Nyong'o) tells Rey: "The belonging you seek is not behind you but ahead." What I can reveal is that Dan Mindel's cinematography is epic and that airborne action is stupendous: in great *Star Wars* tradition, tiny craft go unimaginably fast through narrow spaces, not merely giving the viewer vertigo, but horizontigo. All is tuned to fever pitch by John Williams' soaring orchestral score. Say it quietly, but Abrams, admittedly abetted by new technology, is a better action director than Lucas, although we must bow to the master's original brilliance. As Obi-Wan Kenobi once said, "The Force surrounds us, it penetrates us, it binds the galaxy together," and taking your kids to this new *Star Wars* will probably have a similar effect.

TAXING SUGAR: COMPELLING ARGUMENTS FOR A LEVY

Leading Article

JANUARY 6 2016

EVEN IN THE upper echelons of government few have the power to save thousands of lives by championing one policy over another. Jeremy Hunt, the health secretary, could save tens of thousands of lives and tens of billions of pounds for the taxpayer by facing up to the gravity of Britain's obesity epidemic. This entails cajoling consumers to eat better while heaping pressure on food manufacturers to cut levels of harmful ingredients. It requires tough legislative action, too.

Excessive sugar consumption is closely linked to obesity, which Simon Stevens, the NHS chief, has called "the new smoking". Obesity is a prime cause of type 2 diabetes, which afflicts nearly four million adults (an increase of 70 per cent in a decade) and directly or indirectly costs the health service more than £10 billion a year. It is time for Mr Hunt to accept the advice of two thirds of GPs and his most senior public health officials and insist on a tax on sugar.

The proportion of Britons who are obese or overweight may be a symptom of prosperity. It is also a national scandal affecting a quarter of young children, a third of 11 to 15-year-olds and two thirds of adults. Inadequate exercise is a factor, but poor diet is the main culprit. The levels of physical activity needed to rid our collective waistline of its excess pounds would be "literally Olympic", the head of Diabetes UK tells *The Times* today. We are what we eat. Too much fat contributes to obesity, but cutting back on sugar is the single most efficient strategy for losing weight and limiting the risk of diabetes and its complications.

These complications include heart disease, kidney failure, blindness, loss of hearing and amputations. Obesity more broadly is closely correlated with a high risk of cancer, liver disease and depression. Diabetes and diabetes-related illnesses alone consume a tenth of the NHS budget and cause 24,000 premature deaths a year.

This is a public health disaster that has expanded incrementally, but an incremental response will not suffice. Last year, David Cameron rejected the idea of a sugar tax when it was proposed by Public Health England (PHE) as one of eight courses of action that would cut the nation's intake. PHE's other proposals include a ban on advertising high-sugar food to children and strict limits on two-for-one offers of confectionery and fizzy drinks. Such ideas are likely to be included in the government's forthcoming child obesity strategy. As things stand, a sugar tax is not.

Mr Cameron is thought to oppose a tax because he fears being seen to penalise poorer households that consume large quantities of high-sugar foods. He should not take fright so easily. If a sugar tax hits the poor hardest, they will see its benefits most clearly too. It is, in any case, the height of condescension to assume that the less well-off are also less able to improve their diets in response to good advice. Sir Liam Donaldson, the former chief medical officer, argued strongly for a tax in this newspaper yesterday. Mr Stevens has been coy in public but is thought privately to favour one.

It is reasonable to worry that an unduly complicated tax would be too expensive to enforce, but a 10 per cent tax on high-sugar fizzy drinks would be a simple and practical starting point. It is time for a sugar tax because nothing else is working. As academics and the PHE's chief nutritionist told parliament last year, public education and voluntary agreements with the food industry all have a role but so far have failed to cut sugar consumption.

Smoking in cinemas and restaurants used to be accepted with barely a murmur. Now it is hard to imagine. As Mr Hunt fine-tunes his child obesity strategy, he should consider whether he wants to be remembered as a health secretary shackled by inertia or one who followed the dictates of reason and insisted on reform.

BOWIE: POP'S GREATEST STAR — BRILLIANT, INSPIRING AND BAFFLING TO THE VERY END

Will Hodgkinson

JANUARY 11 2016

THERE'S A SCENE in *Ziggy Stardust And The Spiders From Mars*, D.A. Pennebaker's 1973 concert film on David Bowie's final concert as the Leper Messiah, which underlines why he was an almost religious figure to so many of us. Bowie is performing "Moonage Daydream", but the camera keeps pulling towards a teenage girl in the audience. She's acting out her own drama to the song, singing along to the words keep your electric eye on me, baby with her own eyes closed as she variously clutches her hands to her breast, raises them upwards and generally loses herself in glam rock ecstasy. You know she's listened to *Ziggy Stardust* countless times in her bedroom and now here she is, in the same room as this otherworldly figure in a Kanzai Yamamoto silk kimono, and she's taken to another world.

That's what Bowie did: create a world others could inhabit and by doing so learn to cope with the ones they were in. When I first went to secondary school I wondered why all the most interesting girls I met there loved David Bowie so much; why, in the mid-Eighties, it was Seventies albums like *Hunky Dory*, *Ziggy Stardust* and *Diamond Dogs* that you saw at the front of people's record collections, not *Living In A Box* by Living In A Box or whatever nonsense by men with silly hairstyles was being released at the time.

Because he understands us, one girl told me. Because he's as confused as we are. However strange and otherworldly his personas were, Bowie was oddly relatable: his lyrics may have been hard to decode but the yearning quality of everything — "Space Oddity", "Life On Mars", "Heroes" and countless others — was emotionally direct. He was both a part of us and from a distant galaxy we had no chance of ever reaching. He also never stopped moving, working, and developing. We know now that he made *Blackstar*, released last Friday on his 69th birthday and one of the most musically complex albums of his career, with the shadow of cancer over him, which makes it all the more remarkable that he pushed rock'n'roll into new territories until the very end.

Like all the best Bowie albums *Blackstar*, made with a team of New York jazz musicians while remaining within the essential structure of rock, is lyrically obtuse, but it's beginning to make a bit more sense now. It finishes with "I Can't Give Everything Away", a song that appears to be about how much Bowie will give to the public and keep to himself. It also hints towards his death. I know something is very wrong, the pulse returns the prodigal sons, he sings on the first verse, before concluding: the blackout hearts, the flowered news, with skull designs upon my shoes.

Meanwhile, "Lazarus", from *Blackstar*, referenced his past: in its video he wears the same outfit that features on the back of 1976's *Station To Station*. One way of understanding Bowie is to see his work as a particularly sophisticated take on musical theatre. He created one persona after another in order to play out roles that he could inhabit in public, while keeping private something of himself. Songs on his first album, *David Bowie* (1967), played around with the traditions of music hall while borrowing heavily from the style of the theatrical comic actor/songwriter Antony Newley, the camp humour of Joe Orton and the surreal whimsy of Pink Floyd's first singer Syd Barrett on songs like "Love You Till Tuesday" and "Silly Boy Blue".

Heavily influenced by the mime artist Lindsay Kemp, who would become his sometime lover, Bowie began his lifelong process of creating hyper-realised versions of himself that said something about the wider world. I wondered if I should try and be me, he said, or if I couldn't cope with that, it was much easier to be somebody else. Mike Vernon was the producer of that first album. I remember thinking, this is a really quirky record, says Vernon. But when we did "Love You Till Tuesday" I could see that Bowie was special. I thought: if we can come up with a song which has that certain something, this guy might just go somewhere.

Unfortunately, Bowie's then-label Deram decided the song with that certain something was "The Laughing Gnome", which would cause Bowie no end of embarrassment in the years to come. Today, its Pythonesque humour is rather charming. After Space Oddity, Bowie's first hit from 1969, he had a brief, atypical moment of floundering. The hippy era wasn't quite ready for the sight of a man in a dress, leaving his 1970 album *The Man Who Sold The World* only a minor curio at the time. It can't have been easy to combine genre-bending rock stardom with parenthood in suburban Beckenham, where Bowie and his wife Angie lived with their son Zowie (later Duncan) at the end of the Sixties and the beginning of the Seventies, but the period gave birth to what will, for me, always be his best album. 1971's *Hunky Dory* is an existential reflection on love, mortality and parenthood, and it's the most revealing and least arch of all Bowie's albums.

He tried to do his own version of Frank Sinatra's "My Way" on the heartbreaking "Life On Mars?", tackled Nietzsche on "Oh! You Pretty Things", and promised to be the world's least authoritarian dad in the lovely if undeniably maudlin "Kooks". *Hunky Dory* came out in 1971, the same year a long-haired, floppy-hatted Bowie visited Andy Warhol's Factory and looked distinctly uneasy as he realised that, for the sophisticated, cynical New York milieu he found himself in, long hair and hippy sentimentality was infra dig.

But Bowie was a quick study. The fact that Ziggy Stardust still looks shockingly alien today only underlines how revolutionary Bowie's creation must have seemed in 1972. Spurred on by his equally androgynous wife Angie, taking everything he had learned about artifice from Lindsay Kemp and Andy Warhol and adding a sprinkle of rock'n'roll dirt from Iggy Pop and Lou Reed, Bowie created the world's first space age rock star.

He got the idea for Ziggy after meeting British rocker Vince Taylor, an early user of LSD who had a breakdown and thought he was somewhere between a god and an alien, but Bowie's imagination was such that he took Taylor only as his starting point. Ziggy's one-legged body suit by Kanzai Yamamoto, viciously cropped and dyed hair by hairdresser Suzy Fussey and forehead globe by make-up artist Pierre Laroche made the other glam rockers of the era look like a bunch of builders in lipstick by comparison.

Then there are the songs on *Ziggy Stardust and the Spiders From Mars*: "Soul Love" is glamorous, "Five Years" is apocalyptic, and "Suffragette City" is pure excitement. *Ziggy Stardust* marked the point at which pop turned into art. One of the remarkable things about Bowie is the way in which he used whatever was going on in his life to artistic effect. By 1974 he had effectively fallen apart. Burned by fame, dangerously thin, he was living in Los Angeles on a cocaine diet and hardly going out. That gave birth to another persona, the Thin White Duke, the plastic soul of 1975's *Young Americans*, and to *The Man Who Fell To Earth*. Nic Roeg's film about an alien coming to Earth to bring water to his own planet and becoming increasingly detached from reality offered just another version of Bowie.

For him to move on from there into relative anonymity in late Seventies Berlin and make three of the most artistically challenging albums of his career, *Low*, *Heroes* and *Lodger*, all of them led not by his own persona but by observations, ideas and the influence of experimental German bands such as Can and Kraftwerk, is incredible. Bowie's influence came home to roost by the 1980s — the entire New Romantic movement was essentially an homage to what he had done throughout the 1970s — but after 1980's superb *Scary Monsters (And Super Creeps)* he began to lose his way, chasing after either pure commerciality (*Let's Dance*) or the zeitgeist (*Black Tie White Noise*).

In the last two years, however, he staged one of the most remarkable late career comebacks in modern times with *The Next Day* and *Blackstar*, possibly the former and definitely the latter made, we now realise, at a time when he knew he was dying. As *Blackstar*'s producer Tony Visconti has written, his death was no different from his life — a work of art. He made *Blackstar* for us, his parting gift. And he did it while staging his greatest performance piece yet: disappearing entirely. Brilliant, inspiring and baffling to the very end, David Bowie was the greatest pop star of all time.

Bowie's death has left two layers of grief. Most significantly, his 13-year-old daughter Alexandria and 44-year-old son Duncan Jones have lost their father and his wife Iman has lost a husband. The many musicians, artists and producers he has worked with have lost a colleague and a friend. But on a wider level, those millions of us who never met Bowie but whose music soundtracked our lives, who thought he would always be there, have lost someone who, in his own stylish way, helped make sense of the world.

'ISIS SAYS I'M NEXT. THEY WILL KILL ME. THEY WILL CUT OFF MY HEAD'

Abdel-Aziz al-Hamza interviewed by Damian Whitworth

JANUARY 16 2016

ABDEL-AZIZ AL-HAMZA is such a thorn in the flesh of Islamic State that the fanatics and their supporters subject him to a constant barrage of death threats. He is a co-founder of Raqqa Is Being Slaughtered Silently (RBSS), a group of underground citizen journalists that has been exposing the reality of life in Islamic State's self-proclaimed capital in Syria. They report on everything from crucifixions to long food queues.

Earlier this month they disclosed a fresh level of barbarous insanity with the story of Ali Saqr, a jihadist who shot his own mother because he believed she was guilty of apostasy. In the Isis propaganda video released a few days before that, in which five British "spies" were shot dead by a gang led by an English-speaking jihadist thought to be Siddhartha Dhar from Walthamstow, two of the men "confessed" that they had worked with Hamoud al-Mousa, another founder of RBSS.

In fact, says Hamza, the five murdered men had nothing to do with RBSS, but Isis is so incensed by the effectiveness of the brave and irrepressible citizen journalists in its midst, and so keen to deter Syrians from joining them, that it will seize any opportunity to claim it is executing its supporters. "They say anyone who is an activist is working with us," says Hamza. "They are trying to stop our work."

Several of those who do work for RBSS, or are connected to those who do, have been murdered, and fear of a grisly execution forced Hamza to flee first Raqqa and then Turkey. As we sit in a hotel in the centre of Berlin I ask if he thinks that the lengthening arm of Isis could really reach him here. Yes, he says simply. "They say that I am the next one; they will kill me soon. They will cut off my head." It is an extraordinary situation.

In the heart of Europe, in a city where Cold War spies and dissidents once looked over their shoulders to see if the secret police were coming for them, a 24-year-old writer half-expects the arrival of an assassin sent by a group that controls what is effectively a desert death cult.

Hamza is a tall, brooding figure who arrives for our meeting heavily swaddled against the sub-zero temperatures outside; indeed, he wears a

Nike woolly hat throughout our interview. A friend sits almost silently throughout, nursing a glass of red wine and examining his phone. Hamza, 24, is, understandably given his situation, not one for small talk. He speaks broken English that he picked up "on the street". He sips a vodka and Red Bull, tugs at his beard and is astonishingly phlegmatic about the prospect of dying. "For us, as Syrians, it's a normal thing. If you lose your life, it's not that strange a thing or that important a thing.

"Not only for me, for all of us. After losing all these friends and family members, we decided, anything might happen. I said to my friends and my colleagues, 'If anything happens to me, don't stop this war,' and they told me the same thing. So we decided to stop only if they killed all of us, or when we go back home. It's a war between our group and Isis."

Before the Syrian civil war few had heard of Raqqa, a city of some 220,000 people, that sits on the bank of the Euphrates in the north of the country. "It was a normal city. You could do what you wanted: drink, smoke, whatever," says Hamza. The city is predominantly Sunni, but had some Shia mosques and a Christian population that was later driven out by Isis. When the uprising began against President Assad's regime, Hamza, a biology graduate from Raqqa University with no real previous interest in politics, got involved. "I and my colleagues joined the revolution as activists or media men. The regime didn't allow media organisations to enter; the situation forced us to become citizen journalists."

Hamza and his fellow activists highlighted the attacks and bombings of the Assad regime and then, as the Free Syrian Army jostled for control of the city with the emerging Isis, they brought to light the kidnappings and executions of this new and brutal entity. When Isis secured Raqqa two years ago, Hamza's work was well known enough for jihadists to go after him. "They stormed my house looking for me. Fortunately, I wasn't there." He fled Raqqa after learning that Isis had come for him. "So I escaped from the city." This was in January 2014.

A friend who bears a resemblance to him gave him his ID and he left without saying goodbye to family or friends. "I couldn't take my laptop or anything. I didn't even take a bag, just the clothes I was wearing and my phone." He slipped over the border into Turkey where he joined friends who had also escaped. It was here that they decided to set up RBSS, using social media to relay news from friends back in Raqqa about what Isis was doing. "They started to change the city," he says.

"They painted the city black and started to kidnap its citizens and execute them. But no one heard what was going on, so we decided to show the reality of life in the city, the reality of Isis. It was a duty for us. We used to fight the Syrian government regime, and now we had a regime that was even worse," he says.

When RBSS started, information about life in Raqqa was scarce. "Human rights organisations didn't hear about what was going on. We tried to show the wider international world, so maybe someone could do something to change things. Now I think people know about Raqqa."

RBSS gathered pictures, video and firsthand accounts from its contacts in the city. The group became the key source for international media organisations as stories emerged of beheadings, crucifixions and women being treated as sex slaves. People risked their lives to relay information about the enforcement of a new strict dress code by the all-women morality police. They took to Twitter and Facebook to write about the closure of schools and the opening of Isis education centres at mosques, and posted pictures of snaking queues for food as shortages became normal.

One hallmark of Isis is the slick media operation that aims to spread terror through videos glorying in its treatment of prisoners, and to recruit foreigners whose disaffection and in many cases frustrated machismo make them vulnerable to seduction by images of men in black waving AK-47s in the air. Like all tyrannies, Isis doesn't like to lose control of its own narrative and the level of threats against Hamza while he was still close to the Syrian border in Turkey quickly persuaded him that he needed to get further away.

A legal route to asylum in a European country would take too long. So with the help of a smuggler and a fake Hungarian passport he took a tourist boat to Greece, from where he flew to France and then hired a taxi to take him to Berlin. Relatives outside Syria helped pay the €13,000 (£10,000) cost of his journey. In Germany officials thought his claim that his life was in danger because of his citizen journalism work was "a bulls*** story". But he was granted asylum and can stay for an initial three years. He is urgently looking for work while co-ordinating the RBSS campaign.

He does not have a partner and lives alone in Berlin. He has relatives in Europe but cannot talk about them because of safety concerns. He spends much of his time talking to the international media and working late into the night monitoring the situation back in Syria and liaising with his network of contacts. The threats have only got worse as RBSS has received more attention, winning an award from the Committee to Protect

Journalists in New York last November. "Actually, I don't care about the threats. I don't tell the police. For me it's OK. Our colleagues in Raqqa are risking their lives and I am here in Europe."

Information from Raqqa indicates there is a price on Hamza's head — and those of his RBSS colleagues. "There are rewards for anyone who kills one of us. We don't know the amount, but I am sure it's a big number." Three members of RBSS have been murdered by Isis. Two were captured in Syria; one, Ibrahim Abdul Qader, was beheaded in a house across the border in Turkey in October last year. A film-maker and friend of the group, Naji Jerf, was killed in Turkey, the day before he was due to fly to France, in December. Isis has also gone after relatives of RBSS members and killed one founder's father last summer.

Other RBSS contributors are living in Europe anonymously, but Hamza decided not to do the same — he thinks the organisation needs a public face. "I am the spokesman. If I was anonymous, we'd be accused of being in intelligence, or being a governmental group." He takes precautions, such as never revealing in real time on social media where he is. But, Hamza says, "I don't want to be under pressure, under protection. I want to be as normal as possible here."

The executions of RBSS sources and their associates have not deterred the people of Raqqa from telling their stories. Hamza says RBSS has 70 contributors inside the city and surrounding area. "They caught people but we didn't stop." However, the logistics of getting the news out have become trickier. "They cut the internet inside the city. Now there are four internet shops, all belonging to Isis. But we find ways to transfer information." Videos are harder to smuggle out, "but we still get the breaking news. We can't tell you how. They get crazy."

The image of Isis officials incensed by news of what's happening still seeping out is a pleasing one, and in talking of this Hamza seems to come close to allowing a hint of a smile to appear on his face. Otherwise, he talks calmly and soberly, without demonstrations of passion but with the air of a man with deep reserves of patience and determination. Hamza says that Raqqa is effectively a prison — only those with special permission to travel for medical reasons can leave. The electricity is often on for only three hours a day and sometimes not at all for as long as a week. The water is often contaminated and food prices have increased tenfold.

He estimates there are still as many as one million people in the Raqqa region, and if they don't join Isis life is even more of a struggle. If a man joins, however, "he gets money, a car, house, woman — whatever he wants. Living under Isis control and not joining them is a kind of resistance. If those people say anything against Isis they will be executed." Realising they can't convert all of the adults, Isis leaders are now targeting children. Most have no school to go to and are roaming the streets. "Isis started to give them money — a dollar as a gift — or mobile phones to recruit them."

As well as its social media work, RBSS supporters in Raqqa have been putting up anti-Isis posters and graffiti, and distributing a magazine that has the same cover as an Isis publication but contains subversive material, including comics designed to appeal to children. It is a small step and Hamza is worried that, despite their efforts, fanatical ideology is being implanted in the brains of the next generation. He is also dismayed that people in Raqqa are so desperate that some, including friends, decide that the only way to survive is to join Isis. "I have a close friend, a doctor. I know he hates Isis a lot. And another friend told me he had joined up. When I called him, he said, 'I joined them. I have children and I should feed them. They wouldn't give me any work unless I joined them.'"

RBSS hopes that one of the consequences of its work is that foreigners contemplating joining Isis will at least see its version of what life is like in the so-called caliphate. "Before our campaign, if you wanted to join Isis, you would see only their material. Right now there are at least two sides. It's important for us to stop the immigration [to Raqqa] and show videos of what people are suffering inside the city. And also show that it is not an Islamic state. These people are criminals."

Although the organisation has become famous for its reporting on Isis, Hamza says that it is not RBSS's primary focus. "Our main enemy is the regime of Assad, because if Isis has killed one, the regime has killed 100." Britain, America and other western allies "have forgotten Assad right now and they focus on Isis. But Isis came because of the Assad regime. When we started we just asked for freedom, then we asked to change the regime. They [the West] promised us they would help us but it was just bulls***. If they had helped us when we started we would have no Isis."

Britain should take more Syrian refugees, Hamza believes, and the welcome he has received in Germany has been warm. "The Germans were very nice and non-Muslims helped me more than Muslims." He is concerned, though, by the reaction to events in Cologne and other German cities over New Year, when women were subjected to violence and sexual assaults by mobs of male migrants. "If I am bad that does not mean all the refugees are bad. There are many bad Germans but not all Germans are bad."

Some politicians and media organisations are exploiting the incidents to stop the flow of refugees, he suggests. "But we will not [stop] because asylum is our right." I wonder if he thinks he will ever go home to Raqqa. "I am very optimistic. It is not easy for me and for the other guys to keep fighting after all that happened to us. Our work is risky. But I am very optimistic that something will change and maybe our work can help, or will be part of any change in the future.

"I hope I will go back, but I am not sure. I want to go back to my home; that's the reason why we keep doing these things. We don't know if we can stay alive until that time. Before the war, if anyone young died it was a very sad thing. Everyone remembered the person for years. But right now if you are killed in the morning you will be forgotten by the evening, because it has started to become a normal thing to lose friends, families, relatives."

He tugs at his beard once more, checks a couple of new messages on his phone, but then says, matter-of-factly, "We believe that one day everything will change."

COMRADE CORBYN DOESN'T BELIEVE IN PARLIAMENT

Daniel Finkelstein

JANUARY 16 2016

HERE'S THE THING about Labour and Jeremy Corbyn. They rejected David Miliband, lost under Ed Miliband and now they've chosen Ralph Miliband. As a schoolboy, I fell in with a group of Maoists. I was helping out at the Wiener Library, my grandfather's great anti-fascist archive, and a number of the other temporary staff were fans of Chairman Mao. They thought of me in a kindly way, as a sort of anti-Nazi mascot. But they couldn't believe my bourgeois politics.

So when I left, they gave me a copy of a book arguing the impossibility of achieving radical change through the parliamentary system. It was called *Parliamentary Socialism* and it was by Ralph Miliband. Ed and David's dad begins his volume with these words: "Of political parties claiming socialism to be their aim, the Labour Party has always been one of the most dogmatic — not about socialism, but about the parliamentary system."

The remainder suggests that this dogmatism is an error that prevents Labour from realising true socialism. There was a political joke doing the rounds while Ed was leader that "Ralph Miliband argued parliamentary socialism was impossible and his son had shown he was right". Ralph would not have seen it as a joke. Watching the mess that is Jeremy Corbyn's reshuffle, indeed that is his entire relationship with the parliamentary party, I realise the problem is not just that the parliamentary party does not believe in Jeremy Corbyn. It is that Jeremy Corbyn does not believe in the parliamentary party.

By this I mean something more fundamental than that he does not believe in those who are currently members of the parliamentary party. I mean that he does not really believe in parliament. The Bennite left to which Corbyn belongs eschews Michael Foot and his reverence for the House of Commons. It takes broadly Ralph Miliband's view. Yes, this view has it, there has to be a parliament, but the idea that you can transform society through it is a delusion. There has been, I think, quite a bit of confusion about Corbyn's idea of the new politics — portrayed as a sort of kindly, bumbling way of asking questions more politely and tolerating debate — and about the creation of Momentum, his campaign arm, which is billed as being anything but kindly and tolerant of dissent.

I think both are being misunderstood. The new politics of Corbyn isn't that parliament should be more kindly and civilised, it is that traditional parliamentary exchange is irrelevant, tiresome and reactionary and the people in it are up themselves. Real change is going to come from outside, from the grassroots. And to this new politics Momentum, far from being a contradiction, is essential. While much of the coverage of this new organisation has been about parliamentary deselection, its own meetings and public statements aren't about that. They talk instead of being community activists, supplementing trade unions by campaigns that organise housing tenants, consumers, parents, students.

To this work, parliament is secondary. The campaigns will be positive and creative, so they at least imagine, building local institutions and a sense of community. At the same time they will politicise normally unpolitical people and turn these people's worries and problems into dissent. Together they will then challenge those who hold power. Jeremy

Corbyn's relationship with — and John McDonnell's statements about — the IRA show that they regard insistence upon obeying the law laid down by parliament as quaint when it gets in the way of the struggle. Direct, extra-parliamentary action is necessary to bring about socialism. And necessary to administer it, too.

Socialism does not consist of a static government administering the state. As Ralph Miliband put it in his final book, *Socialism for a Sceptical Age*, socialism would be "a partnership between a socialist government on the one hand and a variety of grassroots agencies on the other. In no way would activists be mere servants of the government; on the contrary they would have an organised life of their own." The president might wear a posh suit but "on no account will he shave off his beard". Leadership proposals to reorganise the Labour Party and give more power to activists are, of course, partly designed to give Corbynistas greater control of the machine.

There is more to it than that, though. With socialism, the party plays a vital role. At first as a vanguard, but then, as Miliband argues in his *The State in Capitalist Society*, as a model for society. "In its own present structures, in its own present modes of behaviour, attitudes and habits, it must prefigure the society to which it aspires."

So Labour is to be reorganised as a grassroots organisation setting policy by plebiscites and overriding parliament, not just because this helps Mr Corbyn and his allies to win control, but because this is how they see society itself being reorganised. Just before he died, Ralph Miliband had a conversation with Tony Benn that it is appropriate to relate as we contemplate Corbyn's painfully drawn-out reshuffle. "Tony," said the professor, "sometimes my children say to me 'Dad, if everything you recommended were done, would it work?' ". Benn replied: "Well, mine say the same to me."

The children were right to ask. Actually they were being polite. Of course it wouldn't work. The socialist policies of state control of industry and the "end of wage labour" would impoverish the people it was supposed to liberate. And the running of society as a sort of out-of-control demonstration being called to order by a convenor shouting through a loudhailer would be chaotic and ultimately oppressive.

Politically Momentum will, in the end, fail. The people it "organises" will not stay organised and like every left-wing (or, come to think of it, right-wing) vanguard, it will soon splinter as the People's Front of Judea falls out with the Judean People's Front. The idea that thousands of tiny protest movements, seizing local power from rapacious landlords or campaigning to preserve the local parks, will produce a harmonious socialist society is absurd. Their interests will clash with each other as they fight for power and resources. And who will have to decide how to mediate between their different claims? Why parliament, of course.

CHINA IS TRAPPED IN THE ULTIMATE TRILEMMA

Ed Conway

JANUARY 19 2016

HERE IN BRITAIN, pantomime season is drawing to a close but 5,000 miles away in Beijing another farcical annual ritual is only just beginning. For today the Chinese authorities deliver their official estimate of economic growth in 2015.

Much like the panto, this rite has a long and colourful history, a predictable if preposterous plot and a fair bit of hammy acting. The main difference is that in China there are still one or two audience members who believe what they are watching is fact rather than fiction. With markets having suffered their worst start to a year on record and investors particularly worried about the Chinese economy, the release of 2015's big number — expected to be close to the official 7 per cent target — is sodden with irony.

A few years ago most economists believed China had the power to control its economy. Today, not so much. Frankly, the most surprising thing is that this epiphany took so long to come around. For years, it has been clear that China's economy has become reliant on credit to fuel its post-crisis boom. The history of debt bubbles always suggested that this was unlikely to end well: the best outcome being Japan-style stagnation; the worst a full-blown crash. What is particularly unsettling in China's case is that even as Beijing attempts to confront its debt crisis and restructure its economy, it is also embarking on an even more ambitious project: to transform its economic relationship with the rest of the world.

Understanding why this is such a big deal involves understanding one of the golden rules of economics, something called the "trilemma". The idea behind the impossible trinity, to use its other name, is as follows: in a fantasy world a government would like to control domestic monetary policy, to keep its exchange rate fixed and to allow money — capital — to flow in and out of the country at will. But in the real world you can only have two of the three at any one time. Consider the UK. The Bank of England controls monetary policy, raising and cutting interest rates as required. There is free movement of capital in and out. But in return for these two privileges, sterling must float against other currencies (occasionally annoying holidaymakers and damaging exporters).

Those with longer memories will recall that the system is relatively recent. Until 1992, Britain pegged its exchange rate, first to the deutschmark, then to a level determined by the European Exchange Rate Mechanism. Capital moved freely, but the UK ceded control of monetary policy, shadowing the Bundesbank's interest rate. Over the past century and a bit, the world economy has lurched around the extremities of this trilemma. There was the Victorian gold standard, under which everyone's exchange rates were pegged to gold, capital flows were free and there was no domestic monetary policy. There was Bretton Woods, under which everyone's exchange rates were pegged to the dollar, which was in turn pegged to gold. Countries could change their interest rates, but in return they gave up freedom of capital — restrictions were imposed on flows of money.

Every 30 or 40 years the dominant international monetary system collapsed. It happened to the gold standard in 1914, lighting the fuse that exploded in the Great Depression. It happened to Bretton Woods in 1971, paving the way for the oil crises and slumps of the 1970s. And those are the two important things to remember: first that the trilemma is inviolable. Second, that whenever a country, or group of countries, shifts from one regime to another, it invariably sparks a period of instability and economic pain.

Which brings us back to 2016 and China. Beijing's monetary regime was, up until recently, a bit like Britain's under Bretton Woods: a pegged exchange rate for the yuan, independent monetary policy and rigid (if a little leaky) capital controls. But gradually over recent years, and then explicitly over the past six months, Beijing has started to unpeg the yuan from the dollar. The objective is primarily political: to formalise China's prominence in the global economy by turning the yuan into an open globally traded currency, rivalling the dollar.

A few months ago the International Monetary Fund gave its seal of approval, signalling that the Chinese currency would be included in its basket of leading world currencies. Many countries are bending over backwards to accommodate China, ranging from the UK, which wants to become the world's biggest offshore trading post for yuan, to Zimbabwe, which recently made the Chinese currency legal tender after Beijing wrote off $40 million of its debt. But with China also firefighting a slowdown, the shift from one monetary regime to another leaves Beijing in particularly tricky waters.

Unless it ditches its plan to unpeg the yuan, it cannot both support struggling households through lower interest rates and prevent cash from escaping the country. So goes the inexorable logic of the trilemma. The Federal Reserve's decision last month to raise US interest rates has increased the pressure, sucking yet more cash out of China towards America.

This is the crux of the matter. No country has managed a transition in its monetary system such as this without inflicting pain and disturbance on its citizens and the rest of the world. Think of Britain's break with the gold standard in 1931, or Black Wednesday in 1992. Remember all of that as you digest those Chinese growth numbers today. The real drama is going on beneath the surface.

RED MARK OF SHAME OPENS DOOR TO ATTACKS ON ASYLUM SEEKERS

Andrew Norfolk

JANUARY 20 2016

SCREENS OF GREY steel mask the doors and windows of abandoned houses on dreary streets. The rows of boarded Victorian terraces were scheduled for demolition in 2005. Bulldozers eventually moved in but their work is incomplete. What survives in the Gresham area of Middlesbrough is a skeletal collection of half-streets.

Ray Mallon, a former mayor, seeking to justify a plan to reduce 1,500 homes to rubble ten years ago, explained that "if a person has cancer a surgeon cuts a big piece out to save the rest of the body". If Gresham was the town's tumour, further surgery is required. A recent visitor would have noticed that lines of grey symmetry were sometimes fractured by a house with no metal sheeting. Here, instead, were windows with grubby net curtains. Behind some shone a pale light. Not all wastelands are uninhabited.

No one sane would choose to live on a ghost street but these are the temporary homes of those who have no choice. Asylum seekers go where they are sent. In the poorest parts of town their spartan houses are all too easy to identify, even on roads where every house is occupied. The clue lies in the chipboard front doors. With few exceptions, they are painted red. On Gresham's broken streets, night-time haunt of drug dealers and prostitutes, the colour feels like a stain. For the would-be refugees who live behind them, red doors are a badge of shame that "shows the difference between normal people and us".

"When people see them, everyone knows it means asylum seekers," a man in his thirties said. "They put us behind red doors. We feel ashamed. I didn't think your country would allow something like this." A multimillionaire owns every red-door asylum property on the demolition streets of Gresham, plus hundreds more across Middlesbrough and its neighbouring local authority, Stockton-on-Tees. His name is Stuart Monk. Last year *The Sunday Times* Rich List estimated his wealth at £175 million.

His property company, Jomast, 100 per cent owned by Mr Monk, 66, his wife and their two children, houses every asylum seeker placed in temporary accommodation in northeast England. It is paid by G4S, the security and outsourcing company which in 2012 was awarded the government's asylum housing contract for the region. Riada Kullani, 32, was one of their "service users". The Albanian, whose asylum application was recently accepted, described months of misery behind a Jomast red door in Stockton. The house, shared by five women, was routinely targeted for abuse by a teenage gang. "They knocked on the door, threw stones at the windows. They were shouting all the time and used rude words," she said. "They said, 'F*** you, dirty women. Get out of our country. You don't belong here.'

"It was every day, for two months. I felt ashamed to go outside because all the neighbours could hear it. One of my friends was crying all the time.

We told Jomast. They said, 'There's nothing we can do, just ignore it.' We reported it many times to the police." In common with dozens of asylum seekers with whom *The Times* has spoken in Middlesbrough and Stockton, Ms Kullani, who says she fled Albania because her life was in danger, is convinced that young thugs targeted her house because of its red front door. "Why are all the doors red? It makes it obvious that we're different," she said. "It makes us feel separated. When I first came here, I thought it was maybe deliberate, to warn the English people that they shouldn't talk to us. It made me feel really sad, but now I know that other cities are not like this."

At the most recent count there were 2,713 asylum seekers in the northeast, among a UK total of 28,620, each awaiting the outcome of their applications for refugee status. Behind some red doors live traumatised men, women and children who fled their homelands in genuine fear for their lives. As of last September, 74 of them were from Syria. They lacked the good fortune to be awarded the gold-star service reserved for 20,000 of their fellow citizens whom the government has promised to accept after selecting them from camps under a Syrian vulnerable persons relocation scheme. Asylum seekers are not allowed to earn money and must survive on £36.95 per person per week. For the first six months of their stay, they are entitled to no support to help to pay for English language classes. Most are terrified to make any complaint about their living conditions in case it jeopardises their claim.

In the northeast they all live in properties owned by Mr Monk. Since 2012 asylum housing has been a for-profit operation. If a company receives a fixed sum of money per asylum seeker per day, it makes business sense to place them in the cheapest properties. Invariably, as in Middlesbrough, these are in the most deprived neighbourhoods.

Much of Mr Monk's asylum housing lies in the terraced streets of Gresham, near Teesside University, or North Ormesby. Each is among the poorest 0.5 per cent of neighbourhoods in England. Middlesbrough has 800 asylum seekers; a neighbouring local authority, Redcar and Cleveland, with its own pockets of deprivation, has eight. The disparity has an explanation: Mr Monk owns 290 asylum properties in Middlesbrough; in the adjoining authority he has two. His company Jomast, is breaking no laws or rules. Dame Margaret Hodge, the former chairwoman of the Commons public accounts committee, has warned that "the last thing you want is a huge concentration of asylum seekers in one area because it has a terrible effect on social cohesion".

Concerns about the red-door branding have been raised with Mr Monk and senior employees of Jomast and G4S on several occasions. Stephen Small, a G4S executive, was challenged in February 2014 by Ian Swales, then the Liberal Democrat MP for Redcar. At a parliamentary committee hearing, the MP asked: "Do you think that painting the doors a different colour so that the whole neighbourhood knows who the asylum seekers are is likely to make that accommodation more safe?" Mr Small promised to "take that point away". Nothing changed. Of 168 Jomast properties identified by *The Times* in Middlesbrough, 155 had red doors.

Andy McDonald, Middlesbrough's Labour MP, views Mr Monk's red doors as "a way of marking people out that is reprehensible". For Mr Swales, they are a "mark of separation" that "reminds you of Germany in the 1930s. I thought it was shocking. I assumed the management of G4S would be equally shocked and would do something about it. To find out nearly two years later that nothing's been done is appalling." Mr Monk lives in an early 18th-century manor house. More than 200 years ago it was described as a "desirable country residence for a genteel family". Its front door is not red.

IF I COULD WALK AGAIN
FOR ONE DAY ONLY

Melanie Reid

JANUARY 30 2016

AUNT AVRIL, WHO DIED when I was small, will never know how dear she has become to me. As I write, she meets my eyes from a picture stuck on my computer: she's glancing up from a book, with an appraising expression. Her chair is parked outside in the sun, her hunched shoulders supported by pillows, her hair unbrushed, her hands welded into fists.

Often I talk to her. "Crap, isn't it? And I have it a million times easier than you did," I mutter. And silently she comforts me. As I have recounted once before, Avril caught encephalitis lethargica, the mysterious disease that struck down thousands, randomly, across the globe after the First World War. She was left an active brain trapped in a paralysed body. Around the time she died in the Sixties, the late, great Oliver Sacks discovered that the drug L-dopa, prescribed to sufferers, gave them a brief, extraordinary period of recovery. Heartbreakingly, the effects lapsed very quickly and their bodies froze again, their voices swiftly silenced.

It was, nevertheless, one of the most phenomenal pharmaceutical events ever known. Now, can we hope for even better from the "miraculous" — a doctor's word — effect that a new procedure is having upon some cases of multiple sclerosis? The treatment, as revealed by a recent BBC *Panorama*, has encouraged enough neurological improvement to let some patients start to walk and cycle again. Their very own L-dopa awakening — only so far the honeymoon has been lasting; there's been no bitter curtailment yet.

Please, dear scientists, may the experiments widen in scope and the amazing results persist. Please, God, if you could assist them, and make these drugs reverse or alleviate all MS, and Parkinson's (already helped by L-dopa), and motor neurone disease, and all other vile neurological complaints, I will start believing in you. And if you could stretch it to effective spinal repair, well, I'd gladly become a nun or wear a burka for the rest of my life.

Sometimes, when I'm bored, as a mild form of torture, I imagine what I'd do if I had an L-dopa moment, even if it were just for 24 hours. Trivial things to start with, to prepare a better environment for when the spell broke. Leap around the house, doing all the high-up, hard-to-reach stuff that six-footers do effortlessly, the tiny things I've spent almost six years gazing at impotently.

I'd dance, make love, go for a walk, twirling this way and that in the wind for fun. I'd put on a dress and elegant accessories and jump in Dave's big car, because I've always wanted to know how it handles, and drive to the airport. We'd fly south, take Dougie out for a meal, order something normally impossible to eat. Before we leave we'd have one of our standing-up group hugs, and chant the Sister Sledge song *We Are Family*. Back home, finally, we'd climb the hill behind our house, in the dark, holding hands, and look up at the sky. And refuse to cry.

A *Times* reader who has had Parkinson's for the past 12 years, which has robbed her of the ability to move around, ride horses and — the final frontier of indignity — her hair, tells me that she too has L-dopa fantasies. She imagines what it would be like to knock it back and half an hour later get to walk, talk and move "just like", as her granddaughter recently wrote, "a normal walking, talking granny". That all-Christmasses-at-once-plus-a-brigade-of-fairy-godmothers moment.

Anyway, fantasies are an indulgence. Back in the here and now, I am doing the only thing I can, which is to keep going. And laugh. The sheer eccentricity of my body, its inconstancy, infuriates me. Some nights I go to bed and my left foot is freezing cold, my right foot warm. The next night, vice versa. The third night, both cold. I cannot differentiate — to me, they merely burn with discomfort. Why? Why, when I tap my chin, do my feet tingle? Why could I stagger 50 feet before Christmas, yet this week struggle with 15? February will come, and the weaker new year resolutionists will revert to the couch; the dedicated will progress. And me, I'll just be stuck in bloody January for the rest of my life. Unless ...

Melanie Reid is tetraplegic after breaking her neck and back in a riding accident in April 2010.

SIR TERRY WOGAN

Obituary

February 1 2016

Terry Wogan had a strong claim to being Britain's favourite broadcaster. For the vast swathes of Middle England who tuned into his breakfast show on Radio 2, which, with more than eight million listeners was the most popular in Europe, that was certainly the case. Ironically as an Irishman, Wogan was lauded for his ability to make Britons feel good about themselves with his masterful use of gentle self-mockery that was laced with great personal warmth. In a rare moment of seriousness, he once said: "I think the most important thing in life is kindness."

In a 50-year broadcasting career, which included vocalising the nation's mirth at the absurdity of the Eurovision Song Contest, he exuded a whimsical Irish charm. His seemingly effortless drollery, delivered in soft, slightly croaky, world-weary tones, never transgressed into flippancy and won him both lasting friendship with millions of viewers and listeners and the admiration of his broadcasting peers. The Queen once told Wogan that she listened to him every morning and on espying him at a Buckingham Palace reception she once cried "flab" in reference to his "fight the flab" campaign on the *Wake Up to Wogan* radio show in the Seventies. When she asked, "How long have you worked at the BBC?" he replied, "Your Majesty, I've never worked here", in reference to the fact to that he was simply doing what he loved.

His retirement in 2009 was national news. Gordon Brown led the tributes and *The Times* published an ode: "Stop all the clocks, cut off the telephone, Terry Wogan is abandoning his microphone." Wogan, who took British citizenship in 2005 and was knighted the same year, never rose to accusations from his countrymen that he somehow betrayed the land of his birth. Indeed, he said he always regarded himself as a "West Brit from the start"; among his earliest memories were listening to the BBC on the wireless. "I'm a kind of child of the Pale," he said. "I'm an effete, urban Irishman. I think I was born to succeed here [in Britain]."

He would become as well known, if not quite as well loved, as a television presenter for the BBC — a cuddly doyen of light entertainment in his well-tailored pastel suits with handkerchief in breast pocket. His mobile eyebrows would arch ironically and his turquoise eyes would twinkle beneath a generous mop of hair that in latter years was reputedly replaced by a toupee. Presenting his own primetime chat show, *Wogan*, he provided some of the most memorable and notorious television moments of the Eighties, including an interview with the sports presenter David Icke, who had metamorphosed into a religious prophet in a garish shell suit. When Icke revealed that he was the "son of the godhead", Wogan told him that the audience was "laughing at him, not with him".

The actress Anne Bancroft, whom he recalled being in a "catatonic trance", gave monosyllabic answers and thunderous looks to his increasingly desperate questions. Vanessa Redgrave once got up and left. Through it all, Wogan was assuredly composed, though he gave the impression of managing a shambles with haphazard bonhomie. The only time he was lost for words was in 1990 when an inebriated George Best said: "Terry, I like screwing," and all Wogan could say in return was "Ladies and Gentlemen, George Best" before rapidly bringing the interview to a close.

The show ran for a decade from 1982 and at its peak drew a thrice-weekly audience of eight million. It was ignominiously pulled from the schedules in 1992 to be replaced by the Spanish-set soap opera *Eldorado*. It proved a flop. In a rare moment when he allowed his guard to drop, he admitted that *Wogan*'s peremptory end was the low point of his career and that he had also been deeply hurt by the "envious and vitriolic" knocking of the programme by TV critics in the broadsheets. "There is a confusion in this country on the distinction between a talk show host and an interviewer," he said.

Talk shows were "about having a look at a famous face, a bit of stand up comedy, knockabout stuff. An interview is what Barbara Walters does. There was a lot of unfair criticism, and also there was the perception that the show had failed, which really annoyed me, because it never did." Licking his wounds, Wogan returned triumphantly to his greatest professional love, and started presenting *Wake Up to Wogan* again on Radio 2 in 1993 after a nine-year gap. He based the show on reading through the 500-plus letters and emails he received every morning and the result would be a stream of consciousness that he would "make up as I go along".

Describing himself as a "bit of a conman", he said: "Everyone thinks I'm brilliant. In fact I'm nothing of the sort. My TV and radio work is little more than an extension of myself." His listeners, whom he dubbed Togs (Terry's old geezers and gals) happily connived in running gags, double entendres and dreadful poems, while Wogan delighted in reading out the "banter" which came his way. Much of the material would echo the surrealism of the Irish writers James Joyce and Flann O'Brien whom he much admired. "I'm looking for a keen eye for the ridiculous, lateral thinking, a laugh at life," he said.

Wogan even attended Togs conventions. He described them as people who can "live without sex but not without glasses". Away from the camera and the airwaves, Wogan admitted to being a shy man who was the antipathy of the Irish notion of "craic". Curiously for someone who in his professional life was blessed with the gift of the gab, he confessed to being hopeless with small talk; he always left parties early, especially those of the BBC. He said he was "Terry no mates" in comparison with his gregarious wife, Helen, a former model. He lived quietly with her just off the M4 in Berkshire, within a manageable chauffeur-driven journey to Broadcasting House.

The height of his excitement might be a visit to one of Heston Blumenthal's gourmet restaurants in the area, but he preferred being at home with his wife, draining a large vodka Martini before enjoying her homecooked food. Tabloid hacks on the hunt for any whiff of scandal gave up on him. "There's nothing to be said for being famous," he said. "It's a pain. You can't be rude to people, it's inexcusable not to be nice."

His most sardonic comments were reserved for whoever happened to be the BBC director-general. Running jokes while he was presenting *Wake Up to Wogan*, included imaginary sightings of the DG emerging from his penthouse in a "hideous Chinese dressing gown" to pick up his milk. In 1975, he received a directive to "lay off" the then director-general, Sir Charles Curran. Wogan professed in serious moments that the BBC was the "greatest broadcasting company in the world". So much so, that he rejected a lucrative opportunity to present a chat show for Disney Corporation in 1988. Attending meetings in Beverly Hills, he recalled "feeling the stultifying weight of boredom drag me beneath the table". When "someone ordered a decaffeinated camomile tea", that was the last straw. "Helen and I were on the next plane out of there."

In any case, Wogan felt that he was fulfilling an important role as a bridge between Britain and the Irish Republic. Having joined the BBC in 1969 as the Troubles in Northern Ireland were beginning, he said it was "very difficult to come up with a cheery morning voice after a horrific bombing incident" but that many Irish people would approach him "grateful to me for being an Irish voice without apology". In 1994 a parcel bomb addressed to him was sent to Broadcasting House. It was defused and Wogan's "blarney" continued unabated.

When being interviewed about his life, Wogan was rarely serious. Asked about his health he said: "One has to keep at the very peak of physical fitness to do what one does and I don't like to have an ounce of superfluous flesh on me — it's corded muscle, the old corrugated iron stomach. I'm not going to take my clothes off to show you — you'll have to take my word for it." The endless self-mockery masked high intelligence. To charges that he shortchanged his listeners by being lightweight and middle of the road, he said: "They're only half listening anyway. It's a mistake to think that everyone is clinging to your every word."

Michael Terence Wogan was born into a lower middle-class Catholic family in Limerick in 1938. His father, Michael, had worked his way up from the relative childhood poverty — he walked barefoot to school — to manage of the Limerick branch of Leverette and Frye, grocers and wine merchants, which is still there. He had met Wogan's mother, Rose, née Byrne, while they were both working in the store's Dublin branch. Terry Wogan later admitted that his broadcasting career was a reaction against his "hard-working, diligent and meticulous father". "Anything which doesn't come freely and easily to me is something from which I will stride away, with a spring in my step and a light laugh."

Limerick was a town where, in Wogan's own words, there was "not a lot of Christianity but plenty of religion". At his schools, a primary in Limerick and Belvedere College in Dublin, where James Joyce was among the alumni, he felt the full force of an austere atmosphere. He later became an atheist. "The Jesuits were very clever men," he recalled. "My mother said it was Jesuits' fault I didn't believe [in God] because they made me think. Faith is a wonderful gift. I personally believe in people. I suppose you could call it humanist ... I think that people are born good rather than evil. I've never accepted the concept of original sin."

The often brutal Jesuit regime of school was softened by the affection that was showered on him by his maiden aunts; one of them owned a bookstore in Dublin and fostered in Wogan a lifelong love of reading. On leaving school he became a clerk with the Royal Bank of Ireland in Dublin earning £5 a week. It was the solid, respectable job his parents had wished for him. The boredom was leavened with practical jokes that included wet sponges flying across the counter when he was serving customers. "There was one old farmer who really stank," he said. "When he came in, it was heads down, and we all disappeared behind the counter until he walked out again."

After four years in the bank he spotted a newspaper advertisement for Radio Eireann, which was looking for announcers and newsreaders. He was one of 10,000 applicants. He smooth-talked his way through the interview, pretending to a facility with foreign languages he did not possess, and was offered a place on the station's training course. His favourite assignment was Hospitals' Requests, in which he had to sort through hundreds of cards and letters and construct a two-hour programme. Wogan realised that ad-libbing between records was something that came easily. It was the prototype for his BBC breakfast shows.

At the end of 1962 Radio Telefís Eireann (RTE), the Irish television service, started, and although Wogan initially failed a newsreader's audition, he was soon reading the news anyway. "Nobody knew what they were doing," he recalled, adding that "a lot of chancers" from the UK and Australia masquerading as directors and producers managed to get jobs there. The result was often a shambles but the benefit was he quickly learnt to keep his head while all about him were losing theirs and he was cured of his nerves in front of the camera. He took over a live quiz show, *Jackpot*, from another leading Irish broadcaster, Gay Byrne. Under Wogan *Jackpot* continued to top the ratings, but RTE decided without telling him to replace it with another quiz show. Wogan felt slighted and decided to look for opportunities in Britain.

He sent a sample of his work to the BBC Light Programme and although the tape was back to front, he was offered a half-hour record programme called *Midday Spin* which he presented from Dublin. In 1967 Wogan landed the job of presenting a nightly show, *Late Night Extra*, on the new Radio 1 and Radio 2 channels and soon joined the corporation full-time. He had married Helen Joyce in 1965 — she was reputed to be one of the most beautiful women in the Emerald Isle. They had met at a party in Dublin.

"She had been let down by a boyfriend which I found very extraordinary … I gave her a lift home in my Morris Minor with the broken passenger seat. We went off and had some soup and sandwiches," he said, adding with a quip: "I know how to get round girls." Once, when taking her home from a ball he was as "drunk as a skunk". As he saw her to the door at 6am, her mother came out to attend early morning Mass. "I staggered a few yards and was terribly ill before her very eyes."

Their early married life was rocked by tragedy when their first daughter, Vanessa, died at three weeks. In his anguish, any remnant of his Catholic faith was extinguished. They went on to have two sons and a daughter. He joked that because he presented the breakfast show he escaped the morning chaos of getting them ready but by late afternoon he was on hand for the easier job of picking them up at the school gates. "I had the best of both worlds. It's no wonder I'm such a family man," he quipped. Appropriately for a family of "foodies", all his children ended up running restaurants. Mark Wogan, a former chef at Carluccio's and the Groucho Club, and Alan Wogan, run the Homeslice Pizza chain. Katherine Wogan, and her husband Henry, run a chain of gastro pubs in Berkshire. They all survive him along with his wife.

From 1972 he presented *Wake Up to Wogan*, which ran on Radio 2 until 1984. Among the chief targets for his mockery was the American soap opera *Dallas* and Wogan is credited with turning the show into a cult. He would pick on the fact that the super-rich Ewing family had only one telephone and used wire coat hangers.

One of his longest stints, just short of 30 years, was on the Eurovision Song Contest on which he would drily comment on the increasingly kitsch entries and a scoring system which most years left Norway on "nil points". He said that he loved the show, "for its grandiose awfulness and manifest foolishness". He finally passed on the baton to Graham Norton in 2009, claiming that the contest had been ruined by the tactical voting from former Eastern Bloc countries. His own suitably silly excursion into song, *The Floral Dance*, resulted in an unexpected Top 30 hit in 1978.

Wogan's status as a bankable BBC commodity was cemented by his fronting of the game show *Blankety Blank* from 1979. Presenting with a trademark wand-like microphone, Wogan revelled in parodying the format as he hammed around the cheesy set, presented underwhelming prizes — including the *Blankety Blank* cheque book and pen — and wheeled out of a panel of "slightly has-been celebrities". A highlight would be the appearances of his old Radio 1 stablemate Kenny Everett who would delight in turning Wogan's microphone horseshoe-shaped.

Around the same time he began hosting the annual Children in Need appeal, an annual telethon which has raised more than £300 million for children's charities. He sat on the board of trustees and regarded it as one of the best things the BBC had done and the thing in his career that he was most proud of. When it emerged that he was too ill to present *Children in Need* in November 2015, it was the first time he had not fronted the campaign since it began in 1980. Wogan won many awards and was appointed OBE in 1997. His passions were rugby and opera, dating back to his early days as an extra for the Dublin Opera Society during which he played an Assyrian slave and a Venetian doge. In later life he was involved in the Garsington Opera.

He also enjoyed spending time with his wife at their home in the Gers region of southwest France. He liked the fact that he could shop without being recognised, although he was critical of French cooking. His considerable earnings enabled him to enjoy the good things of life, including a crimson Rolls-Royce. However, he was at his happiest at home enjoying his wife's cooking. Her duck in a bordelaise sauce and "beautifully roasted potatoes would absolutely be my last meal", he said.

He was determined to retire from his daily breakfast show before people started saying "clear off, you old fool". When he hung up his microphone in 2009, he said that his gentler presenting style had become outdated and that the "in yer face" style of his successor Chris Evans was more in tune with the times. "I don't want to be in anyone's face, I could never be Chris Evans." He added that he was a fan of Evans, but disliked the abrasive style of Anne Robinson, who he described as "a cross between Lucretia Borgia and Hitler's mother. It's quite unnecessary you know."

He continued to present a weekend show on Radio 2, describing the medium as his favourite. "Radio stimulates the brain, the imagination, it provokes reaction," he said. "Television, by providing the picture to go with the thought, stunts the imagination, makes it redundant." Wogan devoted more time to writing, completing a book of short stories, *Those Were The Days*, set in the Ireland of his youth. He had earlier published two autobiographies.

After making a career out of his lighthearted take on life, he said the only thing he had really taken seriously was his family, because "It's the only important thing in life". Reflecting on a career in which he rose to become the highest-paid broadcaster at the BBC with an estimated salary of £800,000, he said he was worth it. "If you do the maths, factoring in my 8 million listeners, I cost the BBC about 2p a fortnight. I think I'm cheap at the price."

Sir Terry Wogan, OBE, broadcaster, was born on August 3, 1938. He died of cancer on January 31, 2016, aged 77.

LORD LUCAN

Obituary

FEBRUARY 4 2016

FOR ALL THAT IT fascinated the British public for so long, only two facts were ever certain in the murder case which centred on the 7th Earl of Lucan, whose obituary we publish here today, 42 years after his disappearance. The first was that a young woman, Sandra Rivett, the family's nanny, had had her life taken from her. The second was that no one has ever established if Lucan was her killer.

All the rest — the decades and decades of words, of talk, of images — was largely conjecture. It filled in the gaps in the story, but what it used as wadding told us more about ourselves than it did about the cast in the drama. For a murder mystery is what it became, increasingly slipping the bonds of fact for the realms of fantasy. Certainly, it was easy to see the ingredients which people found so compelling: the murder in a domestic setting which George Orwell identified as giving so much pleasure to the English; a suspect so splendidly handsome that he was once screen-tested for the part of James Bond; and, above all, class. At the time, the Lucan case was dubbed the "Upstairs, Downstairs Murder", referring to the television programme that was to the 1970s what *Downton Abbey* is to today.

From the start, those involved both at its centre and its periphery were given roles that seemed more to reinforce viewers' prejudices than to take account of the complexity of real life. Now is perhaps the time to put the well-thumbed bestseller back on the shelf. Most of what has been written about the crime has done little to solve it, nor allowed the Lucan and Rivett families to move on with their lives. May it be that this unprecedented and belated obituary goes some way towards allowing them — and all of us — to do that.

Richard John Bingham was born in Marylebone, London, in 1931. He was the eldest son of the 6th Earl of Lucan, whose family had once had substantial lands in Ireland but latterly more slender means. The Lucans had something of a reputation as soldiers — the 3rd Earl was held responsible for the Charge of the Light Brigade. John's father, Pat, won the Military Cross during the Great War, but his real interest was politics. A Labour supporter, by the mid-1950s he rose to be opposition chief whip in the House of Lords.

John's mother Kaitlin was the daughter of a naval officer, and the granddaughter of a peer; her mother had been a lady-in-waiting to Queen Mary. The Binghams lived in Eaton Square for the first few years of John's life, but on the outbreak of war, he and his brother and their two sisters were evacuated to America. There they lived with a wealthy family, the Tuckers, and lacked for nothing. They found it a shock returning to the tired Britain of 1945. The windows of their home had been blown out, and in any event their parents preferred a frugal way of life to that of the Tuckers.

That vision of the easy life was to exert a powerful influence on John, as perhaps did the psychological impact of having been separated from his mother and father. He appeared to settle well at his prep school, where the future polymath Jonathan Miller was a friend — the two would sneak off to the West End to watch films. He seemed to take to Eton too. Although he was often described later as having been unintelligent, contemporaries there such as Stuart Wheeler, the spread betting pioneer, recall him as having been a bright boy. Certainly, he was clever enough to become the school's bookmaker, though unlike James Goldsmith, who left after winning big at the races, he stayed the course.

Bingham undertook his National Service in the Coldstream Guards, competing in bobsleigh events for the army. After leaving in 1955, he joined Brandt's, a small merchant bank in the City. "He thought that through eugenics he ought to be a success," a contemporary later said of him. Yet the prospect of years of deskwork was at odds with the image he now had of himself. He would escape to bet on the greyhounds at Haringay, or to play the tables at Deauville. It was there that he was spotted by the Italian film director Vittorio De Sica, who was so struck by Bingham's looks that he arranged a film test. When Bingham found himself sitting next to Shirley MacLaine on a sofa and asked to ad-lib a few lines, his mind went blank.

Yet he found the means to free himself from his job when one night at chemin-de-fer he won £26,000 (£534,000 in today's money) — ten times his annual salary. With the optimism of youth, Bingham began to believe in the aptness of his nickname, "Lucky". In truth, he had already had several large losses that he could not afford and which absorbed most of the money he received from family investments. Nonetheless, he began to dedicate himself to gambling, his need to prevail all the greater after he lost £10,000 in an attempt to win a powerboat race along the south coast; having led early on, his craft sank.

In the autumn of 1963, to the surprise of his family and his friends, Bingham announced his engagement. The wedding took place a month later, and was followed by a honeymoon on the Orient Express. His bride was Veronica Duncan, the daughter of an army officer who had died in a car accident when she and her sister Christina were very young. Their mother had remarried and later kept an inn near Basingstoke, Hampshire. Veronica was petite and attractive, but often thought to be overshadowed by the livelier Christina, who had married Bill Shand Kydd, heir to a wallpaper fortune. Nonetheless, like Bingham, she had endured shocks in her childhood, and perhaps like him felt less alone in the world with someone at her side. She later said she "was looking for a god, and he was a dream figure".

Veronica much enjoyed keeping company with the friends of the Shand Kydds, but the gambling cronies of her husband's made her less welcome. By now, Lucan — he inherited the title when his father died soon after the wedding — was spending most of his days, and often his nights, at the Clermont Club, in Berkeley Square. This was run by John Aspinall, its other habitués including the entrepreneur James Goldsmith and Aspinall's mother Lady Osborne (the present chancellor's grandmother). Restrictions on gambling had recently been overturned, and for its male patrons, at least, the club undoubtedly had a certain glamour. One might encounter the Duke of Devonshire, Lucian Freud or the Greek tycoons Onassis and Niarchos.

However, Veronica Bingham found herself spending long hours in an alcove known as "the widows' bench", and her fondness for speaking her mind did not endear her to Aspinall. In 1972, he barred her after she snapped and threw a glass of wine in another woman's face.

Drinking steadily from midday onwards, Lucan preferred to put the world to rights with his friends. However, he was not a philistine. He played the piano and taught himself Bach and Scott Joplin rags. By then, the Lucans' marriage had also soured. They had had three children by 1970 —Frances, George and Camilla — but Veronica had suffered from postnatal depression. This may have exacerbated a brittleness in her temperament attested to by her friends. In 1971, her behaviour worried Lucan sufficiently to try to get her to see a psychiatrist, and when she became distressed again he took her to a nursing home, from which she ran away.

Lucan began spending still more time at the club, returning home only to change into evening dress before dining unchangingly on lamb cutlets. He was now heavily indebted to Aspinall, although he hid the extent of the losses from his wife. Lucan also refused to trim expenses, such as trainer's fees for his racehorses. After Christmas 1972, he moved out of the family home in Lower Belgrave Street. The following year brought matters to a head. In March, the children were made wards of court on Lucan's application, obliging Lady Lucan to surrender custody of them. They were later returned to her, and at a hearing in June to decide with whom they should live, she painted a highly unflattering picture of her estranged husband.

Lucan had been certain that he would win — and employed private detectives to follow his wife — but when the judge, Sir Stanley Rees, found against him it seemed to shatter his faith in both the law and his destiny. The cost of losing the case — some £20,000, including his wife's lawyer's fees — tipped the balance of Lucan's finances. The Clermont Club had been bought out by Victor Lownes, the owner of the Playboy Club, but Lucan continued to haunt it, gambling ever more heavily in an attempt to make good his debts, which would total £65,000 (£605,000 in today's money).

With those who would listen — for he talked of little else — he discussed the outcome of the court case and how to set it right. Relations with Veronica were now toxic, and he fretted at the high turnover of nannies who were looking after the children. In August 1974, Sandra Rivett was offered the job. When she later gave a statement to the police, Lucan's daughter Frances said that "Daddy asked me when Sandra had her days off. I said her day off was Thursday."

Some time after 9 o'clock on the night of November 7, 1974, Lady Lucan left her bedroom, where she had been watching television with Frances, and went in search of the nanny. Her other two children were asleep. When she reached the ground floor, she could see that there was no light on in the basement, where Sandra had gone to make tea. She later told police that she then heard a sound behind her, before someone rushed at her and hit her about four times. When she screamed, a voice told her to shut up: "It was my husband." The pair fought, with the intruder thrusting a gloved hand into her throat and trying to throttle her. She managed to grab his testicles, at which point the attack abruptly ended. The Lucans went upstairs to wash their wounds, where they found Frances, who was told by Veronica to go to bed.

After she heard her husband turn on the taps, Lady Lucan ran down the stairs and out of the house. She burst into the Plumbers Arms across the street screaming: "Murder, murder ... I think he tried to kill me." When the police entered the house, they found the body of Sandra Rivett lying in a mail bag. She had been bludgeoned to death. In an interview in 2012, Lucan's son George recalled being woken by the police and, with his sisters, guided out of the house in darkness so that they would not see the blood on the walls. It was nine months before he was told that his nanny had been killed and that his father was the suspect.

Detectives quickly decided that Lucan had lain in wait for his wife in the darkened basement, expecting Rivett to be out, and had murdered her by mistake. Their theory appeared to be confirmed when a Ford Corsair which Lucan had borrowed was found at Newhaven. In the boot was a length of lead pipe similar to one found at the murder scene. Of the earl there was no sign. All that emerged was that late on the night of the 7th, he had gone to the home in Sussex of a friend and fellow gambler, Ian Maxwell-Scott, with whose wife Susan he had spoken. While there, he had written a letter to his brother-in-law, Bill Shand Kydd, describing a "traumatic night of unbelievable coincidence". Lucan told Susan Maxwell-Scott that while passing the house, he had seen through the blinds in the basement a man attacking his wife. He had run in to help, but the assailant had escaped.

There were no more sightings of Lord Lucan after he left the Maxwell-Scotts. News of the murder, and of his disappearance, created a sensation. Deprived of Lucan himself, the media focused chiefly on his former friends, who became known as the Clermont Set. A withering portrait of them by the journalist James Fox in *The Sunday Times*, and complaints by the police that they had been met by a wall of silence, meant that some saw the crime as indicting upper class values, rather than simply as a family tragedy. Yet at least some of Lucan's acquaintances gave the press as good as they got. When Lady Osborne was asked what had happened to the missing peer, she said: "The last I heard, he was being fed to the tigers at my son's zoo," a reference to Aspinall's private menagerie. Fleet Street duly descended on Howletts, in Kent, to be met with scorn by its owner. "My tigers are only fed the choicest cuts. Do you really think they are going to eat stringy old 'Lucky'?"

In his letter to Shand Kydd, Lucan asked him to arrange for the children to live with him and Christina. That eventually happened, as relations between them and their mother became increasingly strained. Lady Frances later trained as a solicitor, while Lady Camilla is a QC. George, who now inherits as 8th Earl of Lucan, has had a career in finance and has recently married. In June 1975, a full inquest was conducted into Sandra Rivett's death. The jury held that she had been murdered by Lord Lucan. It was the last time that a coroner's court exercised the power to commit a murderer to trial, with Lucan becoming the first member of the Lords to be so named in two centuries.

Ignoring the prospect of libel, the national press unanimously reported Lucan as Rivett's killer — and continued to do so for the next 40 years. As it turned out, the inquest settled nothing. Journalists conjectured at once that he had killed himself — "the code of the gentleman" — but the absence of a body allowed speculation to flourish. Soon he was being sighted all over the world. When John Stonehouse, the politician who had faked his own death, was found to be alive in Australia, it was because of his resemblance to Lucan. Rumours whirled that Lucan had been shot by the IRA, by an army comrade embarrassed by his behaviour, or by a vengeful casino owner over his debts.

He was said to have escaped to the Philippines, Hong Kong or Mexico, where Goldsmith was hiding him. When his daughter Frances visited Zimbabwe, inevitably it was to see her father (in fact it was a boyfriend). The landlady of the Grand Hotel, Cherbourg, told the press that Lucan had arrived from England looking very tired, had paid in cash and had never eaten in the restaurant. By 1976, he was in Guatemala answering to the name "Carlos" and, as the Cold War hotted up, holed up in Reykjavik. A folk musician in Goa — "Jungly Barry"— a waiter in San Francisco, a recovering alcoholic in Brisbane and an expat living in the back of his van with a goat in New Zealand were among those misidentified as Lucan. He was seen in an ex-Nazi colony in Paraguay and backpacking near Mount Etna. And he had taken a girl out to dinner in the Channel Islands, or was secreted in a Midlands nursing home.

Africa was a favourite location for sightings. One account had him posing as the manager of a clothing store in South Africa. A tourist reported that he had spotted Lucan in Mozambique drinking beer and "weeping over his prawns" that he could not return home. A personal assistant to Aspinall claimed that she had arranged tickets for Lucan's children to travel to Kenya and Gabon, so "their father would observe them ... just to see how they were growing up". Only the nobility's works of reference retained a certain decorum. *Burke's Peerage* styled him as "The Earl of Lucan, wheresoever," while *Who's Who* informed readers that "The Earl has been missing since Nov 1974".

A small industry grew around the films, television programmes and books that purported to examine the case. Even Muriel Spark joined in the fun, with *Aiding and Abetting* (2000). Each offered its solution to this national game of Cluedo, as did those who had actually known Lucan. Speaking in 1994, Aspinall remained convinced that Lucan was "lying 250ft under the Channel". He believed that Lucan "tied a stone around his body and scuttled the powerboat he kept at Newhaven, and down he went". In the same year, Lady Lucan, by then suffering from osteoarthritis and rarely seen outside of her mews house, said: "I am sure he is dead. My husband was — is — a nobleman and he would behave in a noble way." She is still alive.

Earlier this week, a former acquaintance of Lucan's, Philippe Marcq, revealed that he had been told by Lucan's mentor as a gambler, Stephen Raphael, that the earl had shot himself at Howletts and been fed to a tiger. This was to ensure that, by avoiding imprisonment, his trust funds would go to his children rather than being controlled by his wife. In time, the quest to find Lucan outran even his hunters. One Scotland Yard detective devoted his retirement to tracking down the peer, but died in 1994. His disappearance was a mystery which delighted but baffled even those who created them. At the end of her life, the crime novelist Agatha Christie — who had herself once "vanished" without explanation for a fortnight — was said to have asked: "I do wonder what has happened to Lord Lucan?"

Lord Lucan, murder suspect, was born on December 18, 1934. He was officially declared dead on February 3, 2016.

WHY I'M FOOTBALL CRAZY

Henry Winter

FEBRUARY 13 2016

I'VE BEEN SHOT AT, spat at and asked for selfies, sent death threats and a marriage proposal. I've covered seven World Cups, too many fans' riots and far too many failed penalty shoot-outs. I've had run-ins with the Moscow mafia and Sao Paulo police. Thirty years this month as a football journalist has allowed me to see the world and all extremes of human behaviour.

A week after joining *The Times* in November, I finished writing up an interview with Crystal Palace's charismatic manager Alan Pardew, sitting at one of the tables in the breakout areas between departments and looked around. I saw all the pictures on the wall of distinguished figures who have written for *The Times* down the years, particularly Geoffrey Green. It was quite humbling. I've wanted to work here since I was a teenager at Westminster School, reading Green's musings. He kept a Christmas tree in his drawing room all year round because "when you're a football correspondent, every day is Christmas Day". He brought matches in far-off places to life. Players were characters; games were dramas. Green once accepted an award by holding a cassette recorder to the microphone, pressing "play" and allowing the audience to enjoy *What a Wonderful World* by Louis Armstrong.

Football reporting is a wonderful world, a paid privilege, even with such occasional discomforts as an Uzi discharged over my head outside the Ali Sami Yen "Welcome to Hell" home of Galatasaray in Istanbul, or receiving a stream of phlegm outside Wembley for an ill-received verdict on England, or opening menacing missives after criticising actions during one particularly fractious collision between Celtic and Rangers. There's always the intermittent annoyance of a heavy-coated Russian gangster refusing to budge from my press seat in Moscow or an angry Brazilian copper waving his gun in the air when I try to take a short-cut into a stadium.

Occupational hazards aside, football writers are lucky. I report on 120-130 games a year, each one an unscripted play, occasionally a pantomime. I'm always on deadline, praying the wi-fi doesn't disappear or, in days gone by, the copy-takers typing up the telephoned report know their football. I still shudder at the memory of an ad-libbed intro to a match at AC Milan that had "Manchester United running out to the theme tune from Mister Softball". I spent a good few hours replying to confused readers, explaining that the mystery film was *Mission Impossible*, misheard over a crackling line from the San Siro. It still doesn't rival a colleague's report on a Wales international of the Eighties that contained the line, "Russian Jews are the best strikers in Europe." That would be Rush and Hughes.

Nothing beats covering an England international in a World Cup, the brief hope, the tension, the sense of pending doom and astonishing loyalty of the supporters. When *The Telegraph* placed me on gardening leave after I told them I was moving to *The Times*, I travelled as a fan to San Marino, Lithuania and Spain, as well as three trips to Wembley, maintaining a 22-year run of not missing an England game. I left a maternity suite in a Norfolk hospital early to make kick-off for England-Mexico at Wembley in 1997. Teddy Sheringham and Robbie Fowler scored.

It's a variety act of a job, throwing a writer on to *Football Focus* and the *Today* programme, into reporting in 140 characters on Twitter, and spending hours helping footballing legends such as Steven Gerrard, John Barnes and Kenny Dalglish gather their thoughts for their autobiographies. It's not a serious profession. It's a passion. I interviewed the Bolton Wanderers manager, Neil Lennon, last week and he said, "There are nights when I think, 'God, what would I do without football? What would I do without that feeling?'"

It's an adrenaline rush shared by tens of millions in the country. I roll my eyes at football being pigeonholed as the "working class" game. It's the nation's game, an obsession pervading all strata of society, a sport with its roots in the southern public schools such as Eton, as well as in the northern mill towns like Blackburn and Bolton.

People are too fixated with class in this country, too busy worrying about backgrounds when foregrounds are all that really matter. We did ask Prince William, a decent footballer at Eton and now president of the FA, to turn out for the England Press team once when we were a man short. He could probably get a game with his beloved Aston Villa at the moment, given their travails. I gave a talk at Eton last year and it was rammed with football fans, some talented football bloggers including a Stoke City diehard whose life revolved around events at the Britannia Stadium. Football is such a simple, beautiful, intoxicating sport that it transcends all barriers, all borders.

My friends at Westminster School in the Seventies were constantly disappearing to catch matches at Leeds, Millwall, Chelsea or Arsenal, explaining to housemasters that another dear aunt had sadly suddenly passed away from sherry poisoning or some such malady, and the funeral happened by chance to be in the vicinity of Elland Road, the Den, Stamford Bridge or Highbury. As a kid, I stood occasionally in the Shed at Chelsea, on the North Bank at Arsenal or in the Chicken Run at Upton Park, where I heard one of the best succession of chants in tribute to a player: "Trevor Brooking's supersonic ... he's bionic ... he's gin and tonic." It made a slight change from the Purcell and Palestrina that I'd sung in the school choir in Westminster Abbey that morning. I once had to perform in a celebration of the lives of Second World War field marshals in St Paul's Cathedral. As an Abbey boy, I was never a fan of St Paul's (worse acoustics) and I was in a hurry to get to a game at Wolves.

I still remember the dank, dark smell of a police dog's breath as it snapped away at us away fans emerging from a subway near Molineux, Wolves' stadium, back in the Eighties, when fans were treated like animals. Sniffer dogs are regularly encountered going into grounds now. Whenever my bag's checked over by the beautiful spaniel outside Stamford Bridge, I feel a pang of guilt at almost killing one of its brethren at Heathrow after the 2004 European Championships. I'd returned with the England

Press kit which I'd been too tight to have washed in Portugal and it absolutely reeked; the poor sniffer dog in arrivals almost needed peeling off the ceiling.

I'd always wanted a job with football at its heart, a job where every day was different. I grew up first in Regent's Park, near London Zoo, in a building that the press called "the upside-down house". My father, John, an architect, largely built the place himself, although the milkman helped piece together the spiral staircase. Dad put the bedrooms on the ground floor and kitchen on the top as it afforded magnificent views over the zoo. If you peered out to the right, you could spot the giraffes. Mum was a designer, who worked with Terence Conran, and the house was filled with amazing furniture, such as original Mies van der Rohe Barcelona chairs from Dad's time studying at Yale and working in California. I'd come home from school and think that burglars had raided us, only to discover the furniture was being used for films at Pinewood. One sofa was graced by Liz Taylor and Richard Burton in *The VIPs*. (I made sure I snaffled it when my parents passed away recently.)

After Regent's Park, Dad designed a house out of glass and steel overlooking Highgate Cemetery in north London. I was Karl Marx's nearest neighbour, but slept through the 1970 attempt by vandals to blow off the bust adorning his tomb. They tried to shove explosives made from fireworks and weedkiller up his marble nostril but couldn't get enough in. Highgate was lively. Russian spies lived nearby; goths traipsed through our garden on Hallowe'en to reach the cemetery, and I often awoke to models sashaying across the top floor for fashion shoots. For me it was home; for many others it was a site of architectural pilgrimage, and it received a rare (for a modern building) grade II* listing by English Heritage. Fortunately, they didn't notice the window I took out with a javelin. From the inside.

The main benefit of all that lovely glass was that it looked out on to a strip of grass in Waterlow Park, so I could spot when kids from the estate gathered for games on a Sunday. We formed a team, playing ferocious matches against local sides, including a monks' XI with a penchant for brutal tackling far removed from any concept of divine intervention.

My parents had no interest in football. They came once to watch me play at Westminster's Vincent Square ground and spent 45 minutes admiring the architecture, before decamping at half-time for the nearby

Tate Gallery. Dad was on the Royal Fine Arts Commission and they occasionally got to advise on historic football stadia, especially those with façades designed by Archibald Leitch. It was the only time we spoke about football.

But Dad was a great believer in expanding minds. I was shipped out, briefly, to school in Paris. Embarrassingly, my grasp of the language is still shaky. During the 1998 World Cup, I was invited on French national radio to talk live about what should be done with the England fans rioting in Marseilles. I couldn't remember the word for prison, so I just said the hooligans need throwing in the "Bastille". The interview ended abruptly. French friends kindly mention on a fairly regular basis that their word for "prison" is, in fact, "prison".

My German is not much better, despite spending a term at a school in Munich which allowed me to watch Bayern. My daughter, Electra, attended a school near Toulouse. My son, Toby, is currently enrolled in a Shaolin Temple in China learning mandarin, meditation and martial arts. As you do.

Dad gave me only one piece of advice: choose a career you're fanatical about. His own passion for architecture led to us being thrown out of East Berlin in the Seventies; he wanted to photograph a Bauhaus building and didn't notice the Red Army barracks next door. Angry Soviet soldiers ripped the film from his camera and drove us out through Checkpoint Charlie. Dad was still so focused on the architecture that he crashed into the army jeep in front. Whenever I cover a game in Berlin, I always make a point of walking through Checkpoint Charlie, now a tourist sight, and remember what occurred.

The constant opportunity to travel in this job feeds a fascination with history. I've visited Auschwitz-Birkenau six times; whenever England are based nearby, playing Poland, I find a taxi or bus and go. It's important to step out of the bubble, pay respects and see the horrors of history. It's also vital that players visit such places, responding to requests from the Holocaust Educational Trust, spreading the story among a new generation. In 2012, I went with the England players to Auschwitz-Birkenau, and Wayne Rooney's thoughtful questions to the guide reminded me of the unexpected hinterland of footballers. Rooney asked the guide about the mindset of the SS doctor Heinz Thilo, who wrecked family after family during the day and then went off to play with his children in his home. Rooney spoke with a knowledge of the subject. He explained later that he watched the box set of the Laurence Olivier-narrated *World at War* on Manchester United trips.

Footballers are opening their eyes to the outside world more. It's all a long way from the West Brom player on a tour of China in the Seventies rejecting the chance to see a local landmark with the words, "When you've seen one wall, you've seen them all." The more enlightened players of the modern era, such as Rio Ferdinand and Eni Aluko, should be invited not only on to the boardrooms of clubs and governing bodies but also asked to assist government. They have an insight into real life that many civil servants lack.

Learning more about footballers' characters is a frequent motivation, balancing the frequently negative public image. Defender John Stones is hugely popular at Everton for his footballing gifts, and also for his commitment to community initiatives. At Manchester City, Joe Hart is involved with the Homeless FA. Mesut Özil, Arsenal's Germany wizard, has a foundation funding assorted campaigns helping children. Swansea City's Spanish defender, Àngel Rangel, distributes food to the homeless. Of course they should do such conscientious work, people cry, particularly being wealthy individuals, but not every high-profile member of society does.

Having covered the sport for 30 years, I get a few calls from radio and TV to go on and talk about the game. I also get requests (always rejected) to do a joint programme on me and my brother Tim, otherwise known as Shaykh Abdal Hakim Murad, the Islamic scholar at Cambridge (University not United). He's a preacher at Regent's Park Mosque and contributor to Thought for the Day on the *Today* show. My secret hope is that the *Today* programme mixes us up when we're stacking in the system waiting to go on as guests, and Tim has to opine about England's latest failure with penalties while I wing it on Sufism.

Our sister Martha, a painter, is far more talented than the two of us, but Tim is scarily bright. He got a double first from Pembroke College, Cambridge, whereas I was turned down by Cambridge and sloped off to Edinburgh, where I enjoyed a magical four years, writing for the student paper, playing for the university and scraping a 2:2. I'm often asked on Twitter to get Tim on social media. He has more religious followers than I have Twitter followers. One guy, an Arsenal fan, keeps savaging me on Twitter for berating the club's manager, Arsène Wenger, but then pleads with me to introduce him to Tim.

When Tim was voted among the most influential Muslims in the world in 2010, even ahead of Mahmoud Ahmadinejad and Hosni Mubarak, he gave a compelling interview to one newspaper, talking about the Koran, the importance of family and mentioning his thick younger brother. Tim remarked that he'd never expected when I was growing up, spending my childhood watching football, playing football and talking balls, that I would ever make anything of my life, "but look at him now, living in a six-bedroom house with a Bond girl". (She's an actress, who filmed an early version of a Bond opening credits sequence.) Tim's comment prompted a lively response on Twitter. "Next time you speak to the press," I urged him later, "at least say I'm living in a one-bedroom house with six Bond girls."

Twitter's the Wild West. My timeline goes into meltdown when mentioning Luis Suárez, John Terry or José Mourinho, nuanced individuals who cannot be captured in 140 characters. But social media has revolutionised football journalism. Newspapers were once the first draft of history; now Twitter is. If a story breaks, such as Terry telling reporters he's leaving Chelsea or Manuel Pellegrini ending a press conference by remarking he's departing from Manchester City, the story is unleashed within seconds on Twitter. When *The Guardian*'s Jamie Jackson tweeted a picture of City's statement confirming Pep Guardiola's arrival, he got 1,200 retweets.

Social media can be dangerous. I lost a bet with Newcastle United fans about the future of Pardew, their manager at the time, and ended up having to swim the Tyne. I had constant advice from "experts" on Twitter about choosing the colour of my wetsuit carefully because it was the seal-mating season. "Watch out for brown fish," was another piece of laughing Geordie guidance. Fortunately, I didn't encounter any. I've got another bet still live with England supporters that if Mourinho ever becomes England manager I will swim the Thames dressed as Mrs Doubtfire. It beats being shot at and spat at.

SURVIVING KAMIKAZE FLIES
ON AND ON AND ON

Richard Lloyd Parry

February 16 2016

JUN TAKAHASHI IS a pilot but he does not pay excessive attention to his health. He enjoys a gin and tonic before meals and the occasional night of whisky drinking with his friends. He goes to bed late, rises late, and still smokes the occasional cigarette.

Every year his medical check-up confirms his steady heart and perfect vision, and every week he goes to the Fujikawa airfield and takes his Cessna up above the villages on the slopes of Mount Fuji. One fact alone makes all of this remarkable: Mr Takahashi is 93 years old.

Born in 1922, he learnt to fly in the Imperial Navy and was trained as a kamikaze pilot towards the end of the war. Seventy years later, he is listed by *Guinness World Records* as the world's oldest active commercial pilot. In Japan, such a man is far from unique.

As his countrymen live ever longer, and the number of old people increases to unprecedented levels, a new class is emerging: the supergeriatrics, for whom advanced age is no obstacle to professional achievement. In aviation, entertainment, art, and even athletics, a small number of extremely old Japanese are not only surviving, but excelling.

"Most people work for companies, and retire at the age of 60 or 65, but to me, people of that age are still little chickens," Mr Takahashi said. "I don't dwell on the past. I concentrate on what makes me cheerful. Why not do what you love doing for as long as you like?" Two of the country's most distinguished women painters, Yayoi Kusama, 86, and Toko Shinoda, 102, continue to work. The oldest man ever to climb Mount Everest is Yuichiro Miura, who was 80 at the time.

Now 83, he is chasing in the footsteps of his late father, Keizo, who skied down Mont Blanc at the age of 99. In September, Hidekichi Miyazaki, also known as the "Golden Bolt", ran 100m in 42.22 seconds, setting a record in the over-105 class. Yonemaru Katsura, 90, still works as a traditional storyteller, Tatsuro Yamazaki, 95, is a barman and Kinichi Honma, 89, is a lifeguard leader.

Each of them is unique — but in Japan, simply living to 90, 100, and beyond is no longer a marvel. In 1950, there were 97 centenarians in the

*ve: Deep coal
ing came to an
in Britain with the
ure in December
of the Kellingley
iery in Yorkshire.*

*James Glossop recorded
its last days for* The
Times *and took this
portrait of the miner
Jack Robertson after
one of his last shifts*

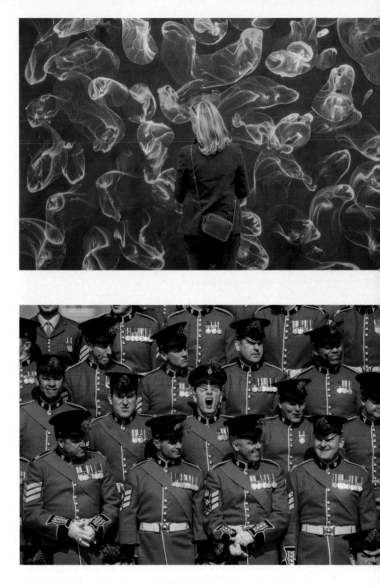

Top: *The hair of a visitor to the Frieze art fair in London echoes an untitled work by Jiri Dokoupil, as captured by Richard Pohle*

Above: *Pohle also caught the variety of emotions among the 1st Battalion Irish Guards at a St Patrick's Day parade in March*

*above: The Exeter
Chiefs and England
rugby player Jack
Nowell photographed
by Marc Aspland in
February exclusively for*
the Times *feature My
Sporting Body. Nowell
told the paper that
since the age of 16 he
had spent more than 70
hours in tattoo parlours*

How our new nuclear submarines could look

Trident II D5 ballistic missile specification

Speed **13,400mph (Mach 17.4)**
Range **7,500 miles**
Weight **58.5 tonnes**
Length **13m**
Diameter **2m**

● A missile fired from the English Channel could reach North Korea

North Korea

● A missile can carry up to 12 warheads. Each warhead has the destructive power of at least eight times the atomic bomb (15 kilotons) that was dropped on Hiroshima

5 Nose faring and second stage jettisoned and third stage fires

4 First stage jettisoned and second-stage rocket fires

3 Missile reaches space and calculates its position from the stars

2 Stage-one rocket ignites and aerospike extends

1 Expanding gas in tube forces missile out

Aerosp
Punch
throug
reduci
extend

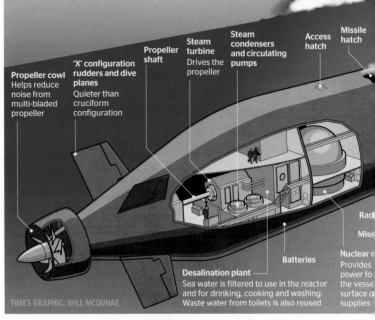

Propeller cowl
Helps reduce noise from multi-bladed propeller

'X' configuration rudders and dive planes
Quieter than cruciform configuration

Propeller shaft

Steam turbine
Drives the propeller

Steam condensers and circulating pumps

Access hatch

Missile hatch

Rad

Miss

Nuclear
Provides
power fo
the vesse
surface o
supplies

Batteries

Desalination plant
Sea water is filtered to use in the reactor and for drinking, cooking and washing. Waste water from toilets is also reused

TIMES GRAPHIC: WILL MCQUHAE

MPs voted in May on a blueprint for the future of Britain's nuclear deterrent. At its

6 Third stage booster ejected when target area reached

7 Thrusters manoeuvre the forward section so each warhead can be independently released in right place to freefall to target, where they detonate

...eads (up to 12)

...-three booster

...l thrusters

...piece
...faring

...-two
...et booster
...ion

...-one
...et booster
...solid fuel
...ellent

...eable
...le to steer

Warhead Mark 4

Neutron generator

Secondary reaction chamber

Primary fission trigger

Re-entry body

Fuse Arming, fusing and firing system

Periscopes, antennae and snorkel

Command and navigation

Forward hydroplane

Computers

Sonar dome

Officers' quarters

Torpedo tubes

Torpedoes

Food storage

...ear
...les

...in

Mess

Galley

...'s bunks
...ockers (crew
...out 120)

...red in a
...er-like
...rial that
...rbs signals
...enemy sonar

Effect of a 100 kiloton bomb on London

Fireball 100% destruction

○ **Air blast at 20psi** Up to 100% fatality rate. Heavy concrete buildings severely damaged

○ **Radiation radius** Up to 90% fatality rate

○ **Air blast 5psi** Most residential buildings collapse. Widespread fatalities and injuries

○ **Thermal radiation radius** 100% third-degree burns

Islington • LONDON • One mile

City • Tower Hamlets

Southwark • Greenwich

Atomic bomb timeline

1945
The US drops atomic bomb on Hiroshima and Nagasaki in world's only nuclear attack

1946
US Congress passes McMahon Act prohibiting nuclear co-operation with any country, including UK

1947
Clement Attlee authorises a British nuclear weapons programme

1952
First British atomic bomb, carried by the Vickers Valiant aircraft, tested in Montebello islands, Australia

1956
Blue Danube free-fall bomb first tested in Maralinga, Australia

1957
Harold Macmillan and President Eisenhower revive nuclear co-operation

1963
United States agrees to provide UK with Polaris ballistic missiles

1965
UK decides to build four Polaris submarines instead of five for cost reasons

1968
Nuclear-armed Polaris submarine, HMS Resolution, conducts first deterrent patrol

1982
Britain buys into Trident missile system from the US

1993
Nuclear-armed Trident submarine HMS Vanguard enters service

2007
MPs vote by 409 to 161 in favour of proposals to replace the Trident fleet, no decision on boat number

2016
MPs vote to replace Vanguard-class fleet

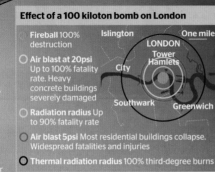

heart is a fleet of nuclear submarines, seen here in a Times *graphic artist's impression*

Top: *The heartbreaking image of Alan Kurdi on a Turkish beach in September 2015 gave* the Times *political cartoonist Peter Brookes inspiration for a powerful political point*

Above: *A more light-hearted influence came from the pages of Lewis Carroll*

Top: Brookes elegantly tied together the Hatton Garden heist and the Labour Party's troubles in January. **Above:** An exciting political year provided no end of subject matter, including an early appearance in July for the new prime minister's leopard-print shoes

Above: Manifest joy in
the faces of the British
hockey team, captured
by Marc Aspland in

Rio de Janeiro, sums up
the response to Great
Britain's performance in
the 2016 Olympic Games

*Morten Morland, named Cartoonist of the Year in the 2016 Press Awards, found a rich seam of material in the EU referendum and its aftermath. **Top:** In June he imagined the reaction of the victorious Brexiteers and, **below**, the lack of team spirit among their rivals*

Top: *The decision by Boris Johnson to back Brexit and turn against his former schoolmate David Cameron suggested a Shakespearean scenario.* **Above:** *Nigel Farage makes an appearance as the wheels seemed to be coming off the Brexit campaign*

Top: The Times photographer Jack Hill was in Lille when the police used pepper spray to suppress violence between England and Wales fans in June. **Above:** Hill also caught a grieving Bowie fan's tattoo matching a memorial to her idol in his birthplace of Brixton

Above: *Deerstalkers in Perthshire, taken by James Glossop in October 2015. "This was towards the end of a long day out," Glossop said. "The light had started to break through the clouds and the scenery was spectacular as we came off the hill"*

Top: *Dancers rehearse* Emergence *at the Edinburgh Festival in August, captured by James Glossop.* **Above:** *Glossop arrived armed* with a pair of fish to photograph David Coburn, the leader of Ukip in Scotland. To his surprise, Coburn agreed to use them as a prop

*Left: Jack Hill photographed Syrian refugees being housed in a warehouse in Cyprus in October 2015. **Above:** Richard Pohle said, after picturing the Queen with the Royal Artillery: "What struck me was how she is seemingly dwarfed by the awesome power of the cannon"*

Above: The transit of Mercury across the Sun captured by Jack Hill in Greenwich with the help of the Flamsteed Astronomy Society

country. Last year, there were 61,568 of them, 54,000 of them women. In 2015, 30,000 Japanese received a silver saké chalice, the equivalent of a telegram from the Queen. Six years ago, the size of the gifts was reduced, because the cost of sending out all that silver was simply too high. The reason for such longevity is not completely clear, but the traditional Japanese diet — rich in fish and lightly cooked vegetables, low in fat, and served in modest portions — has much to do with it.

Longevity is greater in the countryside, where the pace of life is less stressful — but Mr Takahashi lives in Tokyo, and it is only three years since he gave up a 70-year habit of smoking a packet of cigarettes a day. "I can't believe I'm 93," he said. "I don't feel as if I've got older since the age of 70. It's important to stop eating when you are 80 per cent full. I haven't felt completely full for decades. And if you want to live a long time, you need to be stylish." He himself was clad in a pink cardigan and well-cut beige trousers. "And," he added, "have a bit of fun with the young ladies."

Japan's ageing society is seen by many as a disaster. Record numbers of people suffer from dementia, old people are accused of causing accidents on the roads and committing crimes — last year, police registered more geriatric than juvenile offenders. Most importantly, the cost of looking after the elderly is burdening the country's social security system in unsustainable ways.

For Mr Takahashi, who alone among his comrades flew back from the Battle of Okinawa, such anxieties are hard to take seriously. "I dreamt of being a pilot as a child," he said. "And I can still be a pilot now. No one has ever told me I should stop, even my wife. The most she ever says is: 'It's cold on that airfield, and you're getting on a bit. Wrap up well'."

LIBERALS ARE COLLUDING IN CRUELTY AND ABUSE

Alice Thomson

FEBRUARY 24 2016

IT STARTS WITH French women abandoning their miniskirts, then quitting their classrooms and offices to learn to cook. Soon older men are being match-made with submissive young girls. The bestseller *Submission*, set in France in 2022, is chilling because author Michel Houellebecq makes the gradual Islamification of the French republic sound plausible and almost desirable. The charismatic new president, Ben-Abbes, leader of the Muslim Brotherhood, is heading an exotic new coalition. The hero, a middle-aged professor, soon gets used to the idea of being provided with a nubile wife and lucrative job paid for by the Saudis in return for converting. He justifies this because it will give him a stable family life after years of western debauchery.

Surely this could never happen? Certainly not in Britain or America. And yet there are signs that the liberal West is becoming more tolerant of regressive and occasionally repugnant practices in other cultures. Only this week a group of doctors in America said that "mild" female genital mutilation should be accepted as an important cultural rite. In the *Journal of Medical Ethics*, they suggested re-terming this butchery "female genital alteration". Mild FGM, they say, is no different from other cosmetic surgery and they call opponents of the practice "culturally insensitive and supremacist". They are trying to embarrass westerners who speak out against FGM. But we should.

Female genital mutilation is barbaric — even the "lite" version that doesn't remove the whole clitoris. It is designed to prevent women enjoying sex. As one grandmother explained: "If I don't do these things, the girl will grow up horny. She'll be like American girls."

FGM is as antiquated as a chastity belt or the ducking stool discarded in the Middle Ages. Yet where once most in Britain would speak out against obviously outdated and cruel practices such as foot binding and forced marriage, increasingly the West is nervous of condemning antiquated customs we dislike, in case it causes offence.

When I interviewed the evolutionary biologist Richard Dawkins recently, he said: "It is shocking that western feminists are so pusillanimous about condemning misogyny in Islam. Islam is rife with sexism. This ultra-empathising with a culture — what about the poor girls? I would worry if cultural values which are not just alien to our historical ones but are actually unpleasant were to enter our country. If there was a takeover that would be a major tragedy."

He's wrong on one point. This isn't just a feminist issue. It's about how highly both men and women in the West regard equality and freedom above submission. In the 19th century General Sir Charles Napier, commander-in-chief in India, told Hindu priests complaining about the banning of sati: "This burning of widows is your custom; prepare the funeral pile. But my nation also has a custom. When men burn women alive we hang them, and confiscate all their property." We may think he was sounding glib or imperialist, but he had a point.

In many ways he was being more humane than the British High Court judge Mrs Justice Pauffley, who last year said that police and social workers should make allowances when immigrants physically abuse family members. She suggested that within "many communities newly arrived" in the UK, children were slapped in a way that "at first excites the interest of child protection professionals" but warned that their concerns failed to take into account "what is almost certainly a different cultural context". So British-born boys and girls, she implied, mustn't be hit, while foreign-born children can.

But does that also mean that honour killings among newly arrived brides should be ignored? Or that the 1,400 children in Rotherham subjected to serial abuse by offenders of mainly Pakistani heritage should understand this was just a cultural misunderstanding by men who see 13-year-old brides as normal? An inquiry found that frontline staff were afraid of raising "ethnic issues ... for fear of being thought racist".

The West should be more bold. David Cameron was derided when he suggested targeting language classes at the 190,000 British Muslim women who speak little English. Sir Michael Wilshaw, the chief inspector of schools, drew criticism for saying that pupils and teachers should not wear the full veil.

But being unable to speak English means many women are totally dependent on their men. Forcing women into marriage, refusing to give them the choice to work, expecting them to wear a niqab or burka is turning them into lesser beings. A headscarf or hijab is pretty but covering your entire face is a symbol of self-erasure. It is not acceptable to say that these women condone this — it is hard to fight against your own community. The suicide rate of British Asian women is twice that of white women.

However determined we are to be tolerant, we need to speak up for those who are denied the right to be treated equally. This is about the dignity of both sexes. It took a long time for the West to evolve but we should be proud that children are no longer beaten and women can be as well educated as men, dress how they want and choose their partners.

The West is not culturally perfect. Women are still often denied equal pay and suffer domestic violence. But there is a sense that this is wrong. If this country is to keep improving rather than regress to a darker age, everyone needs to stand up for Britain's liberal heritage.

'SO, JACOB REES-MOGG, WHAT IS TWERKING? WHO IS KANYE WEST? DO YOU TAKE OUT THE RUBBISH?'

Interview by Deborah Ross

FEBRUARY 27 2016

THERE SEEMS TO be a lot of love going around at present for Jacob Rees-Mogg, the Conservative MP for North East Somerset, the old Etonian who memorably took his nanny canvassing during his failed bid to win the Labour stronghold that was Central Fife, and who fails my impromptu popular culture quiz time after time. What is twerking? "I know this! Is it working while having a cup of tea?" Who is Kanye West? "I don't even know if that is a man or a woman." His own musical tastes are uniquely his own, shall we say. "I like classical music and jolly tunes. I enjoy Mozart, Verdi, Beethoven, and also *A Frog He Would A-Wooing Go.*"

I thought I might be able to resist Jacob Rees-Mogg, 46, given we have nothing in common, and I do not, as he does, own a miniature of Charles I made with the monarch's hair — "I love things like that. I also have a little memorial brooch embroidered with William Pitt's hair." But here I am, falling at the very first hurdle. Damn.

He is unashamedly himself, which we seem to like. He is a toff who doesn't pretend to be anything other than a toff, which we also seem to like. And everyone is mad for him. Everyone is mad for you, I tell him. "Oh, no, relly," he says. I persist. You may even be a heart-throb. "I am not!" he protests. What about when Victoria Coren Mitchell halted *Have I Got News for You* to tell you how attractive she found you? "I was lost for words. I did not know what to say," he says, blushing. And what about Mumsnet, which subsequently went into a swoon? He was not aware, he insists. "It may not surprise you to know that I do not look at Mumsnet vairy often. But, relly, I'm vairy, vairy flattered."

He also has an unlikely fan in the form of the SNP's Mhairi Black, who has said, "I could sit and listen to him all day. I disagree with him 99.9 per cent of the time ... but I love listening to him. His knowledge is incredible, and he's just so polite." I totally get where Black is coming from. Indeed, his manners are so blissfully exquisite that I very nearly do listen to him all day. We meet at the House of Commons at 5.50pm. I thought we'd be an hour, max, as that is generally the way, but I'm still there at 6.30pm, at 7.30pm and at 8pm. I'm boring him witless, I'm sure, and I'm thinking: is this going to go on for ever? Should I have bought my nightie? And then it suddenly hits: he is too well-mannered to tell me to clear off.

Ultimately, I feel compelled to inform him: "You can, you know, go if you like, at some point." He then confesses he is meeting his younger sister, Annunziata, at Claridge's for dinner — "I shall probably have the steak and I shall probably have the chocolate soufflé" — and that he relly had better shoot. He has yet to dine at Nando's, but he has heard of it: "It's a particularly nasty kind of chicken, isn't it?" Jacob Rees-Mogg is known by many names and phrases: "The Mogg"; "the Bertie Wooster throwback"; "a mini-Boris"; "the honourable member for the early 20th century". (He was born in 1969, but it could just as well have been 1908.)

He has provided endless amusement, intentionally and otherwise. Having been mercilessly teased for taking his nanny canvassing, he responded with, "If I had a valet, you would think it was perfectly normal." He is fiercely right-wing — Europhobic; against same-sex marriages; for the bedroom tax — but his entertainment value means those who would not normally overlook such beliefs, do so.

He employs baroque turns of phrase, accusing his party of "procedural prestidigitation" and "legislative legerdemain", and even "floccinaucinihilipilification", as in, "the estimation of something as valueless". (This is wondrously impressive, of course, but do you know what "WTF" stands for, Jacob? "Is it like WG Grace? Is it the initials of a cricketer?")

It's been reported that he owns no casual clothes and sleeps in double-breasted pyjamas, but he would like to put the record straight about that. "I do not sleep in double-breasted pyjamas, although I would, if I knew where to get them from." I'd read that, at Eton, he paid other boys to clean his shoes and hold an umbrella over him when cross-country running. True? "Yes to the first, but no to the second, although I wish I'd thought of it."

Having been given shares at a young age he was terrorising the City at 11, turning up at shareholders' meetings and castigating the chairmen of GEC (for the company's "pathetic dividend") and of Lonrho (for buying *The Observer*). At this moment, he is most preoccupied with what WTF does mean. I am not as brave as him — I do think he is rather brave — and wimp out. It's like OMG, but a bit different — "OMG" as in "Oh my God." And now that's that, I conclude.

We meet first in the Central Lobby. He is tall and thin and I am not immediately struck by his sex appeal, if I'm honest. He reminds me, in fact, of a beanpole Postman Pat, which is a description he is prepared to go with, if not fully embrace. "I don't own a black and white cat, but will take it as a compliment," he says. He is wearing a Savile Row suit, as per. He once said he had never owned trainers, but has to go back on this now "as I've got a pair of Green Flash, actually. I played cricket last summer. I love cricket. I hadn't played for 20 years, but I got prevailed upon to play and I discovered I had a vairy ancient pair of Green Flash, which I think I must have had at school, but they are still perfectly functional."

I wonder what I would find him wearing if I were to pop in on him unannounced on a Sunday morning. "A jacket and tie," he says. "It may be a suit jacket or it may be a tweed jacket, depending on what I am doing that day." We walk across the Lobby and, as we're doing so, I present him with my gift. Having heard he is fond of Creme Eggs, I have bought him a box of five — £2; Sainsbury's — and he reacts with such stupendous gratitude and enthusiasm, it's as if I'd bought him a Porsche.

"Oh, this is so kind of you, so vairy kind. Thank you, thank you, thank you." It's not a Porsche, Jacob. Calm yourself. "I don't want a Porsche. I want Creme Eggs!" He is still thanking me as we enter the Pugin Room, where we are due to have tea. "I am so pleased with them. I did buy a couple of them in a petrol station last weekend, but I don't have any in the office, so they're extremely welcome. Thank you, thank you, so vairy kind." He adds that when Kraft bought Cadbury it closed down the factory, which was in his constituency, so that was not good. "I thought it reflected very badly on Kraft," he says. Perhaps I should take the eggs back, I say, while making a move to reclaim them. "Definitely not," he says, snatching them back. "I do not believe in pointless protests."

His father, William Rees-Mogg, was editor of *The Times* (1967-81), a governor of the BBC and chairman of the Arts Council. One of the great and the good, in other words, and Jacob adored him. "He was wonderful. He was vairy gentle, vairy kindly, interested in everything, and took everyone seriously." Jacob was brought up between a pile in Somerset and the London house in Smith Square, Westminster. ("I loved the idea of living between the finest Palladian home in north Somerset and one of the best Georgian houses in London," his father, who may also have taken his own self quite seriously, writes in his memoirs.)

When did you realise you were better off than most? "It was probably when I went to school and realised not everybody lived in two places." Was your father any good about the house(s)? He can't recall his father doing a single domestic task, aside from the once. "When I was very little, he was put in charge of putting a cottage pie in the oven and it came out frozen in the middle, so he was never let loose in the kitchen again."

Jacob appears like his father in this respect. Can you cook? "No." Boil an egg? "No." Toast? "I could, but I don't." Could you work a washing machine? "I could not work a washing machine." Do you take out the rubbish? "I do not. I am vairy spoilt." Do you put your dirty plate in the dishwasher? "No." Hang on, Jacob Rees-Mogg has his dinner and then he leaves his plate in situ? God, your poor wife. She's not minded to strangle you? "We do have help," he exclaims. "I'm not leaving it all to her."

He is married to Sue, who used to work in Boots ... Ha ha, good joke. His wife is Helena de Chair. She is the daughter of Somerset Struben de Chair, author and Conservative MP, and Lady Ann Juliet Dorothea Maud Tadgell, who is descended from Thomas Wentworth, first minister to Charles I. "We supposedly first met when Helena was an infant, because our parents knew each other, but we first met in adulthood at a political event run by my younger sister, campaigning for a referendum on the EU constitution. I spent 20 minutes talking to her about her family history, which I think she thought was slightly bonkers, but there you go."

How did the romance progress? "We started dining together." Being a heart-throb, had you had many girlfriends before? "I had not." He proposed in front of one of her mother's five Van Dykes, as engineered by Rees-Mogg. "I just had a word with her mother to see if it would be suitable and her mother gave the all clear." (Apparently, the two Stubbses were on loan to a gallery and the engagement was lengthened until they were returned, so the wedding guests could admire them.)

They have four children: Peter, Thomas, Mary and, um, Anselm. I ask if he thinks Anselm will grow up clamouring to know why he couldn't have been called Peter, Thomas, possibly even Mary. He says, "Anselm came about because Helena was walking through Anselms Court and thought, 'That's a nice name,' and I thought, 'Fantastic, there couldn't be a better name.' He was the most interesting Archbishop of Canterbury (c 1033-1109) and Doctor of the Church. And once we had thought of it, there was no retreat."

I'm intrigued to know what might go down in the Rees-Mogg household on your average Saturday night. *The X Factor*? "I have not watched *The X Factor*. There is a fair chance that my children, after bathtime, would come downstairs and watch a film. This is usually a Seventies James Bond film. The younger two would then go to bed. The older two would stay up a bit later. Then my wife and I would have dinner together and muddle about afterwards." Have you been a hands-on dad? Nappies and all that? "No, no, no. What would nanny say?"

Nanny has been in the family for 50 years. She is Veronica Crook, and now works as nanny to Jacob's children, which is super. "She speaks to them in exactly the same way as she spoke to us. It's a little bit of social history. If they put a large bit of butter on their bread she'll say, 'Do you know that was a week's rations during the war?' They love her stories of growing up in the Forties." I bet. How old is nanny? "She is as old as her little finger but a little bit older than her teeth. That was the answer I was given when I was little." Nanny was due to retire once, he says, and they threw a retirement party for her and everything, "but she was back at work first thing the next day".

Jacob is the second youngest of five children and I wonder if his siblings didn't want nanny. He says yes, they did, but he's the only one with children who also has a house in London (Mayfair) as well as the country (Somerset), and nanny wanted to live in London. So she could go clubbing at weekends? "She is a very respectable, proper nanny who would not do any clubbing," he says. And say you were to make PM one day, would nanny be in the cabinet? What would she be best at? Chancellor? Foreign secretary? "Nanny," he replies excitedly, "would be brilliant at everything."

His earliest memory is of a family holiday to Israel when he was nearly three. "I remember there was a taxi driver, and I asked to be carried, and he said, 'In Israel, we make them walk.' So I did not like him at all. I thought he was vairy bad news." He was reading the *FT* by nine, to check on his shares, and such was his reputation for dressing down company chairmen that, at 12, he was interviewed by Jean Rook of the *Daily Express*. Rook had a formidable reputation and set out to hate him. She wrote, "Braced to interview Master Rees-Mogg — preferably though bulletproof glass — I reminded myself he was only two years older than my son. Otherwise, I'd have turned up in a stocking mask and shot him."

But a few paragraphs in and she's fallen for him, as you do. "I was lost. Down the drain like a dropped 5p. Ready to clasp this pale, paper-thin child to my heart." He told her he had been a Labour supporter temporarily, and I read the quote to him: "I started out Labour to be different from the rest of the family — they're all Tories — but then Labour announced they would bring in a wealth tax. Since I plan to be wealthy, I was very off this, so I buttoned my anorak over dozens of stickers, walked into Transport House and yelled, 'Vote for Maggie.'"

You did that? "Yes, I did do that. I'm not brave enough to do such things now. I was frightfully bumptious." He attended Eton, then studied history at Oxford. "I got a 2:1. It's not a first, but it's better than a poke in the eye with a sharp stick." The student newspaper of the time reveals he had other names even then, including Please-Flogg, Grease-Bog and Rees-Smug. Bizarrely, I find I feel protective, and ask if that hurt him. "Oh no. It was all vairy gentle and amusing." And is it right that nanny came once a week to ensure your room was spick and span? "Not once a week, no," he says. "Just occasionally."

He then became an investment banker and still works 35 hours a month for the company he co-founded, Somerset Capital Management, earning £120,000 a year. What do you spend your money on, aside from hairy miniatures? He says he owns two classic Bentleys, which gobble up a ton of cash, but commutes from Mayfair to Westminster in his Lexus. You wouldn't take the Tube? "From where I live it wouldn't really work.

I'm not against taking the Tube for journeys when it is suitable." So you do take the Tube? "I have done, but I don't with great regularity." When was the last time? "I don't remember."

Have you ever experienced not having money? Have you ever experienced the shame of an ATM telling you "insufficient funds" and then gobbling your card? "I have not. I have had overdrafts, but I have always had an overdraft facility, so I have never had to worry that the bank would not clear my cheques." So when people are poor, or you see them queuing at food banks, or suffering due to the bedroom tax, can you empathise?

Jacob gets as shirty as Jacob ever gets, which isn't that shirty, but I sense him bristling. You don't have to have experienced something personally to have sympathy for individuals, he says. "My role as a constituency MP is that I am always there to support my constituents, and if they are having a difficult time, I am on their side." He is obviously a committed constituency MP and he says he has no ambitions to rise further. "I was ambitious to get into parliament and, having done that, it fulfilled the ambitions such that I had." You don't find the back benches frustrating? "No, no. I'm vairy happy on the back bench. It gives me the freedom to speak on subjects I'm interested in." What do you think David Cameron makes of you? "I don't know, but in the brief conversations we've had he has always been vairy friendly."

We talk about Europe (almost until I have to beg him to stop) and same-sex marriage. He says that, as a Roman Catholic, he could never sanction it. But, I say, isn't the issue about the equal dignity of human beings, which has to be a thoroughly Christian principle? He says, "Marriage is a sacrament, and sacraments are decided by the church, not the state. It is a fairly limited issue. It is this sacramental point."

I put it to him that some would struggle to accept the Catholic church as having the last word on sexual morality, given the endemic child abuse that continues to be uncovered. "The problem is that all institutions have been tainted. Children's homes in the UK, the forcible removal of children to Australia, and also individuals. Yes, there are awful people who do vairy wicked things. Look at Jimmy Savile, but do you still watch the BBC? The difficulty the church faces, which it handled extremely badly, is that it preaches forgiveness and it forgave people who oughtn't to have been forgiven, who should have been rooted out, and who used the mercy of the hierarchy to carry on their wicked behaviour."

But that hierarchy also covered it up. "So how do I reconcile that?" he asks. Indeed. "All human institutions fail to some extent, but that doesn't mean that what they are saying underneath it all isn't true," he says. So it's gay marriage you object to, not gayness? What if, at some point in the future, Peter or Thomas or Mary or, um, Anselm said, "Father, I'm gay." Would that be difficult? "No. I think one's children are one's children and one has to cope with what they decide to do. My quibble is purely with the issue of sacrament." What if Peter or Thomas or Mary or, um, Anselm said, "Father, I'm gay and also I support Labour." The double whammy. "Do the two go together? They have to make their choices in life. Inevitably, one's children won't do, nor should they do, everything that I would want them to do, but we would have some vairy interesting political discussions."

Do you think left-wing people are mad? "Of course I don't. I don't agree with them, but I don't think they are mad." He is quite a fan of Jeremy Corbyn, as it happens. "He is very principled and he is very brave. Also very wrong, but he probably thinks I'm very wrong, too." The two and a half hours fly by, and much is discussed. Does nanny still tick you off? Only, he says, if he arrives home and she's just got the children to bed "and I get them all going. 'Don't get them going,' she says."

He is, himself, a little bit in love with Mary Berry. "I sat next to her at an *Oldie* lunch a couple of years ago. They gave me an award for Wannabe Oldie of the Year. She was wonderful, so charming." He is a fan of Arthur Askey, and takes out his phone to show me Arthur Askey performing *The Bee Song*: "Oh what a wonderful thing to be, a healthy, grown-up, busy, busy bee ..." I say I haven't seen that since *The Good Old Days* was on telly, forgetting that for Jacob every day is possibly a Good Old Day.

I then release him to Claridge's, although not after a fight for the bill. "You will not pay," he says. "You will absolutely not." Readers, I fell for him. But ... WTF?

P.S. A few days after our chat, Jacob Rees-Mogg's fifth child is born. He's called Alfred — or, more properly, Alfred Wulfric Leyson Pius.

I WANTED TO BE RICH AND FAMOUS AND POWERFUL, AND DESIRED BY WOMEN

Giles Coren

February 29 2016

ALL I EVER wanted to be when I grew up was a novelist. But I have failed. And all I ever wanted not to be was a newspaper columnist. So I have failed at that too. Judged according to my childhood aspirations, the whole of my adult life has been a complete and utter failure.

On the last afternoon before my epic life fail began in earnest, I was walking with a friend along a towpath beside a twinkling river, in the week of my final university exams.

"What are you going to do after we leave?" she asked me.

"I'm going to write," I said.

"Like your father and your sister?" she replied.

"What?" I yelled. "No! No! Nothing like that! Jesus Christ. Humorous columns in the newspapers? That's not writing! That's miserable bourgeois ink-pissing! I'm going to write novels. Huge, massive, difficult, brilliant novels. That'll show them! And if nobody wants to read them, fine. Then I'll starve. But I swear to God I will go down a coalmine, I will drive a bus, I will sell my virgin arse for chicken soup on the dockside at Gdansk, before I spend my life hacking out witty bollocks in the national press."

So, anyway. Here I am.

But I would like it noted for the record that I did at least try to be a novelist. Throughout my university years I worked at nights, hunched over a typewriter on the floor of my college room, drinking Scotch and smoking Ducados, on a Joycean memoir called *Portwake of the Ulynan as a Young Fig*, which I used to read aloud, high, to my friends for hours at a time, until I no longer had any friends.

Then after my exams I repaired to the south of France to work on *Non-Fiction – A Novel*, written in the ludic, lipogrammatic style of the Oulipo group of French writers who were as unpopular then, in their heyday, as they are now. And when that failed to get off the ground I moved to Paris to work in a menswear shop (making good on my threat to do menial work rather than succumb to journalism) and in the evenings worked on an untitled project that involved modernising a story-within-a-story from *Don Quixote* and alternating each chapter with the investigations of a detective called Rufus Stone and his Womble sidekick, Orinoco. The Rufus Stone chapters were written, naturally, in verse ("For I am Rufus, Rufus Stone/ Defender of the weak/ Womble or no womble, bad men crumble when I speak").

Now, when I say that I "worked" on these novels, what I mean is that I sat and drank and smoked and stared at a typewriter and imagined what it would be like to be a novelist. Ten years of obsessively reading English literature and three years studying it for a degree had left me with a sense of novel-writing as the only thing worth doing. Though my motivations were not especially pure. I wanted to be rich and famous and powerful and desired by women. And it seemed to me that the best way to achieve that, given that I was easily the best at spelling of anyone I knew, was to be a novelist.

I looked at the lives of Hemingway and Fitzgerald, Orwell and Dickens (though not at their grim, untimely deaths) and thought how if I could get to that sort of level, people would really sit up and take notice. I was also into García Márquez, of course, who had recently won the Nobel prize for literature at the age of 54. I determined to do it by 40.

It sounds mental, I know. But anything less seemed pointless. For at the time I was hatching these hubristic plans, my columnist father was "the funniest writer in Britain" and my 16-year-old sister was appearing on *Wogan* to discuss her own latest book, a collection of the *Daily Telegraph* columns she had been writing since she was 12.

What was to be gained by emulating them? I needed to aim higher. Novel-writing was the thing they hadn't done, couldn't do and never would and was thus my only chance of achieving a status that led people, when they spotted my dad in the street, to whisper, "Isn't that Giles Coren's father?"

In retrospect, if that was all I wanted, I should have just shot one of the remaining Beatles.

The years went by. I wrote endless half-novels, which I locked away and showed to nobody. I worked in bars and clothes shops, smoked a lot of dope and cursed the injustice of the world. At one point, in desperation, my father dug out one of my manuscripts and sent it to his friend Tom Maschler, the legendary publisher of *Catch-22*, who invited me to come in for a meeting. I told my father he had breached my trust and that I would never talk to him again. He replied: "If your plan is to be a f***ing haberdasher then we won't have much to talk about anyway."

Eventually, the old man put me in a half-nelson and frogmarched me into *The Times* where I was indentured as a feature writer on no salary, without hope of reprieve, for as long as I should live. Media-watchers these days give me an endlessly hard time for having "got a leg-up from Daddy". But I wasn't given a leg-up at all. I was frigging shanghaied.

But I did OK. I guess my fury at not being a novelist gave my journalism a bitter urgency that appealed to some people, created a demand for my stuff and allowed me to become first a columnist and then a critic. Which means that, in newspaper terms at least, one is well paid and widely read. You could almost tell yourself that you turned out to be a writer, after all.

But my sense of failure did not lift. As I passed 30, a contemporary of mine from school scored a book deal for £100,000, then so did one from university. And then another, Hari Kunzru, landed an international deal reportedly worth nearly a million. My despair was total. My failure complete.

Rage at the world's injustice poured into my journalism. I was by then writing a daily diary column on the comment page of this paper which grew crazier and crazier, less and less news-based (I was, in truth, making everything up), until the editor finally used the excuse of 9/11 and a sobering of tone across the paper to boot me out into the laughable, dead-end job of restaurant critic, last redoubt of the bloated loser.

Angrier and more defeated than ever, but with time on my hands thanks to a job that involved one morning's writing a week and the occasional spot of lunch, I tried again at a novel. I was at that time obsessed with the details of the Holocaust and the plight of the English Jew (me), and so for the next three years I hammered out the story of Winkler, a defeated young man who meets what he takes to be an Auschwitz survivor, becomes even more angry and then pushes a fat woman under a train.

Except funny.

I sent it to a literary agent, Jonny Geller, who read it in a morning and sold it in a week. I can't remember how much for. I think twenty grand. It wasn't even a tenth of what I thought the book was worth but Jonny said for a first-time literary novel it was pretty good. And what the book had failed to achieve in cash, I reckoned, it would no doubt make up for in world acclaim and major literary prizes.

However, I began to get a sense of just how highly my novel would be valued in the wider world when my publisher, Jonathan Cape, postponed our first editorial meeting because "Ian McEwan is in town", then because

"Julian Barnes is visiting the warehouse" and then, if I remember rightly, "because Will Self is rumoured to be lighting his farts at the Groucho".

But they ascribed me an editor, we did a bit of an edit, and then I delivered my hand-corrected final proof. They lost it. "A cleaner must have thrown it out," they said cheerily. And they hadn't made a copy. So I did it again.

Eventually, there was a book. It had an awful cover, a terrible blurb and was being published in the dead month of August. But at least there would be a publishing party and my career as a major literary figure would be launched.

Actually, they said, there won't be a party. There would just be a lunch on publication day. Then they cancelled the lunch. So on the day that my grand literary opus finally came out, I sat at home in my pants watching cricket on the telly.

The first review was in *The Observer*. "Coren can only fail to live up to … Bellow, Roth, Bashevis Singer," it said.

Sneering leftist bastards. *The Daily Mail* would get it, though.

"More unpleasant even than *Winkler's* plot," wrote the *Mail*, "is the self-referential smugness and unremitting cynicism of Coren's writing."

But these were women. Women don't like serious literary fiction. If I was aiming at women I'd have written a bodice-ripper. Men are going to get it. Men like Anthony Quinn in *The Daily Telegraph*.

"It's difficult to concentrate," wrote Quinn, "against the grinding clank of the book changing gears." Although that was polite compared to the design guru Stephen Bayley, who wrote of *Winkler's* "ocean-going, lavatorial awfulness".

People were surprised when I took umbrage. "You're a critic," they said. "You're supposed to be able to take it!"

"No," I replied. "I'm supposed to be able to dish it out."

Although I'll tell you the truth. The critics who had read my book properly, grasped what I was trying to do and either didn't like it or thought it should have been done better, I didn't really have a gripe with (Quinn and *The Observer*'s Hephzibah Anderson were in that category). It was grudge-bearing illiterates who made short, dumb, *ad hominem* attacks without reading the book that pissed me off. At least when I write a review, I eat what's on my plate before I dump on it.

Then in the autumn I won a prize. Not the Nobel, as it turned out. Nor yet the Booker. Nor even the John Llewellyn Rhys Consolation Medal

For Quite A Bad Book By Someone Who Is At Least Still Quite Young (of which I had agreed to be a judge the previous year in the hope of some quid pro quo). What I won was the Bad Sex Award. And so *Winkler* was headline news from Runcorn to Rawalpindi not for breaking the mould of the modern novel, not for altering the course of British fiction, but for being a crapheap of smutty rubbish.

In the years leading up to the writing and publication of *Winkler*, I had occasionally been invited to do television. But I had always grandly (and quite ridiculously) refused, on the basis that I did not want to sully my name in public in a way that might jeopardise my chances later of being taken seriously as a novelist. But a few months after *Winkler* bombed, one of the producers I had fobbed off called me up and asked, "Will you do telly now?" And I said "Yes." And so in the ten years since Winkler, television has been the thing I do on the side, when I'm not writing for *The Times*.

And because of being on telly I am recognised in the street and paid quite a lot of money and invited to all sorts of exciting and glamorous things. And yes, people want to have sex with me (more men than women, but that's better than nothing). Which is most of what I wanted from novel-writing when I was a kid. Furthermore, I look around at the biggest names in British fiction — Barnes, McEwan, Mantel, Amis — and I think, "Does anyone in the wider world give a f*** what they think about anything?"

So I'll stick with telly, I think. And tonight on Sky Arts you can watch my documentary about the failure of *Winkler*, if you want. It's called *My Failed Novel* and in it you will see me learn, live on camera, exactly how few copies it sold, get called a "greedy little toad" by Jeffrey Archer, chase Stephen Bayley around his kitchen with a carving knife, get pilloried by a ladies' reading circle in Rickmansworth, patronised by a load of whey-faced beginners on a creative writing course in Norwich, and hear from Howard Jacobson how failure is, and must always be, "the stock-in-trade of the serious novelist".

My Failed Novel is fast-paced, well-planned, brilliantly edited and a perfect expression of everything it set out to be. My failed novel, sadly, wasn't.

SPRING

CRICKET IS KEY TO PAKISTAN'S IDENTITY — THE COUNTRY IS STARVED WITHOUT IT

Mike Atherton

MARCH 3 2016

FROM PESHAWAR TO Kotli, from Khyber Pakhtunkhwa on the northwest frontier, to Kashmir in the east on the contested border with India, the enduring love of Pakistan for cricket was clear. The game was being played on street corners, in car parks, on green fields, scrubland, on mountainsides, plains, in orchards and in villages, towns and the great teeming cities of Lahore and Islamabad.

Soldiers sat in the cool night hours outside embassies, huddled next to stone fires, listening on the radio to the final of the Pakistan Super League (PSL), held in the UAE. Schoolchildren at Aitchison College in Lahore, bewitched by the cricket that they had seen in Dubai, wanted to know who would win the World T20. Restaurant owners and kitchen staff demanded selfies, gawping at this former international player as if he were from Mars.

Televisions everywhere were tuned to Dubai and the PSL: viewing figures were higher in Pakistan for the final than for the 2015 World Cup equivalent — according to figures, more than half of those who owned a television tuned in. There was a great sense of pride in the tournament, belonging as it does to Pakistan, and there remains a yearning for cricket, despite the dearth of international players in Pakistan since the terrorist attack on the Sri Lanka team in 2009.

Richie Benaud said that the word "tragedy" should have no place in the sporting lexicon, but Pakistan and cricket has been a tragic affair of late. Not just the absence of cricket, which has prevented Pakistanis from watching their national sport and their national heroes, and these same heroes from playing in front of friends and family, but the very real tragedy when the Sri Lanka team bus was attacked seven years ago, which sparked Pakistan's isolation from the world game, when a number of civilians and policemen were killed and cricketers severely injured.

I stood in the middle of that roundabout in Lahore last week where the attack took place, where bullets were sprayed at Trevor Bayliss and

Paul Farbrace, who were then coaching Sri Lanka, and others. With cars, motorcycles, buses and rickshaws whizzing past, and Lahore going about its daily business, it was hard to think of it as a place of death. In the near distance were the floodlights of the Gaddafi Stadium, near where a suicide bomber blew himself up at the outer security ring during Zimbabwe's one-day return in May last year, the only international cricket in Pakistan since the attack on the Sri Lanka team. That a policeman died that day and the bomber was prevented from getting closer to the stadium is cited as evidence, tragically, that the security arrangements that day worked.

To understand the importance of cricket to Pakistan, you have to remember that its sense of nationhood and international cricket are bound together. Pakistan's first Test match took place five years after the birth of the country. As Omar Kureishi, the late journalist, wrote: "Cricket was intertwined with the process of nation-building. There were few things that Pakistan achieved as a new nation; cricketing success was one of the early bonds of nationhood." As in the Caribbean, cricket is more than just a game. So its absence has been heartfelt.

Now, the first tentative steps are being taken to bring international cricket in some form back to the country. During England's tour to South Africa this winter, Rory Steyn, a security adviser to the ICC and formerly Nelson Mandela's bodyguard, was dispatched on a mission to produce a report on the possibilities for a World XI or Commonwealth XI playing a series of matches against Pakistan in Lahore and Islamabad this year, as a prelude to international teams returning thereafter.

That report is complete and will be discussed during the World T20 by Giles Clarke, who heads what is called the Pakistan task force, and Dave Richardson, the chief executive of the ICC. Recommendations will then be put to the ICC board during the spring meeting. Discussions for the cricket, security notwithstanding, are at an advanced stage, with coaches and players approached, some of whom have given a positive response despite the vast majority of foreign players in the PSL who were asked saying that they would be unwilling to travel to Pakistan.

Although security concerns have been obvious and should not be understated, Pakistan does suffer from adverse perceptions beyond that. Peter Oborne's magisterial history of Pakistan cricket begins with the assertion that cricket writing about Pakistan has sometimes fallen into the wrong hands. "It has been carried out by people who do not like Pakistan, are suspicious of Pakistanis and have their own preconceptions.

Autobiographies by England cricketers, with some exceptions, are blind to the beauty of Pakistan and to the warmth and generosity of its people."

That the world game is dominated by India has not helped either. I spent last week in the company of Imran Khan, making a programme for Sky Sports before Pakistan's visit this summer. It was the first time that I had been back to the country for 15 years, and I too had forgotten the warmth to which Oborne rightly refers. The drip, drip effect of bad news that emanates out of the country, almost on a daily basis, and the western imprint put upon it, obscures other truths too. Another problem is that cricketers, if they returned, would invariably be in lockdown mode, seeing only hotel rooms, airport lounges and stadiums, with heavy security on hand, rather than being allowed to roam freely.

For sure, we had heavily armed security in Khyber Pakhtunkhwa and Kashmir last week, but in Lahore and Islamabad we went around unhindered, taking a tuk-tuk one night in Lahore to dine in a rooftop restaurant overlooking the Old Fort. It is unlikely that international cricketers would be allowed such freedoms, and so they would have a warped and distorted view of the place and the risks involved.

Of course, there are risks, and keen as Clarke is to push for a return of international cricket to Pakistan, he knows that certain conditions must be met: Nawaz Sharif, the prime minister of Pakistan, needs to be on board, as do the intelligence and security services officials; the Pakistan Cricket Board will have to assume the risk, because other boards would be terrified about liability if anything happened to any of their players and the players and coaches would need to assume some risk of their own.

Clarke is determined to succeed, although some in international cricket do not share his enthusiasm. It is unlikely that centrally contracted England players would be given clearance even if they were keen to participate. Players, by and large, seek an easy life, but there may be enough of them with points to prove, with a broader vision to accept some degree of risk or simply keen for a well-paid job. If and when it happens, for cricket-starved Pakistanis it will be an occasion to savour.

CUTS ARE SEVERING LIFELINES
FOR YOUNG AND OLD

Alice Thomson

MARCH 9 2016

TWICE A WEEK a white minibus picks up my 84-year-old father, immaculately dressed in a tie and tweed jacket, at 9am. He always brings a few photos or a book on Alpine birds in a plastic bag and returns six hours later clutching some rose-scented talcum powder or strawberry creams. Neither of which he particularly likes (he prefers toffees) but he thinks he may have won them somewhere.

His mornings at the daycare centre are spent playing competitive Scrabble, doing team quizzes and competing at armchair curling matches. If he is feeling "a bit peckish" there is tea and toast; at lunch he has sausages and mash, bakewell tart and custard or they'll make him an omelette. Afterwards he paints. He once even tried a pedicure. He's not sure where he is but he never wants to wander. There are usually two dozen who join him from around the town of Wallingford in Oxfordshire — retired professors, police officers, engineers, plumbers, actresses and cleaners. Many have dementia, others have physical disabilities, some just need company and medical advice, or feeding up or help with online shopping.

Christmas parties can be quite raucous. No one is lonely and there is a waiting list to join. It means my octogenarian mother, his carer, has a few precious, guilt-free hours on her own without searching for his keys and wallet. Now the centre will close. Oxfordshire County Council is shutting down its adult daycare provision. The elderly of Wallingford have been told they can meet in cafés. They might merit a social worker for 15 minutes twice a week to help open a can of food or fill out a form. They can go to their GP or A&E for their worrying aches, and those who struggle will enter full-time nursing homes or end up on hospital wards. They, their families and the staff will be bereft.

This is not a tale of old people having been abused or abandoned but of a system that worked perfectly for a vulnerable group. It wasn't even expensive. The cost to each elderly person was £17 a day and the council overheads were low thanks to many volunteers. The same is happening to Oxfordshire's children's services. The prime minister's magistrate mother, Mary, has intervened, signing a petition to save the 44 children's centres in the county. She was persuaded to do so by David Cameron's aunt, Clare Currie, who has called the £8 million cuts to the services "a great, great error". They are still going ahead. A lifeline for struggling new parents is being severed.

One mother explained that after she escaped a violent relationship, a centre turned her life around. She met other parents at breastfeeding classes, opened up to the health workers and learnt to care for her baby with advice and kindness. "The NHS couldn't help me. Social services didn't save me. The centre did. They taught me to change a nappy, cook meals and eventually get fit and confident again. Now I have a job."

Another mother explained how the centre saved her when she had post-natal depression. "I was very near to killing myself. But just eating biscuits with other mothers, having a safe crèche, knowing I wasn't alone and learning to enjoy parenthood transformed me." There is help not only for those with babies but older children who may need speech therapy or have hearing impairment or behavioural problems.

These centres for the very old and young may sound like a luxury with cheap coffee, Zumba classes and sympathy for everyone, regardless of their background, but they are crucial. They provide what the prime minister has been talking about in his speeches since Christmas — parenting classes, help with disruptive children, shelter for those with mental and physical illness and respite for carers. More bluntly, these 3,000 children's centres and 59,000 adult day-care places have prevented babies and the elderly clogging up surgeries and lingering in hospital beds, yet the majority of councils are now scrapping them.

The prime minister, as MP for Witney, has written to his Conservative council saying the closures would be "unwelcome and counterproductive". The leader, Ian Hudspeth, has responded with: what do you expect? We have nowhere else to go. Councils everywhere are doing the same. Local government has taken the brunt of cuts since 2010 with funding falling by 37 per cent in real terms. George Osborne last month gave councils a £300 million relief fund but they still insist they can't balance the books.

This isn't just about fortnightly bin collections, overgrown grass verges, fewer hanging baskets and more potholes; this is about services that keep communities and individuals thriving rather than floundering. These Cinderella centres that purée food for babies and sew on buttons for the elderly aren't vital in the short term, but wait a few years.

Since the cuts began in 2010 and 35,000 daycare places for the elderly have been scrapped, the number of times a pensioner visits a GP practice each year has nearly doubled from seven to 13. Bedblocking by the old now costs the NHS £700 million a year. Those who care for the elderly, the physically and mentally ill can't do it 24 hours a day, seven days a week without eventually cracking. Residential homes and hospitals will become the only answer.

JEREMY CLARKSON: MY WORST YEAR

Interview by Charlotte Edwardes

MARCH 19 2016

I AM ON HOLIDAY with Jeremy Clarkson in Barbados. Sorry, I am working and he is working. He's out here filming the new, as yet unnamed Amazon Prime version of *Top Gear*. I am interviewing him. "This is work!" he shouts over the squirrel spray of the jet ski, then skids at 45mph to douse me in seawater. "Work!" he insists as we stroll the length of a spongy beach, look around the island's oldest church, eat warm banana bread and suck at rum sundowners against the bouncing chromatic beat of a steel pan.

But when a woman with a flute of pink fizz floats over in a nightie to ask for a selfie, Clarkson barks, "Can't you see I'm on holiday?" And this is his gruff response (pathetic, may I say, because he always does pose for them) to the other 20-odd random people who ask him for his picture over the course of the weekend.

"The whole thing is an act, of course," he says at one point. What? "My job, my TV persona. 'Jeremy Clarkson.' It's a mask. We all wear masks. It's not the real me." Is he suggesting that the man who's made £30 million from "being himself" is a con? "Yup." Then who is the real you? "I'm not telling you," he laughs.

Instead, he warns against the dangers of catching "c**t flu" in a paradise like this. It affects the rich and famous, he says, and stems from being surrounded by flunkies who won't say no. "It's basically when you see your helicopter and say, 'I want a bigger one.'" He's had a few attacks — once in rural New Zealand, when he couldn't find a board game he felt like playing, so sent someone to Auckland to buy Risk.

"It's one of the reasons rock stars will continue to expire at the age of 27," he explains. "C**t flu kills them. 'I can do what I want, therefore … ' That's c**t flu. It's selfishness, really." Amy Winehouse had c**t flu, he says. "But what a singer."

Still, he has moments of grumpiness, which is down to the "horrible, horrible" time he's had lately: "My luck stopped suddenly three years ago." I suggest it must be wearing to be interrupted to pose every five minutes. "No! It's as Angela Rippon says, 'When it stops is when you have to worry.'"

Actually, his popularity seems undented by his very public defenestration from the BBC's *Top Gear*. A short walk on the beach is like being in *The Truman Show*. There are cries of, "I love you, Jeremy!", "Good luck with the new show, I'll be watching!" and (less reassuringly), "It's you, innit? The one from whatsit?"

No one asks about The Alleged Punch. It's almost exactly a year since Clarkson, 55, gave a cut lip to producer Oisin Tymon in a hotel in North Yorkshire for not, so the story goes, having a steak supper ready after filming. Three and a bit weeks ago he apologised, and Tymon's lawyers said they had settled for an undisclosed fee (rumoured to be in excess of £100,000) for racial discrimination and personal injury (Clarkson allegedly called him "a lazy Irish c**t").

"I can't talk about it — legal reasons," Clarkson says when I ask. Does he have a temper? "I can't talk about it, honestly." Was he really angry? He sighs. Does he argue a lot? "I don't usually argue with people; I discuss. If I'm in a mood and I'm talking to an idiot, I might tell them to eff off. If you and I found a subject we disagreed on, you'd see."

Later, in a harbourside restaurant suggested by TripAdvisor, we do have a disagreement. By then, warmed by sun, swimming and a bottle of rosé, he'll be more relaxed and open about life in general.

I've been chasing Clarkson for this interview for more than a year, and having been batted away with multiple versions of "No, thank you", I'm only here now because, in a moment of "bravado", he texted me something along the lines of, "All right, come on then, but it has to be in Barbados tomorrow."

When I arrive, he has a hangover. He's spent much of the day sitting on the bottom of the swimming pool with an oxygen tank, refusing to be coaxed up by a desperate scuba instructor, on the grounds that he wanted to drown out the world. "It was so nice and peaceful down there. Why would I want to come out?"

All he can bear to recall of the previous evening is that he went down to "Second Street" in nearby Holetown (which develops a mythical quality over the course of the weekend) and bumped into Andrea Corr (of Irish band the Corrs) in a piano bar.

Tonight he's skipped a "pyjama party" to meet me at the Coral Reef Club hotel, which is candlelit and colonial with shutters and palms, although the trees have been castrated of fruit and the area is sprayed with mosquito repellent, erasing the ambience of bugs.

Still, the crickets are going like an itch. And we're drinking banana daiquiris topped with glacé cherries in the smoking area. At all times Clarkson is equipped with three packs of Marlboro Lights, which he spills onto the table along with boxes of matches, lighters, receipts, a "crappy student" cashpoint card and anything else that he can unearth from his pocket.

The confusion over whether this is work or holiday is understandable. This is his itinerary over the next weeks: India, Jordan, America, Mozambique, Sweden. He's already been in Portugal — "and Devon". When I suggest this is all rather five star and enviable, he protests that he often shares a room with co-presenters Richard Hammond and James May, and that May snores like a beast.

Here they're building a coral reef out of old cars. "You need to 'seed' reefs," he explains. "Concrete is best, but steel is good, too. Just over there they sunk a ship not that long ago, and already it's an island of marine life — turtles and fish. Beautiful. One day the ship will rust and dissolve and you'll be left with a coral reef. I was reading about it in an in-flight magazine. I thought, why use ships? There are awful, terrible cars with which you could actually create new life. So that's what we're doing in Barbados. That, and the fact that the crew will think we're brilliant because we're here rather than some godforsaken mountaintop in a country no one has heard of."

His job sounds like the world's longest gap year. In the West Indies he's played drunken dodgems on jet skis. He's been in three plane crashes, including one in Libya and one in Cuba (during which he lit a fag as the plane went down). In Nepal, he remembers dragging his sleeping bag outside their dorm because "May's snoring was worse than the alternative: sleeping on a bench next to a vomiting pig". May regularly holds up their convoy with his 40-minute trips to the lavatory. "He says he can't hold it, which means at least once in his life," Clarkson muses, "that man must've had to interrupt sex in order to take a dump."

There are tales of nervous moments spent confronting armed militias, cross-legged conferences around campfires, negotiations with multiple agencies on borders, and occasional last-minute about-turns — "I was too chicken to go into the DRC [Democratic Republic of Congo]. Got all the way to the border and then thought, 'Actually, no.'"

He flips through his iPhone to show me photos from 2011, larking about in Raqqa (now Islamic State's stronghold) and Homs (now rubble and pock-marked, skeletonised buildings). Of course, jeopardy has always been a part of the show's appeal. This is lads' diplomacy — which at times goes hideously wrong.

While filming a Christmas special in 2014, they had to be evacuated from Argentina after his Porsche's numberplates (H982 FKL) were said to be a deliberately provocative reference to the Falklands conflict. (Clarkson denies this: "It was just an impossibility for us to have chosen that numberplate on purpose. I drive thousands of cars a year; I never look at the registration.")

The situation was so tense for the remaining crew — attempting to reach Chile cross-country — that Clarkson feared they'd be killed. "I rang [David] Cameron, who was out in Afghanistan. 'Get someone over from the Falklands. You've got to help us out here, otherwise you're going to have 40 dead English people.' There were 40 stuck in that convoy. It was one of the most unpleasant nights of my life."

What was the response? "Cameron said there was nothing he could do. And realistically there was nothing he could do. The High Commissioner came out, did his best. He could do about as much as the president of Argentina could do if some Argies got into trouble in England — nothing. Those days when you can send a gunboat, I'm afraid, are over."

It was against a swirling background of "incidents" like this that BBC bosses commissioned a number of investigations into Clarkson's "offensive behaviour". For example, while trying to build a bridge over the River Kwai in Thailand (actually, as it turned out, the River Kok), Clarkson commented, when he saw someone walk across it, "That is a proud moment ... but there's a slope on it."

He makes a noise of exasperation. "No one gave a s*** in Asia. They were alerted to the fact that there was a 'deeply racist' slur in the footage, and said, 'That's not deeply racist,' and transmitted it unedited. Which is what I thought would happen.

"I genuinely don't think it was bad. It was built up to be a huge thing. We don't mind being called 'roast beef'. The Aussies call us Nigel, a lot. Or Poms. We call the French 'frogs'." He has admitted to mumbling the n-word while reciting Eeny, meany, miny, moe and is apologetic for being rude about Mexicans.

"I'd say the one time we made a mistake — not one time, sorry, we made lots of mistakes; everybody does — but the biggest was Mexico. We got carried away in an item about a Mexican sports car and were very rude about Mexico and Mexicans and it was uncalled for. I apologised to the Mexican ambassador."

Against a backdrop of heightened awareness of sexism, the *Top Gear* boys' *Carry On* humour began to be scrutinised. When Clarkson revealed they'd all made up daily injuries as an excuse to see a "rather attractive" paramedic working with them, culminating in Hammond telling her "my willy tastes funny", it provoked a paroxysm — and not of laughter.

Yet Clarkson seemed ever more defiant. I get the impression that he actually enjoyed winding up Danny Cohen, the BBC's director of television at the time. He says Cohen ordered him into his office to ask if it was true he'd called his west highland terrier Didier Dogba (a play on Didier Drogba, the former Chelsea striker; Clarkson is a Blues fan). "I confirmed it was true. He said, 'What colour is it?' And I said, 'It's black.' And he said, 'You can't call your black dog after a black football player.' So I said, 'Why not? Would you rather I called it John Terrier?'"

On another occasion, Clarkson tells me, he sat next to Cohen's economist wife, Noreena Hertz, at dinner and asked her if she was a communist. "No," she said, "a Marxist." "What's the difference?" he replied. "The next time I was in with Tony Hall [the BBC director-general] and Danny Cohen, I said, 'Tony, you do know Danny is a communist, don't you?' Danny got really cross and said, 'Just because two people are married doesn't mean they have the same politics.'"

Today he says, "Danny and I were, and I suspect will remain for ever, very far apart on every single thing. Normally, you could find some common ground with somebody, but I think Danny and I could probably only get on perfectly well so long as we absolutely never had to think about each other for the rest of the time. Because I don't mind anyone having an opinion that's different to mine, just so long as they don't mind my opinion, either. So long as it doesn't impinge on what I want to do."

But it did. Ultimately, Cohen won. Clarkson was sacked from *Top Gear*. "I wasn't sacked. What was it? Oh yes, they 'didn't renew my contract'. I was sacked." There was public outcry. A petition calling for his reinstatement was signed by more than one million people. He says David Cameron quipped, "Well, if you go, they're just left with Hammond and May, and from my experience that'll never work."

In the end, much of the *Top Gear* team — Hammond, May and some key crew members — defected to Amazon Prime with him. (The BBC has rebuilt *Top Gear* with Chris Evans and Matt LeBlanc at the helm, about which Clarkson is entirely nonchalant. "Nobody says, 'What? Someone's doing another cookery programme?' Why shouldn't there be more than one car programme?")

But despite the jibes and the shrugs and the bluff and bravado, these were dark times for Clarkson. When I probe, he swerves, shrugging off tricky questions with, "Wait just a cotton-picking minute. I drive round corners too quickly while shouting. That is my job. Ask me what it's like to have a Ferrari sliding sideways and you've got to do a piece to camera before the power slide is over."

And then he says, "In one year I lost my mother, my house, my job. How do you think I f***ing felt?"

At 10am the following morning we have breakfast. He's been up since dawn with a trainer called Junior. "He has no mercy. I must look close to death and he says, 'Do it more!'" He does daily weights at 8am and plays tennis at 5pm. "It's a new thing. It hasn't had an effect yet." He slaps his stomach.

Clarkson is tall and misshapen with wire-wool hair and tobacco-stained teeth. With the possible exception of Wembley Fraggle, he looks like no one else. He likes to say he was made in God's factory on a Friday evening, when all they had left was two good feet "and a pair of good buttocks. Look at these rubbish hands, this paunch, this hair." Someone like Andrea Corr, he adds, was made on a Monday morning.

He claims to be utterly ham-fisted. "My first memory is peeling a hard-boiled egg. I was only about 18 months apparently, and it's still the most practical thing I've ever done.

"As Hammond always says, I look like an orangutan when I'm presented with simple tasks, like opening a bottle of wine. He says, 'You look perfectly happy, just baffled.' I have no sense of how an engine works at all."

He must be good at something? "I promise faithfully I can do nothing. I can't hang a picture without knocking a wall down. When I play tennis I can hear people saying, 'It is odd because that man is in tennis clothes and he's on a court and he's carrying a racquet, but what's he doing?'

"Skiing is the same. I look like a bus driver having a crap. I can't cook. I tried to make some soup the other day. My daughter was staggered that it could go that wrong. You know that footage of people in the London sewers with all the congealed fat? It looked like that."

Top Gear was the only thing he's done well, he claims. At one point in his 27-year association with the show, he left to pursue a "solo" career. "I thought, 'I'm brilliant at this; I can do anything.' So I did a range of not at all successful programmes: a chat show, a programme on the history of cars. They tanked. One was so bad that it never got shown at all. So I reinvented [*Top Gear*] with Andy [Wilman, the show's producer] and went back."

He's known Wilman since he boarded at Repton School — "He was my fag." Was Clarkson a fag, too? "Yes. We had to sweep the corridors — and then they'd come and empty their bins in them, so you'd have to start again. We'd clean the changing room, the bathrooms, make the beds."

Was he bullied? "Yes. I got beaten every night with empty Globe-Trotter suitcases. There's more give in a Globe-Trotter suitcase than there is in a skull. So you were fine. Head, back, shoulders, buttocks. Maybe you'd get the odd bruise from the corner. It was annoying and uncomfortable.

"In the morning, we were woken up and hurled into the plunge pool, which was freezing." He pauses. "Does you a power of good. I was a cocky little s*** coming to a private school at 13. God, it knocks it out of you."

He says the experience had "a profound effect because I can remember the day, the moment, that I thought: this isn't working just being me. It doesn't work. I'm going to have to make people laugh. Because once someone's made you laugh, you can't be cross with them. And it stopped from that day onwards. I was 14. It was a useful tool, making people laugh." He tells me he's also the world's best liar — that he can fool anyone — but I think he underestimates his audiences.

At school, he continues, "I was simply unaware of any homosexuality. We were remarkably naive. I assume some of the teachers were gay but we didn't notice." What he did notice was the racism. "I'm sad to say it was the Seventies and *Till Death Us Do Part* was on the television and there was definitely racism. We had a few Asian kids, [a] few blacks." He's "100 per cent certain I did not take part in racist bullying" and believes that the leap from his generation, "when racism was institutionalised", to today is remarkable.

"Our generation needs the biggest pat on the back of any generation for the changes we've overseen. When I talk to my children I realise they are completely colour-blind."

In other ways his childhood was perfect. He had a Blytonic middle-class upbringing in a 400-year-old farmhouse. "Prince Charles would get an erection if he thought about my childhood."

His dad, Eddie, "cooked and cooked. And when he ran out of people to cook for, he made cake for the birds." His mum, Shirley, sat at the kitchen table sewing Paddington Bears (they owned the toy company that made them). After school, Clarkson would help sew them before he was allowed to do his homework. "If you've got a Paddington Bear in your attic and it's badly sewn up the back, then that's one of mine."

They holidayed in Padstow, Cornwall, and later in a campsite in Brittany. "And twice a year we went to the Berni Inn in Doncaster, where you could have choice of starters: either grapefruit, pineapple or orange juice. Then you could have steak or breaded plaice. I once saw Leonard Parkin, who was an ITV newsreader, in there. It was like the Ivy."

His childhood hero was Alan Whicker and he even got to meet him. "But afterwards I heard him call me 'an irritating little s***'."

Most of the time he built dens with his sister — now a successful lawyer — and two girls "from up the way". Were they honorary boys? "Nope. I was the honorary girl," he says. "To this day 80 per cent of my closest friends are women."

He says, "Of all the 'ists' I've been accused of, sexist is the most stupid. I'm not sexist. The idea that you can't be pretty and have a brain makes me absolutely livid. Some of the girls were the fastest drivers – and why wouldn't they be? Just because you have breasts doesn't mean you can't drive a car.

"There's a standard thing in *The Guardian* that *Top Gear* was misogynistic. What people who'd never seen it assumed was that we used words like 'lady garden' to be misogynistic, but we didn't. It was primary-school language. We also said 'gentlemen's sausages'."

So who are his female heroes? He pauses. "Um. The Thatch? Although not massively so. She did do remarkable things in that time. Female heroes, um ... "

In the nick of time he remembers Twenties Hearst reporter Grace Hay Drummond-Hay, the first woman to travel around the world in a Zeppelin. "The descriptions are brilliant: the one about crossing the Russian tundra under this remarkable moonlit sky, my God. Then someone else smuggled a record player on board, so they were able to play music and do the charleston."

Later he spoils all his enlightened feminist talk. In a bar surrounded by elderly men and women with sticks and hearing aids, he suddenly stops talking. "Sssh! Can you hear that rustling noise?" No, I say. What? "Listen. Can you hear it now? That is the sound of dried-out old vagina."

Every five minutes or so we stand by the surf for a cigarette. A beach trader stops to ask if he can bum one. "You want any weed? Coke?" he asks after it's lit. When we decline, he offers us paintings, plaited bracelets, sunglasses. Clarkson laughs. "You really are a mobile shop. Do you have any Weetabix or Alphabetti spaghetti?"

At 11.15am, Clarkson switches from espressos to beer. Boy, can he put it away. I ask him about reports that he was drinking too hard and rumours that Tony Hall had told him he could keep his job if he went to rehab. "I still can't drink as much as James May," he deflects. He relates a time at Heathrow when May "just looked at me and said, 'Have you ever had red wine for breakfast?' It was 7.30am. I said, 'No, James. I haven't.' So off he toddled and he came back with two glasses. It was actually delicious. It's an experiment I haven't revisited, I'm relieved to tell you."

Last summer he disappeared for a month (when I ask where he went, he says "somewhere that was like prison"), and subsequently gave up drinking for four or five months. Initially, he says this was to "stay sharp" while negotiating his Amazon Prime deal. "You can't deal with Californian lawyers if you've had a couple of glasses of wine." Later he clarifies that his stint away was not rehab, but helped him clear out his head and think straight. "I'm a lot calmer now. There's the same s***, but I can deal with it."

Over dinner we talk about exes. His first kiss was at the age of 13 (in a boiler room at Repton) with a sixth-former. One of his many flats in Fulham was nicknamed "the vomitorium". "If you got a girl back there she stuck to the carpet and that was the end of it."

He admits to a massive crush on Kristin Scott Thomas, the actress, and boils with inexplicable rage whenever anyone pronounces her name incorrectly. "Sadly, I am unable to string a sentence together in her presence."

On marriage he is silent. His first wife, Alexandra Hall, left him after six months for one of his friends, and he's currently in friendly divorce proceedings with his second wife, Frances Cain — also his manager — to whom he has been married for 26 years. (Although he does tell me their wedding was in the Fulham church used in *The Omen* in the scene where a priest gets skewered by a lightning rod.) His recent split with girlfriend Phillipa Sage is off-limits, too, because, he reasons, "It's unfair on them — they didn't ask to be dragged into this."

It's his view that women are far tougher than men in break-ups. "How are you all so cold?" he asks. "Are you really so deeply unmoved when you get that mixtape of romantic songs, and the really bad poetry?"

Did he have lots of girlfriends? "We're not going there. Nobody's interested." So it's not true that he was "a right shagger"? He looks absolutely mortified and says he's been inaccurately linked with multiple women, among them Jemima Khan, a friend of many years. "Although

I thought her denial of our affair was a little strong," he says. "'No, no! This is the most revolting, disgusting, worst thing that's ever been said about me!' A simple no, Jemima, would probably suffice."

Our argument is over whether it's possible to change as a person. He is a fatalist who believes people can't. For this reason, Clarkson doesn't see the point in therapy. "I don't believe in a human's capacity to change," he says. "We are who we were born and, bar some very early nurturing, that is set for the rest of our lives. Everything else is a mask." (In the morning he says, "I had to really think about it after I said it yesterday. I thought last night, 'Do I really think that?' And I do. I stand by it.")

What he talks a lot about are his kids (Emily, 21, a writer; Finlo, 19, who's at Manchester University; Katya, 17, who's at school). He shows me photos of them on his phone and reflects how much they'd like to be in Barbados now. "They practically grew up here." One thing he breaks his work schedule for is the kids. "I've yet to miss one of Katya's school plays," he says.

His farm in Chipping Norton, he loves that, too. He has dogs, sheep and kunekune pigs (they are pets: Zeppelin and Walter). But he doesn't mention his other properties — in the Isle of Man and London — and actually he's oddly unmaterialistic as a person, carrying his "clean clothes" (denim shirt and jeans) in a black plastic bag, which, from time to time, he asks the reception desk to look after.

There are so many predictable things about Clarkson, such as his dislike of poetry, musicals — "I just want to shout: stop singing!" — and Uber. He's only been in an Uber once (I took him in one in London and he grumbled all the way: "Oh, I see, a quick trip from the top of Notting Hill to the bottom, via Dewsbury. Oh, and a Magic Tree. Anyone who has anything hanging from their rearview mirror can't drive").

But there are surprising things, too, like his love of ornithology (he's constantly looking for a sugarbird to show me), and AA Milne ("Every character you'll meet in life is a character from *Winnie-the-Pooh*: May is Wol [how Owl spells his name], Hammond is Piglet, I am Tigger").

Also, he tells me that he has no pubic hair. "None. Never have. I'm bald down there." How did you know when you were going through puberty? "My voice broke." (Later he tells me this is not true and that he does have pubes.) I'm astonished to hear he has a driver, a man called Andy, but he quickly corrects this to say he's "a Man Friday" who does a little bit of everything. Like drive.

He's doggedly loyal, saying without question that he'd rather go to prison than sneak on a friend, something ingrained since school. "Under any circumstances, you never, ever rat on a friend. That is for ever. I can think of a million other things I'd rather be than a sneak."

I ask about his mother's death last year from breast cancer that spread over five years. He'd just arrived in Moscow to do a live show when he was told over the phone by her nurse, "which was very sad".

"We didn't know how long she had. We didn't know if it was going to be a day or a week or a month – you just didn't know. But you have to be pragmatic. She's lying in bed barely conscious. My sister and I effectively said goodbye in her last bits of consciousness. And then I thought, well, I can either continue to sit in her bedroom for what could be a month … What do you do? It's very difficult to know. We had Moscow planned and I had to go. I thought, 'Well, I'm only going for four days. I'll be back in four days.' But she didn't make it."

Clarkson received the news shortly before he was supposed to be on stage in front of 15,000 people. He hesitated over what to do. "I thought, 'Let's just say I fly home, what would I do? Nothing. I may as well be here.' So I did the show. But the BBC … No, I won't say it."

He looks sour. "Let's say they were very unhelpful." It was the time of the BBC inquiry into "the slope thing". He was fielding calls. He mutters something about someone being "a s***".

"I said, 'My mother's just died. Please leave me alone.' But they wouldn't. And it was bad. We were doing the TV show and the live shows, and three newspaper columns a week and endless investigations into whether or not we'd said this or done that or whether or not my hair was straight or my teeth were cleaned. It went on and on and on. It was very tricky. So there was quite a lot of pressure that year even for a jovial soul like me to handle. I was very close to my mum."

He misses her. "Even now I think, 'I must tell my mother about that.' And then you think … Even just now at the Coral Reef, I thought, 'Oh, mother likes it here.' It just floats in. But" – he takes a deep breath and I can see his eyes are damp behind his sunglasses – "I just tend to think of her as a benign presence around." He sniffs. "Do you mind if I pop to the loo?"

And then he returns, and like all moments of pathos with Jeremy Clarkson, this one is harpooned. "By the way," he says, "all the time I was talking about my mother, I could see your knickers."

STARVATION, CROCODILES, ANTS? ALL I WANTED WAS TO AVOID MY BUILDERS

Sathnam Sanghera

MARCH 24 2016

IT'S DAY THREE OF my stay on a desert island in the Pacific, and as it rains ceaselessly in London and temperatures hit zero, I am lying under a tree on a white beach alongside two young women who have quickly become friends, watching the Moon shimmering over the surface of the sea and listening to the crashing of waves and the chirruping of exotic wildlife.

Sound like paradise? Well, not quite. Having grown up in the landlocked West Midlands, and having poor swimming skills, I've long struggled with the popular notion that the sound of the sea is soothing. I'll tell you what the ocean sounds like in the dark and in a gust: like a fighter jet coming in to crash land. As for the wildlife, not only is the hum of insects and sand flies deafening, but all three of us have been bitten mercilessly. On the plane back people will ask to be seated away from us, weeks later I will be seeking medical attention and in spring we will still be comparing scars.

Then there is the temperature, which is less balmy than boiling hot. Yet, to avoid being stung by the bugs, we are sleeping in multiple layers of clothing, which is making me sweat like a typhoid victim. Meanwhile, my stomach is growling from hunger in a way that suggests I might die, I have a headache from dehydration and I cannot get rid of a salty taste on my top lip, perhaps the result of sweat, the lashing sea or tears.

Welcome to one of the uninhabited islands that make up the Las Perlas Archipelago off the coast of Panama. Or, to be specific, to *The Island with Bear Grylls*, the Channel 4 survival skills reality show, in its third series, in which volunteers are stranded on a Pacific island for more than a month. I have been chosen, along with Edwina Langley, a journalist from a woman's magazine, and the Channel 4 publicist Kate Conway, to get an unscientific taste of the unscientific TV experiment in which a bunch of sadomasochists are left alone with nothing but 24 hours' worth of water and a few tools.

Though I come with low expectations, the experience is nevertheless lowering. Frankly, I only agree to go to escape interminable building work at home. Yet it becomes apparent that it would have been easier to sack the builders, set off a grenade in my flat then reassemble the whole thing myself by hand. The best thing I can say about the experience is I don't, at least, fare as badly as my companions.

My concern for Conway grows over our 36-hour journey to the island, as she reveals, variously, that she so fears insects she can't "even look" at a woodlouse; that she once didn't go in her sitting room "for a year, because there was a spider in it"; and that she is so fair she "can get sunburnt on a rainy day in Wales". Once we arrive, her agony is hard to witness. Even now, if someone asks about my time on the island, I shock them by showing them the picture we took of her bite-ridden face on our return to civilisation.

As for Langley, she comes with a more positive attitude, but the memos in my notebook convey plummeting morale. On arriving there is excited talk about "going to see the crocodiles in the freshwater lagoon". She claims she is "all for killing a wild turkey for food" and wishes "we were here longer". Yet this upbeat talk quickly descends into admissions that she is "counting down the hours", complaints about swollen feet and nausea triggered by a coconut, the only food we have during our stay. My lasting image of her is of her standing on the beach at dawn, a bug going up her nose as she retches in the semidarkness and declares: "Who are we kidding? This is f***ing s*** all round."

In short, we may survive, but the experience leaves us barely wanting to live. Which is not to suggest we are not provided with advice and assistance before getting on to the island. We have about an hour with Grylls himself on the nearby production island of Contadora, and are dropped off on our desert island by some survival experts. Yet we spend our time with the former, asking whimsical questions such as "why do so many Etonians become survivalists and explorers?" and "are men suffering a crisis in masculinity?" instead of posing more pertinent queries such as "what should you do if you wake up to the sight of crocodile footprints on the beach?" (as we did).

Meanwhile, the survival experts, understandably exhausted from six weeks of filming, and, assuming that it is quite hard to get yourself killed in three days, give us about an hour of training, whereas the contestants got two days. According to my smudged notes we are told how to make friction fire using the "bow drill" method. Then we are advised, among other things, of the following: beware of the "death apple tree" because "in the rain, the poison from the tree can drop down and cause blistering and one apple can kill four people".

Don't fear the native crocodiles: "They might eat a dog, not a person". Don't fear the even "bigger American crocodiles" because "they are not aggressive, and protected, so don't kill them for food". Don't fear the boa constrictor snakes: "They are more scared of you than the other way round". Avoid swimming out too far: "There are treacherous currents". Avoid wearing black because it is "the worst thing for heat and mosquitoes" (I am entirely in black). And don't sleep under palm trees because "a falling coconut can kill you".

Then they leave us with a radio in case of emergency, a machete, a small knife, a big dressing in case one of us gets "a big bleeder", a metal canteen with enough water for one day and the concluding remark "If you slash your femoral artery, we won't be able to get here in time. You will bleed to death." The desolation I feel when they depart is total. The only thing I can compare it to is being left at school for the first time, aged four.

My irritation at my fellow survivalists is instant: we land on the island late in the afternoon and while I gather wood and coconuts in aimless panic, they go for a leisurely wander, a splash in the sea and some light sunbathing. Needless to say, when the darkness comes, as it does abruptly, like God has switched off a bedside lamp, we are unprepared for the night ahead. It turns out that sleeping on palm fronds under a tree is about as comfortable as lying on a bed of seashells. Not long into the night we discover we are lying on an ants' nest. We move only to have to get up again when it starts raining and we have to put on waterproofs. Lying on the beach, we have to get up again to avoid being swept out to sea at high tide.

That night and the early hours of the following morning provide us with an important lesson: survival is basically a bunch of bad choices. You can sleep under the shelter of trees in the jungle, but then it is dark and it is impossible to tell the difference between snakes and scorpions and things you've imagined. You can sleep on a beach, where there is better visibility, but then there is no shelter, you risk being swept out by tides and bitten half to death by sand flies.

The second key lesson comes later that morning when the three of us set about the increasingly urgent business of attempting to build a fire, light it and boil some water so we don't die of dehydration. It is this: everything takes a very long time in the heat. To start a fire using the bow drill method you need to make and assemble, from raw materials lying around, a hearth board, a drill, a bow with string, a bearing block, an ember pan and some tinder. It takes me about two hours to carve the drill with a small knife. It takes Conway, in between leisurely swims, some time longer to craft the hearth board. Then it takes Langley, in between some persistent and heroic sunbathing, longer than all these times combined to assemble everything.

In the end it doesn't work: I have carved the drill from wood that isn't dry enough. Gasping and dehydrated, we decide to regroup and partially rehydrate ourselves with the content of the coconuts we have gathered. Unfortunately it takes three of us 45 minutes to open a single coconut with a machete — and having sweated so much in the process, it leaves us more dehydrated than ever. It is only while we gasp and panic quietly in the shade, where it still feels as if it is about 39°C, that I notice Conway is smoking a fag. She only has a bloody lighter!

There ensues a lengthy debate. Conway is of the view that she isn't really taking part, is only there to facilitate a "realistic" experience for Langley and me, and that we cannot "cheat" by using any of the materials left by the cast or any of the modern luxuries she has brought. I am of the view that if we want to make the survival experience truly authentic, we should be allowed to use whatever is available. In the end we reach a sort of compromise, which makes a perverted kind of sense in the heat: we can use the lighter to start a fire, but we will all, including Conway, have to go into the jungle to find some fresh water.

Gathering vessels in which to ferry the water turns out to be simple: depressingly, plastic bottles are forever being washed up on beaches in this part of the world. However, walking into the jungle, up a small cliff and through bush in the hot afternoon sun is shattering. Already dehydrated, we stop to nap and complain every couple of hundred yards or so. Grylls had instructed us to choose a "positive attitude" on the island, "even though it might hurt and you don't feel like it", but the brutal reality of the wilderness means we mainly opt for lethargy and whining.

Fortunately Langley is made of stronger stuff than Conway and I, and, brandishing the machete, she drags us through the acres of foreboding flora and spikes and thorns until, incredibly, we actually find a freshwater lagoon. Ignoring the threat of crocodiles, she immediately volunteers to fill the vessels with water, which, as a feminist, I am more than happy to let her do. Then I realise I will probably be outed as a coward in the glossy press, so I volunteer to fill the bottles, with Langley holding a machete over my head in case a crocodile makes an appearance. Afterwards, we leg it back to our "camp", feeling, frankly, disproportionately exhilarated. Did we boil and drink the water? Of course not. It looked like urine.

The thing most people ask when you mention you've met Bear Grylls is whether he made you drink your own piss, but I wasn't going to contract cholera for a *Times2* feature. Without properly discussing it, we all individually reach the conclusion that the best strategy is to lie still under a tree until we are rescued, which, as it happens, is exactly what I would do in the event of being an actual castaway on a desert island. We drink the final thimble of water in the metal canteen as if it were a rare whisky and settle in for the longest and thirstiest night of our lives.

Did I learn anything from the experience? Yes. I learnt that the experience of "survival", at least as it is created for TV, is packed with ironies: not least that it increases significantly the chance of sudden injury and death. I learnt that we don't need to eat as much as we do: we pigged out when we had food put in front of us on our return, but we weren't exactly dying of hunger at the end of the exercise. I learnt that there is nothing sexy about the desert island experience: it leaves you dirty and smelly and full of self-disgust. Indeed, we had all been grossed out when we heard that the cast had found a toothbrush on the beach and shared it, but by day three I was almost ready to do the same.

Yet none of it was, as Grylls had forecast, profound or life-changing. I went knowing that the secret of happiness is love and work, and it was no particular surprise that it made me unhappy to be deprived of both. I am full of respect for the people who managed to survive six weeks of the torment and I can't wait to see the show, but I am also bemused why anyone would want to volunteer.

Which brings me to the island's final gift to us. On a recent train journey, Langley found herself talking to someone who was a contestant on the new series. They had a hoot laughing about the mosquitoes, the crocodiles, the plastic bottles. Then she discovered that the tree we had slept under was actually where the cast went to the toilet. They called it "the dumping tree". So basically, we slept on a cesspit.

THE WORK AND IDEAS OF CRUYFF WILL LIVE ON LONG AFTER THE MAESTRO HIMSELF

Matt Dickinson

MARCH 25 2016

RIGHT UNTIL THE awful news of his death, *The Times* had been negotiating with Johan Cruyff about a series of columns during the summer's

European Championship finals. For the privilege of "ghostwriting" those pieces, I had been willing to walk to Barcelona (or swim, if necessary) and take down every word, a disciple at his feet. To listen to Cruyff would have been worth any trouble because he was — still is — the most interesting, influential figure in postwar football. As relevant today as ever.

Michel Platini has departed football in disgrace; Franz Beckenbauer might yet walk the same gangplank; Diego Maradona is compelling, but barking; Pelé sells blue pills to help you to get better erections. The game moves so fast that Sir Alex Ferguson must wonder whatever happened to his legacy at Manchester United. Cruyff? His influence endures and surpasses them all. He had not taken a frontline role in the game for almost two decades and yet he is all around us, even in death, in wonderful Cruyffian football. He is still here in the mesmerising passing patterns of Barcelona, the boldness of Pep Guardiola's Bayern Munich, on the coaching fields of Ajax, where acolytes such as Dennis Bergkamp still spread his simple gospel: "The idea is to dominate the ball."

The work, the ideas of Cruyff, will live on long after the maestro himself was struck down by lung cancer, aged 68. To have spread the gospel of Cruyff this summer would have been a joy because he could not be dull. I know that because I was once lucky enough to spend an afternoon in the shade of a tree in Barcelona, listening to his soulful reflections. When the terrible news came out in October that he had cancer, I wrote about that meeting. Forgive the retelling but it was one of the most cherished days of my career.

We spoke in the garden outside his office before the Champions League final between Barcelona and Manchester United in 2011. An argument was at large that Barcelona had to win a second trophy in three seasons to cement their reputation as a truly great team. "That's absurd," Cruyff responded, with characteristic refusal to bow to the prevailing mood. He talked about the majestic style with which Guardiola's team had played throughout the season, and cited Holland's defeat in the 1974 World Cup final and the number of people who continued to congratulate him on their vanquished beauty. "Winning is just one day, a reputation can last a lifetime," Cruyff explained. "Winning is an important thing, but to have your own style, to have people copy you, to admire you, that is the greatest gift."

As I wrote then, it felt like a religious sermon from the Pope of football. Winning is not everything. Beauty matters. Amen. I had marvelled at Cruyff the player, admired the coach, but what I came to love most in Cruyff was the idealist, the self-proclaimed romantic. Football has so very few of them. How I wish I could have talked to him through the summer tournament; to see if idealism would triumph, to talk about the thrilling moments, the great players, the inevitable controversies. He would have raged against diving and feigning injuries.

"As a manager, I would never accept it," Cruyff told me. "If you have someone who is a faker, you get someone to kick him in training. There's too much of it." He would have been amusingly acerbic about those who did not play football to his unyielding principles, just as he was often rude about José Mourinho, the anti-Cruyff. He spoke as someone who was not quite the greatest player of all time, or the most successful manager, but uniquely prominent in both categories and unarguably one of the game's true originals, a visionary, the most famous and creative Dutchman since Van Gogh.

Holland had no great pedigree in football before Cruyff came along. Until that point, some of us assumed that you had to be Brazilian to be blessed with such flair. Playgrounds filled with small boys trying to pull off that Cruyff turn. It was the hallmark of a player who did not so much beat a man as flummox them with his grace. As a coach, he took the Barcajax concept nurtured by Rinus Michels to new heights. Barcelona and their academy became "the university of the pass", as Simon Kuper, the Anglo-Dutch writer, once wrote. No Cruyff, no modern Barcelona. No Cruyff, no Guardiola, the fragile player he moulded into the fulcrum of his Dream Team, and perhaps not even Lionel Messi, Xavi Hernández or Andrés Iniesta.

He championed those whom others would dismiss as too small or weak. He instilled into Bergkamp the notion that football was a pursuit not of triumph but perfection. That is his legacy just as much as his triumphs — his three consecutive European Cups and three Ballons d'Or with Ajax as a player, and four consecutive league titles and another European Cup as coach of Barcelona. He never did win that World Cup medal but Cruyff, and his Dutch team of 1974, are revered much more than many teams who did. The memories will live on, as do so many stories of a famously argumentative man who, among many quarrels, insisted on wearing only two stripes rather than Adidas's usual three down the arm of his Holland shirt at the 1974 World Cup so as to satisfy his sponsor Puma.

He has fallen out with countless people thanks to his unwavering self-certainty. Asked if there was ever an occasion when he was wrong, Cruyff once replied: "If there was, I would never talk about it." Even in death, Cruyff will insist on having the last word. His own memoir — appositely titled *My Turn* — will come out posthumously in the autumn and there will be high expectations that it will be outspoken and unconventional. We will expect something different from a footballer who once explained that, if his team were winning comfortably, he would prefer to hit a post than score "because I just love that sound". Good luck to the Holland and French players should they try that tonight in a match that will be a celebration of Cruyff.

The match will be halted in the 14th minute to mark the shirt number that he wore, with typical non-conformity, as a nominal centre forward. Stopping the match? Better, surely, to stick the number 14 on every shirt and get both coaches to demand that their teams seek the ball and try to play with the attacking verve with which Cruyff will always be synonymous. "Cruyff built the cathedral. Our job is to maintain and renovate it," Guardiola, his protégé, once said. A great man has gone, but he has bequeathed us his ideals.

TORIES HAVE GOT TO END THEIR AFFAIR WITH BORIS

Matthew Parris

MARCH 26 2016

PARODY IS NOW EXTINCT. Boris Johnson has killed the distinction between reality and satire. Remember the Tory who as a wannabe MP called Labour's repeal of Section 28 "appalling", who joked about "tank-topped bum-boys", who sneakily rowed back from homophobia by asking "what's not to like?" about gays who leave the field of available women clear for straight men? He is now urging gay men to vote Leave because, he says, some Eastern European countries have legislation that represses them.

"It was us," he burbles on a new Out & Proud video, "the British people, that created [an] environment of happiness and contentment for LGBT people." It may well have been us. It ruddy well wasn't him. But now, even into gay saunas creeps the smell of his damp tweed. Look, this is a joke but this is not a joke. Somebody has to call a halt to the gathering pretence that if only you're sufficiently comical in politics you can laugh everything off.

Somebody has to remind us that it's not enough for those who seek to govern us simply to be: they have to do. Incompetence is not funny.

Policy vacuum is not funny. Administrative sloth is not funny. Breaking promises is not funny. A careless disregard for the truth is not funny. Advising old mates planning to beat somebody up is not funny. Abortions and gagging orders are not funny. Creeping ambition in a jester's cap is not funny. Vacuity posing as merriment, cynicism posing as savviness, a wink and smile covering for betrayal ... these things are not funny.

So I present you with a mystery. How did we get here, with Boris Johnson? Steadily, almost imperceptibly, an absurd idea has crept upon us. Had it been ventured nine years ago when the Tories desperately sought a candidate for the London mayoralty, it would have met a hollow laugh. Since then nothing that's happened adds to its plausibility. Much has occurred to rob it of any plausibility it ever had.

Yet still the idea has grown: shrewdly, assiduously, flamboyantly puffed by its only conceivable beneficiary. Where else in politics can such self-validating, self-inflating nonsense be found? It isn't — believe me, it really isn't — that Britain could ever want Boris Johnson as prime minister. Travel north of Watford and you'll abandon that thought. It is that the Conservative party could have the effrontery even to ask us to.

I feel uncomfortable writing this: writing about a fellow columnist, my former *Spectator* editor, an essentially liberal-minded fellow Tory, a wonderful entertainer, and a man who has never been anything but friendly towards me. Scores of media colleagues would say something similar of Boris, would feel the same discomfort, the same sneaking affection, the same restraining instinct to keep quiet ... which perhaps explains the silence. I feel uncomfortable too about touching upon sexual impropriety, of which I've certainly had my own share, and which (if sexual indiscretion alone disqualified a person from political office) would disqualify some of the best. And I hesitate to condemn a man for political ambition.

But there's a pattern to Boris's life, and it isn't the lust for office, or for applause, or for susceptible women, that mark out this pattern in red warning ink. It's the casual dishonesty, the cruelty, the betrayal; and, beneath the betrayal, the emptiness of real ambition: the ambition to do anything useful with office once it is attained.

I will not name two of the women he impregnated, one of whom had an abortion and a miscarriage (she had believed he would marry her); the other bearing his child; and the Court of Appeal judge, refusing a "gagging order" in 2013 to conceal her existence, remarking that the public had a right to know about what he called Johnson's "reckless" behaviour.

Nor is there space to elaborate on his lies about the first case to Michael Howard, then his party leader, for which Howard sacked him. Nor on his sacking many years earlier from this newspaper for making up quotes. Nor the broken promise to his proprietors not to run for parliament while editing *The Spectator*.

Have we forgotten all this? In parliament Boris has never shone. He was lacklustre as a junior spokesman (the highest Commons post he reached). His eight years as mayor are characterised by success as a celebrity figurehead and almost no mayoral achievements at all.

But if you want to see for yourself a blustering, bantering hole in the air, watch online his encounter on Wednesday this week with Andrew Tyrie, MP, chairman of the Treasury select committee. Watch him refusing to admit that his *Telegraph* claims, that the EU has banned the recycling of teabags and the inflation of balloons by children, were simply false. Watch a portrait-in-miniature of Johnson the politician: underprepared, jolly, sly, dishonest and unapologetic but (and this is the worrying part) horrifyingly vulnerable.

If Leave win the coming referendum, as I begin to think they may, a leadership bid by Boris will be imminent. If Remain win, the bid will be delayed but still formidable. Though I am an admirer of George Osborne, another likely bidder, I accept that he is in serious trouble from which he should not be confident of emerging. Theresa May has been underrated but she struggles, like Mr Osborne, with the W-thing: warmth. David Cameron's consummate recent performances only sharpen one's worry about the succession. The Tory party is running out of future prime ministers.

So Conservatives stand, as it were, looking across apparently open country towards Mount Boris. He beckons, and they do not see the great canyon between them and the prize: an abyss into which any electoral adventure would tumble. The abyss is Mr Johnson's public and private record. We don't seem to see it, yet it stares at us from yellowing newspaper print, from an insuppressible internet, from the public record, from judicial statements, from colleagues' judgments, from everything we know or ought to know but have been persuaded, such is his charm, to brush aside and forget.

It is all there, waiting. When the media turn nasty, as it will, his powers of laughing everything off will falter. If Mr Johnson had the sense of nemesis I suspect he has, he should stop now. And if we Conservatives have the instinct for survival that I fear we lack, then before the NoGoBoJo banner tightens around our party's neck we on the centre-right should end our affair with this dangerous charmer.

TRUMP MINES RICH SEAM OF DESPAIR IN 'SICKEST' US TOWN

Rhys Blakely

MARCH 26 2016

THE TOWN OF Grundy should, one theory suggests, be the angriest place in the United States. After all, Donald Trump received nearly 70 per cent of the vote in the local Republican primary — the highest share he has taken anywhere — and the theory says that Mr Trump, the Republican presidential candidate frontrunner, has been able to upend US politics because voters are furious: at immigrants, at their "stupid" leaders in Washington, at being exploited by the "cunning Chinese".

In Grundy, however, people do not talk about being angry. Rather, they describe feeling forgotten and on the cusp of despair. The community was built on coal mining but the well-paid mining jobs that supported families for generations are mostly gone. For a century, blue-collar places like this across the US helped to forge a superpower but now they are crumbling.

Last year Grundy, which has a population of about 1,000, was named the sickest town in America. The landscape is stunning. Grundy is in Buchanan County in southwest Virginia, near the Kentucky border, nestled among the towering, timbered slopes of the Appalachian Mountains which are dotted in spring with linen-white dogwood blossom.

The average lifespan for a man here, though, is 70, about the same as in Iraq and nearly ten years lower than the US average. A quarter of the population live in poverty while unemployment and depression are more than double the national norm. Rates of prescription pill addiction — and lethal overdoses — are soaring. Buchanan County has America's highest rate of pneumoconiosis, the mining disease known as "black lung". One in five people is on government disability benefits. Smoking and obesity levels are among the highest in the country.

It is all very far from the glamorous world that Mr Trump inhabits, as a billionaire in a Manhattan penthouse with a Versailles-style hall of mirrors and ceilings hand-painted with murals in the style of Michelangelo. But he seems to be the candidate whom the mining families of Grundy believe shares their pain. Mr Trump has accused President Obama of waging an "outright war on coal that has uprooted and destroyed families and entire communities". The tycoon has claimed that he can revive the industry by rolling back environmental regulations.

Grundy wants to believe him. Terry Barks, 38, a housewife whose miner husband has been out of work for six months, had voted Democrat all her life until she backed Mr Trump in the Virginia primary this month. "I think he's going to be able to help our coal industry, our way of living," she said. "I don't think he's going for president for popularity, cos he's already popular. He's not doing it for the money, cos he's already rich ... He sees that we're struggling." Wanda Clavinger, 65, a shop worker, said: "Some of the stuff he says about foreigners I don't appreciate. But we have to get some help. We have to get some help or we're going to end up being Third World. That's the way I feel about it."

The landscape of Grundy unfolds like a history lesson: a story of how the evolution of the US economy has left many feeling they are on the wrong end of a bad bargain. On one bank of the Levisa Fork River stands what is left of the old town: a courthouse, a memorial to the "gallant Confederate soldiers" who fought in the Civil War, a post office and a motley collection of dilapidated shops, most out of business.

On a recent afternoon, under a flawless, cobalt-blue sky, two drunks explained that the old town was nearly always deserted, except on the days when the post office gives out disability cheques. They sat in the shadow of a handsome bronze statue of a coal miner that looks towards the new town: a vast Walmart supermarket, rising like a giant Aztec temple, with a handful of smaller shops clustered around it — a nail salon, a doughnut place and a discount fashion store. The new town was built on elevated land five years ago with federal government money after the old town was hit by flooding.

The Walmart sells everything from sewing machines to shotguns, which helps explain the dearth of other shops in Grundy. It is often attacked for importing cheap goods that critics say have displaced or destroyed hundreds of thousands of American manufacturing jobs. The average local mining job pays $1,705 a week while the average retail job pays $351 but the locals agree that Walmart is just about the only thing Grundy has going for it. "Walmart pays almost $10 an hour and that's the best you've got," Suzy Cleet, 25, said. The only other business in Grundy that seems to be thriving is Advance America which offers payday loans.

The coal industry arrived in Buchanan County in the 1930s. In the 1970s, accelerated by the Arab oil boycott, it expanded. In 1978 *The New York Times* described how the streets of Grundy were jammed with traffic as 500 coal lorries rumbled through each day. For a while, the one factor that limited the building of houses was a shortage of flat land because 90 per cent of the ground slopes at 20 degrees or more.

Those times are long gone. The school-age population of Buchanan County has fallen from nearly 10,000 in the late 1990s to fewer than 2,800; parents urge their children to leave. Mention Hillary Clinton's promises that America can became the global superpower of clean energy and the people of Grundy scoff. The price of a ton of Appalachian coal has dropped nearly 65 per cent since 2008, and nearly half of America's pits have closed in the past 15 years.

Patrick Baker, of the Appalachian School of Law, says that its decline has four main causes: "First, cheap natural gas. Second, tougher regulations by the Obama administration as they seek to reduce greenhouse gases. Third, central Appalachian coal is getting tougher to mine, the coal seams are smaller and harder to access, reducing profits. Finally, Buchanan County has large metallurgical coal reserves which is essential for steel production, so as China and the world economy slows, demand for met coal declines."

Mr Baker added: "If Trump is elected president, he may be able to stymie some pending regulations and slow down some of the reforms that may protect current jobs. However, most of the changes cannot be undone."

Even Mr Trump's supporters in Grundy sound sceptical about whether he really can bring back the coal jobs, but he is offering a glimpse of hope, and that seems to be enough for many.

Sandra Kennedy, 44, works in a shoe shop and is married to an out-of-work miner. "The politicians ... took the heart out of Grundy. I would like them to live a month in our environment, to see how we struggle," she said. "Trump said he was for the coalminers, that he would bring back coal."

Does she trust that he really can? "Well, he didn't become a multibillionaire over nothing. And he can't be no worse than Obama. I don't know. I know a lot of 'em will say anything just to get in there."

THE TIDE IS COMING IN ON KING GEORGE

Alistair Osborne

April 2 2016

Sometimes you just can't make it up. The British steel industry is collapsing around his ears, so where do you find George Osborne? Well, let him tell you via Twitter: "Great to visit King Canute exhibition at Knutsford Heritage Centre today, marking 1,000th anniversary of coronation of town's namesake."

How could he miss that yesterday? Not when you can have a nice historical debate over what Canute was really up to: proving the heights of his delusion or the limits of his powers? You decide. Either way, the chancellor has brought us an apt image for those waves of Chinese steel dumping that even he's been powerless to stop.

Except it's not as apt as it seems. Mr Osborne did have powers to at least defend Port Talbot against the tide. It's just that he chose not to use them. First, he rejected big industry's pleas to bring UK energy costs into line with Europe's and to stop penalising them for investing in plant and machinery with higher business rates. And second, Mr Osborne blocked the lifting of the EU's so-called "lesser duty rule", so stopping Europe slap higher tariffs on Chinese steel imports.

Or that, at least, is the allegation doing the rounds now that the European Steel Association has called Britain the "ringleader" in blocking a change to the rules. Why would the UK do that? Well, maybe for one principled reason: that trade wars usually don't work and bring unintended consequences. Jack up tariffs on Chinese steel imports into Europe, so helping Port Talbot-owner Tata Steel, and before you know it there are tit-for-tat tariffs on UK car exports to China, so punishing Tata's other key British business, Jaguar Land Rover.

Yet maybe there is another reason more damaging to Mr Osborne. That he didn't want Europe to do anything to frustrate his love affair with China, especially when he wants it to fund the insane Hinkley Point C nuclear project. Who can forget how Mr Osborne's trip to Beijing went down in the local press last September when the state-owned *Global Times* held him up as a model of "diplomatic etiquette" because he did not "confront China by raising the human rights issue" (or steel dumping, for that matter)? Or how, to a room of UK business leaders in Davos in January, Mr Osborne baldly stated: "We want to be China's best partner in the West"?

One consequence, perhaps, is that 40,000 UK workers now have their jobs on the line. When it comes to standing up to China, there must be a better role model than King Canute.

CHAD'S GENTLE GIANTS
ARE CHARGING BACK

Jerome Starkey

APRIL 2 2016

THE PARK DIRECTOR stepped off his verandah and strode across the sunbaked scrub towards a group of six bull elephants basking by a muddy pool yards from his house. "Come, you lazy thing. Come and drink some water," Rian Labuschagne told one, a 10ft-tall giant with only one tusk. "Kom!" he called again, in his native Afrikaans, and the elephant obeyed, ambling over to where Mr Labuschagne stood. "You going to have some water?" he asked again. There was nowhere to hide if it charged, but the director appeared unconcerned. "This one, I know him. He's not aggressive," he said, as he turned and walked back to the house.

The elephant followed, a few steps behind, until it was close enough to flop his trunk onto the verandah, where Mr Labuschagne provided him with water from a hosepipe. "An elephant is just so incredibly intelligent. They communicate, they understand and they definitely have a feeling for what is secure and what is not," he said. If elephants never forget, their behaviour here in the Zakouma National Park in Chad suggests they can at least forgive. Men, usually heavily armed guerrillas or nomadic Arab horsemen, have slaughtered 90 per cent of the park's elephants in a series of massacres that peaked between 2005 and 2009.

From a herd of 4,350 in 2002, there were no more than 443 left in 2014. "I wonder why they accept us so easily," Mr Labuschagne said. One of the worst incidents occurred in 2008, when 64 carcasses were found scattered on a patch of savannah about the size of a football pitch. The poachers had used a belt-fed machine gun wedged in a tree to shoot indiscriminately into a large herd. They took only half the tusks and abandoned the ones they could not carry. Two days later, closer to the park's southern boundary, they shot another 32 elephants. Largely unnoticed by the rest of the world, Zakouma has endured some of the bloodiest incidents in the slaughter of Africa's elephants, according to Darren Potgieter, the park's head of field operations. "Zakouma was really where the poaching crisis started," he said.

The park's 1,200 square miles of seasonal rivers and rust-coloured acacia thickets make unlikely killing fields, but this dry-season refuge, on the edge of the Sahara, has attracted elephants and their human predators for centuries. Yet today it is one of the few places where the tide is turning in the elephants' favour. For the first time in a decade, Zakouma's herd is showing signs of a recovery. When Mr Potgieter, 35, conducted an aerial survey last month he recorded 483 elephants, including 81 calves under three years old, making it one of the largest herds, perhaps the largest, in Africa. "It was an 8 per cent increase," he told colleagues.

"This is the best news we have had about Zakouma's elephants. The population is actually in a recovery stage." The staff were especially pleased about the number of calves, because the herd had stopped breeding when the poaching was at its worst. Calves that were not shot were often trampled in stampedes. The injured, lost or orphaned, were eaten by lions. "When we first got here there were no baby elephants," said Lorna Labuschagne, Zakouma's head of special projects. She moved to the reserve with her husband in 2011 after African Parks, a South African non-profit group, won a mandate to run it for the Chad government. It was two years before she saw a newborn elephant.

"Everybody six years ago thought this population was doomed," she added. "But it is encouraging that it is possible to turn the tide." African Parks made a number of changes. Instead of closing the reserve when it floods in the wet season, it has put anti-poaching teams on horseback to reach otherwise inaccessible areas. Rangers use satellite collars to track the elephants, and never stray far from the herds. A plane patrols the park most days. African Parks has built a school, and put airstrips in neighbouring settlements where it pays radio operators to inform on poachers. It also built a simple, grass-hut tourist camp, which is free for Chadian guests, and supplies lorries to ferry in more than 2,400 visitors a year from surrounding towns and villages. The operation costs £1.4 million a year.

"There are a few things that were a huge advantage to us," Mr Labuschagne said. "The poachers shot the elephants down to such a low number it became very difficult for them to get to the elephants, and much easier for us to protect them." In China, the world's biggest ivory market, prices for tusks have dropped from £1,500 a kilogram in 2014, to £750 last year. Vendors in Beijing said a government crackdown on corruption had cooled demand, and the economy as a whole had slowed.

Poaching has not stopped, however. Six guards were murdered in 2012, and two elephants were killed in August last year. In October, four poachers shot a bull, and in January two men on horseback killed four elephants in a single raid. One of the females fell on her calf, which brought the toll to five. Rangers did, at least, hear the sound of the poachers' guns in each of those cases and were able to get to the scene in time to prevent them hacking out and carrying off the tusks.

"We're never going to stop everything," Mr Labuschagne said. "But we can stop the poachers being successful. We can stop them shooting an elephant and getting rich, and that should stop an influx of more poachers." He believes that intensive management of this kind is the elephants' only possible future. "There's always going to be elephants," he said. "But only in pockets where they are really protected."

BRITAIN'S TO BLAME FOR THE TAX HAVEN MONSTER

Ed Conway

APRIL 8 2016

MY INTRODUCTION TO tax havens came in a grotty tavern somewhere on the Caribbean coast of central America. Slouched at the bar was an American bragging that he had a yacht moored in the marina. Given that we were in a dingy town in a developing country, I scoffed. Half an hour later I found myself on a small dinghy heading out with him into the bay. We turned into a cove and I saw what could only be described as a mega-yacht.

Why had he sailed his boat to this benighted place, I asked. Wouldn't he have been better off mooring it off the Cote d'Azur or St Lucia? "No," he replied. "This is where we come to park our money." We were in Panama.

This was a decade and a half ago and I failed to ask whether the man was stashing his money legally or unlawfully, but these days it seems the distinction hardly matters. Whoever you are, if you're leaving your cash overseas we must assume, to judge from the outcry after the Mossack Fonseca scandal, that you're probably up to no good. But the prurient coverage of the leaks has mostly missed the point.

There is nothing new about dodgy dictators and plutocrats avoiding or evading tax — however titillating the details. The real question is how tax avoidance became such an entrenched part of modern economics. For the answer you need to look not at Panama but far closer to home. For while the Swiss have had their secret bank accounts since before the modern era of finance, the country that has done tax havens with most gusto is the United Kingdom.

The story starts with George Bolton, a Bank of England official who, 70 years ago, was sent out to New Hampshire with John Maynard Keynes to rebuild the postwar world economy. The system devised at Bretton Woods involved fixed exchange rates and controls on movement of capital between countries. This was a disaster for the City, and by extension the Bank, since financiers benefited from free flows of money, but far better news for the wider economy. In the following years economic growth was strong and stable, but gradually the bankers prised open cracks in the system of capital controls.

The biggest crack of all was chipped open by Bolton who, having left the Bank, pushed in the 1960s for the creation of a new international financial market, free from those restrictions. Gradually, informally, the eurodollar market came into being: commercial banks could trade in London in a foreign currency (mostly dollars) without being subject to British regulations. Transactions could be classified as "offshore" without leaving the City. It marked the beginning of the modern City of London and the beginning of the end for Bretton Woods, whose capital controls soon became ineffective, rendering the rest of the system vulnerable to its eventual collapse in the early 1970s.

London had another competitive advantage: a network of overseas territories from Gibraltar and Bermuda to the Cayman Islands and British Virgin Islands, which were British enough to have strong links with the homeland but independent enough to have their own permissive tax regimes. Today's City would be much diminished without them. On its own the UK accounts for 16.5 per cent of international financial assets, compared with 11 per cent in the US. But add the overseas territories and Britain's share rises to 22.6 per cent.

We're not only talking about rich folks' money, but the very foundations of the international financial system. These days most big international companies, not just Google and Starbucks, sit atop a complex pyramid of financial structures designed to reduce tax bills and circumvent regulations. Some 55 per cent of US companies' international profits are booked in tax havens, compared with about 15 per cent in the early 1980s, according to economist Gabriel Zucman.

In other words, tax havens are a symptom of a far deeper issue, a global financial system that encourages those who can afford it to shift money overseas. Given the incentives built into the international tax infrastructure, the question is not why big companies take advantage of financial engineering, but why wouldn't they? Given that this business is Britain's most lucrative, is it any surprise that David Cameron and his Labour predecessors have quietly sought to defend it?

None of this is inevitable. The most interesting nugget to emerge from the Panama papers was that even before the leaks Mossack Fonseca was in decline. In 2005 the firm was setting up 12,287 shell companies for customers to hide money in. By last year it was creating 4,341 and deactivating 8,864. In the face of a public backlash, the tectonic plates are shifting.

Today it is far easier for investigators to discover whether corrupt Fifa officials or Brazilian politicians are hiding money in Swiss accounts. This week US pharmaceutical giant Pfizer cancelled its $160 billion merger with Allergan amid outrage that the deal largely hinged on plans to relocate Pfizer's tax bill outside the US — so-called tax inversion.

Tax havens evolved almost by accident as a result of the gradual deregulation of financial flows from the 1960s onwards. They thrive because the international tax system still works on the basis of principles established by the League of Nations in the 1920s, leaving plenty of loopholes to crawl through. This is, in other words, not about Panama, yachts or even tax dodging. It comes back to the very shape of the global financial system. Time we started thinking how to overhaul it. And time Britain contemplated why it allowed London to become the capital of this sordid merry-go-round.

HOW I JOINED THE WAG CLUB

Lucy Bannerman

April 9 2016

The faux lesbianism begins just before 11pm. Two girls at the bar pout for sapphic selfies, kissing and fawning over each other with formidable fembot efficiency, keeping one eye to the camera while clutching fistfuls of immaculately glossy hair. Then, they spend the next few minutes in silence, editing and uploading the photos on their iPhones for instant titillation on social media.

The hashtag might as well be #AttentionAllFootballers — for we are in Libertine, the Mayfair nightclub that has risen from the trashy ashes of the original Chinawhite, the legendary WAG factory of its day, to return, revamped and rebooted, as the venue of choice for partying stars of the Premier League and the women who want to date them. It is, as its own blurb declares, "a decadent amphitheatre where the misfits and rule-breakers come to party".

Such is the club's pulling power on the Premier League that Arsenal and Spurs put aside their rivalry to have their Christmas parties here last year — on the same night. It's the sort of place where Rihanna drops in with a hip-hop star during Fashion Week, and Lewis Hamilton hangs out with 20-year-old supermodels related to Kim Kardashian.

But most weeks, it's where girls compete to meet footballers, and the footballers take their pick of a new generation of lip-plumped, Instagram-addicted millennials, who were probably still in primary school when the old guard of WAGs made the 2006 World Cup their own. To this lot, Baden-Baden probably sounds like a rapper. It certainly makes for interesting people-watching on an otherwise average Wednesday night.

I'd heard mixed reports about getting in. Anyone can do it in theory by arranging a place on the guest list with promoters who are easily found online. Mine calls beforehand to check my lie that I'm bringing guests — "All girls?" he asks. I soon discover that gaining entry proves much, much easier than trying to do something as passé as being female and buying your own drink. Passport (a requirement) scanned, wrist stamped, I'm guided into the upstairs bar, more like a holding pen for early arrivals, where a barman is standing at a fully stocked bar, underneath a red neon sign that says, "What's your poison?" I ask for a gin and tonic, like the 36-year-old rogue imposter that I am. Sorry, he says, no can do.

"We have only sushi. And free wine." But I don't want sushi. Or the house vinegar. Doesn't matter. Someone hands me a black plastic goblet of the plonk that's circulating around the room, and I watch the bar fill up with young women: some fellow first-timers, lots of international students, and more and more girls with glossy manes and tiny handbags who are invariably the first to start kissing each other. The only men seem to be staff or promoters.

At 11pm, when the club officially opens, we are escorted downstairs by men in braces to our allocated tables, past the burly security guards who are blocking off the empty bar. By this time, I'm really needing a drink — so try, and fail, once again to order my own. The young French guy looking after our table seems bewildered by this withered old hag who can't seem to understand the concept of free booze.

"You like ze vodka," he says. It's not a question. Eventually, giant fluorescent bottles of Belvedere vodka are delivered to the ice buckets on each table. The male promoters do the pouring; the girls drink what they are given. Just out of interest, I ask, can women go to the bar at all? I'm beginning to freak him out. "Eet's not necessary."

Help, I beg a pneumatic girl in a bodycon dress in the toilets. Tell me the rules. "The guy comes and fills you up. You drink whatever's going." What are you drinking? "I don't even know," she giggles. She invites me to join her table, where I surrender control of my glass and realise I'm the only one who is getting uptight about not being able to see how much is being free-poured, or who is doing the pouring. Then, we dance around an empty vodka bottle, dead-eyed and vacant, for a few excruciating minutes, awaiting replenishment.

"Where are all the men? I was told there would be a million to choose from!" says a lively Kardashian klone from Las Vegas. "The ratio is about 5:2 right now, am I right? If they don't come by 1am, I'm going to Cirque." Maybe that's why they're all snogging each other — necessity. She need not panic. The party's getting started. Someone's just ordered champagne, so the music changes, and staff parade through the dancefloor, holding aloft flaming jeroboams of Dom Pérignon to their table. It's West End code for, "Woohoo! The big spenders are here."

Bodycon Girl casts a gimlet eye over her shoulder to check out the competition. A guy walks past in a baseball cap, and there is a brief frisson of excitement — but it's only Calum Best. I totter around aimlessly on my gold heels, trying not to look like somebody's mum, until a man with a plastic wire coiled behind his ear taps me on the arm and nods to a bouncer, who stands aside to allow me into the mezzanine area. I've just been promoted!

This is the first, and most lowly, of the VIP areas. (There are back rooms way beyond my reach.) Up here, the drink is flowing much more freely, and I'm now standing next to short men watching hot girls twerk, while dancers on podiums in flashing corsets heroically disguise their boredom. I've run out of anything to say, so all I can offer the gorgeous brunette, who's dancing magnificently bralessly in a cutaway vest on the same table is, "Great sideboob." Thankfully, she laughs and we start chatting.

She's not here for the footballers, she says. "I once partied all night with the whole Manchester City team and didn't know who they were till after." I don't get the chance to say, we've all been there, love, because she and her friend are tapped on the shoulder again, and whisked away to yet another table, which I can only assume is the Libertine lady equivalent of the Champions League. It's at this moment, trying to look aloof and mysterious and not at all on my own at a nightclub at 1.30am, I realise I wouldn't recognise any players if I tried, so I ask the guy next to me, dead casual, "Erm, many footballers out tonight?" My chat really is stellar.

He laughs. "You're talking to one." Oh. He googles himself to prove he has played in the Premier League, and it would appear that he — or his twin — did indeed play for ... Watford. Still. His friend confirms this dazzling news. More vodka materialises, along with a test tube rack of shots, but he's not drinking much — he's got training tomorrow. I suggest he doesn't look like he's particularly enjoying himself. He's not, he says.

"This place is ... what's the word?" Mercenary? "Pretentious!" he says. "That's it." But it must be great having all these women throwing themselves at you? He sighs, looking across the dancefloor at the podium dancers in their thongs and yet another parade of flaming bottles, celebrating more champagne drinkers, like they're kids at a birthday party. (As the night wears on, it gets more and more like a fratboy Garfunkel's.) "It's boring," he says. "I won't lie. It was great fun when I was 16, 18. I was out all the time. But when you've been doing it for years ..." He shrugs. Meh. He's in his early twenties. He gestures to the girls circling his table to prove his point. "I only actually know two of them. We have a nickname for the rest." Pray tell. "Table whores. They just hang around for the drinks."

We look down at my freshly replenished glass, which has just appeared from nowhere. I will leave this club having paid nothing. "Not you though." He says, rather sweetly, he doesn't think I'm a whore. "Wanna come to an after-party?" So, what did I learn after my night on the town with the wannabe WAGs? Mainly that, provided your clothes are tight and your heels are high, a night out at an "exclusive" Mayfair club can be cheaper than a pint and a packet of peanuts at a Wetherspoons.

Generally, the unwritten rules of the West End nightclub scene work like this: a network of club promoters are paid — around £10-£20 per girl — to bring in a critical mass of female flesh to the dancefloor. Though the majority will be drinking for free, often from promotional stock provided by drinks companies keen to have high brand visibility in such celebrity haunts, the clubs are gambling that the "pretty but poor" crowd will bring in enough high-rollers to subsidise the rest of the party. Women should outnumber men: "No one wants a sausage party," as one promoter puts it. The door host will be keeping a tab of how many people each promoter brings to the guest list (and, crucially, the calibre) and promoters will be rewarded accordingly. Those who bring in the big spenders will get a cut from the table. It's flaming jeroboams all round.

"It's a crazy world," says a former promoter, who used to be paid £700 for bringing his best-looking friends for a free night out. "It's an alternative reality. You can lose yourself in it, but if you just laugh at it, and enjoy it, it can be fun." There are always some "bad egg" promoters who treat girls like a commodity, he says. "A lot of them are nobodies during the day, who live with their mums. But at night they feel like a king."

Ronnie Joice, 28, was making £1,000 a week for two nights' work as a promoter in the West End, but left the scene in disgust. "We were paid to give these places a rock'n'roll atmosphere, because these posh Chelsea boys don't have a bit of rock'n'roll in their bones, and couldn't create it if they tried. The rich, uncool people can feel cool, the girls drink free — the equilibrium all works out. If you convince yourself that no one is getting hurt, it's all fun." He compares the job to "a concierge service, only a bit dirtier". "If you're not bringing in enough girls, the club will drop you. If they decide half the girls aren't up to scratch, you'll only get half your money."

Joice tells me the men blowing £20,000 on a table often rely on the promoters to find women to join them. "The promoter will be in the club, thinking, who's the most fit, the most up for it. He'll make the introductions. There's almost an unwritten code. The girls are eyeing up the bottles of vodka. Some have boyfriends and won't do anything, but some are looking for a way to never work again. They know the rules as much as the men do."

After six years, he felt burnt out. "False relationships start to replace your real ones. It becomes normal to have one-word conversations. It starts to replace your real life. It's a very murky world, a really horrible, ugly experience and I'm glad I'm out of it." This was Francesca Amber Sawyer's scene for several years when she was in her early twenties. Her advice: keep your eyes on the prize and don't fall in love. Amber, from Canvey Island, Essex, wanted to be a writer, "but I didn't go to university, or study English. Those opportunities weren't there for me."

So she went out five nights a week in the West End to meet footballers, and wrote about that instead, in her book *WAG Don't Wannabe: How to Date Footballers — and Survive!*. She's known millionaire midfielders who were nothing but gentlemen, and love rats who paid off girls to ensure kissing and telling was nowhere near as lucrative as kissing and keeping quiet. (Confiding in a tabloid might buy five minutes of fame, but silence buys a BMW.) Now 30, she's married with a baby on the way and a spray tan salon, Never Too Tanned, and lash extension service, Never Too Lashed, to her name. "It was fun and a great experience, but I'd say to girls now, if you're going to do it, make it work to your advantage," she says.

"If you want to become a photographer, use those contacts to become a photographer. Do something to make those contacts worthwhile — because if you use your twenties being a slag, you're going to look back with regret." She began an affair with a well-known Premier League footballer, whom she met at a nightclub in Kensington. They'd meet three times a week at her friend's flat, while he'd pay a guy £300 to keep an eye on the Bentley parked illegally outside, and hook up again at the nightclubs and hotel after-parties. "If it's the night before a game, they are kept in these hotels together, so they don't have sex with their partners. But it was counterproductive. All that would happen is that they'd invite all these girls back to their hotels instead.

"There were loads of orgies. Loads," she says, recalling one at a penthouse in Mayfair, involving around 10 to 15 people. "It was like some ancient Roman orgy. My friend and I left — it was just gross." When the affair came to an end a year later, she claims she was driven to the office of a top sports lawyer, and coerced into signing statements denying she'd ever known said footballer. She signed.

"I was scared. I didn't know what I was getting into. To the [football] clubs, the lawyers, the agents, that person is worth £10 million. They're going to throw everything they've got at protecting their asset. How can you compete? They have got money and money is power. As a young girl, there's no way, you're going to win against that. You are worth nothing to them. No one is looking after you and that can be terrifying."

She refused his offers to buy her an apartment, because she wanted to prove she loved him. "What a fool. I should have just taken the money and run." Did she ever? Only once, she laughs. "£7,000." In cash. It was "an apology" for that day at the lawyer's, apparently. The money was left at her office, in an envelope, at reception. "Well, I didn't want it going to the security guard …" She believes she did better out of the WAG party scene than her ex. "He went off the rails. He was getting thrown out of nightclubs, wetting himself in the street outside Chinawhite." When they bumped into each other in a nightclub years later, she told him she hated him. "He said, 'I hate me, too.'"

"For many of these guys, it all happens so suddenly," she says. "When you have that many women after you, it doesn't matter who you are, you're probably going to become a bit of a bell-end. You become a product of your environment. If you're in that culture, it takes a very strong character not to get sucked in."

Australian journalist Anna Krien grappled with the tricky issues of feminism, sport and fandom in her award-winning book, *Night Games: a Journey to the Dark Side of Sport*, which examines the macho culture of Aussie rules football through the courtroom drama of a rape trial. She says she is still "tussling" with the big questions raised by the subculture of sexual entitlement within male team sports: "Are groupies complicit in promoting a rape culture? Should they even be part of the same conversation?"

Some cases, she says, such as that of Adam Johnson, the former Sunderland player who was recently jailed for six years for grooming and sexual activity with a 15-year-old fan, are so clearly wrong, "so clearly exploitative", they're easy to categorise — you simply file them under "criminal".

What she finds much more difficult to explain is the grey area of consenting (adult) groupies. And by groupie, she is keen to stress, she means both genders — "from the lawyers who keep them out of court, police who cover up their misdeeds, club officials who just say, 'Boys will be boys,' to star-struck journalists who write more like fans than reporters".

I tell her about my night out in the West End. Aren't we being prudish to criticise the cattle markets? If it's all fun and legal, what's the problem? Her conversations with players led Krien to believe the easy availability of sex had a corrosive effect on the men, too. "Normal consent filters [are] definitely jeopardised." In other words, when so many say yes, it becomes more problematic when someone says no. "In a way, women had been so dehumanised and the ritual so repetitive that if one female suddenly became an exception to their norm, there'd be serious trouble." On the other hand, she says, there are the women who seek a certain status from the sexual attentions of these men — "a woman in charge of her sexuality, a woman empowered".

"Some of the women I met would say that in a gangbang scenario she was not a victim, but a powerful woman in control. Who was I to say this wasn't so?" This is exactly the kind of woman described by Ariel Levy in her book *Female Chauvinist Pigs*, when she despairs of a "raunch culture" that has given rise to a new generation of girls who now see lap-dancing and lipstick lesbianism as a form of women's liberation. The kind of girl, in short, you might see snogging her friend for a selfie on a Wednesday night in the West End.

It is with all these questions in mind, that I return to Libertine. There's no free entry this time. "£10 for both of you," sniffs the door host, looking my friend and me up and down, while a Swedish teenager in a snakeskin bikini top swans in free of charge. Once again, the place is full of international students. There's a Russian girl studying accountancy, a Polish girl studying economics and applied mathematics. We meet undergraduates from Imperial College, London School of Economics, Royal Holloway ... The attitude of every single one appears to be, we'll drink the free drink, have fun with our friends but more fool them, if they think they're getting any more.

A Swedish promoter, in particular, has been busy. There are Swedish girls everywhere, including a party of college girls, and another Swedish waitress who's training to become an electrician. Our promoter, Jake (not his real name), seats us at our table but this time, the free vodka is on diversion to the Swedish students; we remain thirsty. A student from Azerbaijan explains why she comes here. "Celebrities." And rich men, in general. "They all come to the same Mayfair clubs, so there's a one in six chance you'll meet one of them," she says, confidently.

Don't you feel pimped out by the promoters? "No! They don't care. They don't hit on you," she says. "Just don't kiss Jake — he's short and horrible." (We didn't, and he was.) In the toilets, another girl, a marketing manager from Nottingham — let's call her Megan — knows exactly what's going on. And it doesn't bother her in the slightest.

"Sometimes they charge me £20 to get in, sometimes it's £3 or £5. They make it up on the spot," she laughs, rolling her eyes. Tonight she's naked but for a black lacy bra and miniskirt, showing off her toned, tanned midriff, and therefore paid nothing. "I love this music. I come here to dance. It's just an advantage I have a vagina," she says, pulling a can from her handbag and spraying a mist of hairspray to keep her diamanté cat ears in place.

Are you on the pull? Looking to hook up with anyone in particular? "No!" she laughs. "I've never gone with anyone from here. The men can look but if they're sleazy I'll tell them to f*** off. It's not acceptable. I'm here to dance. If the club wants women to bring in the men who'll spend 2k on a table, fine. The girls enjoy being here and enjoy drinking at the tables. The men like seeing them. What's the problem? Everyone gets what they want. Everyone wins."

It's even busier than last time. There seem to be conga lines of totty — promoters leading girls from table to table — but perhaps I'm just noticing it more. Over at one of the big-spending tables, a paralytically drunk ginger guy is counting a wad of purple notes, under the torchlight of his friend's iPhone — there are so many £20 notes he needs both hands. About ten minutes later, he disappears behind a red velvet curtain. Apart from catching a glimpse of a dancer with cat's ears, I can't see what's going on, so I ask the bouncer. "It's really, really private," he says with a wink. "It's dangerous."

I spy a promoter leading the Swede in the snakeskin bikini somewhere and shamelessly ask to join them. "You want to go to table one?" he whispers. In for a penny … Sure, I say, really pushing my luck. However, once we arrive at the table, where an older man in a polo neck and blazer is drinking with his friends, the Swedes slip through, but another promoter's arm blocks my way. His smile says nice try. "Table one is full tonight," he whispers in my ear, stroking my elbow. It's confirmed. In the Libertine league of female attractiveness, I'm the Barnet of tits and arse.

By now, the revolting ginger guy is back. I make the mistake of trying to talk to him. He can barely speak, see or stand. "I want you on top of me," he slurs. Then he taps his sweaty thighs as if to say, "Hop on." Tempted though I am by the chivalrous offer, he gropes another girl and places her hand on his groin. My loss. (It's so busy, I'm stuck beside him on the back seat. It takes three noes for him to release his grip of my ankle.)

"Oh, you'll get a lot of groping here," another girl shouts over the music. She's a sweet sociology student on a birthday night out, with a boyfriend at home. "The men are so sleazy!" she yells. "And dirty. First time we came here we kept getting asked to go to after-parties." The promoters were asking on behalf of the big tables. Where were they asking you to go? "The Dorchester. Four Seasons." So why do you keep coming here? Simple, she says. "It's the best club in London. The best music, the best party."

She's not going to let the ginger menace kill the buzz. At 2.30am, my friend and I have had enough. On our way out, we pass the Nottingham girl with the advantageous vagina, who's locked in an embrace with a promoter. You've pulled, I say. "No, he's just a promoter," she shouts. "Absolutely not a pull," as he feels her breasts. I'm defeated. I want home. "Get home safe," she waves.

My friend can't get in the taxi quick enough, kicking off the high heels that have been killing her. She says, "Now I know what hell looks like."

THE POT-BELLIED FANATIC WHO RADICALISED A BOMBING CELL

David Charter, Bruno Waterfield, Adam Sage

APRIL 16 2016

AT FIRST, INVESTIGATORS could not understand the appeal of the mysterious unkempt man holding suspicious meetings with a group of young friends on the fringes of the Brussels criminal underworld. Khalid Zerkani was a bizarre combination of Islamist fanatic — his forehead scarred from obsessive prayer — and profane criminal. He was pot-bellied, had plenty of money but no discernible job, and was overheard talking of the need for armed attacks against the "principal adversary of Islam".

The alarm was raised in April 2012. That was the date of a secret memo to the state security office, obtained by a Belgian newspaper, reporting concerns about gatherings in the Rue de Ribaucourt, the main road through Molenbeek, an inner city area of Brussels known for high unemployment and low hopes. The meetings took place at the home of Gelel Attar, a man now under arrest in Morocco for links to the Paris attacks, and were attended by his friend Chakib Akrouh, one of the Paris attackers. Zerkani gained increasing influence over their close-knit circle of Molenbeek "brothers" including Abdelhamid Abaaoud, a charismatic drug addict who would become the logistical ringleader of the Paris assailants.

Abaaoud recruited Mohamed Abrini (now known as "the man in the hat" from the Brussels airport attack) and the Abdeslam brothers, Salah and Brahim. Ahmed Dahmani (arrested in Turkey in November over links to the Paris attacks) and Bilal Hadfi (later a Paris suicide bomber) also came from the same streets.

Belgian security services began to monitor Zerkani, although he was not arrested for two years, partly because he was hard to track. He never owned a mobile phone and in telephone conversations he spoke in code and often used street slang. This left him free to propel the young friends along a path to mass murder in the name of Islamic State. Akrouh, Brahim Abdeslam and Abaaoud teamed up to carry out the attacks on bars and restaurants in Paris, while Hadfi blew himself up at the Stade de France.

Numerous others came under Zerkani's malign influence. These included Khalid and Ibrahim el-Bakraoui from the northern Brussels suburb of Laken, and Najim Laachraoui, from the more prosperous district of Schaerbeek. All three died in the Brussels attacks. Prosecutors estimated that Zerkani encouraged at least 18 people to fight in Syria before he was arrested in February 2014 on charges of recruiting for a terrorist organisation. Pieter Van Ostaeyen, an expert on Belgian jihadism, puts the figure at 59. Zerkani did not make the journey to Syria himself.

"Mr Zerkani has perverted a whole generation, particularly the youth of Molenbeek," said Bernard Michel, the prosecutor, in February during an appeal over Zerkani's jail sentence, which has been increased to 15 years. Like a latterday Fagin, the Moroccan-born zealot used gifts of stolen camcorders or iPods to lure recruits into his gang of petty criminals, earning himself the nickname Papa Noël Salafiste [Salafi Father Christmas] or Santa Jihad. He soon turned the second or third-generation Moroccan Belgians into "gangster jihadists", encouraging their criminality as part of his struggle against western values.

Funds raised from break-ins and pickpocketing at the Gare du Midi, the Eurostar terminal in Brussels, helped to send recruits, including Abaaoud, Attar, Akrouh and Laachraoui, to fight in Syria. Witnesses told prosecutors that he would incite teenagers to rob, telling them "they had to steal from the disbelievers as it was accepted by Allah" as ghanima, the legitimate spoils of war against unbelievers, *Le Soir* newspaper reported. Mohamed Karim Haddad, whose brother was recruited by Zerkani, described him as "a charlatan who manipulates young men or socially awkward men, for the wrong cause and probably for his own business".

Scruffy, with dirty hair and a penchant for tracksuits, Zerkani's charisma baffled the authorities and most of the Moroccan community. Prison psychiatrists described him as foul-mouthed, provocative and vindictive. His bigotry was notorious — once when he was arrested, he refused to touch anything "that was handled by a kafir", or non-Muslim. He shunned public attention, unlike his press hungry and better known fellow founder of Sharia4Belgium, Fouad Belkacem, who was jailed for recruiting jihadists in Antwerp.

Zerkani's star recruit, Abdelhamid Abaaoud, epitomised the gangster jihadist. He had been in and out of prison for petty crime, serving a sentence in 2010 with Salah Abdeslam for breaking into a garage. A year after going to fight in Syria in 2013, Abaaoud recruited his 13-year-old brother Younes and persuaded him to join him fighting with Isis. Photos of a heavily armed Younes were used as propaganda by Isis in 2014. Their father, Omar, a greengrocer, accused Abaaoud of kidnapping him. Abaaoud was filmed by Isis driving a pick-up truck, dragging the bodies of Syrian adversaries behind it.

Early last year, with Zerkani behind bars, Abaaoud had a new mission — to follow the Charlie Hebdo attacks with another "spectacular", for which he was to be recruiter and organiser. Security services believe that he was a matter of hours away from fulfilling that mission when Belgian police broke up a cell he had organised by raiding an apartment in Verviers on January 16, killing two of the gang. The dead men, Redouane Hagaoui, 22, and Tarik Jadaoun, 24, were both from Molenbeek.

Police were now on to Abaaoud. At the conclusion of Zerkani's trial process in July last year, Abaaoud was sentenced in absentia to 20 years in jail for being part of a terrorist network along with a Frenchman from Zerkani's circle called Reda Kriket. Akrouh and Attar were each given five-year terms in their absence. Before the Paris attacks last November, when Yasmina, Abaaoud's older sister, received a false report from Syria that he had been killed fighting for Islamic State, she rejoiced. "We are praying that Abdelhamid really is dead," she said. This was a smokescreen put out by Islamic State.

In its propaganda material, Abaaoud boasted how easily he could slip between Syria and Europe and claimed that more than 90 Isis fighters had used the migrant crisis to enter Europe. One was Najim Laachraoui, the eldest of five, who was born in Morocco but grew up in Brussels and fell into the orbit of Zerkani in 2013. Laachraoui had studied engineering and electromechanics but dropped out of university when he became radicalised. He broke off contact with his family and in 2013 travelled to Syria, where he got to know Abaaoud. Together they helped to prepare the Paris attacks.

Abaaoud was the organiser of the shootings, while Laachraoui was the bomb maker. DNA material found on suicide bombs in both the Bataclan concert hall and the Stade de France was found to come from Laachraoui. After Zerkani's conviction, Laachraoui was a wanted man under an international arrest warrant issued by Belgian prosecutors. Like Abaaoud, he managed to avoid capture by travelling to and from Syria, with the help of Zerkani's network, on the migrant route.

Laachraoui was picked up last September from Budapest by Salah Abdeslam and another man called Mohammed Belkaid, an Algerian jihadist. Travelling under the false Belgian identity of Soufiane Kayal, Laachraoui was able to avoid arrest at a routine border roadblock. Once in Brussels Laachraoui and Belkaid assumed immediate control of the plan to attack Paris, and were in touch with Abaaoud, who was there.

Laachraoui turned an apartment on Rue Henri Bergé in Schaerbeek into a bomb factory, manufacturing triacetone triperoxide (TATP), the explosive used in the Paris attacks, as well as suicide belts for the attackers. A second Laachraoui bomb factory was found 1,500m away from the first, on Rue Max Roos, also in Schaerbeek. The text message sent at 9.42pm from the Samsung phone found later in a bin outside the Bataclan theatre, which said "We're off, we're beginning" was sent to Laachraoui and Belkaid in Brussels. Abaaoud was called later that evening from a Brussels phone emitting a signal from the same area, either by Laachraoui or Belkaid.

In the attacks that killed 130 people in Paris, Brahim Abdeslam blew himself up in a café on the Boulevard Voltaire, but his fellow members of the Zerkani network, Abaaoud and Akrouh, had nowhere to go. Police were unsure whether they intended to die that night or simply did not think about the aftermath. They hid in bushes in Aubervilliers by the A86 motorway in what police called a "vegetable igloo", made with sticks and leaves, probably by tramps. Laachraoui and Belkaid turned to a cousin of Abaaoud to help him out. She was Hasna Ait Boulahcen, who grew up in Clichy-la-Garenne, a suburb close to Saint-Denis, and had a crush on Abaaoud and had told friends that they were due to marry.

At 15, she had run away from her foster family and spent the next decade without a stable base, sometimes with her father, sometimes her mother, sometimes friends from the Paris region. She took drugs, liked vodka and hung out with dealers. One of these friends was "Sonia" — not her real name. All that is known about Sonia is that she is about 40, lives in the Paris region, and that between 2011 and 2015 Boulahcen would turn up to "crash out on her sofa" when she had nowhere to go.

Boulahcen was staying with Sonia when the call came through to help Abaaoud and Akrouh. She took Sonia with her to meet the men. Abaaoud gave Boulahcen €5,000 (£4,000) to find an apartment to hide in, which she secured in Saint-Denis. As police closed in on the apartment on November 18 in a blaze of gunfire, Akrouh detonated a suicide belt which brought much of the building down and Boulahcen died alongside him and Abaaoud. François Molins, the Paris prosecutor, said that a key witness had led them to the hideout. This is now known to be Sonia, the friend who was revolted by Abaaoud and the Paris attacks.

Other members of the Zerkani network were nearing the end, but not before one more "spectacular". After the attacks in Paris, Laachraoui did not maintain close links with Belkaid, who was killed by a police sniper in a raid on an apartment in the Forest district of Brussels on March 15. This was the raid that led to arrest of Salah Abdeslam, which disrupted plans for a second gun and bomb attack on Paris but hastened last month's attack on Brussels. In the security camera picture of the three airport bombers, Laachraoui is on the left. Alongside him was Ibrahim el-Bakraoui and then Mohamed Abrini, the man in the hat.

Shortly after the Brussels atrocities, Reda Kriket, another of the old Zerkani network, was arrested near Paris on suspicion of planning yet another attack. His apartment contained rifles, handguns and TATP.

A few years earlier, the path of these men to jihad began when they shared Khalid Zerkani's coffee and crazed convictions in the back rooms of Molenbeek. Zerkani would hand out gifts while promising that none of their transgressions was shameful but in fact part of their great fight against a western value system he despised. "I am a pacifist!" Zerkani shouted at his trial. "I refuse to be called a jihadist. I am not Satan. I do not decide what others do," he told the judges. An unknown number of those who fell under his spell remain at large.

TSAR VLADIMIR IS PLOTTING
AN ARCTIC COLD WAR

Roger Boyes

APRIL 20 2016

RUSSIA HAS HAD GOOD tsars and bad tsars and has contrived to love them equally. Vladimir Putin, not much bothered about love (he has his labrador), would still rather go down as a Peter the Great than an Ivan the Terrible and you can see his point: Tsar Pete wanted to use the Russian north as a springboard to global influence and to build up Russia as a maritime power. Other plus points: he hated the Ottomans, crushed opponents, had an early adviser chucked into a nunnery. For Putin, Peter must seem like the very model of a modernising megalomaniac.

The salient fact about Vladimir Putin is that he will almost certainly seek and, barring attack by a Siberian tiger, almost certainly win re-election in 2018. If he serves out that term he will have been at the helm of Russia for a quarter of a century; the narrow-chested Soviet teenager who hung out in the tenements of what would again become St Petersburg, will then have ruled for almost as long as his favourite tsar.

That final presidential stint is likely to be dominated by a single commanding idea: the assertion of Russian power in the Arctic, an endeavour worthy of Peter. The melting of the Arctic ice could change the fortunes of Russia. Some 30 per cent of the world's undiscovered natural gas and 13 per cent of its undiscovered oil is estimated to be in the region. By 2030 the Northern Sea Route, which can only be navigated at the moment with the help of Russia's nuclear-powered ice breakers, could become a profitable alternative to the Suez Canal for transporting goods from Asia to Europe. Travel time would be cut by 40 per cent and Russia, with its long Arctic littoral, would grow wealthy.

This then is Putin's prize, the kind of project that captures his imagination in a way that the bloody Russian interventions in Ukraine and Syria do not. Those were tactical manoeuvres by comparison, attempts to thwart the West and gain temporary advantage. The Arctic, I like to imagine, is what the Kremlin court — the Gazprom and Rosneft bosses, the head of the rail network, the spooks committed to national resurgence — like to shoot the breeze about. That and property prices in Knightsbridge.

Dmitry Rogozin, the deputy premier who watches over the Russian arms industry, says: "We must study the Arctic and colonise it in a positive and civilised way." As civilised perhaps as the airborne troops who are currently training for a parachute drop close to the North Pole. Other military exercises seem to flout the Svalbard treaty which bans military use of the glacial archipelago between Norway and the North Pole.

No one takes very seriously the resumption of strategic talks today between Nato and Russia, the first encounter since 2014. Whatever Nato says, Russia will do what it wants. Moscow is determined to stop any further attempt to enlarge Nato, to undermine those countries that have already done so, and to trample on international law in the process. And it works: the US and Germany are opposing a plan to build a permanent Nato base in Poland for fear that it might upset Putin.

This is short-sighted. Russia attacks Georgia because it does not want a Nato member in the Caucasus. It snatches Crimea because it knows neither Nato nor the EU wants a permanently unstable Ukraine. It almost scrapes the communication mast of a US warship in the Baltic and lets its subs loose in Swedish waters because it wants to demonstrate the Baltic is part of its sphere of interest.

How big, then, is this Russian backyard? The answer, as we are beginning to glimpse in the Arctic, is very big indeed. Russia's military planning for the Arctic stretches from the European Baltic to the Bering Sea bordering Alaska: 3,500miles. Under Putin, Russia has been restoring the Soviet infrastructure from Murmansk in the northwest to Magadan in the east. It has created an Arctic Joint Strategic Command in Severomorsk on the Barents Sea and set up an Arctic brigade. A new fleet of ice-breakers is under construction. The Northern Fleet, boosted by oil revenue when the price was high, now includes 35 submarines and 50 surface warships. The flagship, a nuclear-powered guided missile cruiser, is appropriately called Peter the Great.

The Arctic mission has slowed down because of sanctions and the slump in the oil price. Exploration has become costly and difficult. The militarisation of the Arctic, however, continues apace. Russia's force there will soon be larger than all the other Arctic states — the US, Canada, Norway, Denmark, Finland and Iceland — combined. This force is doing more than securing Russian economic interests and its claims on the continental shelf. From a defrosted north it poses a strategic challenge and cows Nato.

The more China uses the northern sea lanes, the more the Sino-Russian relationship will swing in Moscow's favour. Britain hasn't been counted as an Arctic power since 1907 when Newfoundland became a dominion and we lost Labrador. We should, though, be watching carefully the unfolding of Russian policy. Putin is determined that, far from being made vulnerable by its geography, Russia should become more powerful. Given his taste for brinkmanship, we should be ready for plenty of trouble Up North.

TRUTH, TEARS AND TIME TO ACKNOWLEDGE A TRAGEDY

Patrick Kidd

APRIL 28 2016

THE ATMOSPHERE IN the House of Commons can change in an instant, like flicking a switch. The playground becomes a churchyard, the bearpit replaced by a cloister. One minute MPs are screeching "shame" and "disgrace" across the chamber, the next is a breathless hush.

Theresa May rose in silence to deliver her statement on the Hillsborough inquiry and condemn 27 years of lies and cover-up, smears and pain. "It is this country's worst disaster at a sporting event," the home secretary said.

Watched from the gallery by the former Bishop of Liverpool, the Right Rev James Jones, the vicar's daughter spoke with evident sorrow about the "extraordinary dignity and determination" of the Hillsborough victims' families in pursuing justice. "They never faltered."

As she read in full the jury's determinations, thus placing the verdict on the parliamentary record, I could see Steve Rotheram (Lab, Liverpool Walton), a former bricklayer who had exchanged his Leppings Lane ticket for one in the Hillsborough stand 15 minutes before kick-off, wipe a tear from his eye.

"Thank you from the families," he later told Mrs May. "It took political intervention to force the judicial process of this country to recognise what we knew from day one: that Hillsborough was not an accident; that fans did not open a gate; that drunken and ticketless fans did not turn up late, hell-bent on getting in; and that it was not caused by a drunken, 'tanked-up mob'." Alec Shelbrooke (C, Elmet and Rothwell) made the valid, yet seldom heard, point that, by definition, those who had been crushed at the front of the pens had arrived early with tickets.

"The state said it was their fault," he said. "It was obvious from day one that it could not be." He said that South Yorkshire police now had an indelible stain on its name, and should be abolished through merger with another force.

Andy Burnham, the shadow home secretary, was applauded at the end of a powerful and emotional speech. "It took too long in coming and the struggle for it took too great a toll on too many," he said. Many relatives had died without getting justice. He spoke of the further pain that was caused to the families even in the past two years as lawyers threw "disgusting slurs" around the Warrington courtroom. "They put the families through hell once again," he said. Smearing the dead during the trial was "beyond cruel".

Alex Salmond (SNP, Gordon) added that perjury and perversion of justice were "where the real evil lies".

Many MPs wore black ties or dresses to match the mood, but there were splashes of red all around, like poppies in tribute to Liverpool Football Club. Several wore "justice for the 96" red badges; Mrs May had red nail varnish; Alison McGovern (Lab, Wirral South) wore red lipstick and spoke of the support for Liverpool from the entire football family. Fans were "united in grief", she said.

So, yesterday, was the House of Commons. As Mr Burnham said: "This was not just Liverpool's tragedy but the country's."

THE MAN WHO MISTOOK
HIMSELF FOR A GOAT

Damian Whitworth

MAY 3 2016

WHEN A MAN WALKS into a field full of goats in Kent, the goats do not panic like sheep and bolt. The goats assess the interloper briefly then approach purposefully, using their mouths to explore his coat, his notebook and his pockets. When another man enters the field on all fours, however, wearing strange, springy prosthetics strapped to his legs and firmer, hoof-like attachments on his arms, they don't make friends quite so quickly. They stand perfectly still and stare at this odd quadruped.

Slowly, cautiously, they approach. A few bolder animals close in, then skitter away. Eventually, one is overcome by a need to discover what this intruder might have in his pockets and gently butts his thigh. Another lowers its head against his cycle helmet. The man smiles in delight at this hint that he is being accepted by the herd. His name is Thomas Thwaites and he wants to be a goat.

These are interesting times for those conducting reconnaissance of the wild frontiers of trans-speciesism. There have been reports of a woman in Norway who thinks she's a cat and an American student who claims that he, in that dread phrase, self-identifies as a penguin. For his book *Being a Beast*, published earlier this year, Charles Foster ate worms, slept in a homemade badger sett and encouraged his kids to sniff each other's dung as he tried to experience life as a badger, a fox, an otter, a red deer and a swift.

Thwaites went to even more extraordinary lengths to transform himself into Billy Goat Gruff. Three years ago, when he was aged 32, things weren't going as well as he had hoped in the world of people. A highly educated freelance designer, he had achieved success with *The Toaster Project*, a book about building a toaster from scratch and an accompanying exhibition that was bought by the Victoria and Albert Museum. He feared, however, that he had peaked and was in decline. He lacked a "real" job, effectively lived with his dad and had no means of clambering on to the London property ladder. He and his girlfriend had rowed the night before and that morning he had been turned down for a bank account. His self-esteem was "sunk".

He found himself looking at his niece's dog, Noggin, envying his worry-free existence. He asked himself: "Wouldn't it be nice to be an animal just for a bit?", and decided to take a holiday from being human. The Wellcome Trust's arts awards programme gave him some money to try to become an elephant. He quickly concluded that he would need to build himself an exoskeleton bigger than a family car. There was also worrying evidence that elephants might be aware of their mortality and be prone to sadness, even depression. On a trip to Denmark he visited a shaman who suggested an elephant was too alien an animal for an Englishman and he should focus instead on transforming himself into a goat. He was inspired.

Thwaites was certainly imaginative in his quest to become a goat, but early successes were few. He explored using transcranial magnetic stimulation to inhibit those areas of his brain that are different from a goat's, but was told he should come back in 50 years when the technology might have advanced sufficiently to help. He tried to create an artificial rumen from silicone so that he could digest the cellulose in plant matter. When he ordered some cellulase enzyme, which he hoped to use to break down cellulose into nourishing sugars, the worried supplier contacted the Wellcome Trust. The trust said it was alarmed that he was endangering his safety. It also asked why he was now trying to be a goat and not an elephant. Eventually, it agreed to let him continue as long as he promised not to consume the cellulase.

He had more joy with the prosthetic limbs. Designers created back ankle-foot orthotics that look like Paralympic blades and solid front "legs" to strap to his arms. Thus equipped he set off for a goat farm in the Swiss Alps, sleeping above the herd in the hayloft of a barn. He roamed the pastures on his artificial limbs, wearing a waterproof body suit and a bicycle helmet (he never managed to create horns). Thwaites discovered quickly that walking downhill in his prosthetics was hard. He lets me have a go on his limbs at the Buttercups goat sanctuary in Kent. I find them so painful I have to tear them off after five minutes. "My trouble is that I am a bit of a fantasist," says Thwaites. "When I set out I thought it would be so nice to be able to jump off a ledge. I was hoping to be able to gallop and trot. You think it shouldn't be that difficult. There are videos on YouTube of amazing four-legged robots that are running along, but the reality is your body isn't made of metal and if you fall over, especially if you are on a mountain, it is actually desperately serious."

The original plan was to cross the Alps into Italy. That didn't quite happen. He clattered up on to a glacier along the border but did not descend the other side. "It's all fun until you actually do yourself some damage. I was like: 'Sod this.'" Nevertheless, Thwaites spent a few days with the herd. He grazed by ripping up grass in his mouth, chewing it and spitting it into his artificial "rumen" bag and later putting it in an army surplus pressure cooker to break down the cellulose. The resulting burnt-grass stew was so unappetising he recognised it had potential to be marketed as the Goat Diet.

There was a tricky moment one day when he inadvertently climbed higher on the mountain than all the goats. He realised that they were still and staring at him. It dawned on him that he had unwittingly challenged the dominance hierarchy. Eventually, one of the female goats broke the tension by walking off and the herd carried on grazing. He was thrilled when the farmer said the goats had accepted him.

So if they thought he was a goat, did he? "I think that was probably the closest I came. That was a beautiful moment for me. I never achieved the springiness of being a goat but maybe I achieved a bit of the mental outlook just by being in that environment." Strangely, Thwaites, now 35, hasn't had enough of being a goat. He wants to develop a proper exoskeleton and work out how to feed like a goat. "Imagine if we could genetically engineer ourselves to eat grass. It would solve a lot of problems." He warms to his theme.

"Imagine if I progress this project, devote the next decades of my life to perfecting this way of living — the goat way. You could happily trot and gallop and eat foliage and derive nutrition from it. Would you like to spend a couple of weeks doing that as a holiday somewhere up in Scotland or Ireland? It would be kind of great, wouldn't it?" I try to make encouraging noises. "It just needs a little bit of development," he insists. "I'd need some help." He's thinking of technology companies. He already has pledges of support from individuals, including a goat farmer in the Czech Republic. "I've had lots of emails from people saying 'I would like to join you.' Maybe not lots. I've had a few."

You could start a herd. "A herd!" He starts laughing but likes the idea. And he could lead the herd. He'd like that wouldn't he? "Yes and no. I think if people were going to take it seriously it would be nice to have a herd, but you obviously have to test each other's strength and stuff like that and it would become quite competitive." Surely, he wouldn't let some other human goat barge him out? "Butting and stuff like that would be a part of it and then you would know where you were in the pecking order. I think you wouldn't want to go too far." Well how far do you want to take it? "Probably not to the mating level. I think that would be going too far. If you managed to become a goat so well that you did want to mate with another goat, in one sense that would be a massive success. But again you see my humanness coming through: you would want to step back from that."

The writer Edward Albee wrote a taboo-exploring play *The Goat, or Who Is Sylvia?* about a married man who has sex with a goat, to the outrage of his family and friends. "I have grown up with these exact same taboos so I can't really bring myself to, at the moment, want to have sex with a goat, but you know it does happen," says Thwaites. His girlfriend supported the project. "She's a tolerant person but when I was clomping around the flat she did get a bit cross. I would come up and butt her leg and stuff like that."

I start to ask about those people he meets who don't want to be goats but he cuts in. "Who doesn't? I haven't encountered one person yet." Well, what about me? I had a go at being a goat just now and I have to say it wasn't entirely satisfactory. "But they're brilliant animals!" They are, I admit, very appealing, friendly animals. Why doesn't he just keep some? "Oh, well that would be so nice," he says dreamily. "But I'm in Peckham."

In one way the project has been a triumph. Everyone wants to talk to Goat Man. He has a potential success on his hands which should be good for his self-esteem. "But in another way," he says, "I feel like I would like to gallop away."

'YOU THINK YOU KNOW ME. CHRIS GAYLE. WORLD BOSS. THE SIX MACHINE. KING OF THE PARTY SCENE. YOU'RE WRONG'

Interview by Charlotte Edwardes

MAY 21 2016

I'M HAVING A DRINK with Chris Gayle. Yup, I'm doing what Mel McLaughlin, the Australian sports broadcaster, declined to do when the cricketing superstar and former West Indies captain propositioned her during a live interview in January, and sitting in a spangly bar with the self-styled Six Machine and a mojito. We're in Bangalore, where Gayle, 36, plays for the Royal Challengers in the Indian Premier League, and we're talking about sexism and, "What's that t'ing — womanism?" Is he joking?

Gayle responded to McLaughlin's question about his cricketing form — he'd been playing for the Melbourne Renegades in a Big Bash contest with the Adelaide Strikers — by purring, "I'm here just to see your eyes for the first time ... Hopefully we can win this game and we can have a drink afterwards. Don't blush, baby." Off camera, his teammates can be heard wheezing with laughter. McLaughlin, it's fair to say, seems nonplussed.

The controversy wrapped itself around him like a stripper around a pole. Female journalists called him an "idiot" and a "d***head". Fellow cricketers accused him of "setting a bad example to younger players" and the remark earned him a £4,800 fine from his club (although given his £5.3 million pay packet last year, it was a pretty limp slap on the wrist). But Gayle is his own worst enemy if this evening's interview is anything to go by.

Before two hours are up, he's boasting about having "a very, very big bat, the biggest in the wooooorld", adding, "You think you could lift it? You'd need two hands." He asks how many black men I've "had", goading me when I deflect the question, and whether I've ever had a "t'eesome" — "I bet you have. Tell me." "Do you dye your hair?" he asks at one point. It's highlighted, I reply. "But do you dye your hair?" His eyes flick down. When I rebuke him, he squawks, lifting his shoulders in ham offence: "But it's only fair! Why do you get to ask all the questions?"

Am I letting down the sisterhood by engaging with Gayle, a man who installed a strip club in the basement of his house in Jamaica without telling his girlfriend? A man who, after listening to John Barclay, old Etonian batsman, ex-England manager and former MCC president, hold forth on his sporting record over lunch, was said to have asked, "So, do you get much pussy?" As it turns out, his pantomime bad boy is a bit of a buffer. Later, Gayle will lean forward, his voice changing from laid-back singsong into a deep, rapid-fire rat-a-tat, to tell me that I just don't get it.

"If that had been a white footballer saying that," he says of his comments to McLaughlin, "nothing would've happened. Rugby player, nothing would've happened. Hollywood actor? Tsk." What does he mean? "Successful black men are struggling because people do things to put them down," he says. "They would cover for other people, but not for a black man." Is that true? Would David Beckham have been so roundly criticised? Or Leonardo DiCaprio? Is this an issue as much about racism as sexism?

Here in India, where cricket "is a religion", focus is firmly on his on-field reputation. And that reputation is of a god. With his ginormous bat ("My piece of wood"), he's heroically smashed multiple records and is one of the best — and certainly the most flamboyant — batsmen in the world.

While the fortunes of the West Indies team outside of T20 (20-over) contests have ebbed in the past 15 years, he's one of only four players to have scored two triple centuries in Test matches. In 2012 he became the first (and so far only) batsman to score a six from the first ball of a Test match — a move of characteristic chutzpah: conventional wisdom has it that in a five-day contest, a batsman has the time to adjust to the conditions before taking any big shots.

Last year in Australia, he became the first cricketer in World Cup history to score a double century (against Zimbabwe). And for the Bangalore Challengers he scored a 30-ball century as part of the highest individual score — 175 — in a T20 match. In June he'll play for Somerset in the NatWest T20 Blast. Last year the series was a sellout, largely because of his signing. The county's director of cricket, Matt Maynard, described him as "box office". "I am an entertainer," he says, when I ask about dance moves that accompany his big hits. "I like to entertain."

When I first catch sight of Gayle in person, it's at an evening match in the M Chinnaswamy Stadium. The air is charged with the breathless anticipation of 40,000 spectators. He walks onto the field with his slow, hip-rolling stroll, a cross between a shire horse and a panther. (This is something he inherited from his dad: "Always take your own time, in your own world. Easy-going and nice.")

For the uninitiated, Indian T20 is a long way from the sedate leather on willow and pattering applause of the old-school English game. It's commercial cricket: fast, flash, loud and brash. Sixes and fours spin out of screens like stings from an ITV game show. Scores are accompanied by catchy jingles. Cheerleaders scissor and wind, drums beat dementedly. Most importantly, this is where talented superstars from all over the world earn millions. And Gayle loves it, visibly absorbing the adoration of the crowd. When he hits, screens flash: "INTER-GAYLECTIC".

And the cash flows not just from the steaming crowds of spectators but from big-money endorsements. From advertising hoardings along the exhaust-polluted highways, Gayle's image glowers, along with those of his teammates (South Africa Test captain AB de Villiers, Indian Test captain Virat Kohli), selling everything from sports gear, bikes, casual slacks and — puzzlingly — pimple cream. But even without this notoriety, Gayle is not exactly inconspicuous: a swaggering 6ft 2in black man, broad as the Blue Mountains, is hard to miss in this distinctly Asian city. So his hotel, for all its ritzy glitz, is like "a prison," he jokes, when we meet in the air-conditioned bar. If there is a place in the world where he would not be recognised, "I haven't found it yet."

I'm here because Gayle has written a memoir called — inevitably — *Six Machine* (the man cannot resist a double entendre). In addition to detailing his extraordinary career, he narrates the story of a life "coming up" in cramped poverty amid gang violence in Kingston, Jamaica. His Twitter profile picture has him chilling in full gold and green Jamaican rig against a hazy backdrop of Kingston town. Away from the crease he favours rapper clobber, cigars, fast cars in primary colours, girls twerking in bikinis and diamond studs. He owns a bar in Kingston — the Triple Century — where he drinks Hennessy and Appleton rum with Usain Bolt and Shaggy, and snaps himself for Instagram draped in gold swag.

A strong theme is that he is a man of many sides. "Complex," is how he describes himself. The book opens thus: "You think you know me? You don't know me. Yuh cyaan read me. Yuh cyaan study me. Doh' even try study me. You think you know Chris Gayle. World Boss. The Six Machine. Destroyer of bowlers, demolisher of records, king of the party scene. You're right. You also wrong. I am complicated. I am all you see and much more you don't."

At first sight you'd be forgiven for thinking Gayle has a colossal ego. As well as World Boss, he calls himself Universe Boss, even "da ba'ass of all ba'ass Universe Boss". (British diffidence he admits to finding utterly baffling.) His on-field persona is "this fierce batsman that no one wants to mess with", he says. In the past he engaged in "sledging", the act of intimidating rivals by whispering "a lotta nasty t'ings" in their ears — and "bumping".

This is right but also wrong, he explains, because all cricketers "have that alter ego. They might be absolutely arrogant on the cricket field, and then off the field they are like a baby. They have two sides. One you bring out: the superhuman you bring out in the middle there; the other is the normal person. It's natural to transform into someone else when you play a competitive game," he says. "You're not looking for friends. It's a battle."

What about his mantra that he hates running — "The World Boss don't run." Is that part of the showmanship? "People think that [my] attitude towards the game stink. That's how it come across: lazy. But to score a triple century, that's not lazy. You cannot be lazy and do such things." I ask about his love of "parties with a capital P". Is it true he'll party till dawn and sleep all day (our interview is delayed for an hour and a half, and he finally emerges from his room at 3.30pm after a "lie-in")? "I like to blow off some steam," he says with a shrug.

Initially he tells me he'll take me out partying when he comes to London, but decides I'll be rubbish when I stop at two drinks. "You need a baby-sitter!" But I'm relieved to hear he's human, too. "I will throw up sometimes," he laughs. "I'm not Iron Man. If you're going hard, you gotta suffer the consequence. If you lie down, the room spinning with you, for sure. Then the next day you say, 'I'm not doing it again.' You take a break, then you find yourself doing the same again. You live. That's part of it."

His diet is certainly novel for a world-class athlete: hot chocolate, piles of pancakes and burgers. Surely he can't subsist on junk? "Why not?" he counters. "Usain [Bolt] won a gold medal on chicken nuggets." Later, I'm relieved to see him scarf through a steak and vegetables. He also has a splendidly ungangsterish cappuccino.

So, then, who is the "normal" Gayle, the Gayle we "don't see"? He flips through one of his pile of phones to show me photographs. There's his girlfriend of ten years, Natasha Berridge, whom he met on the neighbouring Caribbean island of St Kitts. He's known her since she was 19 and she's "one of the very few who really knows me". They've recently had a baby whom he cheekily told the world they had named Blush, although he tells me her name is Crisalina.

Berridge, he says, is "a strong character". "Very strong. A lot of people put things in her face and say, 'Chris is this, and Chris is doing that,' all sorts of things. But she's very strong." He adds: "And she got the booty." He shows me a photo from the birth in a hospital in Miami (he wants his daughter to have a US passport). He's wearing his trademark baseball cap with a 333 logo wedged over a do-rag and dip-dyed braids along with a surgical mask. There's Crisalina, with a bow round her head like a gift. "His mother says she has my eyes," he says, smiling broadly.

He asks me if I have kids and — I think out of genuine interest — whether I had a caesarean or a vaginal birth. "It's a nice experience being a father," he continues. "But I only had a short stint there. I'm looking forward to seeing her again." Many of his teammates in India have partners, and I think he's lonely. Last night, he watched English football until the small hours. "They all busy," he says when I ask if they all go out together.

Will he get married? He says he's contemplating it, and asks me what I think. What if she says no? He looks horrified and amused at the same time. "I'll have to accept it. No is no. I can't do anything. I can't force anything down anyone's throat." But, he says, "I've accomplished everything else. If there's one thing left to do, there's that. But it's not a big t'ing in Jamaica." His parents aren't married. "It's a different culture."

Gayle's memoir tells of the cramped conditions of his childhood home in Rollington, a neighbourhood of Kingston, the permanent hunger, belt whippings from teachers (school rules included, "NO hair rollers. NO weapons"), as well as losing his virginity aged 16 to a stripper. "Jamaica is a tough place, it's no secret. You grew up tough. In my childhood days, t'ings were even more outrageous than now. T'ings a bit quiet now, but there are still bad areas, still violence, and we can't hide away from that."

Five children shared a bedroom with two beds: his sister in one, the four brothers taking it in turns on the other. "It was sometimes 40 degrees. No fan. No AC. No electricity when I was little so no TV, no not'ing." The sound of gunshots wasn't uncommon, but his parents (his father was a policeman) shielded the boys from gang culture. "They always sceptical of the company you keep," he says. "They don't want you out late because you can get caught in some gang." Cigarettes, or even marijuana, were never a temptation. "When you go around that's a customary thing: Jamaican sitting on the corner having a smoke. Not only Rasta; general. But I never ever tried it. I swear on my life." And his parents' vigilance — and eyewatering discipline: "Broomstick, mop stick, you misbehave, you getting it" — meant hot afternoons after school were spent at Lucas Cricket Club, the local ground.

Back then he was skinny — "The muscles won't come till later" — and not particularly tough in the wider landscape. Yet he was obsessive: "Batting, batting, batting. I bat long periods as a kid. Bat for days. I'm not like the live-wire person, but I put in the hours." His brothers were naturally gifted at cricket, but he was the one who stuck at it. What he wrestled with was a dark and persistent fear of dying. "As a kid, I don't know why, but I would lie down and think about death. 'Damn, your eyes will close and you're not going to see any more. You're not going to see Mumma or Dada.' And I thought, 'I don't want to die.' And tears would come to my eye."

Since then, and through his life, he has tried to develop ways of dealing with it, mantras such as, "Breathe, let in the light." Yoga, too. Therapy? "I'm not that crazy," he shrieks. "They crazier than us. Therapists need therapy." He said that he overcame his fear "a bit", but when he underwent heart surgery for a congenital heart defect causing cardiac dysrhythmia, he says, "That's when I started to take life not too seriously, tried not to be too tense. I thought, 'I'm only playing cricket. I'm not spending any time really and truly doing things.' So as soon as I get a break, I do those things."

When he retires he wants to be "busy with the family and catching up with life". Will that be soon? After all, the average age for a player to retire is around 38 years, and, at the time of writing, he has scored just 19 runs in 5 matches in the IPL (he missed four games to be at the birth). Virat Kohli dropped him completely from a recent match, prompting one

Indian newspaper to ask, "Is this the beginning of the end for Gayle?" He bats the question for six. "It's not over yet. Not for a while."

About many things, Gayle is open-minded. He wouldn't beat his kids like his parents beat him, for example, but "counsel" them instead. About homophobia — a deep-seated problem in the Jamaica of old — he is thoughtful. "The culture I grew up in, gays were negative," he says. Partly because of his exposure to the rest of the world through cricket, he realised, "People can do whatever they want. You can't tell someone how to live their life. It's a free world." It's odd, then, that he can sound so confused on the subject of women.

"Women should have equality and they do have equality," he argues. "They have more than equality. Women can do what they want. Jamaican women are very vocal. They will let you know what time is it, for sure." And yet he also believes this: "Women should please their man." In what way? "When he comes home, food is on the table. Serious. You ask your husband what he likes and then you make it." What if she's been up all night with a newborn? "No, that OK. Then she doesn't have to. We can stop and buy a meal." What if she's working? "Then they share. First person home, cooks." Would he cook? "No." Clean? "That is not going to happen." He would change a nappy. "I've changed many of my nieces and nephews. I have no problem with that."

He says one huge cultural difference that we totally misunderstand in England (and Australia) is that Jamaicans "are more relaxed about sex. We're not so hung up about it. This is what people like doing. It's no big deal." Right. Does that mean that he's faithful? "I haven't had a shag since I been here," he says, not quite answering the question. "Sometimes I get into trouble because I give a woman a compliment. Natasha will say, 'You see? You and your big mouth.' But most of the time I just love joking around, and she knows that." And then later he boasts, "Ten t'ousand women will throw themselves at me. The fact is that I am damn good-looking." But does he throw himself at women? He sighs a big tired sigh. "Your questions, you suck me dry."

After a couple of drinks Gayle returns to the subject of McLaughlin repeatedly, like a tongue probing a sore tooth. He's not upset about it "any more", he insists. "It was a joke. She knew that. That's who I am, the joker." His hand trembles slightly when he reaches for his drink. "If she didn't like it she could say, 'Chris, I didn't appreciate that.' Simple as that." After the braggadocio (his bar has a cocktail called Don't Blush Baby), the boasting, the bawdy questions ("Dye it blue!"), Gayle does tell me what he really thinks. That the underlying issue is one of racism more than sexism.

"As a genuine statement, and I would say this anywhere in the world, in any sporting arena, right now in 2016: racism is still the case for a black man. Trust me. They just want to get a little sniff of the dirt. They find out some s*** and they want to sink you. It's reality. You have to deal with that as a successful black man — especially if you had a poor man's lifestyle, coming from nothing to something.

"Usain Bolt has the same," he says. He tells me a story: a female reporter (he thinks English) flew to Jamaica to write an article on Bolt. "She was trying to get close to him by being friendly with a local reporter. She didn't want anything but dirt. You see? Reporters come just to dig things up on a successful black man. The Jamaican reporter was like, 'I'm not a part of that. I want no part of that.'

"She just wanted negative stuff. Negative. I say this because I want to open people's eyes. If they want to use me as a scapegoat, fine. But who's coming after [me], they will learn." He says Australia is more explicitly racist "off the field than on". Following the "don't blush" incident, a number of female reporters said they'd experienced similar "creepy" behaviour from him. One said, "He's a big guy. It makes you feel intimidated." Gayle believes this was a form of dogwhistle racism.

"And another of the presenters who said she wasn't happy with it, later she was interviewing a man and sitting in his lap. And she's married. She was flirting. They were playing *Let's Get It On*. She didn't get any trouble. Double standards, that's what it is."

WELCOME TO KYRGYZSTAN: AN UNSPOILT WILDERNESS ON THE ANCIENT SILK ROAD

Giles Whittell

MAY 28 2016

IF YOUR IDEA OF paradise is a bit rustic, I think I can help. Imagine a valley lost in mountains a thousand miles from anywhere you've ever heard of. Add horses, yurts and hot springs. In the bottom of the valley a light fall of snow is melting. Higher up, eagles are hunting marmots, and a long way ahead a huge white mountain marks the Chinese border. Voilà: my rustic paradise.

We were in Kyrgyzstan. Not Kurdistan or Kazakhstan, but Kyrgyzstan, halfway from London to Tokyo and halfway, as the Kyrgyz say, between Earth and space. This was my second visit and a confession is probably needed. I believe in Kyrgyzstan the way that some people believe in God or Arsenal. I have done since buying a fat Russian motorbike with a sidecar and riding it all over this wild and unjustly beautiful country 24 years ago.

I went back a generation after the Soviet collapse to see how much had changed. Eastern Europe has since rushed to join the West, but the ex-Soviet "stans" have barely registered as destinations. Uzbekistan and Turkmenistan are still run by tyrants. Kazakhstan is still a gas-powered kleptocracy. Tajikistan is always on the brink of war — its own or Afghanistan's. Kyrgyzstan has occasionally felt the spill-over effect of its neighbours' troubles, but most of the country is insulated from them by the mighty northern Pamirs. And it's the only "stan" to have made a serious go of democracy and openness. It has even scrapped most visas, sacrificing a precious source of hard currency in the hope that, if they make it easy for us, we will come.

It's worth it. It really is. You fly to Kyrgyzstan via Moscow or Istanbul. Both routes cross the steppe — three hours of grey-brown nothing. Yet suddenly, at 43 degrees latitude, the Earth's crust tips to form the mighty Tien Shan, marching towards Mongolia from the junction of the Himalayas and the Hindu Kush. At the foot of the mountains the Kyrgyz capital, Bishkek, has doubled in size since independence. It has 39 new suburbs, traffic jams and a giant outdoor bazaar where shuttle traders sell Chinese tat. Thankfully the old bazaar is still there too, a place of flat bread and *samovars*, and saffron and raw tobacco brought here along the web of horse tracks known for six centuries as the Silk Road.

With the crush of people, Bishkek has acquired hotels and restaurants. I stayed at the Futuro, a postmodern capsule of cleanliness and comfort in the shadow of a Soviet-era power station. From here a guide called Artyom picked me up in a large black Mercedes. In the old days it would have been a steel-sprung Russian Jeep equivalent, but the Silk Road has had an upgrade. The first 100 miles of the road to China are now a dual carriageway. It skirts the mountains for an hour, then dives into them up a gorge leading to Issyk-Kul, the most extraordinary mountain lake in Asia.

Here is the mystery of Issyk-Kul: 80 rivers flow in but none flow out, and despite its altitude it never freezes. Legend says that the lake is drained and heated by a cleft leading to the centre of the Earth. The truth is that the sun shines here for 300 days a year, driving a benevolent local water cycle: evaporation, rain and snow over the mountains, and hundreds of pristine streams worthy of the northern Rockies.

Across the water the snows of the first rampart of mountains on the way to China looked close enough to swim to. They were actually 100 miles away. I was hoping that our base for the next two days, the town of Karakol, would have evolved into a Kyrgyz sort of Chamonix. It'll get there. For now, Karakol is what you get when a tsarist mountain town turns gradually towards the West. There are half a dozen local agencies ready to lay on river-rafting trips, and heli-skiing in winter. There's a boutique trekkers' lodge across from the old wooden church and peppery beef stroganoff for dinner. At Karakol Coffee there are fresh brownies, decent espresso and a stack of large-scale maps of the mountains.

This was high-grade map porn, not widely available, updated and transliterated by the Norwegian Trekking Union. I drooled. Ladakh and La Paz are all very well, but nowhere has undiscovered mountains like Kyrgyzstan, and even its most visited places are still largely unspoilt. Lake Song-Kul, west of Issyk-Kul, is a high-altitude saucer of water fringed with grazing yaks and yurt encampments. Tash Rabat, in a high, green defile south of Song-Kul, is a Silk Road *caravanserai* unchanged since the Middle Ages.

No one visiting central Asia for the monuments of Samarkand should miss it. Marco Polo probably passed through, and I've no doubt he would have made a grand detour to Karakol as well if he'd only packed his climbing boots. Yuri Gagarin certainly paid a visit. Legend has it that the first man in space peered down from orbit and picked out a high, green Shangri-La, smack in the middle of Asia that he asked about when his spacecraft returned to Earth. "That's Kyrgyzstan," he was told, and luxury dachas were promptly built in the valleys south of Karakol for his official R&R.

The valley that Artyom wanted to show me is called Altyn Arashan. To get there we swapped the Merc for a vintage off-road van that thought it was a goat. For two hours we lurched round hairpins and along cliff edges. At last the mountains stood back a bit and I got out and walked.

"Monochrome and colour at the same time and a fantastic windy silence," I wrote in my notebook. Bliss. The track climbed to a rocky knoll. From here the valley opened into a perfect post-glacial U with a few log cabins in its grassy bottom.

Some of the cabins had rooms that would be taken by trekkers in the high summer season. One had a bathing hut built around a hot spring supposedly for Gagarin, but first we had to earn it. We walked for three hours up into what might conservatively be called the most perfect mountainscape on Earth. Are you allowed to say that? When words fail, surely. Here Neitzsche himself would have been happy.

Every half an hour or so the valley would bend with its river, revealing new tributaries, new meadows carpeted with edelweiss where they weren't being grazed by sheep or horses, new angles on the white north face of Pik Palatka. The topography was alpine but the scale Himalayan. This was Nepal without the crowds, Peru without the Shining Path. More than anything, it was Kyrgyzstan, where herdsmen on horses still disappear into the mountains each spring and don't come down until the snow returns.

Our morning snow melted quickly. The grass beneath it — the Kyrgyz alp — is a precious national resource known as dzhailoo, which I'd thought rhymed with "my loo". Not so. "J-Lo," said Artyom. Later in the season it would be possible to hike up over the J-Lo, past Alakjol Lake and over three high passes to the red cliffs of Dzhety-Oguz and the cabin where Gagarin holed up for his post-orbital holiday. The traverse is one of the world's great treks, but for now the passes were still snowbound and the lake frozen.

The river was shallow and wide, pushing round almond-shaped islands as the volume of meltwater rose with the warmth of the day. We crossed it on a series of log bridges and headed back down the west side of the valley to soak. Artyom's pride in the hot springs was justified. From deep under the mountains came 48 degrees of pure geothermal therapy. We sat up to our necks in it, reflecting on what Gagarin had missed by choosing Dzhety-Oguz over Altyn Arashan.

Afterwards I met an old man I recognised. He was gruff and in a hurry, but when I told him he'd once helped me to fix my motorbike down in Karakol 24 years earlier, he stopped in his tracks. He dragged me into a cabin and introduced me to his wife. "This is him — the one I keep telling you about," he said. "The first, from '92!" It turned out that thanks to something I'd written about him at the time, he'd met a series of trans-Asian bikers, starting with a winner of the Paris-Dakar rally. Which felt like good karma, and reassuring too. This whole Kyrgyzstan obsession hadn't been a dream.

Giles Whittell was a guest of Regent Holidays.

'I'M A DIFFERENT PERSON NOW. YOU CAN'T TELL ME WHAT I CAN'T DO'

Nadiya Hussain interviewed by Janice Turner

MAY 28 2016

A CAKE SHOULDN'T make you cry. But when Nadiya Hussain presented her final creation at *The Great British Bake Off* final, I confess my eyes filled. She'd made the wedding cake she'd never had because she'd married in Bangladesh — lemon drizzle, her husband's favourite — adorned it with her jewels and her red, white and blue sari. Here was Bengali and English, Muslim and Christian, whipped together like butter and sugar to make something beautiful all Britain could share. Mary Berry wept too when she presented her trophy. Nadiya moves people.

As we leave the restaurant after lunch, an Asian man stops her. "My mother and sister love you," he says with feeling. "You're such an inspiration." But search Twitter and you also find accounts covered in Ukip symbols and union flags saying, "Isn't she lovely!" The day after the Paris bombings was her first week as this magazine's baker and to see her friendly face framed by a hijab above *The Times* masthead and headlines about Islamic terror, I felt amid so much horror, reassurance and hope.

This barely 5ft tall 31-year-old, who until last summer lived a very sheltered life, is not just a symbol of interfaith friendship. She has also, as they say on reality TV, had a "journey". But while most are confected for the cameras, her emerging confidence — via soggy bottoms and showstoppers, ending in a victory watched by 13.4 million people — was real. In the course of the programme, she changed for ever.

As she held her trophy, Nadiya tells me, she could hear her little girl say, "But Mummy never wins anything." That prompted her heartfelt speech: "I'm never going to put boundaries on myself ever again. I'm never going to say I can't do it. I am never going to say maybe; I'm never going to say I don't think I can. I can. I will … " And she has.

The morning we meet she's already given a motivational speech to 200 NHS workers. She'd never done this before so wrote it all down, but in the end just spoke from her heart. A few days before, accepting a Bafta for *Bake Off*, Mary Berry looked petrified, while Nadiya — resplendent in gold lurex hijab — beamed like a star: "I wasn't frightened at all. I don't know why." Then she presented the Queen with the 90th birthday cake she'd designed and made. "The old me would have said, 'No way — you're not doing that.' The new me says, 'Yes, you can do that, and if you mess up, you mess up.'"

Seven months after winning, she retains an air of wonder not just at her good fortune, but at every new experience. In this trendy pasta joint, she orders smoked eel tagliatelle because she's never tried eel. A tart contains nespoli and the waitress brings one over, an orange fruit like an apricot. "Can I have this?" Nadiya asks cheekily and plans to cook it at home. Her life now is beyond her wildest imagining — her agent is bombarded with requests from schools, companies, TV and radio — but all she'd hoped for from *Bake Off* was a book deal. *Nadiya's Kitchen* is full of recipes she makes at home: her kids' favourite biscuits; her father's tandoori kebabs; her mother's green mango curry. It is also endearingly uncool: her griddled halloumi was inspired by a trip to Nando's. Indeed, until she won *Bake Off*, family was the outer boundary of her world.

Nadiya grew up in Luton, with three sisters and two brothers. Her father, who'd begun as a waiter, has ended up owning several Bangladeshi restaurants in Hertfordshire. Her mother stayed at home, making sure there were never fewer than four curries for dinner, preferably six. Nadiya went to an all-girls state school where 85 per cent of the pupils were Muslim and she didn't have white friends: "Not a single one".

Her cookery teacher, Mrs Marshall, however, inspired her love of baking, allowing her to hang around the school kitchen at lunchtime and encouraging her to make English sweets unknown in Bengali homes. At 16, she moved to a sixth-form college with a broader social mix. "It was a massive shock, like, 'Whoa, I have to integrate with people who aren't Bangladeshi or Pakistani.' Over time she made new friends, got decent A levels, loved English in particular, and won a place at King's College London to study psychology.

"There are certain rules," she says, "being Bangladeshi. There are certain things you can and can't do, certain ways of being a Muslim, being a woman. I really wanted to go to university. You know, that was the one thing I wasn't allowed to do because it was outside of my home town." They just said you can't go? "You are raised with this duty towards your parents. And if they say, 'No,' you don't." I am, I must admit, shocked. This was only 12 years ago, in Britain not Afghanistan. In fact, none of her sisters was allowed to study. "It was just the way it was," Nadiya says, without bitterness. Did you have a big fight? "No. No big fight," she says evenly.

We turn to our pasta. Nadiya tells me off for seasoning before tasting. After school, she worked for a few years as a medical dispatcher and a PA. Her parents were keen for her to marry; her eldest sister wed at just 17. Nadiya's father came to her with photos of a young man, the son of another Bangladeshi businessman who lived in Leeds. She was given the mobile number of Abdal, four years her senior, and they spoke often for six months but never met. Looking back she thinks how brave she was at 19, "to ask the right questions, to find someone who suited me. It was hard; I didn't really know him at all." They were engaged on the day they met and married three weeks later. Is it awkward, I wonder, moving in with a virtual stranger? "Yes, it is a bit. But I've seen my own family members do it. I think when you grow up in a culture where arranged marriages are completely normal you learn to persevere, regardless." Her parents are first cousins: "Again, that is very normal."

Nadiya moved into Abdal's family home in Leeds. "I remember we had a wardrobe in our bedroom with all his clothes in. And I said, 'Where am I going to put my stuff?' And he goes, 'Do you need a wardrobe? You don't need all that stuff. Get rid of some of it.' And I was like [she gasps]. That for me was the biggest blow. He hadn't made room for my stuff." This is all related as a funny story, but there is distress in her voice. And you can imagine the fear, aged just 20, that she had made a huge mistake, had married someone who didn't think she merited any consideration. In the end, they shared the wardrobe and she threw nothing away.

Did they fall in love straight away or over time? "I think you think you fall in love immediately, but that's more lust. But it took me years to appreciate what a wonderful person my husband is. Even now we laugh and he says, 'I was not ready to take on a wife! I could barely look after myself.'" A week after their first wedding anniversary, their eldest son, now ten, was born. A second boy and a daughter came quickly afterwards. Aged 25, she had three children under four.

Nadiya says it was her choice to give up work; Abdal, an IT consultant, earned much more. Her wage would barely cover childcare. She channelled all her intelligence, energy and creativity into motherhood. Her children could read English and Arabic before starting school. "We went out every day; we were baking, making dens out of duvets." These were happy times, but she'd go to bed dissatisfied, the words echoing in her head, "Is that all you do?" She started an Open University degree, but found it hard to study with children at home.

She expressed her domestic frustrations through writing poetry and monologues. She'd linger outside nursery talking to other mothers in lieu of a social life. Cooking became her passion: eastern and western dishes, cakes and curries. She learnt from books and YouTube. She started baking initially to enjoy Abdal's pleasure when he arrived home to a gorgeous new cake. Even now, she will arrive home at 6pm from a hectic day, put on her apron and knock up a brioche dough. But she put on lots of weight, sometimes never brushed her hair. "I looked at photos and didn't like what I saw. I felt like a slob." But Abdal, who saw not only his wife's unhappiness but her huge potential, is the opposite of the stereotypical controlling Muslim husband.

"I mean, I'm not saying that doesn't exist — it does. Oh, yes! Family members, friends, absolutely. But he's definitely one of the good ones. He's so open to change. We've never followed rules. We've always made our own." Abdal is clearly besotted with his wife. "He's used to being behind a laptop and not really communicating with humans. 'Don't be like me, I'm boring!' he says. He knows how much I love being out there and talking to people." Abdal would say, "You've got the personality to do anything you want," or "I feel like you're so wasted sometimes." But the phrase he'd use most was: "I feel like your wings have been clipped." He wanted his wife to fly.

A year ago, he came to her with the *Great British Bake Off* application form: he'd filled in the first 11 pages and needed her to complete the technical cooking part. It must be this year, he argued. Next year their daughter would be at school, and Nadiya might find a job. She sent it off to humour him. And, just as Abdal predicted, on *Bake Off* Nadiya soared. In the tent she was amazed by the mix of people — the gay Indian, the bodybuilder, the firefighter — but says that hanging around her father's restaurants as a girl had made her gregarious and an easy mixer. For the first time in ten years she was away from her children. Abdal had never looked after them alone before, but didn't complain.

"He has been with me every step of the way, supporting me continuously. He's had to adapt his life a lot for me." While Nadiya received Islamophobic remarks — *Mail* journalist Amanda Platell wrote a losing white contestant should have "made a chocolate mosque" — Abdal had his own critics. It was disgraceful enough this immodest woman was hugging strange men in public, tweeted conservative Muslims, but he was worse for letting his wife do it. "They said, 'Can he not provide for her, so he sent her out to work?'" says Nadiya. "They said he wasn't a proper man. It doesn't affect him. Not one bit."

Throughout the contest, while she tested recipes, Abdal would keep her company into the early hours, washing up — she still doesn't own a dishwasher — and calming her down. "In my culture, it's not normal for a man to do the housework," she says. "Last night, I was in bed, pottering on Twitter, and he was doing the ironing at the foot of the bed! If any of my kind of elders had seen that, I think they would have just died."

What do her family think of him? "That's he's really odd. A bit feminine. They're like, 'Ooh, what's wrong with him?'" Although parental matchmaking worked for her, she is determined her own children will find their own partners and marry older: "An arranged marriage is a gamble." That her youngest sister waited until 27, she sees as a small step forward. Her daughter, she says, will have more choice still.

Muslim girls mob Nadiya in the street. When she returned to her school she looked out at the mass of bottle-green hijabs and told them they could do anything. "I feel I've been given this voice and I want to help someone who thinks they can't break away or needs confidence." With similar encouragement, perhaps she might have persuaded her parents to let her go to university? "Yes, I wasn't strong then. I'm a different person now. If my parents or anyone tells me, 'You can't do that,' I'm the first to challenge them and say, 'You can't tell me what I can't do.'"

Nadiya is a conciliator by nature; she sees progress as gradual change, built upon by each generation. Her grandfather, who came over in the Sixties to work in Luton factories, was spat on by skinheads. Her father arrived aged seven, battled racism, but built successful businesses. In wearing the hijab, she knows she is more vulnerable to abuse. "It would be easier to say, I'd rather blend in. But I am proud of who I am, despite all the negativity that we get. After every Islamic terrorist attack I walk out of the door with a cloud over my head. If I'm on the train, people will sit away from me, or God forbid I've got a rucksack or a suitcase ... I've been shoved waiting for a bus, had things thrown at me."

After the Paris atrocities, her brother was verbally abused and came round to her house, visibly upset. "He said, 'Why do people do that?'" When she made the Queen's cake, someone wrote that she should bleach her brown skin before shaking hands. Others deemed her cake wonky, but Nadiya shrugs. "I gave it to the Queen, and she took the top tier home, and we had a chat … What they want is for me to defend myself, to argue back with expletives and profanity. But there's a dignity in silence."

Yet she is critical of Muslims who refuse to integrate. "I'm a third-generation Bangladeshi, and it's taken up to the third generation to just about get comfortable. Even then, I've got people in my generation who live in these insular societies." She thinks ghettos are now unnecessary. "The bits that haven't integrated are the minority and I think that things will change." In looking for her latest home in Milton Keynes she didn't feel a need to find a Bangladeshi area. "I don't need that to confirm my identity. Some people said, 'You must live no more than two streets from a mosque.' I said, 'Why? I can drive.' Living next to a mosque doesn't make you more of a Muslim."

Through lunch she glances down delightedly at her new Union Jack fingernails. She vows to wear rubber gloves to preserve them for when she speaks at a school in Manchester. "It's nice living in England, and we are, I like to think, a very integrated society. The negative people are definitely in the minority." She wants her children to grow up with a sense of possibility. "I won't say, 'This will happen to you because you're Bangladeshi or because you're a Muslim.' I don't want to create a chip on their shoulder."

Many assume *Bake Off* has made her rich. Someone complained to her brother-in-law that she hadn't given any of her £1 million prize money to the Bangladeshi community. "I didn't win £1 million. I just got a trophy and I'm very happy with that. But it's quite uncomfortable that everyone wants a piece of me."

Unlike previous *Bake Off* winners, Nadiya hasn't disappeared back into anonymity. Her children's baking book is out in September; she's working on a novel with a team of writers, about the travails of four Muslim sisters, inspired by her family. She is back from travelling across Bangladesh for a two-part documentary about its food and people. I ask if she is well known there. "I could barely go out," she says. "I got mobbed." It didn't help, she says, that her father erected a sign outside her family's village saying, "Nadiya is here."

Brand Nadiya has big potential. To a mass audience, her lovable and easygoing nature is balm. I ask what she'd do to bring communities together and she says, "Afternoon tea! Get people talking over tea and cake. Why not?" And there is a large female Muslim audience eager to rejoice in a devout woman, who prays, fasts and eats only halal, but is nonetheless a dazzling, confident and beloved British public figure. A British Muslim Oprah, maybe.

WHY WE MUST GO ON SNEERING AT POSH BOYS

Matthew Parris

MAY 28 2016

ONE SHOULD NEVER disparage modest reforms. "I like small, British ideas," my *Times* colleague Daniel Finkelstein once said. "Big ideas murdered my grandmother." Besides, "life chances" need not be an empty phrase. Measures in the Queen's Speech that were debated in the Commons this week, such as improving our arrangements for adoption, for childcare support and for the supply of starter homes, could all make a material difference to people's lives. But national progress needs big ideas, too. One of my own was planted in the mind quite early in life. It, too, is about life chances.

I arrived in England for university aged 19 with a white skin, fair hair, and an "educated" middle-class accent that in no way distinguished me from nearly all my fellow undergraduates at Cambridge. But I had hardly lived in Britain. Society in the places I'd grown up in (Cyprus, Africa and latterly Jamaica) had seemed to consist of two worlds: us and them. England, I'd supposed, would be different. Everybody would be "us". Not so. It was just that the "them" were now the vast majority of my fellow citizens.

I was feeling my way into an establishment social network remarkably similar to the society of colonial masters from which I'd come. I owe the whole course of my life thereafter to having become assimilated within this network. I had joined that small minority of my fellow citizens from whom most appointments to most of the senior levels of most of the professions, trades, administrative classes, churches and military officers in my country would be drawn. To climb the ladder we still needed talent but how had we accessed the ladder? Not on merit alone.

I used to wonder about the tens of millions of boys and girls in the Britain outside, and ask myself whether they could really all be of inferior potential. It was a question to which I knew the answer. These lessons made a deep impression, to be reinforced later as I learnt that even within the walled city I'd entered there was an inner citadel: those who had attended "top" public schools. Asked by *Newsnight*'s Michael Crick if he could name his closest male relative who hadn't been to Eton, David Cameron replied "There's a cousin of mine. I think he went to Marlborough."

I'd guess the inexperienced Mr Cameron (this was 11 years ago) was joking. But what a joke. Class advantage in Britain is a disgrace and that isn't just a social thing, it's a life-chances thing. Private education is key to its maintenance. Because we've become inured to the disgrace does not lessen the unfairness or the waste of talent. We should step back and recognise it.

Look, I know these stats are forever being trotted out — but don't be numbed, be angry. Taking into account that only 7 per cent — one in 14 — of our population is privately educated, get this: according to the Sutton Trust education think tank, almost three quarters of top military officers, three quarters of senior judges, half of leading print journalists, three fifths of the top ranks of the medical profession, four fifths of leading newspaper editors, two fifths of Bafta winners, a fifth of British music awards winners, nearly a third of MPs and half the cabinet were educated at independent schools.

Even Jeremy Corbyn's Labour shadow cabinet has twice as big a proportion as the population as a whole. National ability and potential cannot possibly be so concentrated in the ranks of the privately educated. So what to do? Here's the good news. State schools have improved a lot under both parties, and are still improving. From Kenneth Baker in the 1980s to Andrew Adonis to Michael Gove, politicians have led a real rise in standards. Across much of Britain the academic (as opposed to the social) case for choosing an independent school has never been weaker. The state now puts up stiff competition. And, except at the top, the independent sector is in some difficulty.

Costs and fees have risen fast, parents demand state-of-the-art facilities, the British struggle to afford this, and schools are increasingly dependent on rich Russians, Indians and Far Eastern pupils to fill the gap. Slowly, the educational as well as the social cachet attached to an education at a second-rank independent school is diminishing. Our "top public schools" are the exception. Their grip on the commanding heights of career and status is undiminished. That inner citadel remains inviolate. There's something risible about ministers, under fire for being "posh boys", whimpering that people should not be judged on where they went to school. Why do they think their parents sent them to Eton?

So for levellers like me the interim conclusion is that we're advancing through the foothills but have yet to storm the commanding heights. How? There's much to be said for sending state-sponsored day pupils to the best independent schools, and the Sutton Trust's Sir Peter Lampl made a strong case in his *Times* column last year. But as one Tory friend put it to me, "while rejoicing that Oliver Twist was adopted by kindly Mr Brownlow, Oliver joined the toffs. How did that help the Artful Dodger and the rest of Fagin's pathetic troupe?"

Airlifting a minority of state pupils into posh public schools could feed smug misconceptions about the porousness of our class system. If a boy from the back streets can get a scholarship at a top public school, then this must be a meritocratic society, right? Wrong. If assisted places is to work, we must be talking of hundreds of thousands. And we levellers must be honest. The aim must be to level down, as well as up. All right, I'll say it: we must break the exclusivity that is the top public schools' unique selling point. If they want to trade on educational excellence alone, fine: but share it. Shed the social cachet.

Now I must reach a conclusion many fellow Tories will hate. The present public mood of sneering at public school toffs is healthy. The brand must be trashed. People must be made to feel sheepish about going to Eton or Harrow. It was welcome news yesterday that the cabinet office minister, Matt Hancock, is drawing up a list of questions that employers may ask job applicants about their socio-economic background.

This column sounds aggressive. I mean it to be. We're in a zero-sum game here. A competitive advantage conferred upon 7 per cent is a competitive disadvantage imposed on the rest. And if that isn't about life chances, what is?

SUMMER

FOLLOWING MY FRIEND ALI, FROM OLYMPIC GLORY TO A LATE-NIGHT JOG IN THE JUNGLE

Neil Allen

June 6 2016

THE LAST TIME I spoke with The Greatest, also known as Muhammad Ali, he was long retired from the boxing ring that he had once adorned but still yet far from being the slowly moving, barely speaking physical wreck that, through long abuse of his dangerous sport, he was to become.

Leaving my home phone number at his London hotel, the message added that we two went as far back as the Rome Olympics of 1960 where the then Cassius Marcellus Clay, of the United States team, had won the light-heavyweight gold medal. "I still remember, champ," I concluded. "The crush you had at those Games on your champion sprinter Wilma Rudolph." Later that day the phone rang and a husky voice asked: "How you bin, my man?" Fine, I replied, but it sounds as if you've got a cold. "Sounds to me," he replied, "as if you were one of the few who used to listen." Maybe I wasn't quite as dumb as I looked, I replied, and he started chuckling huskily.

"And how about you recalling that wonderful triple gold medallist Wilma, that cool Skeeter as we called her. I was so dumb, just a teenager, chasing that beautiful lady, my heart so full of love, all over that Olympic village, when my legs didn't have a chance of catching her ... " We laughed together and that is how I choose to remember him now, the No1 man of all my years in writing about sport, whose bubbling, mischievous, occasionally spiteful mind could transform a press conference or a one-on-one chat just as, in his prime, he could turn the hardest game into a balletic demonstration of speed and skill through dancing feet, flying fists and utter fearlessness.

Recalling those Rome Games, my second of six for *The Times*, the 18-year-old Clay from Louisville, Kentucky was wide-eyed, shy and so afraid of flying ("he insisted you could get to Rome from the States by train", a contemporary said) that he sat on a private parachute all the way across the Atlantic. My first ringside view of "the most" saw him have some trouble in his Olympic semi-final against experienced Australian Tony Madigan, later twice Commonwealth Games champion.

For the final against the tongue-twisting Zbigniew Pietrzykowski, Poland's triple European amateur champion, young Cassius had to be more than "mean and hungry". Tongue in cheek for his first international press conference, he told us: "I'm gonna hit that Pole with two fast jabs, a right cross and a left hook. If he's still standing after that, and the ref ain't holding him up, then ... I run."

In Rome's splendid Palazzo dello Sport, the experienced Pietrzykowski, superb exponent of the eastern European state-backed amateur style, held the centre of the ring like a gladiator, clearly had the best of the first round against the retreating youngster and most of the second except that, just before the bell, the inexperienced American landed four thudding right hands. By the end of the third the Pole was reeling, bleeding and beaten.

At the post-fight interview, a Soviet reporter predictably asked the young black American how he would cope with racism when he returned home. "We got qualified people working on that," was the reply, "but the US is the best country in the world" added the gold medal-winner who would subsequently refuse to serve in the American forces because "I ain't got no quarrel with them Viet Cong". The teenager from the black equivalent of the American middle class, added carefully: "It's hard sometimes to get something to eat but I ain't fighting alligators and living in a mud hut."

By the next time one listened to the most active mouth in sport it was November 1962 in Los Angeles with a brief stop, on the way to report the Commonwealth Games in Perth, before young Clay (he did not embrace the Black Muslim faith and become Muhammad Ali until after he had won the world title from Sonny Liston in 1964) predictably beat the great but now elderly light-heavyweight Archie Moore. Facing a visibly affronted audience of mainly middle-aged sports writers, Clay declared: "The existing heavyweights are bums, if you'll pardon the vulgar description. They are inept bums who were employed to keep the trade surviving until I arrived."

After beating veteran Moore with what he described as "a pension punch" the youngster added, almost as if he had surprised himself: "I'm not the greatest — I'm the double greatest." The one time I saw the motormouth shut tight was in July 1963 when Clay came to London to box, in the first of their two bouts, Britain's popular Henry Cooper. Clay had stripped right down for an official pre-fight medical examination when the British Boxing Board's chairman, Jack Onslow Fane, with all the confidence of an Old Etonian, remarked: "My dear Mr Cassius, I must say you have the most magnificent a***."

Just a couple of nights later the Clay posterior was bouncing on the Wembley canvas only inches away from my front-row seat after he had been dropped at the end of the 4th round by a cracking Cooper left hook while, just behind, Richard Burton and Elizabeth Taylor were screaming the British hero on. Incidentally, exact BBC radio recordings of the sound of the bell to end the 4th round, and then to start the 5th, disprove the legend that Clay's astute, influential trainer Angelo Dundee had gained his man vital recovery time by widening a tear in one of his gloves. The time gained was definitely less than ten seconds.

When the "reborn" Muhammad Ali, having controversially renounced his "slave name" and embraced Allah, returned to London in May 1966 he had won the world heavyweight title from Liston and defended it three times. But when I met him for *The Times* in a little cubby hole in a London White City gym, we were completely alone, as on several occasions in the years ahead. "He likes company," Dundee explained, "and you guys get him rapping." Training over, stretched out in a rickety chair, his fine brown frame clothed in a white towelling robe, Ali began chatting to me, the athletics as well as boxing correspondent, about the importance of road work in preparation.

"Everyone's talking about mah style, mah speed and that it's all natural to me. Well I may have been given both mental and physical gifts, but you still got to work yourself and I run every day so that in the ring I can move, make them miss and then hit them. I'm good for another six years [sadly, he kept boxing until 1981] and another $3 million because my heart is pure and my legs are strong. Soon, you know, I'll have beaten not only Sonny Liston and Cooper and just about every other heavyweight in this whole planet."

What will you do then, I asked, feeding the wonderful ego? "Go to the moon or Mars, man, and fight whoever or whatever is up there." But what if those moon men and Martians got no heads, I wondered. "Just go to the body, man, go to the body," the chuckling champion of this world kept laughing, almost rolling off his little gym chair with the sheer joy of living. "Y'all take care now," he said. "And keep marking my words. I'm a wise young fool ... "

One of the most challenging tasks this newspaper ever gave me was in October 1970 in Atlanta, Georgia, heart of the redneck country, where Ali, destined to be the once and future king after enforced exile, made his comeback against the white American Jerry Quarry. Already, in his Miami training camp, Ali had received a parcel containing the decapitated body of a little dog plus a note reading: "We know how to handle draft dodgers in Georgia." Charles Douglas Home, then deputy editor, proposed I write a feature, to be published when the fight result was already known, explaining how American blacks would regard Ali, win or lose against Quarry.

Arriving in Atlanta 16 hours late through flight problems, my investigation started with a black Maoist threatening to throw me off the 12th-floor balcony of our hotel. Happily, just a mile from the grave of the murdered black leader Martin Luther King, I met a Reverend Lee, director of Atlanta's Southern Christian Conference and ready to talk about what Joe Louis, Ali's heavyweight champ precursor, had meant "when I was a poor young kid living in Virginia and Joe, out of Alabama but living in Detroit, was at his peak.

"We'd go carefully into the local store and creep under the counter so we could hear the radio commentary of Joe's fights. At the end, when he'd won again, the white men in the store would grumble and complain, 'Ah guess they still ain't found someone to lick that n*****.' But we black kids would just shuffle down the road, that special black man's shuffle in the south. And then, when we'd got safely past the last street lamp, we'd stop in the darkness and all holler, 'Yeah, ain't nobody can beat him down.' He was our hero and so, win or lose, is Muhammad Ali ... "

Ali cut and stopped Quarry in three rounds before the most glittering gathering of black America ever seen down south and then, in March 1971, in New York's Madison Square Garden came an event billed simply as "The Fight", though later it was known as Ali-Joe Frazier 1. I recall writing in the *Times* preview to that world-title clash that I would not wish to be anywhere else in the whole wide world, the anticipation building as the press officer John Condon handed us press caps to wear "so the cops know which heads not to hit in a riot".

Dustin Hoffman and Diana Ross were ejected from the press seats, but Frank Sinatra stayed, accredited, taking *Life* magazine's cover of the fight that Frazier won on points after a 15th-round knockdown, though he could also have been credited with another in the 11th. Completely sober, I described the match as "a drama written by a drunken genius". Sadly, Ali's pre-match behaviour, taunting Frazier, who had known white racism in his poverty-stricken youth in Beaufort, South Carolina, as "ignorant" and even an "Uncle Tom fighter" was unforgivable.

I raised the matter later in a quiet talk with Ali and he claimed he had just been trying to sell tickets. Smokin' Joe, who was to fight him twice more, including the frighteningly damaging Thrilla in Manila, never forgave the taunts although, at the end of the first clash, he stood in the ring and acknowledged: "You fought one helluva fight. We both bad n*****s. We don't do no crawling."

Zaire, October 1974, the Rumble in the Jungle was the most memorable assignment of my life and I guess the one fight for which Ali ("I'm back with my kinfolk in Africa") earned the most kudos as well as $5,450,000. But he and defending champion George Foreman were driven to distraction by the length of time they spent far from the US. Hearing me speak French to a Zairois lady, Ali moaned from his bungalow in isolated N'sele: "Man, you only just got here and already you makin' out with the little foxes. Best Angelo and I can do is bet on which sunbathing lizard is going to move first."

Unforgettable was the atmosphere in the dictatorship of Mobutu Sese Seko, who, to discourage the local villains, hanged 24 of them, 12 of them on each crossbar, in the main football stadium, where the fight was to be staged. On fight night, around 3am, my second-row press seat was close to that of a woman from an African embassy busy suckling her baby while just above us Ali was taunting big-hitting Foreman: "That all you got, sucker? You in trouble, boy." The jabs and right crosses, which Ali had demonstrated to me on his jungle bungalow sofa, sent Foreman sprawling in the 8th, dazed and dethroned.

Ali, whose three fights with Frazier officially netted him a total of $11 million, received $6 million for a narrow 1976 title win over Ken Norton in New York which I covered, then heard him admit to his doctor, Ferdie Pacheco: "I'm so tired I don't think I have it any more." Two fights, the first lost the second won, against the undisciplined, inexperienced Leon Spinks brought Muhammad a total payday of $6.75 million and he had at least another eight fights, which earned him cheques ranging from $3 million (Earnie Shavers) to a "mere" million bucks.

Watching the once dashing gladiator at ringside range became increasingly painful, including hearing him actually scream from a body punch by his former sparring partner Larry Holmes who, that Las Vegas evening in 1980, visited his bed-ridden victim to whisper: "You're still the best and I love you." Most of the avalanche of dollars disappeared through indifferent or corrupt husbandry, extraordinary acts of personal charity and the self-indulgence of those hangers-on, (nicknamed "The Faithful Fifty"), who seemed to float round the world on the dressing robe tails of the Champ.

Still, a handful of us with press cards stayed on to the very end, in Nassau, December 1981, when a tatty promotion by the egregious Don King saw Ali helplessly battered about by the Jamaican Trevor Berbick and then announce: "I'm finished." The Associated Press's Ed Schuyler spoke for us all when he replied: "Thanks Muhammad, you gave us a helluva ride." "You can't write a movie no better than this," Ali had once said of his life and he was right.

Why, on the very eve of that last beating, he reluctantly revealed to me that he had recently turned down an offer of $10 million to represent a Texas oilman in the Middle East where his adopted faith then made him so welcome. "What do you mean, how could I be mad enough to turn it down and stop fighting? I just couldn't stand it, having to go to some office every day of my whole life. Man, this is what I do, this is who I am." A sadly inevitable, yet still admirably honest, response.

Now I prefer to recall a late night in Kuala Lumpur, before a wearisome 1975 win over Britain's Joe Bugner. A solitary Ali and I met, slowly jogging together in the jungle, and then, pursued by two rabid dogs, fled back to our deserted hotel lobby, where we shared the world champion's towel and water, chatting together towards the dawn about family life, with the night porter's little daughter perched upon his knee.

On the morrow's daily press conference, Ali loudly declared: "While you was all sleeping last night I was out running six hard miles." Seeing me crouched by his feet, notebook and pen raised, he gave a slow, deliberate wink. As his personal cook, the late, loveable Lana Shabazz, used to say: "Being with Ali, most every day was a sunshine day."

Allen was boxing, athletics and Olympic Games Correspondent of The Times *from 1955 to 1976 and continued to cover Ali through to his final bout.*

I'D SIT ON THE STAIRS UNTIL I WAS READY TO OPEN THE FRONT DOOR. IT COULD TAKE AN HOUR

Oliver Kamm

JUNE 11 2016

A FEW YEARS AGO I had a disagreement on social media with Sally Brampton, the *Sunday Times* agony columnist, about some impossibly trivial issue. The next day she decided she was wrong and sent me not one but three gracious and totally unnecessary messages of apology. They exemplified a generous nature and also a ruthless self-criticism. I only properly realised the second of those characteristics when reading a month ago that she'd died after walking into the sea near her home.

The *Times* obituary quoted her memoir of depression, published in 2008: "We don't kill ourselves. We are simply defeated by the long, hard struggle to stay alive." I can only guess at the anguish she suffered. There's no bleaker place than the human mind when it's unmoored from reason. I lost hold of mine at the tail end of 2013; the condition was diagnosed as severe clinical depression and it dominated my life, everything I did and thought in every waking moment, for a year till I managed to piece my rationality back together. For great stretches of that time my overwhelming thought was a fervent wish not to see another day. Through the herculean efforts of others to reach me, I came out the other side.

Depression can afflict anyone of any age. It can be a constant demoralising presence or a terrifying precipitous descent yet, unlike a broken limb, its effects are observable to others only indirectly. The intangibility and stigma of mental illness remain a powerful deterrent to admitting to it, even to yourself. Yet the evidence is that it's as old as civilisation and that it's treatable. I resolved to write about it one day in the hope that it would help others in the same state.

My disorder gestated slowly but emerged suddenly. One day I went to pay for something in a shop, only to be told by the surprised assistant that I'd done it already. Realising there was a problem, I decided to get a taxi home but my plan fell apart. Normally I can recall obscure details of things I've read or seen, or names and faces from years past. Now I was unable to remember my home address.

I sat by the road. In a line that came back to me but I couldn't immediately place, it was curiouser and curiouser. I was fully awake, but nothing could come to mind beyond immediate sensations: the traffic in front of me and spots of rain, amid an overwhelming oppression, darkness and exhaustion. There was no definable trigger for this state other than the vicissitudes of life. My difficulties were common and have been known by many others too, but they were experienced by me with peculiar vividness under a carapace of stoicism while I confided in no one. Even my closest friends had barely known me and rarely seen me for years.

In that time my professional persona was ostensibly successful but my personal life felt like a long catalogue of stumbles. The gulf weighed on me. A caring but unsuitable marriage and separation produced loneliness for both of us. Bereavement, the death in 2011 of a father I loved and realised I'd insufficiently spoken to, compounded a sense of failure and of falling short. I brought up two young children on my own and found it hard.

I'd had the unlikely and unanticipated good fortune meanwhile to meet the woman of my dreams. She was a single mother with two young children. We fell intensely in love, were fascinated to follow the tributaries of each other's thoughts, and seemed to have found our personal refuges. And I messed it up spectacularly. She persevered for a couple of years, but was driven to distraction and despair by my seeming distance and tardiness to commit, and reasonably concluded that I was not the quality of man she'd assumed. We parted in perplexity. In that same summer of 2013, my children finished primary school and left to live overseas. There they didn't flourish, and I worried. Self-reproach incubated, hatched and turned to execration.

Grief and sadness are part of living, and so are their eventual softening amid the solace of friends, work and recreation. Knowing this, I waited. Yet the darkness didn't dissipate. It deepened. Colleagues began to notice oddities but were too polite to say. My journalism hinges on what I know: the minutiae of recondite subjects, literary quotations, the footnotes of history and the fruits of my reading. Now I was having difficulty recalling things I'd been told only a few minutes earlier. My writing had become excruciatingly slow and was strewn with grammatical errors. My friends were alarmed. I'd send them barely coherent emails in the middle of the night. Trying to make sense of these communications, they patiently responded when they awoke and called at my home in the evening to discreetly check on me.

It was at that stage, and in that state, that memory fled. How the mind works is one of science's great remaining questions. We know that genes control brain development, and neurons firing within the brain produce consciousness, but not the mechanisms that produce thought. Perhaps my mind shutting down was its way of coping with a condition that had built up over a long time, but I can only guess.

What filled the vacuum was a state unlike anything I'd known. I told myself I had stress. Mental illness was just a label to me: I had no history of it and no real notion even of what it meant. The everyday sense of being depressed is to feel sad, but clinical depression isn't like this. I didn't just feel low or sad: it was a constant torment to be awake at all. I was overwhelmed with feelings of guilt, shame and worthlessness, amid a searing anguish that never lifted.

I was haunted by the conviction that I was evil. I would imagine mocking, derisive voices. (There is an evocative description of this state in Evelyn Waugh's novel *The Ordeal of Gilbert Pinfold*.) The simplest pleasures, such as reading a book or listening to music, were beyond me. The most trivial tasks, such as opening the front door, became near-insurmountable challenges. All I could think of, on and on, was the oblivion of sleep, which wouldn't come, and how merciful it would be not to wake up again.

I was desperately fortunate. Close friends came together to ensure I wasn't on my own. They planned the thankless daily task of meeting me at lunchtime or calling on me in the evening with food they'd bought or cooked for me. They'd also have me to stay for part of every week to make sure I ate and slept and was capable of travelling to work. For all their care, they still couldn't displace my stubborn, ineradicable certainty that I was monstrous. One evening, when I was at home, I phoned a counselling hotline I'd seen on a noticeboard in the office. My usual manner, on a public platform or on the radio, is to talk. And here the words wouldn't come, just choking sobs.

The friendly voice at the other end did her best. She took me through her checklist of symptoms. The next day she emailed with a referral to a therapist. That was a new one to me. I had no inclination to find myself through psychotherapy — no belief that fishing through my memories would tell me anything reliable, let alone useful or interesting. But I was in a state, and my friends, knowing I was not myself and unable to get me back again, thought it sensible that I meet a dispassionate professional outsider. So I phoned the therapist and made an appointment. She detected a note of urgency in my voice and advised me to visit a GP. That was not only good advice but, sadly, the only useful thing I got out of the hours we spent together.

I turned up one afternoon for my first appointment at a red-brick residential Edwardian block. The therapist was a slight woman in late middle age, in carpet slippers and with a shock of grey hair. I wanted to like her, and her manner was reassuring. Seeing I was in distress, she suggested we meet three times a week over the next three months and then take stock. I readily agreed, believing I'd found a confidante, and told her of the things that I believed had brought me low.

They seemed mundane when spoken out loud and my concerns bizarrely exaggerated. I could recount the loneliness, guilt and ennui but not the darkness they brought in their wake. On departing my first session, I extended my hand — which the therapist was extremely reluctant to take. It surprised me, but I realised in that instant that she believed she was applying a professional method of greater significance than the mere acts of listening, talking and advising. Her premise was that the reasons behind my distress would be uncovered by exploring my feelings about past events. Her role was not to befriend me. Rather, under her therapeutic guidance we'd identify persistent themes in my life that had caused my present mental disorder.

So it went. I would turn up, morning or afternoon, and the therapist would wait for me to begin. Her intentions were good-hearted, but it was a disastrous encounter. Not going at all would have been a better course. I realised that if you start from the premise that there is some catalyst waiting to be uncovered you'll look for it in every word or recollection over the allotted 50-minute session. And she did. I saw no prospect of a cure by this route and asked that we terminate the appointments. Her parting words were that she was sorry not to be seeing me again because I was a nice person inside. The caveat would normally have made me laugh. It was a model put-down.

Having nowhere to go and believing I was a burden to all, I wrote to someone who I thought might be able to help break the impasse. Mark Henderson had been science editor at *The Times* before moving to the Wellcome Trust. He put me in touch with the redoubtable mental-health campaigner Lord (Dennis) Stevenson, who invited me to see him at his home in Westminster one Sunday. It was an ambitious plan just to get there.

I wasn't particularly safe to cross roads because I didn't always notice traffic. For weeks, apart from trips to the therapist, I'd travelled on just two routes: between my home in east London and the *Times* offices, and between home and close friends in north London who I knew would — extraordinarily — welcome me and give me their spare room at any time and in whatever state they found me.

But I got to the Stevenson family home and again could scarcely get the words out. Dennis listened and then explained at length his view of mental affliction, the struggles and as yet rudimentary progress of neuroscience in decoding the mysteries of the brain, and the plight of the many people he'd individually tried to help who were in my position. He asked me what I most enjoyed doing, comparable to his enthusiasm for Arsenal and Beethoven. So I mentioned literature and music and that I no longer got pleasure out of them. "Well," said Dennis, "you almost certainly have clinical depression!" This was his way of distinguishing it from conventional misery.

He wrote to me the next day and phoned me every few days thereafter to check how I was. He still does. I didn't take in much that he said. I just knew there was someone who was interested in where I'd ended up and wasn't going to judge me. He told me I was brave to admit to it.

I did admit to it, not through courage but through weight of evidence. As I couldn't function normally and my published output was pitiful, I belatedly spoke to my employers. They were hugely sympathetic and impressed on me that I could and should get help. First, they sent me to the in-house clinic, where the doctor showed me a health information sheet listing the symptoms of depression. I had the lot: sleeplessness, listlessness, hopelessness, sluggish speech and movement, a total loss of appetite for recreation or pleasure, and some things I couldn't explain at all. My problem of short-term memory loss was acute, and the fear of it has never quite left me. (I do almost all shopping online so that I'm not at risk of inadvertently leaving without paying.) Tearfulness could come at any moment, whether or not I was ruminating. Just being in a crowded place would render me anxious and desperate to escape. Underlying everything was the constant guilt and mental flagellation.

It took a long time but the professional help was effective. With powerful prescription drugs, antidepressants and sedatives, my wilder imaginings began to stabilise. The doctor referred me to an expert clinical psychologist, who literally taught me to think again. Our first meeting was pretty much my darkest day. Arriving at the consulting room, I wept uncontrollably for no reason. But it proved to be a lifeline. Instead of going on a trawling expedition through my memories looking for a key, the psychologist showed me over weeks and months how to act directly on depressive thoughts and overcome them.

That's how we proceeded. At our sessions I would describe not distant memories but what I had thought and accomplished in the previous few days. Her clinical approach, known as cognitive-behavioural therapy, made no grandiose claims to uncover the role of the unconscious. It was more about getting me to talk to myself. That may sound pedestrian, but it helped pacify me if I woke in the middle of the night and my demons came calling. The treatment was not Freud but Socrates: a process of dialogue to test and change destructive ways of thinking. The psychologist explained that my depression was a severe illness but not at root a mystery: it was born of cognitive error. Recovery, and then guarding against a relapse, could come by interrogating the beliefs that had caused my mental collapse and replacing them with better ones.

On that model, we devised techniques for coping with day-to-day tasks. Just to leave home in the morning was an ordeal so I tackled it in stages. I'd sit on the stairs and wait until I was ready to open the front door. This could take an hour or more. When I got to the office I would switch on the computer and count this an achievement. Sometimes I couldn't write anything and switched the computer off again. That was a day's work. All I could do was pretend I'd accomplished something and try again tomorrow. My colleagues connived in the fiction.

It was hard and I had many setbacks. The most severe were when I visited my children and was concerned not to alarm them with what I knew was an unfamiliar demeanour. The effort generally became too much by the end of the weekend, when I sat alone in the airport terminal and felt sick with misery. Less seriously, I'd agreed months in advance to do an Intelligence Squared debate on the "language wars", alongside the classicist Mary Beard and against the journalists Simon Heffer and John Humphrys. I went through with it. And as I sat on the stage listening to the first speaker (Humphrys), I realised I'd forgotten any argument I'd intended to make and didn't know what to say. I looked out across the auditorium in desolation.

As part of the recovery plan I devised with the psychologist, I'd email a different friend each week whom I hadn't seen for a while, to get back in touch and say that they'd been on my mind. If they were in London we'd arrange to meet. Often, retreating in anxiety, I'd cancel at the last minute. It must have seemed, and was, very discourteous. One of those friends, a Tamil lawyer, had the kindness and presence of mind to insist gently I turn up for our dinner reservation anyway. So I did, told her all that had gone wrong and realised that, like many others, she understood what I was saying because she'd seen people who were clinically depressed. The commonness of the scourge was a revelation to me.

In private, too, my faculties of memory and reason could depart abruptly. I took a day off work to do minor final revisions on a book whose text I'd managed to deliver before the deluge of depression. Looking at the proofs, I could recall virtually nothing of the book or its themes. By evening I found I'd frittered the day away by looking at suicide websites — not with any view to self-harm but because this was all I could think about. I had the notion that if only I knew in principle there was an easy and painless way out, then the knowledge, even though never acted upon, would calm me. It didn't (and there isn't). That was an exceptional day.

Antidepressants can paradoxically increase suicidal thoughts in some patients but I've no doubt their net effect on me was beneficial. I managed things more easily by having less erratic emotions. There were side-effects, too, that the information sheet advised might appear. Already torpid and exhausted through depression, I lost any trace of physical desire.

In his final years Tony Benn remarked of himself that "as you get older, all desire goes — medical conditions help with that — so I think of myself now as a biological Buddhist". Medication did the same to me. Yet the darkness did dissipate. At first it was sporadic. I got the bus home one evening from the City and as it passed the Palladian elegance of Shoreditch Church I quite suddenly had a sense not of peace but of recollection. I could remember what it felt like not to have depression. A religious person, unlike me, might have seen in it an act of grace.

I began to take pleasure in things once more. The psychologist advised me to resume reading books. If I got only 10 per cent of my previous enjoyment of a Wodehouse novel or I took in only a few words, she said, it was still an advance. I was invited by the Stevensons to a concert — their friend Steven Isserlis, the cellist, playing Elgar at the Royal Festival Hall — and I didn't pull out. It was like hearing music for the first time. There was no defining moment when I was cured but the difference was not one merely of degree, nor was I precisely the same person as before.

It took me two goes to come off medication. Dennis recounted a comment he'd heard from Alastair Campbell, another sufferer: depression is like being in a trench and you have no idea how to get out; when you're out, you have no idea how you ever fell in. Recovery doesn't solve external problems, but it puts you in a better place to confront, resolve or just live with them.

Depression was known by our forebears in identical form, although described in different terminology. Robert Burton wrote in *The Anatomy of Melancholy* (1621) that "fear and sorrow are the true characters and inseparable companions of melancholy", which strikes down the sufferer "without any apparent occasion". That's how it is. It's a sudden transport to a landscape of incapacitating strangeness, where rescuers blessedly came to find me when I cried out.

REMAKING EUROPE

Leading Article

June 18 2016

THE EUROPEAN REFERENDUM will shape the character of this country for decades to come. It will decide how Britain's laws are made and how its borders are monitored. It will signal to the world what sort of welcome we intend to offer to those hoping to live and work here. It will alert financial markets about our faith in an imperfect present or an unknown future. And, whatever the result, it will send a powerful message to Brussels that must be heeded.

"Remain" should be a vote for continued access to the single market and more British influence over it. For most this would be a pragmatic rather than enthusiastic choice, made despite the behaviour of Brussels rather than because of it. "Leave" would be a vote of no confidence in the European project so shattering that it would rock it to the core, with unknown and possibly alarming consequences. This referendum is a choice between change and a version of the status quo; between risk and risk aversion. Only one side has inspired voters because change is more exciting than continuity, and because the status quo has become a byword for frustration.

Five years ago, in a speech to the House of Lords, Shirley Williams professed astonishment at Britain's inability to recognise the scale of the EU's two greatest achievements — preserving peace in western Europe after the Second World War and bringing democracy to eastern Europe after the collapse of communism. Her bewilderment was understandable, but since that speech the EU's agenda has narrowed and its effectiveness has dramatically diminished. The institutions that run the world's biggest trading bloc foster democracy in new member states but are themselves undemocratic, meddling and short-sighted.

When Britain bucked the European trend to record robust economic growth three years ago, Brussels' response was to demand an extra £1.7 billion from the Treasury. When the 2015 refugee crisis threatened to overwhelm the European asylum system, the EU failed to prevent it doing so. Germany broke ranks and opened its borders, leaving Hungary and the western Balkans to improvise with razorwire fences. When David Cameron sought a new EU relationship for Britain, he was offered token concessions on benefit rules and the rubric of the Lisbon treaty.

This was not a Europe that was truly listening or open to reform. It is a Europe that has ceded all the best lines to its critics. In a nation divided, it is the Brexiteers who seem to stand for freedom. Their dream may once have seemed unlikely but is now close enough to touch. Their vision is of a proud new independence and their account of how to get there has the romance of adventure. A clean break, they argue, will end uncontrolled immigration and confound unelected authority. They are freebooting cavaliers to Remain's sturdy roundheads.

In their joint TV debate appearance, Boris Johnson and Gisela Stuart performed a duet with the refrain "take back control". No wonder. The need for greater control of Britain's borders and legislative processes is evident to many voters. So is the appeal of action over inertia. Tory Remain campaigners would have been hard put to show enthusiasm for their cause even if most were not already Eurosceptics. Flailing for a narrative half as compelling as Brexit, they have slumped in opinion polls while their opponents have been, to put it kindly, cavalier with the truth.

The Leave campaign has not needed to varnish reality, but has done so anyway. It is not true that Britain sends £350 million a week to Brussels.

According to the UK Statistics Authority, the actual figure is £136 million. It is not true that EU migration is the main cause of pressure on the NHS. That pressure comes from an ageing population and the rising cost of treatments. It is not true that Turkey is on a path to EU membership, for all that Mr Cameron was a supporter of the idea until as recently as 2014. Since then, Ankara under President Erdogan has shown decreasing interest in accession, which takes a minimum of 15 years and which France and Germany would veto anyway. It is not true, finally, that Brexit would answer at a stroke the prayers of those Vote Leave is wooing.

This is especially so in Labour strongholds where most social problems predate the EU's expansion and most immigration is from outside Europe. What is true is that EU migration to Britain is more than three times higher than Mr Cameron promised before the last election. It is bringing change and anxiety about change, and successive governments have failed to invest adequately in extra capacity where schools and public services are strained.

Immigration has for centuries fuelled this country's enterprise and creativity. Its net effect on the economy is to boost employment and tax revenues. It has brought Slovak hotel staff to Lerwick and given London an energy and bustle to rival New York's a century ago. Nonetheless concerns about a population rising towards 80 million are broadly felt and Remain may be severely punished for neglecting them. By addressing them Brexit has touched a chord. For those who fear Britain is losing control of its destiny, seizing back control is an appealing notion.

Sovereignty is precious. Yet it is never absolute. Every alliance and international body that Britain has joined for its own good, from the International Monetary Fund to Nato, demands some pooling of sovereignty. The question for many undecided voters is practical: would Brexit deliver on its promises or be overwhelmed by unintended consequences? It is impossible to say. As Martin Lewis, the consumer champion, has written in *The Times*: "Anyone who tells you they know what will happen if we leave the EU is lying."

That said, a vote for Brexit is unquestionably economically riskier than a vote to remain. Experts overwhelmingly concur. Paul Johnson, of the fiercely independent Institute for Fiscal Studies, puts the chances of Britain being worse off after a vote to leave at 90 per cent. The Treasury has projected an "immediate and profound" downturn in the short term in the event of a Brexit win, and a 15-year outlook of less trade, less investment and less growth than if Britain stayed in. The Bank of England, the US Federal Reserve, the IMF, the World Bank, the World Trade Organisation (WTO), the Organisation for Economic Co-operation and Development (OECD) and nine out of ten economists polled by Ipsos MORI broadly agree.

It is fashionable among Leave campaigners to disdain expert opinion, but fashion is not a good guide for so serious a decision. The best-informed deserve the most consideration. These include Sir David Ramsden, who oversaw the Treasury's analysis of the risks of Brexit, and who produced the civil service's sound advice to stay out of the euro. The leaders of Rolls-Royce, BT, BAE Systems, Centrica and Carphone Warehouse are among an overwhelming majority of employers who back Remain. Every business that trades with Europe, small, medium or large, benefits from the single market. The people who own and run these companies have a high tolerance for risk in general, but not in this case. When entrepreneurs as diverse as Michael Bloomberg, Lord Sugar and Sir Charles Dunstone say the danger is too great, the British people should take note.

Hundreds of thousands of well-paid jobs depend on the judgment of top executives and there is no good reason to disregard it. Even allowing for campaign hyperbole, the economic perils of leaving the EU are clear. Forging new trading relationships with Brussels and other big economies could take much longer than the two years forecast by the most optimistic Brexiteers. If so, the short-term shock that both sides agree is likely would stretch into a long period of lost growth.

EU trade deals on the Swiss or Norwegian model would entail stiff payments and continued free movement of labour. Alternative arrangements would still involve compromises, as all deals do. Relying on existing WTO rules would allow tighter control of immigration but would expose exporters to external EU tariffs that average 6 per cent, rising to 18 per cent for agricultural produce.

The City would survive Brexit but would not thrive. Banks that chose London as an EU foothold would no longer have one. HSBC and Goldman Sachs have already indicated they would move their euro-denominated securities businesses elsewhere. Vote Leave insists that staying in the union carries its own risks. And so it does, but these are less severe than if Britain were shackled to the eurozone. As it is, the United Kingdom has done well in Europe. In the 43 years since the country joined what was then the EEC, per capita GDP has grown by 103 per cent in Britain. That is faster than in France, Germany or the United States and more than twice as fast as in our imperial heyday before the First World War.

Since joining as the sick man of Europe, Britain has grown into its most vibrant economy, at least for the moment. Elsewhere, Mr Johnson's description of the eurozone as a "graveyard of low growth" is apt. Average youth unemployment across the area stands at 21 per cent. In Greece it is more than double that. Resentment towards the EU is widespread. A recent Pew survey showed that the EU was as unpopular in Spain, Greece, France and Germany as it was in Britain. Across northern Europe, Eurosceptics watch Britain's referendum campaign with fascination and not a little envy.

There is enough truth to the cliché that the EU is run by a pampered and arrogant elite to corrode the union to its foundations. It faces an imperative to reform, including reform of the rules on freedom of movement. If enough countries want a brake on numbers, they should be allowed to have one. There is a real risk of the EU collapsing if it fails to rise to the challenge. Brexit would heighten that risk, especially if Brussels' response were to drag out withdrawal negotiations *pour encourager les autres.*

The spectacle of a European existential crisis would delight the world's autocrats, none more than Vladimir Putin. Nato remains the guarantor of European security but the EU is a symbol of western soft power that Mr Putin scorns and seeks to undermine. Were the union to fail, the danger of tension between its members would rise, and so would the risk of more Russian adventurism along Europe's eastern fringe. That is not scaremongering but a simple lesson of history.

Were the EU to survive Brexit, a different union would be under renewed strain — that of England and Scotland, whose ruling nationalists would mobilise again for independence within Europe. In either scenario, Britain would be diminished. Three million EU migrants live in Britain. Two million Britons live elsewhere in Europe. The EU has given them the right to live and work there, but also low air fares, easy access to health care and the rule of law. Regulation is easy to caricature (and we should remember that much of it is generated within this country) but not all of it is infuriating.

The Times may once have been regarded as part of the establishment. If so, those times are past. We will take a maverick view where logic and the evidence support it. We have considered every aspect of the European argument with the seriousness and scepticism it deserves. We respect the arguments of those who would have Britain leave, but on balance we believe Britain would be better off leading a renewed drive for reform within the EU rather than starting afresh outside it.

By the same token a win for Remain followed by a limp return to business as usual would be a dismal outcome. This referendum has rightly been a thunderous rebuke to Europe and a solid Brexit vote should shake Brussels out of its complacency. If Mr Cameron wins, he must seize the moment to galvanise other disgruntled allies from Denmark to Dubrovnik for a new assault on waste, red tape and anti-democratic interference.

The Germans and the Dutch, among others, are desperate for Britain to remain because they know we can still play a key role in energising change and preventing France from being a hindrance to free market reform. Such a campaign would be a legacy worth having in the limited time that remains to Mr Cameron as prime minister.

A leader who has won a general election last year against the odds, and then a referendum against formidable opponents such as Michael Gove and Mr Johnson, plus against the groundswell of national distaste for Europe and for unhindered immigration, would be at the peak of his powers. He could go down in history as both an effective campaigner and the leader of a reform movement in Europe that would prevent it sliding into a disharmonious federal state that would ultimately rip it apart. No one should underestimate how tough a task that would be. It may not sound as exhilarating or romantic as a defiant march to Brexit, but it is the better choice for Britain and Europe.

IT WILL TAKE AN AGE TO RECOVER FROM THIS VICTORY FOR THE EXIT FANTASISTS

Philip Collins

JUNE 24 2016

IT IS ONE of those phrases which goes straight into the memory as soon as you read it. The landslide for the Liberal government in 1906 was, wrote George Dangerfield, "a victory from which the Liberal party would never recover". Boris Johnson, foolishly, has set himself a task in which he does not believe. He will assuredly become prime minister in due course and has ensured that his time in office will be dominated by an issue that he has pretended to care about in order to appeal to the fixated ideological obsessives in his party.

For all the pious invocation of "democracy" by the campaign to leave the European Union it is worth noting that, not much more than a year ago, this country had a general election. It entered a clear verdict. The Conservative Party, led by David Cameron, won an overall majority of 12 seats. The question of Europe was not a big issue. Yet, an unlucky 13 months later, the Conservative Party has decided, collectively, that its own internal squabbling is important enough to override that decision. The arrogance of these people.

If we are all permitted some pious preaching about democracy then I, as someone who did not vote for Mr Cameron's government, regard that as a democratic outrage. No, Mr and Ms Exit-fantasist the country did not vote for an excessively ambitious clown in Downing Street. No, it did not vote for Nigel Farage to be anywhere near power. Before you lecture the rest of us on taking back control and getting our country back you might like to regard the democratic settlement of May 2015 as something more than an inconvenience to be swept away.

My, but politics is brutal. Mr Cameron has been destroyed by his friends. His career is over and, with his usual dignity and his voice cracking, he resigned in Downing Street. He has been humiliated by a party which, astonishingly, has never regarded him as a proper Conservative. The irony of it. A collection of utopian dreamers, blathering on about romantic nationalism and freeing Britain from the bonds of servitude, have humiliated and slaughtered their prime minister, and his chancellor, for not being real conservatives.

I thought from the beginning that the referendum was a colossal error on the prime minister's part and so it has proved. I always believed that it was avoidable and that, with every concession to Eurosceptics who cannot take yes for an answer, he simply encouraged the march of madness in his party. Mr Cameron was never as adept a politician as his friends believed. He was lucky to get away with his Scottish gamble. He rolled the dice again and this time was handed the pearl revolver. He deserved better than this. Mr Cameron led a party I could not vote for but he was a good prime minister at a difficult time for Britain and he should be given thanks for being a good ambassador for the country.

Not that his enemies on his own side really care about that. They knew the referendum was a plebiscite on his leadership and they wanted him out. The view of the rest of the nation on the identity of the prime minister they regard as a decision to be made in their own closed rooms. It is not just the sheer arrogance of it. It is the absence of coherence. It will not be long before we discover that power migrated to a band who are even more divided than the fledgling, fractious government that has just been deposed. Even in the jubilant scenes of the Leave victory two competing ideas of the immediate future could be glimpsed, neither of them especially appealing.

The first is the Daniel Hannan world in which Britain, a serf-nation under the European yoke, gains control of its economy and sweeps away the burdens of regulation and tax. The second is the vision, if that is the right word for so murky a prospect, of Nigel Farage, who wants to turn off the clocks. Mr Farage has only one issue, which is immigration. He wants fewer foreigners and nothing more. It is not coincidental that Marine Le Pen, leader of the National Front in France, welcomed the result.

I have bad news for the Hannans and Goves and Johnsons of this world. This is not your victory. You are free riders on the back of Mr Farage. You have smuggled through your sixth-form reading list politics on the back of Mr Farage's stoking up of immigration fears. I hope you are proud of yourself and I hope, though I do not expect, that you are ready for what is coming. You have made a promise, whether you realise it or not, to bring down immigration. Even if you find, as you will, that employers rebel because they need the labour, you have promised. You have condemned yourself to leading a government for whom the number of foreigners in the country is the primary issue.

You will then find, of course, that when the white working class says "immigration" it means something more than the presence of Polish plumbers and Romanian fruit pickers. It means that life is hard, that employment prospects are bleak and that work is either unavailable or of really low quality. It is beyond laughable that the exit fantasists have the first idea what to do about this. Frankly most of them have never shown the slightest concern about that before. Well, it's their problem now.

They are going to find that everything is their problem now. So then exit fantasist, it is time to make good on your histrionic promise of liberty. Everything that happens is on your watch. All the tribulations and vicissitudes of the economy are yours. The pound fell to its lowest point since 1985 and the Bank of England is poised to intervene. Standard and Poor's have said that the UK will lose its fine credit rating. The stock market was down 8.5 per cent in early trading. This is not just a downgrade in the value of assets. It is a leading indicator of the financial turmoil to come. If there is a recession, it is your recession. If inflation goes up and interest rates follow with an attendant spate of repossessions, it's all yours. Well done.

And for what, exit fantasist? For what? The notion that Britain was not free until the early hours of this morning is the single most childish claim I have ever heard in British politics. I have heard grown people, who ought to know better, talk of serfdom and calling June 23rd "independence day". This is thinking that is profoundly unconservative, placing an abstract idea above the concrete facts of life. When the sun came up this morning — a new dawn was it not? — it meant nothing to pretend that we have passed from servitude into liberty. It is the emptiest campaign slogan, the self-satisfied bluster of a fluent intellectual dwarf. It is a victory but a victory from which it is going to take an age to recover.

FORWARD WITHOUT RANCOUR

Leading Article

June 25 2016

The people have spoken. Their decision has split the nation but it is stunningly clear. Democracy demands that Britain's choice to withdraw from the European Union be respected by those who disagree with it and implemented by parliament. The die is cast. Brexit is happening.

After a love-hate relationship spanning five decades, this country has voted to leave the EU in a protest against political elites that will echo down the ages. The prime minister has tendered his resignation because he had no choice. He called the referendum and lost it, and rightly concluded that the country needs a new captain for the uncharted voyage to its new destination.

The United Kingdom could break up before that destination is reached. David Cameron's successor must answer a renewed drive for Scottish secession with a case for union that stands the test of time. He or she must plot a new course to prosperity, especially for the millions who have let Brussels and London know loud and clear that in the EU prosperity has eluded them.

The union itself is now shaken to the core. Other states may demand referendums of their own and Brussels cannot quash these yearnings. They are appeals for more accountability and less interference which the EU must heed for its own sake. Britain should find a way to help this process from the outside, because whatever else will change in the coming months and years, geography will not. We must strive for new trade deals with emerging economies and the anchor nations of the Commonwealth, but Europe will remain our closest neighbour. Its stability will always be in Britain's strategic national interest.

The chief executive of Airbus called Brexit yesterday a "lose-lose" result for Britain and Europe. It is time to consign doom-mongering to history and aim to realise the Eurosceptic dream of a "win-win". Britain must seize this chance to rein in migration, cut its regulatory burden and exploit its unique status as an English-speaking business powerhouse midway between New York and Asia. Brussels must be persuaded to swallow its injured pride and co-operate in forging a mutually beneficial relationship with the first big power to leave the EU.

It is true that success is not a certainty, but only because this move has not been tried before. Nor is it happening in isolation. Britain's rejection of the EU is the most dramatic expression yet of a global wave of populism that has upended political establishments from Rome and Athens to Washington DC. In London, the post-mortems will be exhaustive. They will be carried out by politicians convinced that Brexit could have been avoided. Perhaps it could have been. Had Michael Gove and Boris Johnson not opted to lead the Leave campaign it would have offered voters only a parade of second-raters. Had Angela Merkel understood the depth of anti-European feeling that Mr Cameron was trying to contain with his ill-fated renegotiation, she might have consented to an emergency brake on migration that would have impressed undecided voters.

In Labour corridors the recriminations will be brutal. What if Jeremy Corbyn had given the EU more than a half-hearted seven out of ten? What if Ed Miliband had tackled head-on voters' anger over immigration in the party's heartlands? Such questions will intrigue historians. But it was hard yesterday not to conclude that this revolution was only a matter of time. Nigel Farage called his win a victory for ordinary people. Stephen Crabb, the work and pensions secretary, saw it as the result of a fundamental breach of trust. He said voters were saying, "sorry, we just don't believe the Labour Party or the government in the way they tell us that the EU is good for us".

Both grasped something that most of the Westminster bubble missed. Brexit is born of a glaring disconnect between council estates and leafy London terraces; between farmers and fishermen and bankers and estate agents; between solid country folk and bearded hipsters; between Scottish nationalists who feel the EU speaks for them, and English nationalists who don't. This disconnect was never bridged. Project Fear failed to frighten. Experts' dire economic warnings were trumped by something deeper and more visceral — a conviction felt everywhere, except in London and Scotland, that the political class has allowed unchecked immigration to change the very fabric and identity of Britain.

And so the citizens have risen in revolt. The result is a political crisis more acute and far-reaching than any to have seized this country since Suez. That humiliation marked the end of British imperial ambition and a collapse in national self-confidence. This must be a turning point leading to something better. To make sure of this, the government assembled by the next prime minister must, as Mr Gove said yesterday, commit itself to "a shared mission of securing the best possible terms" for Britain in its future trading relationship with Europe.

Jean-Claude Juncker, the European Commission president, said moments later that there could be no renegotiation of the British position. This is itself a negotiating position. Britain may have slipped for a time yesterday from Europe's fifth largest economy to its sixth. But it does not have to settle for trading arrangements based on those agreed for Norway or Switzerland. With a \$2.6 trillion GDP and a substantial trade deficit in Europe's favour, a tailored deal is an entirely reasonable expectation.

The incoming government must secure continued passporting rights for foreign banks with a London presence, enabling them to go on trading across the EU. British negotiators will have to fight hard to preserve London's right to host trading in euro-denominated securities. There will be fewer obstacles to setting up new bilateral trade deals with emerging economies beyond the EU, but they will be just as important. More than that, they will be a genuine Brexit dividend. A divorce is coming, and it must be handled deftly.

Mr Johnson is right that Article 50, which provides for EU withdrawal, does not have to be invoked at once. That said, Brussels' concerns about drift are legitimate. Each day's uncertainty delays vital investment decisions. Once invoked, Article 50 will set the clock ticking on a two-year process after which Britain can reassert control of borders and immigration. Nothing about this referendum has diminished immigration's value to this country's economy and culture. EU migrant workers resident here when new controls come into force should be allowed to stay. Having promised an Australian-style points-based immigration system, together with work permits for those hoping to come in the future, the new government must make it a priority.

World markets struggled yesterday to shake off the shock of Brexit, but there is stoicism among the anxiety. Energy and pharmaceutical companies in particular said that EU withdrawal would have negligible impact on their businesses. The impact it will have on Scotland is already becoming clear. Nicola Sturgeon has warned that a second independence referendum is now "highly likely". Yet she knows it cannot go ahead without Westminster's co-operation, and that even now a win for independence would be far from certain. She cannot be confident of victory when oil prices stay low and there is no convincing solution to Scotland's currency.

Donald Trump, in Scotland yesterday, hailed Brexit as "fantastic". Some 16 million Britons who voted for Remain will not agree, but the only course for the nation's new captain is to get the best deal possible in the tough navigation that lies ahead.

RAGTAG REBELS WHO HAD NOTHING LEFT TO LOSE

Janice Turner

JUNE 25 2016

A REFERENDUM IS a binary choice: yes or no, stay or leave. As was the breakdown of results: north or south, working or middle class, young or old, city or shire. But what if, like me, you are — to borrow the jargon of the "gender fluidity" brigade — Brexit non-binary? Prole roots but bourgeois life; northerner living in London. Sitting at the fulcrum made a voting decision more tortuous but the result less of surprise.

Travelling back and forth to South Yorkshire, I've marvelled for years at the contempt such communities are held in by London friends, supposed progressives, people with power. You could see a ragtag rebellion kicking up dust, gathering strength, a long way off if you'd bothered to look. In London I hear people rave about the "gig economy", the cheapness of Uber, the snap-your-fingers-and-it's-here Amazon Prime and Deliveroo. So modern, and the people who serve you, well, they're young dudes or hard-working migrants. It's cool!

Outside cities, the gig economy means fifty-something ex-miners turned minicab drivers, the job centre presenting you with a list not of sits-vac but temp agencies that may give you six weeks packing salad or a week of warehouse night shifts. Success has a thousand fathers and Farage, Gove and Johnson will be writ large on Brexit's birth certificate. I'd add plenty more. Sneering Remain sophisticates banging on about how the EU means Bach and Bergman; second-homers Instagramming burgundy passports and weeping they'll never see Paris again; any narcissist with a man-bag who characterised the British working class as wholly bigots, loudmouths, ugly chavs, racists and fools.

Are you surprised they disdained "experts" when bankers and politicians have ravaged their life chances, or that they ignored George Osborne when his "£4,300 worse off" claim just echoed his endless austerity budgets? Of course, when they finally got a chance, they'd stick two fingers in your face. Those whose forebears fuelled the industrial revolution, whose parents fought for and lost whole communities, are now told they're no longer the workers we need. They're not flexible, eager, young Stakhanovites who don't mind being strip-searched before minimum-wage shifts. They want — the outrage! — training, job security, to raise families, pay mortgages.

Mike Ashley and Sir Philip Green, Next, Amazon ... every employer that treated its workers like interchangeable slave-bots helped take us out of the EU. Hearing the left proclaim Brexit would mean a bonfire of employment rights, I'd wonder where trade unions have been in this zero-hours decade protecting workers who already have no rights at all. Immigration was, let's not pretend otherwise, the central issue here. The unsaid was now said, often and crudely, feeding viciousness and rancour. However, 52 per cent of Britain is not racist: we have long absorbed great shifts of people, are more inclusive of other cultures, have more interracial relationships than any nation in Europe: we've made foreign dishes our national cuisine. We have not changed.

Rather, a specific angst had incubated for years about unrestricted freedom of movement, a concept I believe for many — especially the most economically insecure — is psychologically unendurable. Stripped back, it is a mind-blowing proposition: all of Greece, say, could move here tomorrow. Yes, of course, they won't. But they could! No, they won't. But what if they do? This principle, regardless of numbers, activates a primal fear, a nagging worry that your back door is unlocked but you're forbidden to shut it, while people tell you it will be fine.

Free movement suits big business, which benefits from cheap, limitless labour; it suits a young, educated cosmopolitan workforce; it suits our now-stymied children who long to study abroad; it suits me. But try selling it in poor provincial towns to people who may not even have a passport; those who feel no benefits from this shiny fast-flowing global world; who are lectured by all parties about the GDP benefits of migration while their own wages are undercut.

That towns with the fewest migrants fear immigration most is always seen as a measure of working-class stupidity. But in a diverse city, migrants are just a few extra pixels in the frame; in a small town they are a distinct event, a challenge to a fragile identity. And identity — as we have seen — is not a phantasm but a banner that people are prepared to risk economic destruction to protect. Besides, there are the unprecedented migration numbers — half a million added to our population in a year — which no one ever has the courage to address.

We didn't wake up yesterday in "Nigel Farage's Britain", as hyperbolic Remainers lament. Few want a Ukip government: its charlatans and raging free marketeers offer nothing to the dispossessed. Brexit revealed austerity-weary, frightened voters who want housing, security and proper jobs. Jeremy Corbyn's In campaign may have been half-hearted but after a decade of Labour misleading its voters about migration he could have had Jean-Claude Juncker tattooed on his chest. Far, far too late have Ed Balls and Tom Watson acknowledged that free movement needs reform. Without this the whole European project will fall.

As a Brexit non-binary I had bitter, upsetting rows for weeks with everyone I love. I voted Remain in the end. The Breaking Point poster was my breaking point. These Leavers were not my people and would never deliver social justice. But here we are! Everything to play for, if only the Labour Party can eject Jeremy Corbyn and seize the day. In the meantime, as our eyes shift from our European neighbours to each other, it is time for a less binary Britain — more understanding, less hate.

I KNOW WHY I GO TO RESTAURANTS, BUT WHY DOES ANYONE ELSE?

Giles Coren reviews Piquet, W1

JUNE 25 2016

THE WAY WE eat out has been changing so fast lately, and things have got so intense and exciting, with so many different ways of doing it being invented all the time, that sometimes I genuinely lose sight of why people go to restaurants at all.

"I know why I go to restaurants," I said to Esther last night at Piquet, just off Oxford Street, over a manzanilla and a bowl of olives while we looked at the menu. "But what about these other people? It isn't their job. They don't have to write about it. Why are they here? Why aren't they at home watching *Peaky Blinders* with a bottle of burgundy and last night's roast chicken between two slices of bread, like I would be if I'd had a long hard day at work and didn't have a deadline to hit?"

"Have a drink and pipe down," said Esther, who grew tired of my endless chitchat long ago. "I'm trying to read the menu. It looks fantastic."

So I looked at the menu, and it did indeed look fantastic. But it didn't help my confusion. It contained all the sorts of classic French bistro dishes that I thought I and everyone else was totally over – crab raviolo, pithivier of snails, monkfish casserole, roast veal sweetbreads, asparagus with chopped egg, pig's head croquette with gribiche – and yet I found myself drooling with anticipation. Why? Whatever happened to my newfound predilection for Mexican and Peruvian cuisine, crazy regional Chinese dishes, Nordic foraging and street food? Did I really crave pomme purée, turned vegetables and veal stock reductions all along?

I looked around me and my confusion deepened. Here in the big downstairs dining room, as in the rather vibeless upstairs bar, were acres of brand new oak panelling. Oak panelling? In 2016? Sure, if it has been there since the Victorian age and you want to hang modern art and make a joke of it. But who puts this ridiculous overbearing wall covering in new? In a basement off Oxford Street? What are you saying? That this is basically the Connaught?

And if Edwardian stiffness is what we all want again, then why the extremely open kitchen with a huge, bald Australian chef at the pass shouting, "Less salad on there! I've told you twice already!" If oak-panelled Edwardian hush is what you're after, then for heaven's sake shut the staff away. Ideally underground.

But then, wait, here is a handsome French 1980s charmer in a suit and tie with the wine list, complimenting my choice of wine. He brings us proper white burgundy glasses to drink it from, not jam jars. So perhaps this is the rebirth of swank after all. No, it is not, for he has retreated now (and for the rest of the meal) to let us pour it for ourselves from the copper cooler on the table, instead of serving us himself, dribble by obsequious dribble, as such fellows used to do.

So is he an old-fashioned overbearing fiddler or a modern laid-back waiter who just happens to have no beard or tattoos? I just can't tell. But I like him.

And why are the tables uncovered? And why are they made of shiny, wipe-clean plasticky stuff? You've got oak panels and posh food and serious glassware and waiters in ties. So you should have tablecloths. But then tablecloths wouldn't go with the bald shouty chef, the open kitchen and, what's that ... the smell of bubbling vegetable oil?

"Groundnut oil," corrects Esther. "Dodgy extraction, clearly. I'll have to wash these clothes tomorrow." And she's right. The place hums like a chip shop, at least from our "privileged" position next to the deep-fat fryer.

Open kitchen but no beards or tats, oak panels but no tablecloths, proper glasses but no top-ups, cuisine bourgeoise but kebab van pongs ... I DON'T UNDERSTAND!!!

Ate bloody well though. And at just the right pace. Within 20 minutes of arriving, we had our 3 starters in front of us. Yes, three. Piquet does not claim to be a sharing restaurant, thank God, but it does not insist that it is not one, so we did as we pleased. And after those two mains and two puds and all done in ninety minutes (the optimal restaurant-dinner length).

And it was all top-class cooking from the second half of the 1990s, with flavours that brought back everything I loved about eating out back then, when I first came into this game. My crab raviolo was what critics in those days used to call "well judged", the filling smooth and balanced, the pasta perfectly al dente, soft on the dome but firmer at the pinched edge. The shellfish dressing was beefy, brown, bespeaking long hours of care and bubbling – in the pompous terminology of the 1990s, one would have declared it "accurate". And then little strips of neatly trimmed young samphire and weeny rhomboids of skinless, seedless, tomato flesh imparted freshness. Half a dozen lovely little mouthfuls.

And then a veal pancreas served whole (it was in the 1990s that I learnt to distinguish a pancreas from a thymus when eating "sweetbreads"), crisped to a golden brown on one side and cooked past creamy (when it can be a bit oozy and brain-like) to a perfect blancmange consistency, served with truffled pomme purée and romaine lettuce.

Those two – crab raviolo followed by sweetbreads – were what I ate for probably my first 30 meals as a restaurant critic (for *Tatler* in those days), whether by Ramsay, Wareing, Blanc, Ladenis, Pierre White ... And it was a joy to find myself transported to those days again. And across these I drank a delicious young meursault, something else I learnt to do in early summer in good restaurants on someone else's budget.

The other starters we had were "marinated Scottish sea scallops, coriander cress, pickled apple, cucumber and squid ink" and pressed suckling pig. Now, I come at scallops from an odd direction, loving them so much sliced raw for sashimi and seasoned only with the merest fleck of soy that all additions upset me. These at least were not cooked (I'd sooner apply pan heat to one of my own children than the delicate flesh of the scallop), but they were sliced wafer-thin and then rather lost in the trimmings. I just want to eat the raw scallop, feel the smoothness on my tongue, the fresh planes exposed as I halve it with my teeth, the sugary first flavour, the almost human, unquestionably sexual fleshiness of a lychee, then the faint hint of the sea as it goes down. Squid ink and apple and cucumber and coriander are not indelicate or unsuitable, they are just – even they – too much for me.

I had expected the pressed suckling pig to be thinly sliced and served cold, but it was a proper tranche of sous-vide pork belly crisped on the top and all salty-juicy and delicious, with smooth, rich black pudding and warm, chocolaty prunes that rewarded a carefully constructed "combination mouthful" as well as any fry-up. It was, again, very 1990s and big enough to have served as a main course.

Esther's casserole of monkfish cheeks, baby squid, chorizo, haricot blanc and chopped herb oil was stunning. So clean and refreshing without the quasi-chemical tang of saffron or the addition of "le boaky sludge fish" so prized by the Marseillaises ("rascasse" is what they call it to our faces). This had a lightness, a fruitiness. The haricots were firm and nutty and there was depth and redness and spice from the chorizo but no egregious fattiness. And then strips of baby squid on top, perfectly crisped in the (smelly) fryer and the frazzled tentacle crown dancing on the summit, which I whipped off with my fingers as soon as the bowl landed in front of Esther and crunched through loudly.

For pudding, we retreated to the early 1980s with an impossibly light île flottante, so light, in fact, that it was quite tricky to eat: you went to close your mouth upon a forkful and found nothing there. To make up for it, the apricot tart was as heavy as a dead badger. I had been hoping for something sharp and fruity to end my meal but it was just a lot of mouth-filling pastry with only the merest hint of apricot. Fine for a mouthful with strong coffee but really, teatime cake not a postprandial treat.

So, a grab bag of dislocated restaurant idioms from across the past 35 years, all of them done well but contributing to a slightly confusing experience for a jaded critic of the genre, while providing unquestionably tasty scoff which, from what I remember, is what most normal people are looking for.

TIME TO GO

Leading Article

JUNE 29 2016

"SEUMAS, I'M NOT sure this is a great idea," said Jeremy Corbyn to his head of communications about the plan to film a session of the new shadow cabinet. That line will surely become engraved as the epitaph of Mr Corbyn's troubled reign as Labour leader, which came a big step closer to its end yesterday.

After the rolling resignation of the shadow cabinet and junior ministers, Mr Corbyn lost a confidence vote of MPs by 172 votes to 40. Though it is reasonable to wonder how 40 MPs still retain confidence in his leadership, this makes working in parliament impossible. A ministerial team needs more than 40 people. If Mr Corbyn clings on, as he says he will, citing the mandate he has from Labour Party members, he is declaring that there will be no effective opposition in the Commons. That is more than a local dispute. This is now a constitutional question.

Mr Corbyn needs to reflect on his position, realise it is hopeless and stand down. The vote of no confidence has no legal status and neither does the fact that he cannot assemble a team. There is a dispute about whether Mr Corbyn has an automatic right to stand again if a leadership challenge follows, as it surely will. He may have the numbers in any case. If Mr Corbyn could command the 40 MPs who voted for him and ten of the party's MEPs, then he would be back on the ballot.

The better course would be for him to realise that the game is up. Otherwise he may go down, to quote Chris Bryant MP's resignation letter, as "the man who broke the Labour Party". The early suggestions are that the field will not be opened up. The rebels intend to field only one candidate, to maximise the likelihood of getting rid of Mr Corbyn. That will be either Angela Eagle, who was until yesterday the shadow business secretary, or Tom Watson, the party's deputy leader. Both would be likely to be an interim appointment to stabilise the party and allow a transition to a leader with a wider appeal.

There is a case for Labour skipping this step and going for a new person with popular appeal now. There may, after all, be a general election in a matter of months. It is not hard to define what the nation needs in a leader of the opposition. It needs someone to define a credible, fiscally sound economic policy. It needs someone who resumes the Labour Party's historical position as a supporter of Nato and a guardian of the nation's defence. It needs someone who, in short, looks plausible as an alternative prime minister.

The problem is that the party is not chock-a-block with such talent. There have been renewed attempts to persuade David Miliband to return to Labour politics, though this would look a backward step to a man who dared not seize the crown. Hilary Benn, whose sacking precipitated this crisis, grew in stature during the debate over Syria and presents a generous demeanour that would be welcome in a time of political turmoil. Dan Jarvis is less experienced and may lack the charisma, but the Conservatives might find it hard to attack a former major in the Parachute Regiment.

A country without a government needs an opposition. On Monday Mr Corbyn left a meeting of his parliamentary party to address a rally on Parliament Square. In a torrent of platitudes about justice he did not mention the EU once. He is an irrelevance as a party leader. His MPs have noticed. The question is whether he has.

WE SHOULD IGNORE JUNCKER
AND TALK TO MERKEL

Roger Boyes

JUNE 29 2016

IN THE GRAND investigative tradition of diplomatic journalism, reporters at EU summits are sent out to discover the top-table dinner menu. The point is to contrast the extravagant taste of leaders with their less well-nourished voters. They were saved the trouble yesterday. As David

Cameron sat down with his soon-to-be-former colleagues in Brussels, it was pretty clear what was going to be served up: humble pie, sour grapes and Eton Mess.

Some leaders would have preferred his head on a platter. Not Angela Merkel. Germany is undergoing a fit of righteous indignation about Brexit; in particular, her Social Democrat partners in government think the British should be placed in the stocks for their temerity and ingratitude. Up to a point Chancellor Merkel agrees: she was sure from the outset that Cameron's referendum was a reckless gamble. Rather than In/Out, say the Germans, he could have launched a narrower question. For example: should Britain support further EU enlargement?

The German leader, though, understands that this is not the time for recrimination or punishment. If mishandled by the EU, Brexit will be like the barely visible thin crack in Edgar Allan Poe's *The Fall of the House of Usher* that ends up splitting the building in two. So out of an acute sense of danger she is being flexible about the start of negotiations. Whether this will translate into a greater understanding for Britain remains to be seen. Her priority is to head off a more general dismemberment of Europe and its core policies. For now at least it is important for her not to make a pariah out of Britain but rather find it a place, short of full membership, that slots us into a broader plan for a continent that is already operating at drastically different speeds.

Here's the problem: it's not only Boris Johnson who has mislaid his plan. Despite decades of white papers and leaked memos, the EU does not have a realistic master plan. Once upon a time the destination may have been a European super-state, driven by France, Germany and some core states. Now it's just a jumble of competing ideas. So both Britain and the EU are in flux. That is why Britain should be talking to Merkel, not to the busted flush Jean-Claude Juncker, who as president of the European Commission has set himself up as the lord high executioner. Not difficult to imagine his contribution to future negotiations: Britain will have to suffer, and suffer publicly, in order to scare off any other EU members (France, Italy, the Netherlands, Denmark are part of the long queue) from consulting their citizens.

It cannot be business-as-usual for angry Eurocrats. No one (apart from the plucky Inuits of Greenland) has ever voted to get out of the EU. The talks have to be not just about customs duties but about a fundamental repositioning of the EU. Merkel grasps that in a way that Juncker does not. He takes the *Hotel California* view: you can check in but you can never check out. Merkel-watchers say she has a personal stake in stopping a European break-up. Her mentor Helmut Kohl constructed today's EU. In order to get the top job she had to push him aside. That carried with it a responsibility to make Kohl's Europe bloom.

Now that Europe is disappearing fast, forcing her to compromise some basic German principles of good housekeeping to keep the eurozone intact and stave off a Grexit. Then came the challenge of Putin's war on Ukraine — should Kiev be offered a European perspective or not — and the huge influx of migrants that has blown holes in the Schengen zone. To these fractures in the south and east of the EU comes Brexit in the west. They impact not only on how the EU will shape its present and future, but also on Germany itself.

Brexit — perhaps this is the origin of current German anger — shackles Merkel closer to France, the sick man of Europe. François Hollande thinks that the French and Germans should re-commit to a deeper political union to demonstrate the EU's vitality. It is difficult to imagine a more pointless act. As Europe gets smaller, so German dominance becomes more evident. Merkel is profoundly uncomfortable with that. The Obama administration is suggesting the Germans will now become the primary US conduit into the EU. That's a headache, not a boon, for the German leader.

It will mean demands to step up Germany's contribution to active defence. Chit-chat about a future European army won't do it for a President Trump or a President Clinton. Worse still, the impact of Brexit on the eurozone's fortunes may tip Italy over the brink. The prime minister, Matteo Renzi, faces a referendum on constitutional reform in October. Judging by the insurgent mood in Italy, he may lose. If he does, he has promised to resign. Even if he doesn't there will be an election at a time when the country's banking system is looking wobbly. The Five Star Movement populists are on the rise and they want a referendum on, yes, membership of the eurozone. The euro would go into a tailspin.

So Merkel's eye is as much on Italy as it is on Britain. The next crisis is just around the corner, even before we have engaged on Brexit. The calculation of the Leave team is that Britain is too important to overlook. The fact is, though, that the whole of Europe is erupting with problems and the buck is all too often stopping with Merkel. We need to engage her fast and explain that a fair, undogmatic compromise on the single market and freedom of movement is not only possible but also in the wider interests of a troubled Europe.

MPS ARE FIDDLING WHILE THE ECONOMY BURNS

Ed Conway

July 1 2016

WE BRITONS DON'T do revolutions, or so says the conventional wisdom. Except that that's nonsense. This, after all, is the country of the Peasants' Revolt, Oliver Cromwell, the Reform Act and the Invergordon Mutiny. What happened a week ago had the whiff of revolution. Not because of anything it said about our relationship with Europe, but because of what it said about our relationship with the future — and the light it shed on our broken political system. For it was ultimately a protest vote not just against the EU but against globalisation.

Over the past 70 years Britain's arms have creaked open to the rest of the world. Our borders have been gradually unfastened, barriers to capital flows lifted, tariffs cut, regulations harmonised and the currency floated. The upshot is that we are no longer just citizens of the UK. We are citizens of the IMF, the WTO, Nato. We are citizens of a multilateral world of which the EU is only one particularly visible element. The contract we all have with government was imperceptibly rewritten without much in the way of consultation.

We don't often talk about these changes because, frankly, we don't much understand them, yet their consequences are profound. Immigration has a demonstrable impact on many workers' wages. Free trade boosts the exports of some companies and destroys the livelihoods of others. Too little is known about the impact of untrammelled capital flows, but there is evidence that they contribute to the yawning gaps between the haves and have-nots. By the same token, these shifts have arguably made us all wealthier. They have helped innovation to spread around the world, benefiting everybody. But rather than being aired, this topic has been swept under the carpet for too long.

Those who resisted such shifts were derided as Luddites; those who argued fervently for them were dismissed as neoliberals. The chief message of this referendum is that we cannot ignore the debate any more — and a good thing too. After all, this saga was really a shadow debate about our place in the wider world. Do you want more of the world, or more Britain? More or less immigration? Shared sovereignty or British sovereignty? Do you approve of the past 70 years of ever-closer union with the world, or disapprove? The longer we suppress these conversations from the political mainstream, the more likely they are to be monopolised by crackpots, extremists and racists.

Anyway, these questions are far more relevant to today's politics than left and right. The faultlines that defined 20th-century politics are out of date. Today there is far more consensus over the scope and scale of the welfare state, over a redistributive tax system and over tax and spending levels. In other words, if ever there were a moment we needed new political parties, it is now: not left v right but engagement v isolationism. If not, the chances are that the Labour and Conservative parties, which uncomfortably accommodate both factions, will continue to tear themselves apart. And while they squabble, the economy stutters.

Most likely, we are now on the brink of recession. A Leave vote was always going to cause a short-term slump — it was, after all, a vote for the unknown. Whether that slump can be reversed now depends on political leadership. The longer it takes to establish what kind of European deal we are aiming for, the more businesses will pull investment, consumers will put off spending and incomes will suffer. The longer the pound remains weak, the more inflation will rise and the bigger the squeeze on living standards.

There is a feedback loop here. Economic disappointment fed many voters' resentment towards the political class before the referendum. Things will only fester if such disappointments continue in the coming years. Our politicians are fiddling while Rome burns. Conservative MPs will continue to jostle for the leadership. The Labour Party will tear itself apart. The SNP will dust off its independence plans. All of them risk ignoring the challenge thrust up by the referendum.

At some stage we need to confront what kind of an economy, and a country, we want to be. Much better to have such conversations in a civilised, intelligent manner — that, after all, is the British way. Nor would it be the first time. In the early 1930s workers hissed with frustration over the gold standard, the economic order that their political masters joined without consulting them. At Invergordon in 1931 some naval seamen staged a good-natured mutiny. This small-scale revolution was the final straw; Britain soon left the gold standard.

For a while, the decision was regarded as treachery. A few months later what seemed scandalous was regarded as quite sensible. Britain did not stop engaging with the world; it just started engaging with its people. Time to do it all over again.

GROOM LEFT AT THE ALTAR AFTER BRIDE FLIRTS WITH BEST MAN

Patrick Kidd

JULY 1 2016

IT WAS A fitting backdrop against which to announce the survivors in the leadership bloodbath. As the chairman of the 1922 committee read out the famous five, the eye was drawn to the Kate Blee tapestry behind him, showing a series of large red splodges that resembled Sweeney Todd's kitchen worktop.

How many of the guests who had assembled at St Ermin's Hotel earlier that day for what was supposed to be the launch of Boris Johnson's candidacy had an idea of what was to happen? They had come for a wedding but it turned into a wake.

Nothing in the behaviour of Team Boris suggested that we were there for anything other than the happy union of politician and party. The sun was shining, the bunting was out and the MPs fussily arranged and rearranged their seating plan, deciding in the end to sit boy-girl-boy-girl in the front two rows.

Meanwhile, the groom was having second thoughts. It turned out that his bride didn't love him as much as he thought. In fact, she had been flashing her garter at his best man the night before and Michael Gove had admitted that he fancied trying his luck. The dilemma for the groom was crippling. Should he say his vows and risk becoming a cuckold, or back out gracefully?

St Ermin's was an appropriate venue for a spot of treachery. This hotel near St James's Park was where Burgess, Blunt and Philby liked to meet their Russian handlers. "I'm no communist," Mr Johnson insisted near the beginning of his speech, perhaps aware of this. Yet it was he who had become the victim of a double-cross as those who were once his friends sought to put the Gove into government.

To start with, though, his speech suggested that he was fighting on. "This is not a time to quail, it is not a crisis, nor should we see it as an excuse for wobbling or self-doubt," Mr Johnson said. "It is an excuse for hope and ambition." Marriage on, then. You could almost hear the organ playing Mandelson's wedding march, every Machiavelli's favourite introit. He went on: "This is a time to take the tide of history at the flood and sail on to fortune."

We nodded at the Shakespearean reference. The whole referendum campaign had been a re-enactment of Julius Caesar, with David Cameron as the ruler and Mr Johnson as Brutus at the head of a gang of conspirators. Beware the march of IDS, as they say.

Except that this version had a twist. Brutus stabbed Caesar, but then Cassius Gove, who has had a lean and hungry look of late, stuck one up his old pal's toga.

The audience still did not know, but as Mr Johnson went on a tour of his achievements as London mayor — "We cut bus crime! More people visit the British Museum than Belgium!" — it started to feel more like an obituary than vows.

Then it came. "My friends, you who have waited faithfully for the punchline. Having consulted colleagues, and in view of the circumstances in parliament, I have concluded that person cannot be me." James Cleverly, one of his longest-serving allies, shook his head. Nadine Dorries wiped tears from her eyes. Other MPs just looked shocked, wondering how long it would be decent to leave it before dashing off to pledge their allegiance to someone else.

This is the way of politics. Death will come when it will come. As Brutus/Boris knows, men are masters of our fates. The fault is not in our stars, but in ourselves.

TEARS, BETRAYAL AND BREXECUTIONS: THE WEEK THAT SHOOK THE WORLD

Matt Chorley

JULY 2 2016

As THE DOOR OF No 10 closed behind David Cameron at 8.30am on Friday, June 24, emotions erupted and tears flowed. But the drama inside Downing Street was nothing compared with the chaos about to be unleashed outside.

Saturday marked a truce. Boris Johnson played cricket, Michael Gove played Monopoly, Jeremy Corbyn gave a speech to a Pride rally and Tom Watson danced the night away at Glastonbury. Each would learn new lessons in the brutality of politics. The first sign of trouble was Hilary Benn's rumoured plan to call on Mr Corbyn to quit. The leader texted his shadow foreign secretary and demanded he ring immediately. He did so, told his leader he had lost confidence in him and was sacked.

Dawn on Sunday brought a drip-drip of Labour resignations but Mr Corbyn proved to be almost indestructible. In Islington, Mr Johnson wrote his weekly *Daily Telegraph* column, setting out his vision of Brexit, with Britain part of the single market and freedom of movement. He emailed it to Mr Gove, who replied that it was "overall very, very good" and made only minor changes to present a more "inclusive, positive and optimistic message". Out in the real world the reaction was getting angrier. More than three million people had signed a petition apparently demanding a second referendum. In west London xenophobic graffiti was sprayed across the Polish Social and Cultural Association, as reports emerged of increases in hate crime.

At 7am on Monday, George Osborne finally surfaced to try to calm the markets. Visibly shattered, he insisted that he did not "resile" from his Brexit warnings. He wrote an article for *The Times* conceding: "I am not the person to provide the unity my party needs at this time."

At 9am Mr Watson, Labour's deputy leader, walked into Jeremy Corbyn's office for a crunch meeting. Many wanted him to tell the leader to quit. He did everything but, giving a "blunt but polite" assessment of the state of the party and warning the months ahead were "bound to be brutal". Unknown MPs were quickly promoted to shadow some of the great offices of state.

In his Commons statement at 3.31pm Mr Cameron told the newly elected Tooting MP, Rosena Allin-Khan, "to keep her mobile phone turned on because she might be in the shadow cabinet by the end of the day". As the laughter subsided, he added wistfully: "And I thought I was having a bad day." For Mr Corbyn, the worst was still to come.

At that night's meeting of the parliamentary Labour Party, MPs took their chance to tell him to go. "The attacks were brutal and Jeremy just stood and talked pre-prepared nonsense," said one. Labour MPs heading home that night thought a plan had been hatched: Mr Watson and Rosie Winterton, the chief whip, would resign in the morning, and Mr Corbyn would be finished. They were to be disappointed.

On Tuesday morning Mr Johnson met Sir Lynton Crosby for breakfast, in the hope of securing the services of the general election guru. The Boris bandwagon appeared to be rolling, but something didn't feel right. Anger over his *Telegraph* column was mounting, with friends trying to claim he was "tired" when he wrote it.

With Theresa May on the up, careerists spotted an opportunity. Two Tory MPs went to see her to inquire what jobs they might expect if they supported her. She told them: "I don't do deals. You are going to support me because I'm Theresa May." Hers is a campaign where all talk of deals is banned, and advisers have been warned against negative briefing.

With 60 Labour frontbenchers and aides now resigned, MPs voted on a motion of no confidence in their leader, which was passed by 172 to 40. He still refused to go. TV cameras were invited to film what was left of the shadow cabinet, but caught Mr Corbyn whispering to his spin doctor, Seumas Milne: "I'm not sure this is a good idea."

Mr Cameron left the drama of Westminster behind him as he headed to Brussels for his final summit of EU leaders. It was marked with sadness. "The irony is that during his renegotiation he got to know the other leaders incredibly well," a No 10 source said.

On Wednesday morning Stephen Crabb, the work and pensions secretary, launched his leadership campaign. He mocked Mr Johnson's claim that he would be interested in becoming PM "if the ball came loose from the back of the scrum". Mr Johnson had bigger problems.

At 10am he had been due to address a group of about 50 centrist Tory MPs and ministers, most of whom backed Remain. With 15 minutes to go, he cancelled. People were furious. "They are basically saying get on board now, or you're all f***ing doomed," one MP said, believing the "arrogant" move was evidence that Mr Johnson had the numbers to get on the ballot. It could not have been further from the truth.

Hours later an email emerged from Sarah Vine, Mr Gove's wife, in which she told him not to support Mr Johnson without "specific" assurances. Meanwhile, Mr Corbyn was entering his fourth day of misery. Some suggested he wanted to quit but was being forced to stay. The farce reached a new low when, just before prime minister's questions, Pat Glass said she was quitting as shadow education secretary. After two days.

Mr Cameron's session to prepare for PMQs was shorter than usual. Notable by his absence was Mr Gove, who usually helps. Mr Cameron set off for the Commons without having finalised attacks on Labour's chaos. But after Mr Corbyn referred to the fact the PM has only two months left, he shot back: "It might be in my party's interest for him to sit there, it's not in the national interest and I would say, for heaven's sake man, go!"

That afternoon Mr Watson had arranged to have a "clear the air" meeting with Mr Corbyn as they drove to an event together. But Mr Corbyn was in no mood to talk and sat in silence for much of the journey. Shortly afterwards, Mr Watson gave an interview calling for him to go. Angela Eagle, the former work and pensions minister, had been seen as the candidate to challenge him, but as the day wore on, Owen Smith's name kept coming up. The coup was failing.

The race for Tory leader was widening. Liam Fox announced he would run and Jeremy Hunt made his own pitch to a group of backbenchers. In the evening the group snubbed by Mr Johnson held a hustings for Mrs May. She went down a storm. On the Commons terrace that night, MPs toasted the home secretary as their potential saviour. "She even did jokes," one minister said. "She's a grown-up who can sort out the children's mess," another MP said.

Mr Cameron was at the Conservative summer party in Fulham, west London, where leadership contenders, ministers, MPs, donors and allies drank Pimm's and toasted the prime minister. In the corner of the room, a drama was being played out.

Mr Johnson had written a note for Mrs Leadsom which read: "Dear Andrea, Delighted that you're in our top 3." She never got it. Mr Johnson left it in his desk drawer, and by the time his henchman Nick Boles, a Tory minister, had sent someone to collect it, she had left the party. A promised tweet, due at 8pm announcing it was "great to have Andrea and

The Gover on board", never materialised. This left Mrs Leadsom without the guarantee she wanted.

In the car heading home, Mr Johnson repeatedly tried to call her but she didn't pick up. As the evening wore on, MPs were still getting text messages from Mr Gove's aides after 10.30pm urging them to turn up to Mr Johnson's launch in the morning. Then something changed.

By midnight, Mr Gove had decided he would run himself. At just after 1am, Team Gove took a call to be told that Mrs Leadsom would also be running. On Thursday morning, unaware of the overnight shenanigans, Mr Johnson left home with his leadership speech under his arm. An opinion poll of Tory members in *The Times* showed him trailing Mrs May by 17 points. The frontrunner was falling behind.

At 8.53am Mr Gove called Sir Lynton to tell him he planned to run as leader himself. He said he would call Mr Johnson next, but never did. At 9.02am, Mr Gove fired his exocet missile. "I have come, reluctantly, to the conclusion that Boris cannot provide the leadership or build the team for the task ahead." It was devastating. "It's a stab in the front, right up to the f***ing hilt," one MP said. Another spat: "Michael has made a pact with the devil."

More bad news was to come. At 9.13am, Mrs Leadsom announced her ambition to be leader on Twitter, declaring: "Let's make the most of the Brexit opportunities!" An ally of Mr Johnson said he now would be "s****ing himself". It was quite the backdrop for Mrs May's campaign launch, where, surrounded by rows of books, she declared: "I'm Theresa May and I'm the best person to be prime minister."

A woman not known for cracking gags, she took a swipe at Mr Johnson. "Boris negotiated in Europe. I seem to remember last time he did a deal with the Germans, he came back with three nearly new water cannon." The attack, it later transpired, was redundant. Mr Hunt pulled out and backed Mrs May. Mr Johnson arrived at St Ermin's Hotel for his speech knowing the game was up. In the Cloisters Suite some of his most loyal supporters sat quietly, unaware of the bombshell to come.

The speech lacked his usual bombast. As the clock ticked towards the midday deadline for nominations, it was notable that he hadn't actually mentioned being leader. Then, the bolt from the blue: "My friends, you have waited for the punchline of this speech, that having consulted colleagues and in view of the circumstances in parliament I have concluded that person cannot be me."

Journalists emerged in a state of shock. The destruction of one of Westminster's most enduring political ambitions was incredible and total. Mr Gove missed it because he had the TV sound turned down. Only when the breaking news graphics flashed up did everyone exclaim: "F***ing hell he's pulled out." British politics had seen nothing like it.

Having helped Mr Johnson to finish off the prime minister, Mr Gove had destroyed his sidekick's career. Bewildered MPs and journalists toured Portcullis House, trying to make sense of it all. Mr Cameron walked through, beaming.

And yet still Mr Corbyn felt the need to make news. Launching a report on Labour and antisemitism, he appeared to compare Israel to Islamic State, leading to condemnation from the Chief Rabbi. Keen to show he was still in charge, he fired off a defiant message to supporters and mistakenly signed it "Jeremy Corybn".

Mr Osborne emerged again yesterday to admit that his target of having a surplus by 2020 was as dead as his leadership hopes. Then Mr Gove delivered his leadership speech at the Policy Exchange think tank that he helped set up in 2002. He declared himself the "candidate for change".

Three miles away in Islington, Mr Johnson was surveying the wreckage of his career, telling reporters: "I cannot, unfortunately, get on with doing what I wanted to do, so it'll be up to somebody else now."

It was exactly a week since Mr Cameron, his old friend and political foe, had stood outside his own home and uttered the same sentiment. Which is about the only thing the pair still have in common.

MY ONE-EYED, ONE-ARMED GREAT-GRANDFATHER. HERO OF THE SOMME. AND THE REASON I BECAME A WAR CORRESPONDENT

Anthony Loyd

JULY 2 2016

A FAMILIAR HERO I never knew stares at me most days. With one eye, and an empty sleeve scaled by wound stripes, he watches my comings and goings from the dining room wall. He sees me early in the morning, bleary and tousled, on my way to feed the dogs and let out the chickens. He sees the daily to-ing and fro-ing of my wife and daughters, hears us laugh and shout and curse, and is still watching last thing at night as I lock the front door and turn off the lights.

His fob watch is by my desk. He stopped wearing a wrist watch after a German bullet drove one into his hand, causing a wound so terrible that he was obliged to pull off some of his fingers in a dressing station. His Bible is on my book shelf. And a bullet, pulled from him in France, capped in gold and given to his first wife, my mother's grandmother, the Austrian Countess Friederike Fugger Von Babenhausen, sits in a tin in my bedroom. Some bullet, that. As a German bullet given to an Austrian wife by a wounded, half-Belgian half-Irish British subject, it is the distillation of a complex family history: love and war told in lead and gold.

It is serious, too. That lump of lead that they pulled from Lieutenant-General Sir Adrian Carton de Wiart — the one-eyed, one-armed, 11-times wounded hero of two world wars, great-grandfather of mine, who won his Victoria Cross leading the remnants of a brigade at La Boisselle on day three of the Somme — that bullet makes me wince every time I look at it. It sits so heavy in the palm of my hand — thud, thud it goes as I bounce it — that I would have thought that the shock of impact alone would be enough to kill a man. Not him, though. Despite wounds in the face, head, hand, stomach, groin, hip, leg and ankle, despite two plane crashes and four decades' worth of adventures, which included tunnelling out a PoW camp in Italy during the Second World War and 15 years living in the wilderness of Poland's Pripet Marshes, he died at peace in his home in Co Cork, Ireland, aged 83.

Sometimes he is near to me, my great-grandfather, that old one-armed shrapnel-rattling lead-lined eye-patched death-cheating warrior, but more often far. Render to the brave their deserved respect: he was fearless and I know fear. I recognise the depressions and angers; the yen for excitement and love of the wild. Unified by a bit of family blood and wars, mostly it is our differences that interest me, though.

So the space between us was full of talk as I went walking with his ghost last week, through Picardy fields, up the road from Albert and over the top at La Boisselle, that bullet heavy in my pocket.

What makes men brave? It is the first thing I wonder, standing by the Lochnagar mine crater at La Boisselle, still preserved in the chalky soil a century after it went off at 7.28am on July 1, blowing debris and German soldiers 4,000ft high, starting a battle that was to go on for 141 days and involved an average daily casualty count among Somme combatants of 7,500 men: three times higher than that at Verdun.

Bravery was compulsory in that place, then, if only to suspend men's imagination enough just to move. A hundred years later, those fields and that battle, more than any other in France, are synonymous with Britain's collective memory of the Great War; to unflinching courage, to horror, to loss. Measured in dead men, in those first few days of the Somme, La Boisselle was the worst place to fight in that bloodiest battle of British history.

Two minutes behind the massive mine blasts that signalled the start of the battle on each side of the village, which by then was little more than a smear of rubble in a pitted, shrapnel-shorn wilderness, British troops from the 34th division went over the top and advanced towards the heavily defended German position. Most were killed within a few yards.

By 9am, 80 per cent of the British assault battalions around La Boisselle were casualties: 2,300 were slain by German machinegun and shell fire there before ever reaching the enemy lines. There was no truce, so most of the wounded died in no man's land. The bodies of 1,950 soldiers, killed that first day, were never recovered at all.

Held in reserve for the start of the battle, Carton de Wiart — then a captain in the 4th Dragoon Guards, promoted to acting lieutenant-colonel and put in command of the 8th Battalion of the Gloucestershire Regiment — later wrote of the exuberant innocence of his young soldiers as they prepared for their turn in the cataclysm the following day. Conscription had not yet begun, so each and every soldier was a volunteer, and few had been in action before.

Most of them were formerly clerks and office boys from Bristol, and had been trained only to the most minimal standard of military proficiency. "Though they knew they were going to have a bad time and that casualties would be heavy," my great-grandfather wrote, "they seemed not to have a care in the world, and spent their free time playing games and behaving like schoolboys on a half holiday."

I walk over the gentle crest of Usna Hill, within a few yards of where he led these men on the night of July 2 along St Andrew's Avenue, a communication trench, to their jump-off point in positions along the lip of the narrow country road that runs from La Boisselle to the neighbouring village of Ovillers. Everything looks so small. The hills are not hills at all; they are gentle undulations. The objectives are not forests or towns or cities, but copses, hedge lines, hamlets and villages. Not even the fields, dusted with poppies and alive with June birdsong, seem that large, although large enough, evidently, for thousands of men to be harvested at once.

The sun is shining on me as I walk with the dead general, pulled awkwardly between the conflicting emotions of pride, wonder and sorrow. A warm breeze ripples the crops as I try to reach back to that night of torn, blood-soaked chalk and tangled barbed wire, where the road to glory lay paved with the twisted bodies of dead British soldiers, who slabbed the ground in piles. Traffic hums along the Picardy lanes. Already missing his eye and hand from previous fighting in Africa and Ypres, as he moved forward along the trench Carton de Wiart carried with him just a walking stick and a bag of bombs for the day ahead.

"I never carried a revolver, being afraid that if I lost my temper I might use it against my own people, so my only weapon was a walking stick," he said. Accompanying him was his servant, Holmes, also unarmed. Carton de Wiart had confiscated Holmes' rifle earlier, annoyed by the noise when Holmes shot at a German plane. Reaching their jump-off point, at 3am on July 3, as his men fixed bayonets, Carton de Wiart stepped up a ladder and stood on the edge of the trench above them to survey the field. The closest German trenches were just 150 yards away. Because of the narrow frontage of the advance he could only take 20 officers and 400 soldiers with him. Within a few hours, 302 would be dead, wounded or missing.

"I remember my feelings waiting for the order to go over the top," one of his men, a lance corporal, later recounted. "I was only 18 years of age. I was scared stiff. Just before the order came I saw ... Carton de Wiart standing on the top of the trench in full view of the enemy and he was carrying a stick. The mere sight of this very real soldier standing up there gave me new courage."

At 3.15am the 8th Glosters went over the top. The maelstrom of whistling shot and bursting shell through which these men passed, as they scrambled over the trench line following their one-eyed commanding officer in the darkness before dawn, was more horrific than modern imagination can likely grasp.

Most went forward unquestioningly, their courage contained by a complex set of strictures that are virtually absent from our lives today: patriotism; sense of duty; respect for authority; peer loyalty; belief in the righteousness of cause; fear of the firing squad. They were different from us, those soldiers of the Somme. They thought differently, and they behaved differently. Their war was relatively simple compared to today's multispectrum conflicts: a clash of empires that was monolithic in its demand for huge sacrifice of life.

So careless with his own safety, Carton de Wiart made a chillingly pertinent comment in his 1950 memoir, *Happy Odyssey*, when assessing his feelings over casualties among those he commanded. "It was easy enough to be callous when one went to a new battalion," he wrote, "but when one knew and liked them all and had been through so much together it was a different matter. I felt losses more and more as time went on." Tellingly, he made no remark on any need to preserve lives.

As we walk, the memory of a British colonel in Iraq springs to my mind. I had known him since we first met when we were infantry platoon commanders in the Eighties, during the five years I had spent in the army. It was Basra. Night. 2007. He sat at his desk in his room, alone, his head in his hands. One of his men had just been killed on an operation in the city, right at the tail end of the British occupation there.

The operation had no specific use beyond fulfilling the dictates of fighting spirit and regimental pride. No possible outcome of that mission would have left Britain's people richer, wiser or safer than before. But now a soldier was dead and somewhere there was about to be a knock on a family's door that would send a freight train of grief straight through the wall of their home. The colonel knew it. He knew the value of that dead soldier's life. Not every modern soldier and officer shares similar perceptions, a hundred years after British commanders led their men to death en masse in the Somme day after day for 141 days.

In Helmand five years ago, another British commanding officer had been doing a gym circuit at a patrol base he was visiting. A patrol of his men was beyond the wire. It was hit. A soldier died. Informed of the news, the CO carried on with his gym circuit. Perhaps he thought he was showing some inspiring sang-froid. The men's judgment was different. They despised him for it. Later, when that CO addressed his men at the end of their tour, they heckled him. The regimental sergeant-major stepped up to quieten the troops. He was heckled, too. Today's heroes attach careful value to their lives, and need explanation as a precondition to courage.

Bravery would have come more easily to the less-questioning British soldier of 1916, fighting a mighty enemy just over the channel, than his equivalent in 2016's age of doubt. Nevertheless, it requires a base level of extreme physical courage for human beings to propel themselves deliberately forward into air that scythes with metal, amid the terrible sounds of explosions and screaming, as those around you drop.

One older friend, a hard-drinking hellraiser and fighter with his own searing experience of war, once advised me that good frontline etiquette involved "wearing the right shoes, having a crap beforehand and trying to look lively — even if you don't feel it". It was good advice that I have tried to keep to.

Never having been especially physically brave — I know fear well and fight it often — but up-for-it enough to handle most of the lonely risks of life as a war correspondent, I feel modestly confident in managing the art of moving around the tread of violence without getting whacked. Yet that art is very different from combat. As a person sensitive to the threat of danger, the thought of going over the top at La Boisselle angers and appals me. I suppose I would have achieved it a hundred years ago — for all the same reasons that the men then did so. Not everyone went gladly forward into those deathly fields.

Amid it all, Carton de Wiart described finding a frozen soldier unable to advance. "I asked him the reason for his dawdling," he said, "and he replied that he had been wounded three or four times already, and simply couldn't face it. I told him that I had been hit oftener than he but still had to face it ... and gave him a push in the right direction."

That soldier was lucky. Just a few weeks later, during a desperate assault on nearby High Wood in which he lost most of the remaining survivors from La Boisselle, Carton de Wiart took a revolver from his adjutant to shoot an unwounded malingerer, although the soldier fled over the trench parapet before he had time to use it. Seconds later, Carton de Wiart was himself badly wounded by German machinegun fire.

I have never known what made my great-grandfather quite so spectacularly brave. Any fool can get wounded. Being wounded without the right context is no more suggestive of courage than having a car crash.

But as the human mind naturally adapts to having war metal blown inside the body in a way that usually makes it more difficult to take quite the same risks next time as before, Carton de Wiart's consistent courage in action across decades of operations and woundings makes him a very unusual man.

An avowed fatalist who believed in death at the appointed moment, even among war heroes he was exceptional in his fearlessness. I respect that courage. I am proud to be related to such a man. I envy it, too. To move fearless in war, cradled in a sense of destiny, would be to become an almost celestial entity, surfing terrible reefs unshackled by mortal fear.

Lord Moran, whose book *The Anatomy of Courage* was in its day a groundbreaking work on the study of courage and cowardice in the Great War, argued that each man has a finite ration of courage which is gradually expended. "A man's courage is his capital and he is always spending," he wrote.

Nevertheless, Carton de Wiart seemed an exemption to the rule, and was among only five men Lord Moran had met who did not appear to know fear at all, despite his multiple war injuries. Perhaps this verdict wrongly diminishes him. Perhaps my great-grandfather indeed felt fear, but was stronger-willed than others in overcoming it. Either way, echoes of his example have caused me occasional shame and pain.

Whenever I have been even reasonably frightened in war it bothers me inordinately, and usually requires that I seek redress of shame in new challenge: the perpetual chase of the white stag. War heroes are difficult family members, even dead ones. When I was wounded a couple of years ago, I turned down the offer of morphine in a Syrian dressing station for a catalogue of reasons, the main one being that the pain was at first perfectly manageable.

Not much further down the list, though, was the awareness that Carton de Wiart disliked anaesthetic for his wounds and often refused it. "S***," I thought resentfully, when a doctor offered the morphine. "Now it's my turn." It was another eight hours before anyone else offered me morphine: plenty long enough, as the pain set in, to regret not ignoring the ghostly beckoning of family example.

Fewer than half of his men from the 8th Glosters made it across those 150 yards with Carton de Wiart, who was pulling pins from grenades using his teeth, to the German lines at La Boisselle. Those who did so found themselves in a savage hand-to-hand mêlée with the defenders, as small groups of survivors from each side tore at one another with bomb, bullet and bayonet. Three more British battalions were committed to this desperate fray, but their commanders were immediately hit, so that by dawn Carton de Wiart found himself commanding the fragments of a brigade in a roiling 360-degree fight through the churned soil.

By the time the sun rose across this apocalyptic corner of a foreign field, the British had succeeded in establishing a line through the rubble of the village church, fewer than 400 yards from the day's original front line.

By the standards of the Somme, this was a mighty victory. Beneath the heat of the morning the exhausted British survivors were brought water in unrinsed petrol cans. They slathered at it eagerly. "Our tongues were hanging out for the water," wrote Carton De Wiart, who found himself resting in the wilderness, writing orders, seated on a dead man.

They fought off a series of German counterattacks between late morning and mid-afternoon. Eventually, they were rotated out of the line after dusk and trudged back towards Albert. Fewer than one in four of the soldiers Carton de Wiart had led out of the trench before dawn remained alive or uninjured.

There is a deeper and remarkable peace among those fields now, and I walk across them as if in a strange dream in the warm stillness of that summer afternoon, looking for my great-grandfather's dead soldiers among the cemeteries. I see the graves of thousands of men. "The Lord watch between you and me while we are separated from each other," a widow has inscribed on the stone of one dead soldier, a 48-year-old colonel from Devon. So full of yearning and love, the words sting my eyes.

But although I wander north and south of La Boisselle, and walk as far as High Wood, never properly cleared after the war and where an estimated 8,000 dead British and German troops still lie entangled among the roots of a new generation of trees, I find no trace of the soldiers of the 8th Glosters as I search for those dead 300.

There is no shortage of tenderness for those whose bodies have been found. French gardeners nurse our dead at the Somme, and among the ranks of bright white headstones and tended lawns spring roses, irises and lobelias; every private soldier, every officer, serenaded by the lazy gurgle of summer birdsong. Such beauty there, I think, that it could be so easy to forget the horror from which it sprang.

It is not until the shadows lengthen and the day cools that I realise most of those dead soldiers led by my great-grandfather that fateful day around La Boisselle have no known grave; that the Lutyens memorial to the 72,000 missing of the Somme — its top just visible peeping over the fold of fields at Thiepval — is not a part of militaristic hubris or glorification of war that I once assumed, but a totemic focus of grief; grief on a vast scale; grief for those who were ground into mud.

There is silence between the general and me as we walk back from High Wood towards La Boisselle, amicable strangers in the gathering dusk. The power of what that bullet embodies goes on and on. My daughter will have it in her pocket someday, maybe, when she has her own conversation with the dead general in those Somme fields; when she talks about war and fear and loss and the nature of courage; but mostly, I hope, about all the love in between.

OUR WEEK: EVERYBODY*

* according to Hugo Rifkind

JULY 2 2016

MONDAY

Boris Johnson: Ohgodohgodohgod. Oh God. Ohgodohgodohgod. Oh God. Vom. Right. Feel better. Nope. Vom. Ohgodohgodohgod. Oh God.

David Cameron: Screw you all. I'm going to Ibiza. Point at some fish. Netflix and chill. I can't? I've still got to run the country? FFS. Can't George do it? No, I don't know where he is either. Man, I wish I still had money offshore.

Nigel Farage: You all laughed at me. Well, you're not laughing now! The pound is plummeting, the FTSE is crashing, and for some reason, you don't see the funny side! Also, none of you have ever had a proper job in your lives. A cardiac surgeon? Not surprised you're covering your face. The shame! Jobs for the boys. Who's got a corkscrew?

Sarah Vine: It was a morning like any other in the Gove household. Except it wasn't, because Michael now rules the world. And by "Michael" I mean both of us. And by "both of us", I mean me. As the shower sprang to life, I put the kettle on and reflected on the agony that has been inflicted on our social circle. Many people outside politics don't realise how much friendships can suffer when you stab your friends in the back and jump up and down on their corpses, laughing. But we have learnt, the hard way. It's very sad.

Jean-Claude Juncker: The British are our friends and will always be our friends. And so, we must respect their decision. By filling in the Channel tunnel and sowing your fields with salt. Which we may do already, actually, as part of the common agricultural policy. Who's got a corkscrew?

Jeremy Corbyn: Everybody is resigning. Tom Watson drops by on his way back from Glastonbury and says it's because nobody takes me seriously. "But you're wearing shorts, a wristband and a headband with bobbing alien eyes on springs," I say. "So?" says Tom.

Michael Gove: Boris is the man! And walking through the House of Commons this morning, I spot him, and grab him by the shoulder, and tell him he's going to be the next prime minister. "Thank you," says Angela Eagle, turning around. "Woah," I say. "What?" she says. "It's just ... " I say. "From behind ... Never mind."

TUESDAY

Boris Johnson: We're going to stay in the single market. We're going to leave the single market. Oh God. Ohgodohgod. Wait! We're going to retain access to the single market! Yes! Like a man who leaves his wife, but retains access to her! Which, put like that, sounds totally reasonable! Doesn't it? Sweetheart?

Sarah Vine: I call Michael. I've messed up, I tell him. It's a disaster, and I should never even have pressed send. "Pillow talk again?" says Michael. "Look, you need to stop this. It was one thing to edit Boris's column. I can't edit yours, too." "I meant the email," I say. "What email?" he says.

Nigel Farage: When are the elite going to stop talking down Britain? Don't they know we're the fifth largest economy in the world? What? Oh. Sixth, now? Really?

Tom Watson: Back in to see Jeremy Corbyn. My clothes are all ripped and there are leaves in my hair. "You still haven't washed from Glastonbury?" he says. Of course I have, I tell him. I just got stuck in that massive rosebush he has by the front door. Then I tell him that this confidence vote is a real disaster, and he's got to go. And he says he's still got momentum. "Sure," I say. "Like an anvil falling out of a helicopter has momentum." "Momentum," says Jeremy. "Oh," I say.

Stephen Crabb: A random woman comes up to me at the launch of my leadership campaign and says the big problem with Stephen Crabb is that nobody knows who he is. "But he's me," I say. "Whoops," she says. Then I say it could be worse, anyway, because at least I'm not as obscure as Andrea Leadsom. "But that's me," she says. "Whoops," I say.

Angela Eagle: Maybe I'll launch my leadership challenge tomorrow?

Nicola Sturgeon: I've gone to Brussels. It's awfy big. Don't patronise me. Annoyingly, I've been refused meetings by Angela Merkel, François Hollande and Mariano Rajoy. The good news, though, is that I'm meeting Martin Schulz! Now I just need to figure out who he is.

WEDNESDAY

David Cameron: Seriously? PMQs? We're still doing that? WTF? Right at the end I lose my rag and tell Jeremy Corbyn he's got to go, for the good of the country. People say it's very non-partisan of me. Seriously, though. I'm thinking of the future. I've got to vote for someone.

Seumas Milne: "Don't worry about Cameron," I say to Jeremy after PMQs. "He's just a Tory." "They're all Tories," says Jeremy. "No," I say, "but he actually is one.""He should just go and join the Tories," snarls Jeremy. "I think you're tired," I say.

Ed Miliband: Blimey. And I thought I was bad at this.

Theresa May: I'm getting a lot of support from MPs. I'm the sanity candidate. The only problem is, quite a lot of the party isn't sane at all. Thankfully, I have the support of Chris Grayling. All bases covered.

Boris Johnson: In parliament. Govey catches me on the shoulder. "Oh thank God," he says. "It is you." "Who else would it be?" I say. Michael says it's not important. Then he says that we need to talk about our team, because he wants to bring Whacko Cummings along and he's heard I'm not keen. "Forget him," I say. "We've got more important things to worry about. Such as Article 50." "But it's only Wednesday," sighs Gove. "She can't have written that many already."

Thursday

Boris Johnson: Today's the day! Bojo back on top! I'm going to be PM! Theresa May is toast! Oh hang on. Email from Michael Gove. Back with you in a moment.

Michael Gove: Hum. Look, I appreciate people might think I've been a bit of a bastard. Bit stabby. But everywhere I go, somebody says to me, "Forget Boris! It should be you!" Admittedly, that's because my wife is always there. But still.

Sarah Vine: Michael had to stand. The fact is, he — we — are in charge of everything now. The country. The dawn. Gravity, probably. It is with a heavy heart that I think of the many treasured friends we have lost along the way as I spend the afternoon phoning up a few of them to gloat about it.

Angela Eagle: Look, I'm still thinking, OK?

Mark Carney: Remember me? I'm making a speech today. In precis: screw you people. I mean, seriously. Screw you all. I'm so glad I'm Canadian.

Pat Glass: Two days ago, I was appointed to the shadow cabinet. Now I've quit the shadow cabinet. You'd never heard of me before. Frankly, you still don't even know if I'm a man or a woman. You don't have time to check. This my finest hour.

Jeremy Corbyn: Today, I am proud to launch the Labour Party's report into antisemitism. The fact is, our Jewish friends are no more responsible for Israel than our doctor friends are for all those people killed by Harold Shipman. Still, you know how these people get. Look, I'll text you later.

Shami Chakrabarti: Sort of wish I hadn't bothered with all that, actually.

FRIDAY

Michael Gove: Today I launch my official campaign for leadership. "Whatever charisma is," I say, "I do not have it. I never thought I would be in this position. I did not want it. Indeed, apart from the Boris stuff, and the Cameron stuff, and the lifetime spent hacking my way towards the top of politics, I did almost everything I could to avoid being in it. Still, here we are."

Theresa May: Yes, but I have even less charisma. Damn him. That's my whole pitch. Is John Major backing anyone yet?

Liam Fox: How come nobody is even talking about me?

George Osborne: "It is with a heavy heart," I announce in Manchester, "that I hereby abandon the incomprehensible and frankly unlikely thing I was pretending I was going to do with the nation's finances". Once, this would have been news.

Nigel Farage: Typical! Still talking down Britain! As though we weren't the sixth largest economy in the world! Wait. Seventh? Surely not eighth?

Boris Johnson: Broken. Distraught. Running through the Commons, trying not to be seen. Hoping Dave will let me tag along to Ibiza. Left my trunks in the office. "Launch it already!" shouts Tom Watson as I lumber past. "Be our next prime minister!" "Old chap," I say. "Where have you been?" "Whoops," says Watson. "Thought you were somebody else."

'MAY THE MEN WHO BROUGHT THIS HELL TO IRAQ BE FOREVER DAMNED'

Catherine Philp

July 6 2016

Hurriya's first son, Ghanem, was taken away by Saddam Hussein's secret police and hanged aged 21. Her second, Ali, was killed in a car bomb that ripped through a market near their home in a Shia slum in Baghdad two years after the 2003 invasion. Hussein, another son, died in a bombing four years later, sitting in his taxi outside the Sheraton Hotel in central Baghdad next to Firdous Square, where Saddam's statue was torn down. Her youngest boy, Mohammed, was killed last year on the road to Tikrit, where he had gone as a volunteer with a Shia militia to fight Isis.

"All this loss," she cries. "I wish the invasion had never happened. May those who brought this hell to our lands be forever damned." Few Iraqis are waiting for, or even aware of, the Chilcot report examining the British role in the 2003 invasion. Many, perhaps most, have already concluded that the invasion was the trigger for 13 years of bloodshed. Hurriya had keenly awaited what she saw as liberation from the murderous security state that spirited away her eldest son and repressed her Shia community to keep power in the hands of the Sunni elite.

"It felt like a prison had opened and we would be free," she said. "We hoped we would have a better life." The promises never materialised as Iraq's oil wealth disappeared into the pockets of corrupt politicians ushered in by the new order and sectarian tensions exploded into street violence. Shias, supposedly liberated after years of persecution, found themselves the target of Sunni extremists. The Sunni sect felt disenfranchised, not only from the loss of power but also from the coalition's decision to disband the army and bar former members of Saddam's Baath party from power.

Colonel Talat Issa, a former republican guard from Saddam's home town of Tikrit, had been jailed five years before the invasion so he was allowed to join the new security forces. Many of his former compatriots were not. Today, many of them fill the ranks of Isis, from which he helped wrest back control of his city last year. His base, Saddam's former palace on the banks of the Tigris, is the story of post-invasion Iraq writ in stone; first occupied by US Marines, then the Iraqi security forces after being handed back, then by Isis, who used it as a slaughterhouse for 1,700 Shia troops. Triumphant Shia militias took it back after coalition airstrikes toppled all but its inner walls but few Isis fighters were found as the city was cleared.

"They came from the people and they are back among them," Colonel Issa says. "Without the invasion there would be no Isis." Tikrit is a city heavy with suspicion, where Shia militias "disappear" anyone suspected of Isis links and ordinary Sunnis only recently returned chafe at their double dispossession. The collapse of the Iraqi army, which had failed to become an effective national force, allowed for the rise of the militias. The men who once battled US and British troops are now indispensable in the fight against Isis. Najaf, the Shia holy city once persecuted by Saddam, is now a rare oasis of peace. "We are only Shia here, that's why it's safe," said Yahir Rashid, a gravedigger in Najaf's Valley of Peace, the world's largest cemetery, where five million bodies are buried.

But the rivalries between the armed groups, each loyal to a different Shia cleric or leader, are clear to see within the cemetery walls. Once the dead were interred in family plots; now each militia has staked out its own corner, urging families to have their dead buried with their brothers in arms and not those of their own blood.

Yesterday those killed in Sunday's suicide bombing in Baghdad were being laid to rest. With the death toll now over 250, it is now the single bloodiest attack of the post-invasion period. Rashid waited on his shovel for the arrival of Umm Saif, a mother burnt to death in a fire that followed the explosion. Her grave had been dug next to that of her son, Saif, 20, a volunteer with the Badr brigade, who was killed fighting Isis in Salahuddin in May. The bloodshed was good business for the gravediggers. After the peak of the sectarian conflict between 2006 and 2008, the past two years have been the busiest as Isis's grip tightened.

An estimated 160,000 civilians have met violent deaths since 2003, a smaller number, by any reckoning, than those who died under Saddam's brutal rule. Yet Iraqis talk not so much of numbers as of the nature of the violence, its unpredictability, somehow qualitatively different from that of the dictator they denounced as "unjust". "Someone walks out of the door and you do not know if he will ever come home," Hurriya said. "We have given up on a better life, we just want to survive."

Colonel Issa said: "I would welcome back the British and the Americans if only they could bring us security. The only thing they have done that is worse than the invasion is to leave us in this hell. We had one Saddam before and now we have a thousand Saddams."

The draw of strongman rule is enticing. Before the Isis takeover, Nouri al-Maliki, the prime minister, repressed and marginalised Sunnis in the name of security. His conduct fanned the flames of sectarianism, enabling Isis's rise with the support of many Sunnis who believed that Isis rule could be hardly worse than Baghdad's. The failure of his more emollient successor, Haider al-Abadi, to bring security has left him vulnerable both to challenge and to authoritarian impulses.

The day of the bombing he ordered all death row prisoners to be executed. The next day five were hanged.

CATALOGUE OF FAILURE

Leading Article

JULY 7 2016

IN 1999, AS NATO liberated Kosovo from Serbian tyranny, Tony Blair hailed the operation in a landmark speech in Chicago as "a just war, based not on any territorial ambitions but on values". He implored the United States not to retreat into isolationism, partly because of the presence on the world stage of two "dangerous and ruthless men". One was Slobodan Milosevic. The other was Saddam Hussein.

Two years later the 9/11 attacks reduced the World Trade Center to rubble. It set the stage for two long wars that Mr Blair believed would vindicate a foreign policy doctrine of enlightened interventionism. The Iraq war has instead turned into an unending human tragedy and a humiliating disaster for British diplomacy and statecraft. Saddam is no more, but the price of his removal has been immeasurable.

A total of 179 British service personnel died in a mission never accomplished. Hundreds of thousands of Iraqi civilians have perished in a revival of historical Sunni-Shia bloodletting that grinds on to this day. Trust in British competence abroad has been shattered. To a dismaying degree, so has trust in British governance at home. The Chilcot report had an absurdly long gestation but it compensates with thoroughness. It pulls no punches.

Like the Iraq war itself, the report carries the risk of raising the bar for future British military intervention so high that dictators can rest easy.

Yet Sir John Chilcot has performed an important service by setting out in forensic detail how this country joined an American-led invasion despite the absence of an imminent threat from Saddam. He has laid bare the war's flimsy legal basis, the "wholly inadequate" planning for its aftermath and Downing Street's inflated sense of British influence over Washington. Many details are familiar from earlier reports but this will be the definitive account.

It is doubly sobering that its account of one set of grave miscalculations at the highest level of government is being published as Britain struggles with another. Generations of historians will look back on July 2016 as the month this country's political class received a lesson in how not to lead. As he has before, Mr Blair apologised for mistakes in the execution of the war but not for the decision to embark on it. This was a decision that *The Times* supported. We did so on the basis of intelligence on weapons of mass destruction that remained privy to the prime minister and his closest aides but which he insisted, in private as well as public, was incontrovertible. It was anything but.

Still defiant 13 years on, Mr Blair insisted in a written statement that the Chilcot report alleged "no falsification or improper use of intelligence". In fact the report states that the intelligence "was not challenged and should have been". Many will conclude that amounts to improper use. Mr Blair claimed the report does not accuse him of deceiving his cabinet. This is true, but the question of deception was all but irrelevant since the cabinet was barely consulted. He claimed the report found no evidence of a "secret commitment to war", but it is hard to see his six-page letter to President Bush, pledging "I'm with you whatever", as anything else.

He claimed the report found that the attorney-general, Lord Goldsmith, had decided by March 13, 2003, that there was a legal basis for war even without a second UN security council resolution. Unsurprisingly, Mr Blair does not mention the report's concern about the basis for Lord Goldsmith's decision. In seven years of inquiry, its authors did not find one. The truth is, as Mr Blair admitted in a press conference after publication of the report, that he "took the decision after 9/11 that we should be America's closest ally". His letter to Mr Bush suggests that by the summer of 2002 he had resolved this would be an axis that prevailed through thick and thin.

His two closest advisers begged him to remove the phrase "with you whatever" from the letter, but he insisted on it. He persuaded Mr Bush to seek UN approval for the war, and in the end he made Britain's support unconditional. The value of the transatlantic alliance to global security since the Second World War is hard to overstate. Yet unconditional support is the wrong basis for it in principle, and in practice.

Harold Wilson understood that refusing to send British troops to support America during the Vietnam War might damage the special relationship but not end it. Margaret Thatcher learnt the converse: despite unstinting support for America and her warm personal relationship with President Reagan, he gave her no advance warning of the US invasion of Grenada, and scant public support during the Falklands conflict.

Mr Blair believes that 9/11 changed everything, yet there are lessons from history that he has ignored. The Chilcot report's remit was to seek lessons from Britain's involvement in Iraq from 2001-09. Had his window been wider, Sir John might have noted that the Sunni-Shia schism long predated the allied invasion. In his oral defence Mr Blair also argued with some justification that violence of the sort now tearing Syria apart is to be expected "where we don't intervene to remove the dictator".

It is true that the United States and Britain should have acted to remove Bashar al-Assad three years ago; true, too, that the bloodshed in Syria since then has been even heavier than in Iraq. Yet the West's inability to muster the will to act decisively in the Middle East since the Arab Spring finds its roots in the grotesque mismanagement of the Iraq war.

London and Washington failed utterly to prepare for the peacemaking and nation-building that should have come after the invasion. Chaos followed instead. It was the height of naivety to suppose that a liberal democracy would emerge naturally from the wreckage of the Saddam police state. It was also unforgivable. Downing Street received explicit warnings of the potential for al-Qaeda and Iran to expand their influence and foment conflict after regime change. These warnings were ignored.

With hindsight it is clear that strategic blunders led to tactical disaster. Both main Nato allies should have pressed home the offensive against the Taliban in Afghanistan in 2003 instead of fighting two wars at once on what was, for Britain, a peacetime military budget. The result for British military families who are still grieving today was the dispatch of three army brigades to Basra with Snatch Land Rovers that were sitting ducks for the most basic landmines.

The report is devastating in its critique of the Basra operation. Humiliatingly, stability could be achieved only through prisoner swaps with local death squads. The only consistent trend was the downward number of British troops stationed there. Their bravery is not in doubt. Nor is the short-sightedness of the mandarins in charge of their deployment. Even without hindsight it is clear that expecting Iraq to rebuild itself in peace and pluralism after its army and ruling elite had been dismantled was fantasy. "We trusted what our political masters told us," one former British officer who led under-equipped soldiers into Iraq in 2003 said. "We were wrong to do so."

This war has made mere survival the most that many Iraqis can hope for. In Britain its link to a "dodgy" intelligence dossier has fuelled mistrust of the security services and cynicism about government. This loss of faith has deepened with time and extends now to the scorn shown for "expert" opinion in the recent Brexit campaign. At each end of the period covered by the Chilcot report a British prime minister has faced the consequences of his catastrophic misjudgments — Mr Blair's on Iraq, and David Cameron's on the referendum. Their successors have their work cut out to rebuild the public's trust.

'I'M SURE THERESA WILL BE REALLY SAD THAT SHE DOESN'T HAVE CHILDREN ... '

Andrea Leadsom interviewed by Rachel Sylvester

JULY 9 2016

ANDREA LEADSOM THINKS it is superb that two women are competing to be the next prime minister. "I don't think that all women are better than anyone else, but it's great for this country to have female role models and see women showing the confidence and desire to reach the top."

The energy minister — the outsider in the Tory leadership race who was catapulted into the final two this week — also hopes that a woman at the top may improve the tone and reputation of politics. There is a problem with the "confrontational, aggressive nature of politics" that is fostered by the testosterone-fuelled, male-dominated world of Westminster, she says.

But when asked what she sees as the main difference between her and Theresa May, her rival for the top job, her answer is far from sisterly.

After explaining that, as a former banker, she understands "how the economy works and can really focus on turning it around" — unlike, by implication, the home secretary — she stresses that she is a "member of a huge family and that's important to me. My kids are a huge part of my life, my sisters and my two half brothers are very close so I am very grounded and normal." Mrs May, of course, has spoken of her heartbreak at realising that she could not have children.

In case the contrast is not clear enough, Mrs Leadsom goes on: "I am sure Theresa will be really sad she doesn't have children so I don't want this to be 'Andrea has children, Theresa hasn't' because I think that would be really horrible, but genuinely I feel that being a mum means you have a very real stake in the future of our country, a tangible stake. She possibly has nieces, nephews, lots of people, but I have children who are going to have children who will directly be a part of what happens next."

There is also an empathy that comes from motherhood, she suggests, "when you are thinking about the issues that other people have: you worry about your kids' exam results, what direction their careers are taking, what we are going to eat on Sunday". She must know that to bring motherhood into the leadership contest will be deeply hurtful to Mrs May — but also that "family values" could appeal to the Tory grassroots who will choose the winner.

At times Mrs Leadsom seems naive, and even brittle, but she is clearly ruthless about winning power. MPs, who voted overwhelmingly for Mrs May in this week's ballot, underestimate the MP for South Northamptonshire at their peril. Last week her supporters led a "Peasants' Revolt" march to parliament, chanting "What do we want? Leadsom for leader! When do we want it? Now!" She believes that she has captured the anti-establishment mood surging through politics.

"The vote to leave the EU reflects the fact that people don't feel they have a stake in society," she says. She has been an MP since 2010 and has never served in the cabinet. If she wins on September 9 she will be the least experienced prime minister but she argues that she is no novice in the real world. "In politics the currency is very often what you've done in the Commons or in government, rather than outside. I have had such a wide-ranging career; I would point to the business experience."

Educated as was Mrs May at a grammar school, Mrs Leadsom is

pleased that the era of the "posh boys" is over in the party. "I hugely admire David Cameron ... but I do think that there is something good about people being able to identify with their politicians. There could be an advantage in having people who have gone through the state system. People feel more comfortable with somebody who knew what it was like in their playground or in a class that's too big."

Although she will never support quotas she wants fewer public school boys and more women at the top of government. Mrs Leadsom's own inspiration came from her mother, who brought up three daughters on her own after divorcing at the age of 25. She worked in a dress shop by day and a pub at night to make ends meet. The family lived in a tiny terrace house, where the girls all shared a room. With tears in her eyes, Mrs Leadsom says: "It was tough but it was very formative. She really taught us the world doesn't owe you a living, you don't rely on a man you make your own way.

"I'm not a feminist because I'm not anti-men, I just see people as people. I'm never happy to see women written out of the picture ... but feminism is a term that's been used to abuse men so I don't identify with it." She has been criticised for calling for maternity rights to be scrapped for small businesses employing no more than three people. "When you start a business you are really struggling ... It's not about scrapping rights it's about giving a breathing place to people who are starting out," she says.

"But I'm a huge fan of shared parental leave. I believe maternity rights are absolutely vital." The Tories must, she believes, be much more radical about tackling the failings in capitalism. "I have been in markets and seen some of the excessive behaviour," she says. "The prime minister should be able to say this is a terrible thing, corporate governance has to be about more than just abiding by the rules, your stakeholders are not just your shareholders. There is a moral dimension."

There is a lot of anxiety in the City — and outside it — about the Brexit vote. The pound has plummeted, the markets are unsteady, but Mrs Leadsom says she has a plan. Instead of staying in the single market, she would negotiate a new free trade deal with the EU. "The single market is not a term that is any longer relevant to this discussion," she says. "The size of our economy means we will be the key trading partner for the EU, and we have also had 43 years aligning our goods and services. We start with zero tariffs. All we actually need to do is continue as before." Surely, the EU would impose tariffs? "Why would they do that?" she says.

On free movement, there is no room for negotiation in her view. "Once we leave the EU we will be back in control of immigration. People going on holiday or travelling on business or to collaborate on science will be able to do that but the right to reside and the right to work here will be under work permits." She has already discussed her proposals with the civil service. Unlike Mrs May she insists that "people who have already come here and made their lives here will have their rights protected. I think it would be cruel otherwise".

In order to prevent a massive influx of migrants in the run-up to Brexit, she would immediately remove the right to remain for new entrants. "If I'm prime minister on September 9 what I would then say is people would still be able to come here under free movement until the day we leave the EU but those people who came here under free movement rules would then not be entitled to just remain here. We are a sovereign state. We can do what we want. Under free movement you don't have to guarantee free movement for ever."

The referendum result has left a nasty mood, with a shocking rise in racist attacks. Does she have any remorse about the tone of the Brexit campaign? "I have nothing I regret about my campaign," she says. "In politics, in life, we cannot all be held responsible for some of the vile things that some individuals say." It is "absolutely appalling" that there has been an increase in hate crimes but she says: "I reject the premise that it's to do with the campaign." She is "absolutely not happy" about winning the backing of Arron Banks and Nigel Farage. "I've already made very clear that I will not take money from them, I don't want their support. I'm no Ukip sympathiser, they don't advise me, I don't know them."

Her enemies in the Commons suggest that Mrs Leadsom has been hijacked by the Tory right. She has already promised to hold a vote to bring back fox hunting and review HS2, and has criticised gay marriage, but she says: "That is all part of the 'Let's get Leadsom' techniques. I'm completely pro the modernisation agenda." However, her views will chime with Tory traditionalists. She wants "grammar-school-style streaming" in schools and more single-sex education. She believes the government should do more to support families, saying: "I absolutely accept that couples who don't marry can be every bit as loving to each other and supportive to their children but, if you follow the evidence, that suggests marriage is a very good way to provide a supportive background for children."

Too often "stay-at-home mums feel they've been undervalued", she argues. "I wouldn't like a woman to feel 'I have to go back to work otherwise I can't pay the bills', equally I don't want a woman to feel forced to stay at home." She worries about the abortion limit, which is set at 24 weeks. "I'm absolutely in favour of choice but I also think that as the facts change and the viability of babies ever earlier changes you have to follow the evidence."

Mrs Leadsom describes herself as the "fresh start" candidate after the resignation of Mr Cameron. "I would welcome [the contest] being faster for the sake of the country. I think the country needs to see new leadership." But if she wins she will not call a general election to secure a mandate for the new direction. "I'm not going to have an early election. We have to get a grip, we can't just carry on indulging ourselves."

FAMILY MOURN AT SPOT MOTHER WAS DRAGGED TO DEATH

David Brown, Dominic Kennedy

JULY 18 2016

BRUNO RAZAFITRIMO CLUTCHED his young sons at the site of a smear of dried blood where they had seen their mother dragged under the speeding lorry. As the father struggled to comprehend what they had witnessed, Amaury, six, and Andrew, four, wriggled impatiently towards the beach. "She was here," said Mr Razafitrimo, pointing at the centre of the pavement of Promenade des Anglais in Nice where Mino, 31, had been walking. "Then she was gone."

Robiharivelo, the boys' aunt, whose knee was dislocated when she was hit by the 19-tonne lorry driven by Mohamed Lahouaiej Bouhlel, added: "We saw the lorry swerving towards us. Then it hit Mino but passed straight between my nephews and carried on."

There was increasing anger yesterday at an alleged lack of security at the Bastille Day firework display that ended with 84 dead. It also emerged that Bono, the singer with the rock band U2, had been at a nearby restaurant and that police had arrested a man who had tried to stop the killer.

The Razafitrimos had attended the display with the family of Andrew's friend Yannis Coviaux, also aged four. The fireworks had finished and both families were returning to their cars. Mickaël, Yannis's father, remembered seeing a lorry approach while walking with Samira, his wife, as their only child played with his friends a little further ahead.

"I just had time to grab my wife and pull her out of the way and to dive on to the ground," Mr Coviaux, a lorry driver, said. He then scooped up the body of his son in his arms and ran 600 yards to Nice's children's hospital. Doctors there told him "it's over". In the chaos they handed Yannis's body to him wrapped in a sheet and he carried it back to the promenade where his son had loved to play. Dotted along the promenade were dozens of other bodies, many covered in tablecloths from local restaurants.

The promenade was reopened on Saturday morning before the pools of blood had been cleared. Places where pedestrians had been horribly mutilated had stains up to 18ft long, with the lorry's tracks marked in blood. Initially small groups of relatives and friends gathered at the marks, often laying a single rose or lighting a candle before hugging and sobbing. Then strangers came. Within hours the stains were covered in flowers, more candles, soft toys, children's pictures and chalk drawings.

Some people still had hope. Tahar Mejri, 39, showed strangers a photograph of his son, Killan, four. His son's scooter had been found next to the body of his wife, Olfa. Fourd Manse, 32, carried a photocopied picture of his sister, Bouzaouit Aldjia, 42, whose four children were in hospital.

On Saturday, 16 of the 84 victims remained unidentified but yesterday afternoon the hospital authorities said that only one remained nameless. The victims included Christophe Lyon, the former head of a rugby club, as well as his wife, parents, parents-in-law and his stepson.

A delivery worker at a restaurant described how he had fought to stop Bouhlel. Gwenaël Leriche, 26, said that he had jumped over corpses in pursuit of the lorry after seeing it leave behind a "field of dead people, blood and flesh". When the lorry slowed down, a second man opened the driver's door and Mr Leriche began punching Bouhlel. The killer used his 7.65mm pistol to shoot at Mr Leriche before the police returned fire and the rampage ended. Mr Leriche, who had a small knife, was arrested as a suspected accomplice to Bouhlel and questioned for several hours before being released. Another man chased the lorry on his bicycle and tried to open the cab door. Alexandre Migues said: "I saw the lorry speeding and knocking a lady down." He jumped on to his bike and pursued it. "It was instinctive," he said. "I saw that I could reach the cab, so I got up and tried to open the door two or three times."

"He took a pistol out of his bag and aimed it at me," said Mr Migues, who then let go of the door and saw another man approaching on a scooter who died in an attempt to stop the lorry. "When the scooter hit the lorry I heard shooting," Mr Migues said. "I wish I had been able to hang on for longer so that I could at least have slowed the vehicle down enough to allow more people to escape."

ASTOUNDING WIZARDRY OF HARRY POTTER'S NEW CHAPTER WILL LEAVE YOU SPELLBOUND

Review by Ann Treneman

JULY 26 2016

JK ROWLING HAS never been known for brevity — some of her books can double as doorstops — and her first play is no exception. This, the eighth *Harry Potter* story, is told in two parts, each lasting more than 2½ hours. In between there is a three-hour break. It's not so much a play as a weekend mini-break, a theatrical experience that lasts longer than some relationships.

I am a mere Muggle, of course, which is Potter-speak for those of us without magical powers, but that doesn't mean I can't spot wizardry when I see it. Or ghosts. Theatreland is prone to superstition: normally the owners of the Palace leave two seats empty, locked into sitting position, for their local apparitions. Such is the demand for *Cursed Child*, though, that these seats are filled. What, I wonder, if I am sitting in a ghost's seat? But then "what if" is the overarching plot here. What if things aren't really as they seem? It's the kind of question that Voldemort, evil incarnate, would find very interesting indeed.

It's 19 years since we last saw Harry: he's now an overworked civil servant in the Ministry for Magic. Harry (Jamie Parker) and Ginny (Poppy Miller) have three children but the one we get to know is his youngest son, Albus Severus Potter, named after the beloved (dead) headmaster Dumbledore and the enigmatic potions teacher Snape. Such references are strewn throughout the play(s) but there are plenty of clues dropped in so that it is quite easy to pick it all up and not feel excluded.

We meet Albus, played by Sam Clemmett, as he heads off at King's Cross portal platform 9¾ (I know it well) to Hogwarts for his first year. What a curse it must be to be the son of the famed Harry Potter — Albus isn't happy about it, that's for sure. A classic rebel, he is almost at war with his father who is, in turn, and as always, taking on the entire world of dark magic. "The story is a bit complicated," I said to my companion who had reread all the *Harry Potters* in preparation. "Of course it is but that's JK Rowling," she said.

As I watched the rapt faces round me, I realised that the complexity of this story (there are mazes that are more straightforward) is key. Rowling never treats her audience as dolts. So this is Dickens, with magic. It's a raunchless *Game of Thrones* with heart. Crucially, it's authentic Potter but, most importantly, it's new. It's not the movie of the book. It's the real deal, live in front of you, so much better than any film could be.

The themes are classic Rowling: friendship, love, evil, revenge. She wrote the original story here but the play itself is credited to Jack Thorne, who excels in flowing dialogue. John Tiffany, who also contributed to the story, directs. The team effort means that Rowling's normal tendency to digress at length about almost anything has been stymied: the result is that the pace of Part One is nigh on perfect and Part Two lags only towards the end and could do with a mini-trim.

The acting by the cast of 42 (!) is uniformly good but Parker and Clemmett deserve particular mention for making the marathon look so effortless. Noma Dumezweni plays Hermione (still a swot) so naturally and in a way that makes you assume that the character was always black. The stage design (sets by Christine Jones) is ingenious.

The key, though, lies in the wizardry on display. It is out of this world. It's one thing to read about an invisibility cloak, it's another to see it (or not). The Dementors, evil apparitions that suck you dry, are phenomenal. Nothing has been too much trouble. For one trick the entire inside of the theatre had to be repainted. It's magic — as reflected in my rating of four and three quarter stars — and it's a hit.

'IF I COULD WATCH ONE INNINGS AGAIN, IT WOULD BE COWDREY'S FIRST HUNDRED'

John Woodcock interviewed by Mike Atherton

JULY 30 2016

IN THE FRONT ROOM of The Old Curacy, the anecdotes are flowing. After all, this is a man who can remember being perched on CB Fry's knee, who played golf with Herbert Sutcliffe, Leonard Hutton and Geoffrey Boycott, went duck shooting with Harold Larwood, partridge shooting with Imran Khan, bonefishing with Ian Botham, took a stumping off Tiger O'Reilly and batted alongside Wally Hammond in his last (uncompetitive) match.

"Well, we went duck shooting with Harold in theory. It was the day after England had won their first Test in Australia after the war and dear Harold was there for a newspaper. There was a party in the Windsor Hotel in Melbourne that evening and an Australian racehorse trainer called Murphy asked if anyone wanted to go duck shooting in the morning. I loved all sports, including field sports, and Harold was keen too.

"We had to pick up some guns from down the peninsula and we left Harold on the beach and told him to join us at six o'clock in the morning, when the shooting started. We banged away a bit, not much doing, and when we got back Harold hadn't moved. Fast asleep he was, on the beach. I was very fond of Harold."

We are transported back to a 30-year time frame, 1950s to 1980s, the memories fresh and the recall sharp of separate golf matches with the three Yorkshire legends. "Len was the most natural golfer of the three. Herbert Sutcliffe played like he'd never held a club in his life — most remarkable thing, given the runs he'd scored. Boycott played like a young pro and turned up with a companion, I remember, who at the end of the game gave me his card — I've still got it somewhere. It read, 'Entrepreneurial genius — retired.' Geoff was obviously cultivating him."

What a life. Memories and photographs of every significant England cricketer since the war, all informal, as they would be from a time when journalists and cricketers mixed like rum and water: Hammond, placing his silk handkerchief in his pocket before his last match with the press; Denis Compton, "the incomparable Compton", pulling a horse with a heavy roller when England got caught on a sticky dog in Australia 1950-51; Ted Dexter; Don Bradman; Colin Cowdrey; Alec Bedser and the rest.

The timespan takes some getting my head around, though. After driving for an hour or two, during which time my teenage son extols the virtues of *Pokémon Go*, I then spend three hours in the company of a man who does not have a mobile phone, does not use email and whose grandfather was born before the battle of Waterloo, more than two hundred years ago.

John Woodcock the most illustrious cricket correspondent of *The Times*, will be 90 next weekend. Longparish, the village in Hampshire in which he has spent almost his entire life, is gearing up for a giant celebration with one party reserved just for the villagers. After all, Woodcock knows everyone here: his roots run deep — as deep, surely, as any Englishman alive.

On the western wall of St Nicholas's church, a boundary throw from Woodcock's thatched cottage, where he has lived since 1947, there is a beautiful stained glass window, *The Four Seasons*, commissioned last year to celebrate his family's 250-year connection with the church. The first Woodcock to run the place was Edward, 1765-92; then came Henry, 1795-99, and after that, Woodcock's father, Parry John, who was the rector between 1906 and 1933. Woodcock still opens the church three mornings a week.

Sitting and talking with Woodcock is not just a history lesson on cricket — he went to his first Test in 1936 at Lord's, was this paper's correspondent between 1954-1987 and has continued to write in this space every year without interruption since then — but also a history of English country life. The window contains many of the aspects of it that are dear to him: crab apples, a woodcock, mayflies, butterflies, brown trout, water lilies, fingerlings, snowdrops and the river bed with trout eggs to renew the cycle. The deep connection with the village is best seen in a photograph of him and his brother sitting on a horse and cart, making the morning delivery from a milk churn to the rest of village in the mid-1930s.

Parry John was 70 when Woodcock was born and Woodcock's grandfather, John William, was in his forties when Parry John was born, hence the pre-Waterloo timeline. Despite his father's advanced age, Woodcock remembers his love of fishing — the river Test runs less than 500 yards from the house — and his love of cricket. "He was a renowned fisherman in the village and was mentioned in a famous fishing book, *Where the Bright Waters Meet*. He loved cricket too. I like to think I was born to it, that it runs in the blood. It's been my life really, that and Longparish. I've been so lucky. It's been such a privilege."

Woodcock was a natural ball player and a very decent cricketer, as good as anyone of his age on his prep-school circuit, until tragedy struck. At 15, studying at St Edward's in Oxford, he contracted septic arthritis in his hip and was poisoned badly, spending four months hanging from a frame to prevent it from spreading. His mother was called to his bedside, so close to death did he come — this being before antibiotics were in general use.

He continued to play games after he recovered, but with a limp. He was close to playing a first-class match for Oxford University against Gloucestershire, but is thankful he wasn't selected. "Tom Goddard [Gloucestershire and England] would have got me out for fun. I didn't play forward you see, always back in my crease and Tom's off spinners would have done me easily. All people would have been able to recall, had I played, was a pair, I'm sure of it." He earned a blue in hockey as a goalkeeper instead.

Six hip replacements later, he uses an electric buggy to get around and his springer spaniel, Stumper, is on hand, a little cancerous but still in good spirits. "He'll be my last dog. I've had seven I think. They've all had cricket names, Bouncer, Googly, and so forth but there are only so many cricketing names you can come up with. I can hardly call the next one Persistent Short-Pitched Bowling, can I? No, he'll be the last one."

At Oxford, many of his contemporaries had been in the war. Tommy Macpherson, with whom Woodcock matriculated from Trinity College on the same day, won three Military Crosses and three Croix de Guerre, before taking a first and winning blues in rugby, athletics and hockey. Dick Wakeford, another friend, won a VC. War experiences informed the attitudes of these men. "They saw themselves as immensely fortunate. Few of them talked about their experiences; like the survivors from the Great War, they were almost ashamed to have survived when so many did not. But, my, these men wanted to make up for it afterwards."

Woodcock had intended to go into teaching after Oxford but joined the press corps as Jim Swanton's amanuensis. His first assignment for *The Times* was the 1954-55 Australia and New Zealand tour, which lasted — including travel — for over seven months, during which time journalists and players mixed as friends. The same age as many of the players, Woodcock became very close to many of them. "Probably too close," he says. "We were like a family, really."

But if the desire of many who returned from the war to enjoy life to the full was strong, Woodcock's close-up view of the players in Australia showed him the other side of the Ashes rivalry as well. "Well, you know how it is in Australia as well as anyone, Mike. It is agony at times. Len [Hutton] used to get very stressed. Halfway through that tour I wasn't sure he was going to finish it. On many occasions it was George Duckworth — George was a marvellous man, a father figure to the players — who got Len out on to the park.

"George once saw Colin Cowdrey coming back from church after Colin had holed out to Richie Benaud at Sydney just before the close. 'Been to confession?' he asked Colin in his lovely, humorous way. It's always been a hell of a strain playing against Australia and some showed it more than others. Len was a terrible worrier. I once had a drink with Cowdrey after a hundred in Melbourne on David Sheppard's tour. 'Well done,' I said to him. 'Got to go through it all again next week,' he said. I knew what he meant. Some simply coped better than others."

If he could watch one innings again, Woodcock would transport himself back to Melbourne on that tour to watch the first of Cowdrey's 22 Test hundreds. "It was the most marvellous innings. I don't think he ever played better than that again. [Ray] Lindwall and [Keith] Miller still weren't bad, you know, and we were 40 odd for four. Colin made 102 out of 191 and we won the match. But there's no footage of it and I can't remember it as well as I would like to. But I remember how I felt watching it at the time."

So close was he to these players, that when Cowdrey was sent for in 1974-75, 20 years after his maiden hundred, to take on Dennis Lillee and Jeff Thomson at the Waca, Perth, Woodcock said he felt as shaky as if his own son were walking out to bat. He had to take himself off to the bar to calm his nerves. He was certain that Cowdrey got away with a first-ball shout for leg-before, and then watched in admiration as the old boy got stuck in before being bowled around his legs for 22. "I had such affection for these players, you know."

Woodcock is dismissive of his own journalism but readers of a certain age will know — as will those who read *The Times* on the Ashes anthology produced last year, in which many of his reports were reproduced — that he was a superb writer. Not pretentious, as some contemporary sportswriters can be, but clear, concise, measured, with a natural, flowing style. He was no newshound but he did not shy from passing sharp judgment on those players he knew well. "If I was good at anything I could write a decent match report. I was a decent reader of a match."

It was a different time, of course. "My starting salary was £900 a year, with a £52 cost-of-living bonus. Expenses? They were virtually unlimited. I had a summer suit made from JC Wells next to Savile Row for the '54-55 tour, but Swanton put me up to that. I'm not sure I could do the job now, it's much more stressful. Television has changed everything. I think I had the best of it. It was a different world, Mike." It certainly was: in 1976, he and Henry Blofeld travelled to a tour to India in a 1921 Rolls-Royce.

"*The Times* was a wonderful paper to work for. Sir William Haley was my first editor. A brilliant, formidable man. He had been the director-general of the BBC. He was very well read and wrote book reviews under the name of Oliver Edwards. He had steel eyes. I've gone through a few editors. Harry Evans was the one who nearly rumbled me. He wanted proper journalists. I wasn't really a journalist; I was a cricket writer. Swanton once called me the supreme non-professional. I never knew whether to take that as a compliment."

Television and the internet have reordered the media landscape, and the giants of newspaper journalism, who could be sure to sway public opinion as well as the opinion of decision-makers, no longer exist. Woodcock was one of those, along with Neville Cardus, Swanton, John Arlott and others. The rhythm of the season was different, too, with the County Championship the dominant theme of the summer.

There was camaraderie, of course. Woodcock's press briefing notes from fellow scribe Ron Roberts for the India tour in 1963-64 give a flavour: "If you write about the memorial well of Kanpur," advised Roberts, "remember the rebels put the British down the well and not the other way around, as I wrote a couple of years ago, causing a marked decline in the readership of *The Daily Telegraph* among retired colonels of Bognor Regis."

"I first met Cardus on the boat in 1950-51. He always needed an audience and his colleagues avoided him because they had heard it all before. I was the new boy, so he came to me after dinner with two deckchairs, two cigars and two glasses of port and told me to listen to him rather than waste my time dancing. He was very kind to me."

"Arlott was a brilliant man. He wrote hymns, you know? We used to stay at The Swan at Bucklow Hill before the Manchester Test and Arlott had been invited by a school in Cheshire to attend because they were going to sing one of his hymns. 'Are you going to go?' I asked him. 'No, they've changed one of the lines. Not only that, they've f***ed up the sodding scansion.' "

Woodcock does not wallow in memory. He brought out his photograph albums, thick as a telephone directory, only at my urging. He watches the modern game avidly. He enjoys bits of it but laments the loss of variety, the lack of spin, the brutality of batsmen, the "confounded corridor", the leave, and thinks that the reverse sweep should be outlawed. But he always enjoys watching those who play with a freedom and generosity of spirit, those who share the lineage from Compton to Botham and beyond.

"I'm very particular about greatness. The essence of great batsmanship is calculated risk. That's why I hope Joe Root doesn't have that knocked out of him. He was criticised for his shots at Lord's [in the first Test against Pakistan] but in the second innings I thought he was taking a calculated risk and just played the shot badly. There will always be those who grind out runs but the best players — [Garry] Sobers, Dexter, Compton, Everton Weekes — take risks and play with charm. Root is too good to become a percentage player and it wouldn't be good for the game."

It is time to leave the front room, where Stumper is now snoring and where, many years before, Jack Fingleton wrote a book, *Batting From Memory*, and return to the church. The late afternoon sun catches the iridescent purples, greens and blues of the stained glass window, and has lit up the words of Psalm 1:3, which is the inscription at the bottom.

"And he shall be like a tree, planted by the waterside, that will bring forth his fruit in due season; his leaf also shall not wither and whatsoever he doeth it shall prosper." The Sage of Longparish has lived long and prospered.

CLINTON EDGES AHEAD AS MUSLIM SOLDIER ROW BACKFIRES ON TRUMP

Rhys Blakely

AUGUST 2 2016

HILLARY CLINTON PULLED clear of Donald Trump in a poll yesterday as the Republican tycoon was further embroiled in the most charged feud of the election: his war of words with the parents of a Muslim US soldier who died in Iraq.

Mrs Clinton appears to have had a better bounce from the Democrats' tightly stage-managed convention last week than Mr Trump received from the Republicans' less polished event a week before. She leads her billionaire rival by 52 per cent to 43 per cent, according to a national survey by CNN.

With 97 days until the election, Mr Trump faced some of the most blistering criticism of his political career. Families of fallen soldiers called him repugnant after he disparaged a Muslim couple whose son, a US Army captain, was killed in Iraq.

Humayun Khan died when he put himself between a car bomb and his men in 2004. His father, Khizr, denounced Mr Trump's divisive, racially tinged rhetoric at the Democratic convention last Thursday. Mr Trump retaliated by questioning why Mr Khan's wife, Ghazala, had not spoken, implying that she was not allowed to express herself.

Seventeen families whose loved ones died in battle wrote a scathing open letter to the tycoon. "When you question a mother's pain, by implying that her religion, not her grief, kept her from addressing an arena of people, you are attacking us," they said. "You are not just attacking us, you are cheapening the sacrifice made by those we lost."

John McCain, the Arizona senator whose record as a prisoner of war in Vietnam was disparaged by Mr Trump last year, said: "I hope Americans understand that [Mr Trump's] remarks do not represent the views of our Republican Party."

On Twitter Mr Trump cast himself as a victim: "Mr Khan, who does not know me, viciously attacked me ... Nice!" After Mr Khan held up a copy of the US constitution as he spoke, imploring Mr Trump to read it, sales of the founding document rocketed. A $1 pocket version was the second best-selling book on Amazon yesterday, trailing only the latest Harry Potter spin-off.

Mr Trump's combative, counterpunching style served him well during the primaries. He recovered in the polls from a political firestorm in June when his attack on a judge of Mexican heritage shocked his party. Roger Stone, a former political aide to Mr Trump, tried to smear Mr Khan by suggesting — without any proof — that he was a member of the Muslim Brotherhood and wanted to bring sharia to the US.

Mrs Khan explained that she found it difficult to maintain her composure whenever she saw a picture of her son. "Without saying a thing, all the world, all America, felt my pain," she said.

Yesterday Mr Trump told a rally in the battleground state of Ohio that he was "afraid the election is going to be rigged". He did not say how.

There was speculation last week that Russian government hackers had intervened in the US election to try to help the billionaire. Mr Trump has denied any links with Russia.

A poll by Gallup yesterday showed that 51 per cent of voters were less likely to support Mr Trump after the Republican convention, the worst result for a Republican nominee since Gallup began asking the question in 1984. Mr Trump said that he had raised nearly $36 million from more than 500,000 small donors last month. In June Mrs Clinton raised $35 million.

THE MOT JUSTE

Leading Article

AUGUST 13 2016

ZUT ALORS! Le soi-disant World Congress of French Teachers sont fromage-eating surrender monkeys. La langue française, say ces supposed experts, est trop compliquée pour les pauvres en France.

"We demand the creation of an international commission which would aim to propose a new, coherent and ambitious reform of French spelling, concerning as a priority the most energy consuming and least useful rules," dit la résolution. C'est vrai. La langue française est really,

really difficile, un nightmare veritable. Even le predictive text anglais est horrible.

Mais, so what? Pour centuries, ils manglent les mots anglais. Le Happy Hour (pronounced: ah-pee-owar), Le Weekend (Vendredi, Samedi, Dimanche), Le Brunch (consommé après le petit roll-dans-le-hay le Dimanche), Le Has-Been (M Sarkozy, par exemple), Le Call-Girl (le little something pour Dominique Strauss-Kahn) et le Job (very rare). Vraiment, la langue française est toute over la boutique.

Maintenant, c'est le temps pour un French dictionary for the French, écrit par les anglais. Un Petit Larousse Farage, peut-être. Un guide facile, comme M Farage soi-même.

Quelques phrases indispensibles pour ce handy copain:
Voulez-vous un cuppa?
Nous ne sommes pas stupides
Il pleut les cats et les dogs (tous les jours)
Il y a bugger-tout à la télé
Ce bloke est off son rockeur
Rigide lip supérieur, monsieur!

Vous comprenez le principe? Simplement parlez what you know en français, et faites tout else en anglais. C'est un walk dans le jardin publique. Un doddle. Mais, n'oubliez pas: Brexit means Brexit. Toujours.

MY CHILD-REARING IS DONE

Caitlin Moran

August 13 2016

By the time you read this, my youngest child will have turned 13 — so technically, as of mid-August, I am childless.

Obviously, the grander task of parenting is not over, as I now have two teenage girls: a job not unlike being a roadie-cum-Grand Vizier-cum-zookeeper to two columns of lightning, who oscillate between dreaming of changing the world and dreaming of peroxiding themselves white-blonde

20 minutes before catching a train. And, at some point, their memoir, *Crying in an Uber with Green Hair*, might well be the book that does change the world. But for now, for the first time since February 2001, there are no children in my house. My child-rearing is done.

In many ways, the most profound response to having parented children is, "So — what the f*** was all that, then?" I don't mean those often-repeated homilies about babies arriving with no instruction manuals; the exhaustion; the confusion; the staring at a wailing child, saying, "But why are you crying? Why is it bad that your piece of cheese has been cut into two pieces?" Everyone expects those things. There is a common understanding that parenting is, as the old adage goes, "long periods of boredom, punctuated by moments of sheer Peppa".

No. What I wasn't ready for is how, as you're giving birth, something fundamental happens to your perception of time and space. In that you totally lose it. Or — to be more specific — you totally lose all sense of it being linear, with you in the centre, and the past behind you, and the future in front of you. That's gone. BOOM! Bye!

For the first, vital skill of parenting is: to continually live in the future. Will this approaching dog scare them? Where can I put them down for a nap ... in half an hour? Will scolding them now make them more pleasant during their first job interview in 2025? To make the present successful and peaceful, you have to constantly live in a future that has not yet happened. Mentally and emotionally, that's pretty sci-fi. It's why parents of young children often look like they've just fallen out of a spaceship after being probed by Greys.

As a parent, you gradually lose any sense of what "the present" is, because the future has swirled in, over the edges, and muddied the waters. And, of course, because you've started f***ing with time — you have summoned the future, you amateur warlock, you — there is an equal and opposite reaction, in that the past stops sitting where it should be — behind you — and starts flooding into the present, too. Time is everywhere. It eddies. It is mad. You'll find yourself sitting on the sofa, thinking, "The baby's very quiet. Perhaps I should go and check on her" — and then suddenly remember, in a vertigo rush, that a decade has passed, and the baby is now ten years old, and on a camping trip in Wales.

You catch glimpses of ghost-toddlers out of the corner of your eye, under the kitchen table, with the cat, when the cat died long ago, and the toddler is now taller than you. You'll be on a train, trying to keep a fractious child interested — "Look! Moo-cows!" — only to realise you're on the train alone, surrounded by confused businessmen, and the fractious child has gone to Brent Cross to buy trainers. The answer to those recurrent, panicking nightmares — "Where did I leave the baby?" — is, "You left her in 2005, dude." Over years of parenting, time has become meaningless. You cannot grasp what it is. It goes so fast; it goes so slow. It moves at will.

You remember standing in playgrounds on dull grey days, pushing a swing for what seemed like 50 years. But putting a sleeping baby into a cot seems like it happened one minute ago — even though the cot, the baby and the house are long gone. As the Bravecaptain song about parenting has it, "The minutes pass like mountains/ The years/ Like bullets."

Now my years with children are done, I can tell you what I'm surprised about. I thought we'd spend a lot more time in museums and libraries. I thought we'd spend half our lives in there, on rainy days, but we went twice? Three times? They both loved doll's houses more.

I thought we'd spend a lot more time on the beach. I thought we'd make thousands of sandcastles. We made six. I thought we'd sit round the table more, and play Ludo, and walk the South Downs Way on a sunny day I was sure we'd never forget, but in actual fact, we just never did. I thought we'd climb into abandoned orchards and scrump apples, and light more bonfires, and swim in more streams.

And of course, because I don't understand time any more, I believe we will still do all these things. I am planning that first, magical Christmas. They can still have all those childhood memories. I can still have all those childhood memories.

GREATEST QUALITY OF GAMES
WAS ENCAPSULATED IN
EMOTIONAL EMBRACE

Matthew Syed

AUGUST 16 2016

AT THE END of the match, Andy Murray and Juan Martín del Potro embraced. Almost exactly four hours after they had first started taking chunks out of each other in the Olympic Tennis Centre, the Argentinian placed his head on to the shoulder of the Scot, his head angled to the side, offering whispered congratulations to his conqueror.

Murray, for his part, placed his right arm around the shoulders of his opponent, comforting him, as he took in the acclaim of a marvellously engaged crowd. Up in the commentary box, Simon Reed said: "These two men will for ever share a special bond." I suspect that people up and down Britain, and perhaps in Argentina, too, were shedding tears.

The longer I live, the more I recognise the triviality of sport. Hitting a tennis ball is not like inventing a vaccine. If sports scientists and athletes found a way of improving the world record for the discus by a few inches, it would not have a knock-on effect in the way of, say, a cure for cancer, a technology to improve communication, or a new kind of energy supply.

And yet it is precisely because sport is trivial that it enthrals us. No other branch of human activity more precisely dramatises the human instinct to win, to measure oneself against others, to dare to take on the world, and to learn more about oneself in the trying.

I have watched in amazement these past ten days as my three-year-old daughter has become a devotee of the Olympics. The gymnastics, the diving, the cycling, you name it. She has been transfixed by the drama of sport, the will of the athletes and the shocking realisation that it is possible to fiercely seek to deprive your opponent of that which they most desire, and yet to embrace them in the aftermath, in a spirit of mutual respect.

"Why are they bending over?" she said at the end of a judo bout, having watched Britain's Sally Conway and Bernadette Graf, of Austria, attempt to throw each other to the floor. "They are bowing," I said. "It is a bit like hugging. They are telling each other that they are still friends."

"So you can be friends when you are trying to beat someone?" she said, almost confused. I felt like saying: "Yes, this is why our species has achieved so much. It's what makes us human."

We witness Olympic Games with our lives happening concurrently. Perhaps we are having problems at work, in relationships, with a family illness. Somehow, however, this timeless drama retains its capacity to transport us from these everyday concerns, however serious, and provides solace, even inspiration. I have never been quite so transfixed by any sporting competition, not even London 2012.

Yes, there are drugs. Yes, there are cheats. Yes, there are those who seem to take delight in the negative aspects of sport. And yet when you witness Max Whitlock, the new double Olympic champion, turning a pommel horse into an extension of his body, when you see Jessica Ennis-Hill running her heart out in the 800m of the heptathlon, so vainly, so beautifully, when you watch Laura Trott turning her bike into Pegasus in the omnium, almost taking off from the track on the final bend, how can you fail to be moved?

I have been moved more times than I can remember during these Games. When Murray won, perhaps because of the late hour, my mind flitted to his mother, watching at home in a village in Scotland, doubtless reflecting on the sacrifices she made to help a small, rather shy child develop into the most formidable of champions. "Warrior," she tweeted at the moment Murray found renewed energy to close out the match.

I was moved, too, during the men's team pursuit final, one of the most dramatic sporting events of my lifetime, four British cyclists coming from seven tenths of a second down to win gold even as we feared they had left it too late.

I reflected upon Bradley Wiggins and the astonishing achievement of winning a fifth gold medal, and an eighth overall, by this lad who grew up in a council flat in Kilburn, and who was bullied so badly that cycling became an escape. Last December, I watched him training to his physical limits at the velodrome in Derby. "This is all for one day," he said. "We live in the shadow of that one day."

In a column written 24 hours before travelling to Rio, Constantine Louloudis, a rower who struck gold in the coxless four, wrote elegantly about the pressure of competing in the Olympic Games. "It is exhilarating and terrifying. Those few minutes of such intensity and consequence that they will echo through a person's entire life." He is right, of course, but it is not just success and failure that reverberate down the years. It is also how you play the game, the humanity you display.

Consider that Justin Gatlin was booed when introduced for the 100m final. The audience in Rio, like the watching public around the world, could not warm to a man who has tested not once but twice for banned substances. So fiercely did the American want to win that he lost sight of the meaning of sport. Del Potro, on the other hand, was embraced by the world for his courage and class in defeat. He left that stadium as the loser, but with his reputation infinitely enhanced. Isn't that part of the meaning of sport, too? The grace we show in adversity?

Yes, sport is trivial. Yes, it is inconsequential. But at the same time, it has such rare and beautiful depth. We have witnessed courage with Becky James winning keirin silver in the velodrome after years of tribulation, Fran Halsall daring to take on the world in the 50m freestyle in the pool, losing out to the winner by just six hundredths of a second, Jason Kenny, one of the finest British athletes of this or any other era, redefining man's relationship with two wheels.

The Olympics reveal the best and the worst in human nature. They are corrupt, have been tainted by drug-taking (organised, in the case of Russia, at the highest level of the state) and are run by cowards. And yet we should never allow these defects, these problems, to blind us to why these invented games matter, why they inspire, and why our children watch in wonder, as we once did.

"I did it," Murray said after victory in the early hours of Monday morning. "The feeling is just incredible." He was talking about the emotion of winning a four-hour match, duelled for its duration at the apex of skill and intensity. But, somehow, he was speaking for us too.